always up to date

The law changes, but Nolo is always on top of it! We offer several ways to make sure you and your Nolo products are always up to date:

1 **Nolo's Legal Updater**
We'll send you an email whenever a new edition of your book is published! Sign up at **www.nolo.com/legalupdater**.

2 **Updates @ Nolo.com**
Check **www.nolo.com/update** to find recent changes in the law that affect the current edition of your book.

3 **Nolo Customer Service**
To make sure that this edition of the book is the most recent one, call us at **800-728-3555** and ask one of our friendly customer service representatives. Or find out at **www.nolo.com**.

please note

We believe accurate and current legal information should help you solve many of your own legal problems on a cost-efficient basis. But this text is not a substitute for personalized advice from a knowledgeable lawyer. If you want the help of a trained professional, consult an attorney licensed to practice in your state.

The New Bankruptcy:

Will It Work for You?

By Attorney Stephen Elias

First Edition	JANUARY 2006
Editor	LISA GUERIN
Cover Design	TONI IHARA
Book Design	TERRI HEARSH
Proofreading	ROBERT WELLS
Index	MEDEA MINNICH
Printing	CONSOLIDATED PRINTERS, INC.

Elias, Stephen.
   The new bankruptcy : will it work for you? / by Stephen Elias.--1st ed.
      p. cm.
   Includes index.
   ISBN 1-4133-0439-7 (alk. paper)
   1. Bankruptcy--United States--Popular works. I. Title
   KF1524.6.L468 2005
   346.7307'8--dc22

                         2005051822

Quanity sales: For information on bulk purchases or corporate premium sales, please contact the Special Sales Department. For academic sales or textbook adoptions, ask for Academic Sales. 800-955-4775, Nolo, 950 Parker Street, Berkeley, CA 94710.

Dedication

To my son Rubin, who faithfully reminds me of what bankruptcy is all about.

Acknowledgments

Thanks to Robin Leonard, the original, superlative author of this book's predecessor, and Lisa Guerin, Nolo editor extraordinaire, who did such a great job helping me get this book into the world in a timely manner.

To immerse myself in the new law I attended two wonderful conferences sponsored by the National Association of Consumer Bankruptcy Attorneys. Thanks to Henry Sommer and the NACBA crew for doing such a great job.

Many thanks to Sandy McCarthy and Herb Gura, both bankruptcy petition preparers, who read the manuscript and found that it played in Peoria.

I'm perpetually grateful for my many friends at Nolo. Special kudos to Clark Miller, Nolo PR guru, whose enthusiasm for the book has translated into media gold.

I couldn't have written the book without the support and love I received from my wife, co-author, and partner in life Catherine Elias-Jermany

Table of Contents

Introduction

The New Bankruptcy Law: A Work in Progress

1 What Is Bankruptcy?

2 Who Can File for Bankruptcy

3 How Bankruptcy Affects Your Debts

4 Your Property and Bankruptcy

10 Getting Help With Your Bankruptcy

11 Alternatives to Bankruptcy

Glossary

Appendixes

A Federal and State Exemption Tables

B Charts

C Sample Bankruptcy Forms

D Worksheets

Index

The New Bankruptcy Law:
A Work in Progress

On April 17th, 2005 President Bush signed a bill that made fundamental changes to the American consumer bankruptcy system. These changes, most of which took effect on October 17, 2005, are expected to have a major impact on many who file for bankruptcy to wipe out their debt.

Written primarily by the banking and credit card industries, the new bankruptcy law places a number of new hurdles in the way of those who seek the "fresh start" bankruptcy has traditionally offered. Among the changes enacted by the new law are provisions that make it harder to wipe out certain types of debts; force more debtors to repay a portion of their debts; require debtors to undergo credit and budget counseling; impose more obligations on bankruptcy attorneys (which will drive some attorneys out of the field and cause those who remain to raise their fees); and subject bankruptcy filers to increased scrutiny from the court and the United States Attorney General.

This book explains what you can expect under the new bankruptcy law—how eligibility for Chapter 7 and Chapter 13 bankruptcy is determined, what debts are cancelled (discharged), what happens to your home, car, and other property, what complications might occur, what paperwork is involved, and where you can find help with your bankruptcy. This information will help you decide whether it makes sense to handle your debt problems through bankruptcy and, if so, which type of bankruptcy is the best choice for you.

This book provides valuable guidance for consumers who are considering bankruptcy. However, it is not intended as an authoritative reference on every detail of the new bankruptcy law. Nor should it be viewed as a guide on how to handle your own bankruptcy. For that task, Nolo's more detailed "do-it-yourself" bankruptcy books (*How to File for Chapter 7 Bankruptcy* and *Chapter 13 Bankruptcy: Repay Your Debts*) are being revised to incorporate the requirements of the new law. These resources should be available in early 2006. In the meantime, the debt relief agencies described in Ch. 10 can help you navigate the process, although this type of help will cost more than it used to under the old law.

The rules may change as courts weigh in. Because the new law makes such profound changes to the bankruptcy system, no one can know exactly how courts will interpret its provisions. As bankruptcy cases are filed under the new rules, we will learn how these legal changes play out in actual practice—including how courts will define the new terms included in the law. This book includes the best available information on the effect of the new rules, but of course, we can't predict the future. To make sure you have the latest information, check for updates on Nolo's website, at www.nolo.com.

What Is Bankruptcy?

If you've picked up this book, you probably have more debt than you can handle. Most likely, your debt mushroomed because of circumstances beyond your control—job loss, divorce, business failure, illness, or accident. You may feel overwhelmed by your financial situation, and uncertain about what to do next. Maybe a friend, relative, or even a lawyer suggested bankruptcy, describing it as the best thing in the world for you. Someone else may have said the opposite—that bankruptcy is a huge mistake and will ruin your life.

This book will help you sort through your options and choose the best strategy for dealing with your debts. It explains how the new bankruptcy law works; how filing for bankruptcy under Chapter 7 or Chapter 13 (the two bankruptcy options for consumers, named for their location in the Federal Bankruptcy Court) will affect your debts, property, home, and credit; the procedures you'll have to follow (and paperwork you'll have to complete) to file for bankruptcy; and some alternative ways to handle your debt problems, outside of the bankruptcy system. Armed with this information, you'll be ready to decide whether filing for Chapter 7 or Chapter 13 bankruptcy makes sense for you.

As you consider the strategies available to you, keep in mind that you're not alone. During each of the first five years of the new millennium, more than 1.5 million Americans have filed for bankruptcy. So have thousands of companies. Bankruptcy has become a necessary and pervasive part of our economic system.

And bankruptcy may be right for you. You may be able to stop creditor collection actions (such as foreclosures, wage garnishments, and bank account levies) and:

- wipe out all or most of your debts in a Chapter 7 bankruptcy while hanging on to your home, car, and other necessary items, or
- use Chapter 13 bankruptcy to pay back a portion of your debts over three to five years.

If your debts are overwhelming and your creditors are hounding you, bankruptcy may seem like a magic wand. But bankruptcy also has its drawbacks. And, because everyone's situation is a little bit different, there is no one-size-fits-all formula that will tell you whether you absolutely should or should not file. For many, the need for and advantage of bankruptcy will be obvious. Others will be able to reach a decision only after closely examining their property, debts, income, and recent financial transactions—and how persistent their creditors are. For some, simple non-bankruptcy options might do the trick— these are explained in Ch. 11 of this book.

This chapter provides some basic background information about the two types of bankruptcies most often filed by individuals: Chapter 7 and Chapter 13. In the chapters that follow, you'll find more detailed information on the issues you are likely to face under the new bankruptcy law, including:

- whether you are eligible to file
- which debts will and will not be cancelled
- what will happen to your home, car, and other essential property items
- how your post-bankruptcy credit will be affected,
- how bankruptcy will affect your personal life, and
- whether you need to be represented by a lawyer or can represent yourself with some outside help.

 Bankruptcy laws have changed.
As you know from this book's title, Congress has recently made big changes to the bankruptcy laws—and these changes will affect the filing options and decisions of many readers. One major new requirement has to do with eligibility: Filers with higher incomes (as measured against the median family income for their state) may not be allowed to file for Chapter 7 at all, and will have to pay back more of their debts, over a longer period of time, if they file for Chapter 13. (You can find more on these requirements in Ch. 2.) And this is just one of the many changes. The new law leaves few areas of bankruptcy untouched, so you shouldn't assume that anything you thought you knew about bankruptcy is still correct: You may be unpleasantly surprised. Section D, below, briefly describes the most important changes; each subsequent chapter concludes with a brief summary of the new rules covered in that chapter.

Icons Used in This Book

 This "fast track" arrow indicates that you may be able to skip some material.

 This icon refers you to related information in the book.

 This icon warns you of potential problems.

 The briefcase icon lets you know when you need the advice of an attorney.

 This icon refers you to helpful books or other resources.

 This icon alerts you to a practical tip or good idea.

A. Types of Bankruptcy

There are two kinds of bankruptcy: "liquidation" and "reorganization." In a liquidation bankruptcy (referred to as a Chapter 7 bankruptcy because of its location in the Bankruptcy Code), some of your property might be sold to pay down your debt; in exchange, most or all of your debts will be wiped out. Individuals can file for Chapter 7 (a "consumer" Chapter 7 bankruptcy) as can businesses (a "business" Chapter 7 bankruptcy). A Chapter 7 bankruptcy typically lasts three to six months.

In a reorganization bankruptcy, you devote part of your income to paying down your debt over time. There are three different kinds of reorganization bankruptcies:

- Chapter 13 bankruptcy is for individuals only.
- Chapter 11 bankruptcy is for businesses and for individuals with very large debts.
- Chapter 12 bankruptcy is for individuals whose debts come mainly from the operation of a family farm.

This book focuses exclusively on consumer Chapter 7 bankruptcies and Chapter 13 bankruptcies. However, Chapter 11 and Chapter 12 bankruptcies are briefly described in Ch. 11.

1. Chapter 7 Bankruptcy

This section answers some common questions about Chapter 7 bankruptcy.

a. How a Chapter 7 Case Begins

To begin a Chapter 7 bankruptcy case, you must complete a packet of forms and file them with the bankruptcy court in your area. Perhaps the most important form—made necessary by the new bankruptcy law—requires you to compute your average income during the six months prior to your bankruptcy filing date and compare that to the median income for your state. If your income is above the median, the same form takes you through a series of questions (called the "means test") designed to determine whether you could file a Chapter 13 bankruptcy and pay some of your unsecured debts over time. The outcome of this test will determine whether you can file for Chapter 7 bankruptcy. (See Ch. 2 for detailed information about these calculations and other Chapter 7 eligibility requirements.)

In addition to completing the income form and the petition, you must also complete forms that provide information about your property, debts, current income and expenses, and prefiling economic transactions. If you are making payments on a car or other personal property, you will be required to file another form stating how you wish to handle those debts after bankruptcy. As explained in detail in Ch. 6, you will have the choice of:

- giving the property back to the creditor and wiping out the debt
- paying the value of the property to the creditor in a lump sum and keeping the property (this is called "redemption,") or
- agreeing to continue the contract and make the payments after your bankruptcy is final, so you can keep the property (this is called "reaffirmation").

The laws of some states may give you the additional option of keeping the property as long as you stay current on your payments.

If You File Your Own Papers

If you are filing your own bankruptcy case, the clerk will also require you to sign a form explaining:
- the different types of bankruptcies (Chapters 7, 11, 12, and 13)
- the services available from credit counseling agencies
- the penalties for knowingly and fraudulently concealing assets or making a false statement under penalty of perjury, and
- that all information you supply is subject to examination by the Attorney General.

You can find information in Ch. 9 on all the forms you need to file in a Chapter 7 bankruptcy.

b. Which Debts Are Discharged

In a Chapter 7 bankruptcy, you get to cancel, or "discharge," certain types of debts. As a general rule, most credit card, medical, and legal debts are discharged, as are most court judgments and loans. Many filers can discharge all of their debts.

However, some debts are not discharged in Chapter 7 bankruptcy. The most common of these are:
- debts incurred to pay nondischargeable taxes
- court-imposed fines
- back child support and alimony

- debts owed under marital settlement agreements
- loans owed to a pension plan
- student loans (unless you can show that repaying the loans would be an undue hardship, which is tougher than you might think)
- recent back taxes, and
- debts for personal injuries or death resulting from your drunk driving.

If the creditor successfully objects, debts arising from your fraudulent actions, recent credit card charges for luxuries, and willful and malicious acts causing personal injury or property damages will also survive your bankruptcy. (For more on which debts are and are not discharged in a Chapter 7 bankruptcy, see Ch. 3.)

c. Which Property Is at Risk

The sum total of your property that is subject to the bankruptcy court's control is called your bankruptcy estate. In a Chapter 7 bankruptcy, the person who exercises legal control over your bankruptcy estate is called a trustee (see Section C, below). Your bankruptcy estate consists of all the property you own on the date you file, property you recently gave away to others, and certain types of property you reasonably expect to own in the near future. (See Ch. 4, Section A, for more information about what is and is not in your bankruptcy estate.)

In return for having your debts discharged, the trustee may sell any property in your bankruptcy estate that isn't exempt under applicable state or federal bankruptcy laws, then distribute the proceeds to your creditors. In some cases, an item is exempt regardless of its value (for example, a state's exemption laws might allow you to keep a burial plot, a piano, and/or your clothing). Sometimes, there are limits on an exempt item's value. For example, debtors who use the Georgia state exemptions may keep jewelry only up to a $500 limit. If your wedding ring is worth $1,000, the bankruptcy trustee can take the ring, sell it, give you your $500 exemption, and pay the rest to your unsecured creditors.

In your bankruptcy papers, you must tell the court which property you claim is exempt under the exemption laws available to you. Under the new bankruptcy law, you must use the exemptions for the state where you have been living for the two-year period prior to filing. If you haven't lived in your state for two years, you must use the exemption laws for the state where you were living before that two-year period began. (Some states allow you to choose between their exemption laws and a special set of federal exemptions—you can use whichever rules allow you to keep more of the property you really want.)

Exemptions are a bit complicated—and they are very important, because they determine what you get to keep (and what you may lose) when you file for Chapter 7 bankruptcy. Ch. 4 explains exemptions in detail, including how to figure out which state's exemptions are available to you

and how to apply those exemptions to the property you own.

d. Houses and Cars

Property you are making payments on—such as a house or car—is treated a little differently than property you own outright. If your equity in property you are making payments on doesn't exceed the exemption available to you, you can keep the property as long as you continue making the payments. But if your equity is worth significantly more than the exemption allows, the trustee can:

- sell the property
- pay off the creditor for that property (the bank that lent you the money to buy the car or house, most likely)
- give you what you're entitled to under the applicable exemption law, and
- distribute what remains to your unsecured creditors.

 Later chapters include detailed information on exemptions. Ch. 4 covers exemptions in general, Ch. 5 explains exemptions for a home, and Ch. 6 covers cars and other property that secures a loan.

e. Costs and Fees

The filing fee for a Chapter 7 Bankruptcy is $274. If you can't afford the fee, you can apply for a fee waiver or permission to pay in installments. The form, rules, and eligibility guidelines for getting a few waiver are available at www.uscourts.gov/bankruptcycourts/resources.html. If you want to be represented by a lawyer, you will likely have to pay an additional $1,500 to $2,000 in attorneys' fees.

If you decide to handle your own case, you will need to buy some information. This will typically consist of one or more of the following:

- one or more self-help law books on bankruptcy (roughly $30 a pop)
- telephonic legal advice from a lawyer (roughly $100 an hour), and
- clerical assistance with your forms from a bankruptcy petition preparer (between $150 and $300).

See Ch. 10 for more on resources you can use to file for bankruptcy.

f. The Meeting of Creditors

When your Chapter 7 bankruptcy is filed, the court will set a date for an event called the meeting of creditors. You are required to appear at this meeting, often referred to as a "341 meeting" because it is covered in Section 341 of the Bankruptcy Code. The meeting is seldom held in court; rather, it is conducted in a separate hearing room in the bankruptcy courthouse or another federal building. The bankruptcy trustee who has been assigned to your case runs the meeting. No judge is present.

At the creditors' meeting, your creditors and the trustee are allowed to ask you questions about the information in your filing paperwork and about other issues in your case that might affect your ability to obtain a bankruptcy discharge or have

a particular debt erased. For example, the trustee might inquire further about:

- anticipated tax refunds
- recent large payments you made to creditors or relatives, if applicable
- methods you used to arrive at the value of big-ticket property items you are claiming as exempt, such as a house or car
- whether you should be required to proceed under Chapter 13 rather than Chapter 7
- your failure to file any of the required documents, if applicable (see Ch. 9, Section G, for more on required paperwork)
- inconsistencies in information you provided that might indicate you are being less than honest, and
- if you didn't have a lawyer prepare your papers, how you got the information necessary to make certain choices, such as which property is exempt (your answer would typically be the Internet, a Nolo book, or a telephone advice lawyer).

If you've done a good job on your paperwork, you clearly qualify for Chapter 7, and you filed all required documents, your particular "moment of truth" will likely be brief. Creditors rarely show up at these meetings, and the trustee is typically the only one asking the questions. The trustee may simply ask whether all the information in your papers is 100% correct and end the meeting if you say, "Yes."

g. Issues That Must Be Decided by a Judge

Under the old law, Chapter 7 bankruptcy was designed to run on automatic, without the need for a judge to decide contested issues. Under the new law, however, there are more opportunities for a judge to become involved. For example, you (and/or your attorney, if you have one) will need to appear in court before a judge if:

- your income appears to make you ineligible for Chapter 7 bankruptcy and you want to argue that an exception should be made in your case
- a creditor contests your right to file for Chapter 7 bankruptcy or discharge a particular debt
- you want the judge to rule that you are entitled to discharge a particular type of debt (such as taxes or student loans—see Ch. 3, Section B, for more information on debts that can be discharged in Chapter 7 bankruptcy only with the judge's approval)
- you want to eliminate a lien on your property that will survive bankruptcy if the judge doesn't remove it (see Ch. 9, Section D), or
- you are handling your own case, are making payments on a car or other personal property, and want to keep the property and continue the contract after bankruptcy. This is called "reaffirming" the contract. (See Ch. 6 for more on reaffirmation agreements.)

See Ch. 9 for more on these and other types of issues that require a court decision.

h. How a Chapter 7 Case Ends

Chapter 7 bankruptcy ends with a discharge of all the debts you are entitled to discharge. (For information on which debts can be discharged in Chapter 7, see Ch. 3.) When a debt is discharged, the creditor is forever barred from trying to collect it from you or reporting it to a credit bureau. Government entities may not discriminate against you simply because you've received a bankruptcy discharge, but private companies can in some circumstances. (See Ch. 8 for more on the consequences of receiving a bankruptcy discharge.)

Mandatory Budget Counseling

Under the new law, you are required to participate in a two-hour course on budget management before you can get your discharge. These courses are to be provided by authorized agencies for a reasonable price (or free, if you can't afford the fee). See Ch. 2 for more information about this requirement.

If you file for Chapter 7 bankruptcy and then change your mind, you can ask the court to dismiss your case. As a general rule, the court will do so unless it would not be in the best interests of your creditors. For example, the trustee would probably oppose your request to dismiss if you have nonexempt assets that could be sold to pay your creditors.

> **EXAMPLE:** Jake files for Chapter 7 bankruptcy, thinking all of his property is exempt. Shortly after he files, Jake's mother tells him that he is on the deed for a 20-acre ranchette that he, his sister, and his mother inherited from his father. Under the exemption laws applicable to Jake's bankruptcy, his share of the ranchette is not exempt and can be taken by the trustee for the benefit of Jake's unsecured creditors (which means the property will have to be sold). Upon learning this, Jake moves to dismiss his bankruptcy. The trustee successfully opposes the dismissal because it would not be in the best interest of Jake's creditors. The moral? Don't file Chapter 7 unless and until you know what property you own and what will happen to it in bankruptcy.

If you do dismiss your case, you can file again later, although in some circumstances you may have to wait 180 days and pay a new filing fee. Instead of dismissing your Chapter 7 case, you can always convert it to another type of bankruptcy (typically Chapter 13 for consumers).

2. Chapter 13 Bankruptcy

Chapter 13 bankruptcy works quite differently from Chapter 7 bankruptcy. In Chapter 13, you use a portion of your income to pay some or all of what you owe to your creditors over time (anywhere from three to five years, depending on your income and how much of your debt you can afford to repay). The trick to successfully using Chapter 13 to get out of debt is to make sure you have enough income to meet all of your payment obligations under the Chapter 13 laws. (See Ch. 2, Section D, to learn about the eligibility requirements for filing under Chapter 13.)

a. How a Chapter 13 Case Begins

To begin a Chapter 13 bankruptcy, you fill out a packet of forms—mostly the same forms as you would use in a Chapter 7 bankruptcy, as well as:

- a workable plan to repay some or all of your debts over the plan period (either three or five years, depending on your income)
- proof that you've filed your federal and state income tax returns for the previous four years, and
- your IRS income tax return or transcript for the previous year. (See Ch. 9, Section G, for more on Chapter 13 paperwork.)

b. The Repayment Plan

Under a Chapter 13 plan, you make payments, usually monthly, to the bankruptcy trustee, an official appointed by the bankruptcy court to oversee your case. (Section C, below, discusses the role played by the trustee.) The trustee uses that money to pay the creditors covered by your plan; he or she also collects a statutory fee (usually 10% of the amount you will pay under your plan).

Under Chapter 13, you are required to devote all of your projected disposable income (the amount left over after paying your expenses) to your plan for either a three-year or five-year period. Your repayment period will be three years if your income is below your state's median income and five years if it is above. (See Ch. 2, Section B, for more on making this calculation.)

Some creditors are entitled to receive 100% of what you owe them, while others may receive a much smaller percentage or even nothing at all if you won't have any projected disposable income left over after the mandatory debts are paid. For example, a Chapter 13 plan must propose that any child support you owe to a spouse or child (as opposed to a government agency) will be paid in full over the life of your plan; otherwise, the judge will not approve it. On the other hand, the judge can approve a plan that doesn't repay any portion of your credit card debts if you won't have any projected disposable income left after paying your child support obligations.

One of the oddities of the new law is that your projected disposable income may be different than your actual disposable income. The new law calculates your projected disposable income based on your average income over the six-month period prior to your filing date. For example, if your income was $8,000 a month for the first three months of that period and $4,000 for the second three months, your projected monthly disposable income will be based on the $6,000 figure, even though your income through the life of the plan may only be $4,000. (Ch. 2, Section D, explains projected disposable income in more detail, as well as how these figures and requirements might be juggled to come up with a workable repayment plan that a judge will approve.)

To have your debts discharged under Chapter 13, you must make all payments required by your plan and:

- remain current on your federal and state income taxes
- remain current on any child support or alimony obligations
- annually file your federal income tax return or transcript of the return with the court, and
- annually file an income and expense statement with the court.

You also have to provide your creditors with copies of the income tax returns or transcripts you file with the court, if they request it.

c. Which Debts Are Discharged

If your Chapter 13 bankruptcy pays your unsecured debts in full, then you will receive a complete discharge of those debts no matter what type they are. If your plan pays less than 100%, the balance will be discharged unless they are the type of debts that cannot be discharged in Chapter 13 bankruptcy or the type that can survive your bankruptcy if the creditor appears in court and convinces the judge not to discharge them.

As a general rule, most credit card, medical, and legal debts are discharged, as are most court judgments and loans. Debts that have to be fully paid to be discharged in a Chapter 13 bankruptcy are:

- court-imposed fines and restitution
- back child support and alimony
- student loans
- recent back taxes
- unfiled taxes, and
- debts you owe because of a civil judgment arising out of your willful or malicious acts, or for personal injuries or death caused by your drunk driving.

If the creditor successfully objects, debts arising from your fraudulent actions or recent credit card charges for luxuries will not be discharged. Ch. 3, Section C, explains which debts are discharged in a Chapter 13 bankruptcy.

d. Which Property Is at Risk in Chapter 13 Bankruptcy

Unlike Chapter 7, you are not required to give up any property you own when you file your Chapter 13 bankruptcy case. In Chapter 13, you use your income to pay off some portion of your debt, not your nonexempt property.

e. Houses and Cars

Filing for Chapter 13 bankruptcy lets you keep your house and car as long as you stay current on the payments. You can also use Chapter 13 to pay off arrearages you owe when you file. For instance, if you are $10,000 behind on your mortgage payments, you can pay an extra amount into your plan to pay off the arrearage in a reasonable amount of time. That's why Chapter 13 is the remedy of choice if you are facing foreclosure. (See Ch. 5 for more on what happens to your home when you file for either type of bankruptcy.)

f. Costs and Fees

The filing fee for a Chapter 13 is $189. If you can't afford the fee, you can apply for a fee waiver. If you want to be represented by a lawyer, you will probably have to pay $2,500 to $4,000 in legal fees, which can be paid as a priority debt over the life of your plan.

If you decide to handle your own case (as many do), you will need to buy some information. This will typically consist of one or more of the following:

- one or more self-help law books on Chapter 13 bankruptcy (roughly $30 a pop)
- telephonic legal advice from a lawyer (roughly $100 an hour), and
- clerical assistance with your forms from a bankruptcy petition preparer (between $300 and $600).

See Ch. 10 for more on resources you can use to file for bankruptcy.

g. The Meeting of Creditors

Shortly after you file your Chapter 13 bankruptcy petition (usually within about a month), the court will schedule a meeting of creditors and send an official notice of the bankruptcy filing and the meeting to you and all of your creditors. You (and your spouse if you have filed jointly) are required to attend. You'll need to bring two forms of identification—a picture ID and proof of your Social Security number.

A typical creditors' meeting lasts less than 15 minutes. The trustee will briefly go over your forms with you. No judge will be present. The trustee is likely to be most interested in the fairness and legality of your proposed repayment plan, and your ability to make the payments you have proposed. (See Ch. 2, Section D, for more on Chapter 13 requirements.) The trustee has a vested interest in helping you successfully navigate the Chapter 13 process because the trustee gets paid a percentage of all payments doled out under your plan.

The trustee will also make sure you have filed your tax returns for all taxable periods during the four prior years. If not, the trustee will continue the creditors' meeting to give you a chance to file these returns. You cannot proceed with a Chapter 13 bankruptcy unless and until you bring your tax filings up to date.

When the trustee is finished asking questions, any creditors who show up will have a chance to question you. Secured creditors often come, especially if they have any objections to the plan you have proposed as part of your Chapter 13 filing. They may claim, for example, that your plan isn't feasible, that you're giving yourself too much time to pay your arrears on your car note or mortgage, or that your plan proposes to pay less on a secured debt than the replacement value of the collateral property. (See Ch. 6 for more information on collateral and other property that secures a loan.)

An unsecured creditor who is scheduled to receive very little under your plan might show up, too, if that creditor thinks you should cut your living expenses and thereby increase your disposable income (the amount from which unsecured creditors are paid).

Come to the meeting prepared to negotiate with disgruntled creditors. If you agree to make changes to accommodate their objections, you must submit a modified plan. While the trustee won't use the creditors' meeting to rule on any objections raised by the creditors, the trustee may raise these objections on behalf of the creditors at your confirmation hearing before the judge (see Subsection h, below).

h. Issues That Must Be Decided by a Judge

Unlike Chapter 7, Chapter 13 bankruptcy requires at least one appearance before a bankruptcy judge. At this appearance, called the "confirmation hearing," the judge either confirms (approves of) your proposed plan or sends you back to the drawing board for various reasons— usually because your plan doesn't meet Chapter 13 requirements. (For example, a judge might reject your plan because you don't have enough projected disposable income to at least pay your priority creditors and stay current on your secured debts—such as a car note or mortgage.) For more information on the confirmation hearing, see Ch. 9, Section F.

You are entitled to amend your proposed plan until you get it right or the judge decides that it's hopeless. Each amendment requires a new confirmation hearing and appropriate written notice to your creditors.

In addition to attending the confirmation hearing, you may need to go to court to:

- amend your plan (if necessary)
- value an asset (if your plan proposes to pay less for a car or other property than the creditor thinks it's worth)
- respond to requests by a creditor or the trustee to dismiss your case or amend your plan (see Ch. 9, Section F)
- respond to a creditor who opposes your right to discharge a particular debt (perhaps because you engaged in fraud when incurring the debt— see Ch. 9, Section D)
- discharge a type of debt that can be discharged only if the judge decides that it should be (such as discharging a student loan because of hardship— see Ch. 9, Section D)

- eliminate a lien on your property that will survive your Chapter 13 bankruptcy unless the judge removes it (see Ch. 9, Section D), or
- reaffirm a contract that would otherwise not survive your bankruptcy (see Ch. 6 for more on reaffirmation agreements).

i. How a Chapter 13 Case Ends

If you complete your full three- or five-year repayment plan, are current on your income tax returns and your child support or alimony payments, and complete a budget management course approved by the U.S. Trustee, the remaining unpaid balance on any of your debts that qualify for discharge will be wiped out. If any balance remains on a debt that doesn't qualify for discharge, you will continue to owe the unpaid amount. (The debts that qualify for discharge in a Chapter 13 are explained in Chapter 3, Section C.)

You can't enjoy the benefits of a discharge unless and until the plan is completed—either because you make all your payments or because the court grants you an early discharge. If you don't complete your plan, your remaining debts will not be discharged. For this reason, if you can't make some payments under your plan, you'll want to ask the bankruptcy court for permission to modify it. As long as it's clear that you're acting in good faith, the court is likely to approve a request for a modification. If you can't complete the plan because of circumstances beyond your control, the court might even let you end your case early and discharge the remainder of your debts on the basis of hardship.

If the bankruptcy court won't let you modify your plan or give you a hardship discharge, you can:

- convert your Chapter 13 bankruptcy to a Chapter 7 bankruptcy, unless you received a Chapter 7 discharge within the previous eight years (this is explained in Ch. 9, Section E), or
- dismiss your Chapter 13 case. This means you'll owe your creditors the balances on your debts from before you filed your Chapter 13 case, less the payments you made, plus the interest that accrued while your Chapter 13 case was open.

As you can see, Chapter 13 bankruptcy requires discipline. For the entire length of your case, you will have to live strictly within your means—and even more strictly if your income exceeds the state's median income. The Chapter 13 trustee will not allow you to spend money on anything deemed nonessential. In past years, only about 35% of Chapter 13 plans were successfully completed; this percentage may well drop under the new, stricter, bankruptcy laws. Many Chapter 13 filers have dropped out early in the process, without ever submitting a feasible repayment plan to the court. Nevertheless, for the 35% of those who made it to the end, the rewards often included an earlier and easier path to restoring good credit.

3. Which Type of Bankruptcy Is Right for You

Under the new bankruptcy law, some people will no longer have a choice between Chapter 7 and Chapter 13 bankruptcy— they will have to file Chapter 13 and repay some of their debt. Most of those who still have a choice will probably want to file under Chapter 7, but there are some situations when Chapter 13 will be the better option.

a. Upper Income Filers Must Use Chapter 13

Under the old law, most people could choose to file under either Chapter 7 or Chapter 13 bankruptcy, as long as they met the eligibility requirements for their Chapter of choice. This is still the case under the new bankruptcy law, with one major exception: those whose current monthly income (the average income over the six months prior to filing) is higher than the median monthly income for their state cannot file for Chapter 7 bankruptcy if their projected disposable income would allow them to pay their unsecured creditors at least $166 a month over a five-year period. (Eligibility requirements for Chapter 7 and Chapter 13 bankruptcies are explained in Ch. 2.)

b. Reasons to Choose Chapter 7

Most people who have a choice traditionally have opted to file for Chapter 7 bankruptcy because it was relatively fast, effective, easy to file, and didn't require payments over time. In the typical situation, a case was opened and closed within three to six months, and the filer emerged debt free except for a mortgage, car payments, and certain types of debts that survive bankruptcy (such as student loans, recent taxes, and back child support). In addition, few filers lost any property in Chapter 7 bankruptcy because state and federal exemption rules allowed them to keep most necessities.

The new bankruptcy law has put a few more hurdles in the way of Chapter 7 filers. For example:

- attorneys fees have doubled in many cases
- more types of debts cannot be discharged
- more documents have to be filed, including the most recent tax return and wage stubs for the previous 60 days
- credit counseling and budget management education are mandatory
- property must now be valued at its replacement value (essentially, it's retail value), which will make it harder to hold on to property in Chapter 7 bankruptcy, and
- people who have not lived in the state where they are filing for at least two years now have to use the exemptions for the state where they lived before the two year period (see Ch. 4 for more on this rule).

Nevertheless, assuming they qualify, most people will still find it easier—and more effective—to file for Chapter 7 than to keep up with a long-term payment plan under Chapter 13. And if you do file for Chapter 13 and don't keep up with your repayment plan, you will likely get no benefit from the Chapter 13 process (unless the court lets you off the hook early for hardship reasons).

If your Chapter 13 fails—and historically, most do—you have two options. You may be able to convert your case to Chapter 7 and discharge what remains of your unsecured debts (except those that aren't dischargeable), or you can handle your remaining debt outside of bankruptcy. If you choose to convert to Chapter 7, any money you paid into your plan for dischargeable debts will have been for naught.

EXAMPLE: Frank files for Chapter 13 bankruptcy. His plan includes payment of an arrearage on his mortgage, current payments on his mortgage, and repayment of a portion of $50,000 worth of credit card debt. Frank remains current on his plan for three years, and then loses his job. In that three-year period, Frank, through the Chapter 13 trustee, cured the mortgage arrearage and paid off $12,000 worth of the credit card debt.

If Frank converts his case to Chapter 7, he can discharge all of the remaining credit card debt. But had Frank filed Chapter 7 from the beginning, he could also have discharged the $12,000 that was paid to the credit card companies under his Chapter 13 plan. If Frank decides to skip Chapter 7 and negotiate a repayment schedule for the remaining $38,000, Frank will at least have made a dent in the original $50,000 debt by filing for Chapter 13.

The moral of the story is that you should file for Chapter 7 in the first place if you have significant doubts about your ability to complete a Chapter 13 repayment plan.

c. Reasons to Choose Chapter 13

Although Chapter 7 is easier and doesn't require repayment, there are many good reasons why people who qualify for both types of bankruptcy choose Chapter 13 bankruptcy over Chapter 7 bankruptcy. Generally, you are probably a good candidate for Chapter 13 bankruptcy if you have adequate projected disposable income to fund your plan and are in any of the following situations:

- You are behind on your mortgage or car loan, and want to make up the missed payments over time and reinstate the original agreement. You generally cannot do this in Chapter 7 bankruptcy.
- Your car is reliable and you want to keep it, but it's worth far less than you owe. You can take advantage of Chapter 13 bankruptcy's option (for cars purchased more than 2½

years prior to filing for bankruptcy) to keep the car by paying its retail value—rather than the full amount you owe on the contract—as part of your Chapter 13 plan.
- You have a tax obligation, student loan, or other debt that cannot be discharged in Chapter 7 bankruptcy, but can be paid off over time in a Chapter 13 plan. (Nondischargeable debts are discussed in Ch. 3.)
- You owe debts that can be discharged in a Chapter 13 bankruptcy but not in a Chapter 7 bankruptcy. For instance, nonsupport debts arising from a divorce can't be discharged in Chapter 7 but can be discharged in Chapter 13.
- You have a sincere desire to repay your debts, but you need the protection of the bankruptcy court to do so.
- You want to restore your good credit as soon as possible and a Chapter 13 bankruptcy facilitates that process.

B. How Bankruptcy Stops Collection Efforts

One of the most powerful features of bankruptcy is that it stops most debt collectors dead in their tracks and keeps them at bay for the rest of your case. Once you file, all collection activity (with a few exceptions, explained below) must go through the bankruptcy court—and most creditors cannot take any further action against you directly.

 You don't need bankruptcy to stop your creditors from harassing you. Many people begin thinking about bankruptcy when their creditors start phoning their homes and/or places of employment. Federal law prohibits this activity by debt collectors once you tell the creditor, in writing, that you don't want to be called. And if you orally tell debt collectors that you refuse to pay, they cannot, by law, contact you except to send one last letter making a final demand for payment before filing a lawsuit. While just telling the creditor to stop usually works, you may have to send a written follow-up letter. (See Ch. 11 for a sample letter.)

When you file for any kind of bankruptcy, something called the "automatic stay" goes into effect. The automatic stay prohibits creditors and collection agencies from taking any action to collect most kinds of debts you owe them—unless the law or the bankruptcy court says they can.

Under the new law, however, the stay is not as automatic as it once was. In some circumstances, the creditor can file an action in court to have the stay lifted (called a "Motion to Lift Stay"). In others, the creditor can simply begin collection proceedings without seeking advance permission from the court.

The good news is that most common type of creditor collection actions are still stopped dead by the stay—harassing calls by debt collectors, threatening letters by attorneys, and lawsuits seeking a money judgment for credit card and health care bills. This section explains the collection rules for various types of debts.

1. Credit Card Debts, Medical Debts, and Attorney Fees

Anyone trying to collect credit card debts, medical debts, attorney fees, debts arising from breach of contract, or legal judgments against you (other than child support and alimony) must cease all collection activities after you file your bankruptcy. They cannot:

- file a lawsuit or proceed with a pending lawsuit against you
- record liens against your property
- report the debt to a credit reporting bureau, or
- seize your property or income, such as money in a bank account or your paycheck.

2. Public Benefits

Government entities that are seeking to collect overpayments of public benefits such as SSI, Medicaid, or TANF (welfare) benefits cannot do so by reducing or terminating your benefits while your bankruptcy is pending. If, however, you become ineligible for benefits, including Medicare benefits, bankruptcy doesn't prevent denial or termination of the benefits on that ground.

3. Domestic Relations Proceedings

Almost all proceedings related to a divorce or paternity action continue as before—they are not affected by the automatic stay. These include:

- the setting and collection of current child support and alimony
- the collection of back child support and alimony from property that is not in the bankruptcy estate (see Ch. 4 for more on what's in the bankruptcy estate)
- the determination of child custody and visitation
- a lawsuit to establish paternity
- an action to modify child support and alimony
- proceedings to protect a spouse or child from domestic violence
- withholding of income to collect child support
- reporting of overdue support to credit bureaus
- the interception of tax refunds to pay back child support, and
- withholding, suspension, or restriction of drivers' and professional licenses as leverage to collect child support.

4. Criminal Proceedings

If a case against you can be broken down into criminal and debt components, only the criminal component will be allowed to continue—the debt component will be stayed while your bankruptcy is pending. For example, if you were convicted of writing a bad check and have been sentenced to community service and ordered to pay a fine, your obligation to do community service will not be stopped by the automatic stay (but your obligation to pay the fine will).

5. Landlord-Tenant Proceedings

With a few exceptions, the automatic stay does not stop the eviction of a tenant if:

- the landlord obtained a judgment prior to the bankruptcy filing, or
- the tenant is endangering the property or using controlled substances on it.

Ch. 5, Section C, explains when evictions on these grounds may occur. It also covers the new requirements imposed on both the tenant and the landlord if there is a dispute about whether an eviction can proceed.

6. Tax Proceedings

The IRS can continue certain actions, such as a tax audit, issuing a tax deficiency notice, demanding a tax return, issuing a tax assessment, or demanding payment of an assessment. The automatic stay does, however, stop the IRS from issuing a lien or seizing (levying against) any of your property or income.

7. Pension Loans

The stay doesn't prevent withholding from a debtor's income to repay a loan from an ERISA-qualified pension (this includes most job-related pensions and individual retirement plans). See Ch. 4 for more on how pensions are treated under bankruptcy.

8. Foreclosures

Although foreclosures initially are stayed by your bankruptcy filing, the stay won't apply if you filed another bankruptcy within the previous two years and the court, in that proceeding, lifted the stay and allowed the lender to proceed with the foreclosure. In other words, the law doesn't allow you to prevent a foreclosure by filing serial bankruptcies.

9. Utilities

Companies providing you with utilities (such as gas, heating oil, electricity, telephone, and water) may not discontinue service because you file for bankruptcy. However, they can shut off your service 20 days after you file if you don't provide them with a deposit or other means to assure future payment.

10. Special Rules for Multiple Filers

If you had a bankruptcy case pending during the previous year, then the stay

will terminate after 30 days unless you, the trustee, the U.S. Trustee, or the creditor asks for the stay to continue and proves that the current case was filed in good faith.

This rule doesn't apply to any case that was dismissed because you should have filed under Chapter 13 instead of Chapter 7 (see Ch. 2 for more on when a case may be dismissed on that ground).

If a creditor had a motion to lift the stay pending during the previous case, the court will presume that you acted in bad faith. You will have to overcome this presumption in order to obtain continuing stay relief. If you had more than two cases pending during the previous year, then you will have to seek a court order to obtain any stay relief.

C. The Bankruptcy Trustee

Until your Chapter 7 or Chapter 13 bankruptcy case ends, your financial assets and problems are in the hands of the bankruptcy trustee.

1. The Trustee's General Duties

With few exceptions, the court assumes legal control of your property and debts as of the date you file. If, without the court's consent, you sell or give away property while your case is open, you risk having your case dismissed.

The court exercises its control through a court-appointed person called a bankruptcy trustee. The trustee's primary duties are:

- to see that your unsecured creditors are paid as much as possible on the debts you owe them, and
- to make sure you comply with the bankruptcy laws, under the supervision of the U.S. Trustee for the region where your bankruptcy court is located. (See Section 2, below, for more on the U.S. Trustee's office.)

The trustee may be a local bankruptcy attorney or someone who is very knowledgeable about Chapter 7 or Chapter 13 bankruptcy generally and the local court's rules and procedures in particular. In some courts, trustees are not attorneys but business people with specialized knowledge of finances or personal bankruptcy.

Just a few days after you file your bankruptcy papers, you'll get a Notice of Appointment of Trustee from the court, giving the name, business address, and business phone number of the trustee. The letter may also include a list of any financial documents the trustee wants to see, such as bank statements, property appraisals, or canceled checks, and the date by which the trustee wants them.

As used in this book, the term "trustee" means the trustee who will actually be handling your case on behalf of the bankruptcy court, unless otherwise stated.

2. The U.S. Trustee's Office

In addition to the trustee assigned to your case, another type of trustee—a U.S. Trustee—will be involved, usually behind the scenes. The Office of the U.S. Trustee is a part of the United States Department of Justice. Its role is to supervise the trustees who actually handle cases in the bankruptcy court, to make sure that the bankruptcy laws are being followed and that cases of fraud and other crimes are appropriately handled. There are 21 regional U.S. Trustee offices throughout the country.

If the a U.S. Trustee decides to take an active part in your case, the parties to the case—including you—will be sent a notice about the proposed action. You will have an opportunity in bankruptcy court to oppose the action proposed by the U.S. Trustee. Later chapters in this book suggest some ways to respond to various actions the U.S. Trustee might propose.

Happily, most of you will never have to deal with the U.S. Trustee. It will likely happen only if you file a Chapter 7 bankruptcy and your bankruptcy papers—or your testimony at the creditors' meeting—indicate that:

- your "current monthly income" is more than the median income for your state (see Ch. 2, Section B)
- you earn enough actual income to support a Chapter 13 plan (see Ch. 2, Section D)
- you have apparently engaged in illegal actions that warrant investigative follow-up (such as perjuring yourself in your bankruptcy papers), or
- your case is selected for a random audit (one out of every 250 bankruptcy cases is supposed to be audited under the new bankruptcy rules).

3. Chapter 7 Trustee

In a Chapter 7 bankruptcy, the trustee is mostly interested in what you own and what property you claim as exempt. This is because the court pays the trustee a commission on property that is sold for the benefit of the unsecured creditors. The trustee may receive 25% of the first $5,000, 10% of any amount between $5,000 and $50,000, and 5% of any additional money up to $1,000,000.

If your papers indicate that all of your property is exempt, your case initially is considered a "no-asset" case and your creditors are told not to file claims (because you don't have any property that can be used to pay them). The trustee also won't show much interest in a no-asset case unless your papers suggest that you may be hiding or mischaracterizing assets. After all, if there is no property for the trustee to seize and sell to pay your unsecured creditors, then there is no commission for the trustee.

The first time you will encounter the trustee in a Chapter 7 case is when you appear at your creditors' meeting, which you must attend if you don't want your bankruptcy dismissed. (The Chapter 7 creditors' meeting is covered in Section A1, above.) Typically, if all of your assets are exempt, you will hear nothing further from the trustee. However, if there are (or it appears that there might be) nonexempt assets in your bankruptcy estate, the trustee may continue your creditors' meeting to another date and ask you to submit appropriate documentation in the meantime. More rarely, the trustee may hire an attorney to pursue nonexempt assets you appear to own or even refer your case to the U.S. Trustee's office for further action if it looks like you have engaged in dishonest activity.

If there are nonexempt assets for the trustee to seize and sell, you will be expected to cooperate in getting them to the trustee for disposition. You may also buy the assets back from the trustee at a negotiated price or substitute exempt assets for the nonexempt assets.

If you have nonexempt property that isn't worth very much or would be cumbersome for the trustee to sell, the trustee can—and often will—abandon the property, which means you get to keep it. For example, no matter how much your used furniture may be worth in theory, many trustees won't bother selling it. Arranging to sell used furniture is expensive and rarely produces much profit.

Many people wonder whether a trustee can search their homes to determine whether they are hiding property. While such searches are rare, part of your duty to cooperate with the trustee could consist of a guided tour of your home upon the trustee's request. And if you don't voluntarily cooperate, the trustee can obtain an order from the court to force the issue.

The trustee is also required, under the supervision of the U.S. Trustee, to assess your bankruptcy papers for accuracy and for signs of possible fraud or abuse of the bankruptcy system.

If You Owe Back Child Support

If you owe back support, the trustee is also required to provide notices to the holder of the support claim and the state child support agency to keep them abreast of your bankruptcy and help them find you after your bankruptcy discharge. Specifically, the trustee is required to provide:

- the payee with information about the state child support enforcement agency and his or her rights under the bankruptcy law
- the state child support enforcement agency with information about the back support and the payee, and
- (when you are granted a discharge), the state child support agency and payee with information about the discharge, your last known address, the last known name and address of your employer, and the name of any creditor who holds a nondischargeable claim or a claim that has been reaffirmed.

Both the payee and the child support enforcement agency can ask these creditors to provide your last known address. The laws specifically authorize these creditors to release such information without any penalty.

4. Chapter 13 Trustee

In a Chapter 13 bankruptcy, the trustee's role is to:

- examine your proposed plan and make sure it complies with all legal requirements
- receive the payments you make under the plan and distribute them to your creditors in the manner required by law
- monitor your duty to file tax returns with the appropriate federal and state taxing authorities for the four years previous to your filing date and annually while your Chapter 13 case is pending
- monitor your duty to file an annual financial statement charting your income and expenses (see Ch. 2, Section D), and
- if you owe back child support, provide the payee and your state's child support enforcement agency with information described in "If You Owe Back Child Support," above.

Chapter 13 trustees pay themselves by keeping a percentage of the payments you make—almost always 10%, the maximum allowed under law.

Many Chapter 13 trustees play a fairly active role in the cases they administer. This is especially true in small suburban or rural judicial districts, or in districts with a lot of Chapter 13 bankruptcy cases. For example, a trustee may:

- give you financial advice, such as helping you create a realistic budget

(the trustee cannot, however, give you legal advice)

- actively participate in helping you modify your plan, if necessary
- give you a temporary reprieve or take other steps to help you get back on track if you miss a payment or two, or
- participate at any hearing on the value of an item of property, possibly even hiring an appraiser.

Despite the trustee's great interest in your finances, your financial relationship with the trustee is not as stifling as it may sound. In most situations, you keep complete control over money and property you acquire after filing—as long as you make the payments called for under your repayment plan, and you make all regular payments on your secured debts. However, if your income or property increases during the life of your plan (for instance, you win the lottery), the trustee can seek to amend your plan to pay your creditors 100% of what you owe them rather than a lesser percentage called for in your plan.

D. Changes to the Bankruptcy Laws

As noted throughout this chapter, Congress made major changes to the bankruptcy laws in April 2005. This section describes some of the most important legal changes and the practical effects they are likely to have on those considering or filing for bankruptcy. These changes and others are fully covered in the text of the chapters that follow. In addition, each chapter includes a final section that summarizes the legal changes covered in that chapter.

1. Higher Income Filers Must File Chapter 13

Under the old rules, most filers could choose the bankruptcy type that made the most sense for them—and most preferred Chapter 7 to Chapter 13. The new rules force those with higher incomes to file under Chapter 13. Filers whose average monthly income is higher than the median income for their state will not be allowed to file for Chapter 7 bankruptcy.

Most filers will have a lower median income and, therefore, will still be eligible for Chapter 7 bankruptcy. To find out if you're one of them, you'll have to use the instructions in Ch. 2 to

- compute your average monthly income (a somewhat complicated formula)
- compare it to the state median income, and
- if your income is more than the median income, figure out whether any exceptions apply that will still let you file Chapter 7 bankruptcy.

2. Filings Will Be Scrutinized More Closely

One reason Congress changed the bankruptcy laws was to prevent fraud. Even though studies show that 90% of filers don't engage in fraud, the bankruptcy rules are now explicitly designed to catch cheats. All filers will be notified that they are subject to criminal prosecution for errors in their paperwork, cases will be audited for fraud by lawyers from the Attorney General's office with much greater frequency, and all filers will have to produce their income tax returns—which must also be provided to creditors upon request.

3. Lawyers Will Be Harder to Find and More Expensive

The new laws impose a number of responsibilities on bankruptcy lawyers, which is expected to cause many to get out of the field (and those who remain to charge more for their services). Chief among these new responsibilities is that lawyers must personally vouch for the accuracy of the information their clients provide them. This rule changes the traditional alliance between lawyers and their clients. It will also add to the time and money lawyers will have to spend on bankruptcy cases, which will in turn cause legal fees to go up. (See Ch. 10 for more on working with a lawyer.)

4. Chapter 13 Filers Will Have to Live on Less

Under the old rules, people who filed under Chapter 13 had to devote all of their "disposable income" to their repayment plan. A filer's actual living expenses determined the filer's level of disposable income, as long as the expenses were reasonably necessary. For instance, if your actual reasonable expenses left you with $100 a month extra, you only had to pay $100 a month under your plan.

Under the new law, if your income is higher than your state's median income (see Ch. 2), you must commit to a five-year plan and compute your disposable income using "official" expenses compiled by the Internal Revenue Service. These expenses are often lower than actual costs, which means you may have to pay more each month into your Chapter 13 repayment plan (and live on less). Even worse, because your disposable income will be based on your average income over the six months prior to filing, you may have less income to actually pay into your plan than the law assumes you have.

5. Credit and Budget Counseling Is Required

Under the new law, you must undergo credit counseling before filing a Chapter 7 or Chapter 13 bankruptcy (unless no credit counseling is available where you live). You must pay for this counseling yourself on a sliding scale. In addition, you'll have to complete a course on personal financial management before obtaining final relief from your debts.

6. Property Must Be Valued at Replacement Cost

Under the old law, you could value your property at what you could get for it in a "fire" sale or auction. This meant that used furniture, hobby items, cars, heirlooms, and other property a debtor might want to keep was typically assumed to have little value—and, therefore, that it often fell well within the exemption categories offered by most states.

Under the new law, your property has to be valued at what it would cost to replace it from a retail vendor, taking into account the property's age and condition. This requirement is sure to jack up the value of your property, often in excess of the exemption system you are using— which means more property will be at risk of being taken and sold by the trustee.

7. State Exemptions Aren't Available to Recent State Residents

Under the old bankruptcy law, the personal property you could keep was determined by the exemption laws of your state of residence (as long you lived there for more than three months). Under the new law, you must live in a state for at least two years prior to filing in order to claim that state's personal property exemptions.

EXAMPLE: Al moved from California to Nevada 18 months ago. If he wants to file for Chapter 7 bankruptcy, he will have to use California's personal property exemptions. Instead of being able to claim Nevada's relatively liberal exemption for a motor vehicle ($15,000), Al will have to use California's parsimonious motor vehicle exemption of $2,300.

There are also new residency requirements for homestead exemptions, which determine how much of your equity in a home you can keep when filing a Chapter 7 bankruptcy. Under the old law, the exemptions for the state where your home was located (with rare exceptions) determined how much equity you could keep in your home, as long as you lived in that state for more than three months.

Under the new law, you must live in a state for 40 months prior to filing in order to claim that state's full homestead exemption. For instance, if Al moved from California to Nevada three years ago (36 months) and wants to file a Chapter 7 bankruptcy, his homestead exemption will be capped at $125,000 even though Nevada's homestead is higher.

In this case, it might make sense for Al to wait out the four months before filing. Once he has spent 40 months in Nevada, he will be able to claim Nevada's homestead exemption of $200,000. Otherwise, he will have to use California's homestead exemption, which runs from $50,000 for single people to $150,000 for people over 65 or over 55 and disabled.

Nolo Resources on Bankruptcy and Debt

Nolo publishes self-help bankruptcy books that provide readers with all of the information they need to file for Chapter 7 or Chapter 13 bankruptcy, step by step. Look for the latest editions of these books, which will incorporate the new bankruptcy rules effective October 20, 2005:

- *How to File for Chapter 7 Bankruptcy,* by Stephen R. Elias, Albin Renauer, and Robin Leonard. This do-it-yourself bankruptcy book takes you through the filing process for a liquidation bankruptcy. It gives practical advice, and supplies all the official bankruptcy forms you'll need, with complete instructions. The 13th edition will cover all of the new bankruptcy requirements.

- *Chapter 13 Bankruptcy: Repay Your Debts,* by Robin Leonard. This book takes you through the entire Chapter 13 bankruptcy process, step by step. It provides the official bankruptcy forms, with complete instructions for filling them out. You'll learn how to create a repayment plan, represent yourself in bankruptcy court, and deal with unexpected changes. The 8th edition will incorporate all of the important changes imposed by the new bankruptcy rules.

In addition to these bankruptcy titles, Nolo publishes books that deal with credit, debt, and other money issues. Here are a few you might find helpful:

- *Solve Your Money Troubles: Get Debt Collectors Off Your Back & Regain Financial Freedom*, by Robin Leonard. A practical book to help you prioritize debts, negotiate with creditors, stop collector harassment, challenge wage attachments, contend with repossession, respond to creditor lawsuits, and rebuild your credit. Contains sample letters to creditors as well as worksheets and charts to calculate a budget and create a payment plan.

- *Credit Repair,* by Robin Leonard. This book shows how to fix your credit situation quickly, easily, and legally. It teaches you how to read and understand your credit report, fix mistakes, get positive information added to your credit report, avoid credit discrimination, and defend your good credit from fraud and identity theft. Includes sample credit reports and letters to creditors, as well as lists of agencies and organizations to turn to for additional help.

- *Divorce & Money: How to Make the Best Financial Decisions During Divorce*, by Violet Woodhouse, with Dale Fetherling. This book can help you with the overwhelming

Nolo Resources on Bankruptcy and Debt (continued)

financial decisions of divorce: selling the house, dividing debts, discovering assets, setting alimony and child support, handling retirement benefits and taxes, and negotiating a fair settlement. Contains worksheets, charts, formulas, and tables.

- *Take Control of Your Student Loan Debt*, by Robin Leonard and Deanne Loonin. Comprehensive strategies for paying off debt, deferring repayment, avoiding default, and handling collection efforts. Includes sample forms and letters.

Who Can File for Bankruptcy

Bankruptcy might be a fine solution to your debt problems—but only if you are eligible to file. The new bankruptcy law creates a few new hurdles up front for people seeking to wipe out their debts. For example, you won't be allowed to file for Chapter 7 bankruptcy if you don't first seek credit counseling or if the court believes your income is high enough to allow you to complete a repayment plan under Chapter 13. Before reading the rest of this book to find out what effect bankruptcy will have on your life, you should figure out whether you'll be eligible to file for bankruptcy in the first place.

The new bankruptcy eligibility rules are intended, in large part, to require people to pay back at least a portion of their debts if they are able—in other words, to require people to file for bankruptcy under Chapter 13 rather than Chapter 7. To determine who will still be allowed to file for Chapter 7 and who will be forced into Chapter 13, Congress has created formulas to calculate monthly income and expenses. (As you'll learn below, these equations are likely to yield numbers that are very different from your actual income and expenses.) Unless you can prove that you have almost no income to devote to a repayment plan, Chapter 13 may be your only option.

This chapter explains these new tests, along with the other eligibility rules for Chapter 7 and Chapter 13 bankruptcy. Section A describes the new requirement that all debtors receive credit counseling from an approved agency before filing

for bankruptcy. In Section B, you'll learn how to calculate your monthly income according to the new rules. Section C explains the other eligibility requirements for Chapter 7 bankruptcy, including the much-discussed "means test" that you may have to pass in order to prove that your income is too low to complete a Chapter 13 repayment plan. And Section D describes the other eligibility requirements for Chapter 13 bankruptcy.

A. Credit Counseling

Before you can file for Chapter 7 or Chapter 13 bankruptcy, you must consult a nonprofit credit counseling agency. The purpose of this consultation is to see whether there is a feasible way to handle your debt load outside of bankruptcy, without adding to what you owe.

1. Counseling Requirements

To qualify for bankruptcy relief, you must show that you received credit counseling from an agency approved by the U.S Trustee's office for your region within the 180-day period before you filed. Once you complete the counseling, the agency will give you a certificate showing that you participated. It will also give you a copy of any repayment plan you worked out with the agency. This requirement doesn't apply if no credit counseling agency is available to you in your region. (See Section 3, below, for more on this exception.) You can find out which agencies have been approved for your judicial district by visiting the Office of the U.S. Trustee's website at www .usdoj.gov/ust; click "Credit Counseling and Debtor Education" to see the list.

The purpose of credit counseling is to give you an idea of whether you really need to file for bankruptcy or whether an informal repayment plan would get you back on your economic feet. Counseling is required even if it's pretty obvious that a repayment plan isn't feasible (that is, your debts are too high and your income is too low) or you are facing debts that you find unfair and don't want to pay. (Credit card balances inflated by high interest rates and penalties are particularly unpopular with many filers, as are emergency room bills and deficiency judgments based on auctions of repossessed cars.)

The law requires only that you participate—not that you go along with whatever the agency proposes. Even if a repayment plan is feasible, you aren't required to agree to it. However, if the agency does come up with a plan, you must file it along with the other bankruptcy documents described in Ch. 9.

Rules Counseling Agencies Must Follow

In addition to providing services without regard to the debtor's ability to pay, counseling agencies have to meet a number of other requirements. They must:

- disclose to you their funding sources, their counselor qualifications, the possible impact of their proposed plan on your credit report, the costs of the program, if any, and how much of the costs will be born by you
- provide counseling that includes an analysis of your current financial condition, factors that caused the condition, and how you can develop a plan to respond to the problems without adding to your debt
- use trained counselors who don't receive any commissions or bonuses based on the outcome of the counseling services (that is, kickbacks to individual counselors are not allowed, although kickbacks to the agency may be legal), and
- maintain adequate financial resources to provide continuing support services over the life of any repayment plan (that is, if they propose a three-year payment plan, they must have adequate reserves to service your case for three years).

⚠️ **The court might agree with the agency's plan.** If it's clear from the documents you file that you could complete the repayment plan proposed by the agency, the court may use this as a reason to question your Chapter 7 filing and try to push you into a Chapter 13 repayment plan (see Ch. 9, Section B). If that happens, at least you'll have an opportunity to argue about whether you should have to repay all of your debts.

2. Counseling Costs

Credit counseling agencies may charge a reasonable fee for their services. However, if a debtor cannot afford the fee, the counseling agency must provide services free or at reduced rates. This means that the service must offer a sliding fee scale and a waiver of fees altogether for people below a certain income level. The Office of the U.S. Trustee, the law enforcement agency that oversees credit counseling agencies, has indicated that a "reasonable" fee might range from free to $50, depending on the circumstances.

3. Exceptions to the Counseling Requirement

You don't have to get counseling if the U.S. Trustee certifies that there is no appropriate agency available to you in the district where you will be filing. However, counseling can be provided by telephone or online if the U.S. Trustee approves, so it is unlikely that approved debt counseling will ever be "unavailable."

You can also avoid the requirement if you certify to the court's satisfaction that:

- you had to file for bankruptcy immediately (perhaps to stop a foreclosure), and
- you were unable to obtain counseling within five days after requesting it.

If you can prove that you didn't receive credit counseling for this reason, you must certify that to the court and complete the counseling within 30 days after filing (you can ask the court to extend this deadline by 15 days).

You may also escape the credit counseling requirement if, after notice and hearing, the bankruptcy court determines that you couldn't participate because of:

- a physical disability that prevents you from attending counseling (this exception probably won't apply if the counseling is available on the Internet or over the phone)
- mental incapacity (you are unable to understand and benefit from the counseling), or
- your active duty in a military combat zone.

Incentive for Creditors To Settle?

If a credit counseling agency proposes a settlement that would repay at least 60% of your debt to a creditor, and that creditor refuses to go along with the plan, the creditor may be penalized when and if your property is distributed in bankruptcy. The creditor will be allowed to collect a maximum of 80% of the total claim if you can show, by clear and convincing evidence, that the creditor was offered the deal at least 60 days before you filed and the creditor unreasonably refused the offer.

Although this 20% penalty is billed as an incentive for creditors to accept settlement prior to bankruptcy, the creditor stands to lose only 20 cents on the dollar for turning down an offer to lose 40 cents on the dollar. It's not clear why a creditor should agree to take a large hit early to avoid the possibility of a smaller hit down the road. Also, it will generally cost you more to prove that the creditor's refusal was unreasonable than the penalty is worth. And finally, this will be a factor only in Chapter 13 cases; creditors of Chapter 7 debtors rarely recoup 60% of their debt, let alone 80%.

B. Calculating Your Income Status

The new bankruptcy law divides would-be filers into two classes—people whose "current monthly income" (a legal term defined below) is more than the "family median income" for their state, and those whose current monthly income is less than the median. The term "family median income" means that there are as many families with income above that level as below it; the median is different for families of different sizes.

> **EXAMPLE:** Sarah is single with no children (a family of one). Sarah's current monthly income (calculated as explained below) is $5,000. The family median income in Sarah's state for one-person families, converted to a monthly figure, is $4,500. Because Sarah's monthly income is $500 more than the family median income, Sarah will have to meet an additional requirement (the means test) to prove that she should be allowed to file for Chapter 7 bankruptcy.

If your income is more than the median, you'll face these consequences:

- If you want to file for Chapter 7 bankruptcy—and your debts were incurred primarily for yourself and your family rather than for a business—you must first pass the means test (explained in Section C2, below) to prove that a Chapter 13 repayment plan isn't feasible.

- If you choose to file under Chapter 13 and are otherwise eligible, you must reduce your expenses to a relatively low standard set by the IRS and, after taking some other allowable deductions, commit to paying the rest of your income into the Chapter 13 plan for five years (unless you can pay 100% of the debt included in your plan in a shorter period).

If your income is less than the median, these rules apply:

- If you choose to file for Chapter 7 bankruptcy, you will not be forced into Chapter 13—unless the court finds, upon a motion filed by the court itself or the U.S. Trustee, that allowing you to file for Chapter 7 would be an "abuse" of the bankruptcy system. (See Section C, below.)
- If you choose to file under Chapter 13 and are otherwise eligible, you are not required legally to use the IRS expense standards to determine how much of your income is available for your repayment plan. Also, you can propose a three-year plan unless you need a longer time to pay certain debts in full, as required under Chapter 13. (See Section D, below.)

An Exception for Disabled Veterans

There is one exception to the higher income rule: If you are a disabled veteran and the debts you wish to discharge were incurred when you were on active duty or engaged in homeland defense activity, the court must treat you as if you were in the lower income group, regardless of your actual income. The law doesn't clearly indicate what will happen if some of your debts were incurred when you were on active duty and others prior to or after active duty; we'll have to wait and see how courts interpret this provision.

1. Determine Your Current Monthly Income

The bankruptcy law defines "current monthly income" as your average monthly income received during the six-month period that ends on the last day of the month preceding your filing date—whether or not the income is taxable. When including wages or other sources of income, you must include the gross amount, not the net income you actually receive after deductions and other withholdings are made.

Your current monthly income includes income from all sources except:

- payments you receive under the Social Security Act (including Social Security Retirement, SSI, SSDI, TANF, and (arguably) state unemployment insurance)
- payments to victims of war crimes or crimes against humanity based on their status as victims of such crimes, or
- payments to victims of international or domestic terrorism.

Use *Worksheet A: Current Monthly Income*, below (and in Appendix D), to compute your current monthly income by:

- adding up all of the income you received during that six-month period (except for income that falls into the excluded categories), and
- dividing by six to come up with a monthly average.

EXAMPLE: John and Marcia are married and have two young children. They fell quickly into debt after John was forced out of his job because of a work-related injury on April 1, 2006. Three months later, on July 1, 2006, John and Marcia decide to file for bankruptcy.

To compute their current monthly income, Marcia reviews the family's income for the period between January 1 and June 30, 2006 (the six-month period prior to their bankruptcy filing date). This includes John's *gross* salary for the first three months (he made $8,000 a month as a software engineer), plus $1,800 in workers'

compensation benefits for each of the last three months. Marcia made $1,000 a month during the first three months and had no income for the last three months. The total family income for the six-month period is $32,400. The family's "current monthly income" is $5,400 (the six-month average), even though the monthly amount they actually took in during each of the three months before filing was only $1,800. None of the deductions available for computing current monthly income are available to John and Marcia, so their current monthly income remains at $5,400.

The following types of income should be included in the form:

- wages, salary, tips, bonuses, overtime, commissions
- gross income from the operation of a business, profession, or farm
- interest, dividends, and royalties
- rents and other real property income
- pension and retirement income
- regular contributions to the household expenses of the debtor or the debtor's dependents, including child or spousal support
- regular contributions of the debtor's spouse if he or she isn't a joint debtor in the bankruptcy
- unemployment compensation
- workers' compensation insurance
- state disability insurance, and
- annuity payments.

Worksheet A: Current Monthly Income

Use this worksheet to calculate your current monthly income; use figures for you and your spouse if you plan to file jointly.

Line 1. Calculate your total income over the last six months from wages, salary, tips, bonuses, overtime, and so on.

    A. Month 1 $ _____

    B. Month 2   _____

    C. Month 3   _____

    D. Month 4   _____

    E. Month 5   _____

    F. Month 6   _____

    G. TOTAL WAGES (add Lines A–F) $ _____

Line 2. Add up all other income for the last six months.

    A. Business, profession, or farm income   _____

    B. Interest, dividends, and royalties   _____

    C. Rents and real property income   _____

    D. Pension and retirement income   _____

    E. Alimony or family support   _____

    F. Spousal contributions (if not filing jointly)   _____

    G. Unemployment compensation   _____

    H. Workers' compensation   _____

    I. State disability insurance   _____

    J. Annuity payments   _____

    K. Other   _____

    L. TOTAL OTHER INCOME $ _____

Line 3. Calculate total income over the six months prior to filing.

    A. Enter total wages (Line 1G)   _____

    B. Enter total other income (Line 2L)   _____

    C. TOTAL INCOME OVER THE SIX MONTHS PRIOR TO FILING. Add Lines A and B together. $ _____

Line 4. Average monthly income over the six months prior to filing. This is called your "current monthly income."

    A. Enter total six-month income (Line 3C)   _____

    B. CURRENT MONTHLY INCOME. Divide Line A by six. $ _____

2. Compare Your Income to Your State's Family Median Income

The census bureau publishes *annual* family median income figures for all 50 states. To compare your current *monthly* income to the family median income for your state, you'll need to multiply your current monthly income by 12 (or divide the annual family median income figure by 12). Let's do it the first way. In John and Marcia's case, the family's "current monthly income" ($5,400) multiplied by 12 would be $64,800.

Once you've got your current monthly income and your family median income for the same time period (one month or one year), compare them to see whether your current monthly income is more or less than the median. For the most recent family median income figures, see the "Median Family Income" chart, in Appendix B. You can also find up-to-date figures at the U.S. Trustee's website at www.usdoj.gov/ust (click "Means Testing Information," then "Median Income Figures") or at the website of the United States Census Bureau, www.census.gov (click "State Family Income" from the home page).

You can see from the chart in Appendix B that John and Marcia's current monthly income would be more than the family median income in most states.

For Larger Families

Although the U.S. Census Bureau generates median figures for families that have up to seven members, Congress does not want you to use these figures if you have a larger family. The Census figures are to be used for families that have up to four members (these are the numbers you will find in Appendix B). If there are more than four members of your family, you must add $6,300 per additional person to the four-member family median income figure for your state.

3. If Your Current Monthly Income Is Less Than or Equal to Your State's Family Median Income

If your current monthly income is less than or equal to your state's family median income, you aren't subject to the means test in a Chapter 7 bankruptcy filing. If you decide to file for Chapter 13, you may propose a plan that is based on your actual expenses and lasts for only three years.

4. If Your Current Monthly Income Is More Than Your State's Family Median Income

If your current monthly income, as calculated above, exceeds your state's family median income, the consequences depend on whether you are filing for Chapter 7 or Chapter 13 bankruptcy:

Chapter 7: If your current monthly income is more than the family median income for your state, your debts were incurred primarily for consumer rather than business purposes, and you want to file for Chapter 7 bankruptcy, you will come face to face with what has been called the "means test" (explained step by step in Section C2, below). Under the means test, you can't file for Chapter 7 bankruptcy if, after certain expenses are deducted, your remaining income:

- would exceed $10,000 when projected over a five-year period ($166.66 per month), or
- would be equal to at least $6,000 over five years ($100 per month) and would pay at least 25% of your unsecured, nonpriority debts over that same period. These types of debts include credit card and department store charge card bills, medical bills, utility bills, and student loans (see Section C1, below, for more on unsecured debts).

If your income would be less than $6,000 when projected over the next five years, you will pass the means test and can file for Chapter 7 if you meet the other eligibility requirements explained in Section C below.

EXAMPLE: Jonas makes $4,500 a month as a section manager in a large general-purpose store. His current monthly income is more than the median income for his state, so he has to pass the means test to file for Chapter 7 bankruptcy. He deducts allowable expenses from his income (see Section C2, below) and comes up with $200 a month extra. Because his excess income comes to $12,000 when projected over the next five years ($200 x 60 months), Jonas fails the means test.

If Jonas had only $125 a month extra ($7,500 over a five-year period), he would have to figure out whether this amount would pay 25% of his unsecured, nonpriority debt in that five-year period. For instance, if Jonas owed $36,000 in credit card debt, he would be barred from Chapter 7 if he could pay $9,000 (25% of the debt) over a five-year period. Because Jonas only has $7,500 extra, however, he would pass the means test and be eligible for Chapter 7, as long as he meets the other eligibility factors.

Chapter 13: If your current monthly income is more than the median for your state and you file for Chapter 13, you must propose a five-year repayment plan to which you commit all of your disposable income. You will also have to use the IRS expense standards—and other allowable deductions—to calculate your projected disposable income (the amount of income you'll have to pay into the plan every month for the benefit of your nonpriority, unsecured creditors). These rules are explained in Section D, below.

💡 **Choose your filing date to lower your income.** If your income has been uneven during the six months prior to your projected filing date, you may want delay or speed up your filing if either strategy would move your current monthly income from the high-income to the low-income category. For instance, if you had a high-paying job during the first three months and a low-paying job during the second three months, each month you wait before filing will reduce your current monthly income. On the other hand, if you've recently landed a high-paying job after having a low income, the sooner you file the lower your currently monthly income will be. Either way, by changing the filing date of your bankruptcy, you can cross the line from high filer status to low filer status, which will make your bankruptcy much easier.

C. Chapter 7 Eligibility Requirements

There are several basic eligibility requirements you must meet to file a "consumer" Chapter 7 bankruptcy. In addition, if your current monthly income is more than your state's family median income for a family of your size, and your debts are primarily consumer debts, you will have to pass the "means test," explained in Section 2, below. To figure out whether you can meet these requirements, you'll first need to know how various debts are classified; you can find this information in Section 1, below.

1. How Debts Are Classified

The eligibility requirements for Chapter 7 and Chapter 13 bankruptcy (see Section D, below) are based primarily on your income, living expenses, and debts. Different types of debts are handled differently in these calculations. This section will help you figure out which numbers to use.

a. Secured Debts

A debt is "secured" if you stand to lose specific property when you don't make your payments to the creditor. Most secured debts are created when you sign loan papers giving a creditor a security interest in your property—such as a home loan or car loan. But a debt might also be secured if a creditor has filed a lien (a legal claim against your property that must be paid before the property can be sold). Here is a list of common secured debts and liens:

- **Mortgages.** Called deeds of trust in some states, these are loans to buy or refinance a house or other real estate. If you fail to pay, the lender can foreclose on your house.

- **Home equity loans (second mortgages).** If you fail to pay, the lender (typically a bank or finance company) can foreclose on your house.
- **Loans for cars, boats, tractors, motorcycles, or RVs.** If you fail to pay, the lender can repossess the vehicle.
- **Store charges with a security agreement.** Almost all store purchases on credit cards are unsecured. Some stores, notably Sears and J.C. Penney, however, claim to retain a security interest in all hard goods (durable goods) purchased, or they make customers sign security agreements when they use their store charge card.
- **Personal loans from banks, credit unions, or finance companies.** Often, you must pledge valuable personal property, such as a paid-off motor vehicle, as collateral for these loans. The property can be repossessed if you don't make the payments.
- **Judicial liens.** A judicial lien can be imposed on your property only after somebody sues you and wins a money judgment against you. In most states, the judgment creditor then must record (file) the judgment with the county or state. The recorded judgment creates a lien on your real estate and, in some states, on some of your personal property as well.
- **Statutory liens.** Some liens are automatic, by law. For example, in most states, when you hire someone to work on your house, the worker and the supplier of materials automatically gets a mechanic's lien (sometimes called a materialman's or contractor's lien) on the house if you don't pay.
- **Tax liens.** If you owe money to the IRS or other taxing authority, the debt is secured if the agency has recorded a lien against your property.

b. Unsecured Debts

An unsecured debt is any debt for which you haven't pledged collateral and for which the creditor has not filed a lien against you. If the debt is unsecured, the creditor is not entitled to repossess or seize any of your property if you don't pay.

Most debts are unsecured. Some of the common ones are:

- credit and charge card purchases and cash advances
- department store credit card purchases, unless the store retains a security interest in the items you buy or requires you to sign a security agreement
- gasoline company credit card purchases
- back rent
- medical bills
- alimony and child support
- student loans
- utility bills
- loans from friends or relatives, unless you signed a promissory note secured by some property you own
- health club dues

- lawyers' and accountants' bills
- church or synagogue dues, and
- union dues.

c. Priority Debts

Priority debts are unsecured debts that are considered sufficiently important to jump to the head of the bankruptcy repayment line. This means they are paid first if a Chapter 7 trustee disburses property in the course of the case, and with one exception (child support owed to a government agency) are required to be paid in full in a Chapter 13 plan.

Priority debts that may come up in consumer bankruptcies include:

- wages, salaries, and commissions owed by an employer
- contributions to employee benefit plans
- debts of up to $4,925 (each) owed to certain farmers and fishermen
- up to $2,225 in deposits made for the purchase, lease, or rental of property or services for personal, family, or household use, that were not delivered or provided
- alimony, maintenance, or support and
- income taxes that first became due within the three-year period before the bankruptcy filing date, whether or not the debtor filed a tax return, and taxes that were collected or withheld from an employee (trust fund taxes). Also, customs, duties, and penalties owing to federal, state, and local governmental units.

2. The Means Test

In Section B, above, you found out whether your current monthly income was more than your state's family median income for your family size. If it was, you will have to pass the means test if you want to file Chapter 7.

 You have to take the means test only if your debts are primarily from consumer purchases. If the majority of your debts are not consumer debts, you can skip the means test. Your debts are not primarily consumer debts if more than half of your debt load comes from the operation of a business, back taxes, or debts for personal injury or property damage you caused another (called "tort debts").

 If your current monthly income is less than your state's family median income, your debts were not primarily consumer debts, or you fit into the disabled veteran exception, you can skip this section and jump to Section C3, below, to find out whether you meet the other Chapter 7 eligibility requirements.

Don't get intimidated as you read through this section. Remember, the purpose of the means test is simply to find out whether you have enough disposable income left, after allowable expenses, to propose a feasible Chapter 13 plan. This section outlines the basic steps in the means test—Form B22A, in Appendix C, lays out the test in its entirety.

Most filers won't have to take the means test. According to a survey of 11,000 bankruptcies filed before the new law took effect, only 15% of all Chapter 7 filers would have had to take the means test. If these figures hold true for future filings, most debtors won't have to worry about this new requirement if they file for Chapter 7 bankruptcy.

In a nutshell, the means test requires you to:

- calculate your current monthly income (as defined by Congress)—you already did this in Section B, above
- subtract certain allowable IRS expense amounts (Step 1, below)
- subtract required secured and priority debt payments to calculate what you would have left over each month, called your "monthly disposable income" (Step 2, below), and
- figure out whether your monthly disposable income either exceeds $166.66 a month or is at least $100 a month and could pay more than 25% of your unsecured, nonpriority debts over a five-year period (Step 3, below).

Note: If, at any point during your subtractions, you come up with a monthly income of less than $100, you can stop—you've passed the means test.

To do the calculations in this section, you will need access to the Internet. Although the means test uses some national IRS expense tables that are included in Appendix B, it also uses local expense tables that are too voluminous to include

in this book. If you don't have personal access to the Web, free Internet access is available in most libraries.

Use *Worksheet B: Allowable Monthly Expenses*, below (and in Appendix D), to help you with the actual figures as you work through the following steps.

Step 1: Calculate Your IRS Expenses

First, add up all of the expenses allowed by the IRS. These include:

- **Food, clothing, and so on.** Enter these expenses using the national monthly living standards for food, clothing, housekeeping supplies, personal care, and miscellaneous expenses for your family size published by the IRS (you can find these in the "National Standards for Allowable Living Expenses" chart in Appendix B, but check the U.S. Trustee's website at www.usdoj.gov/ust (click "Means Testing," then look under the heading "IRS Data") to find out whether they have been updated. If you can document that your necessary expenses exceed these amounts, you can deduct up to 5% more than the IRS allows for food and clothing.
- **Transportation.** Use the regional IRS expense standards for transportation (you can find these in the "Allowable Living Expenses for Transportation" chart in Appendix B, but check the U.S. Trustee's website at www.usdoj.gov/ust (click "Means Testing," then look under the heading "IRS Data")

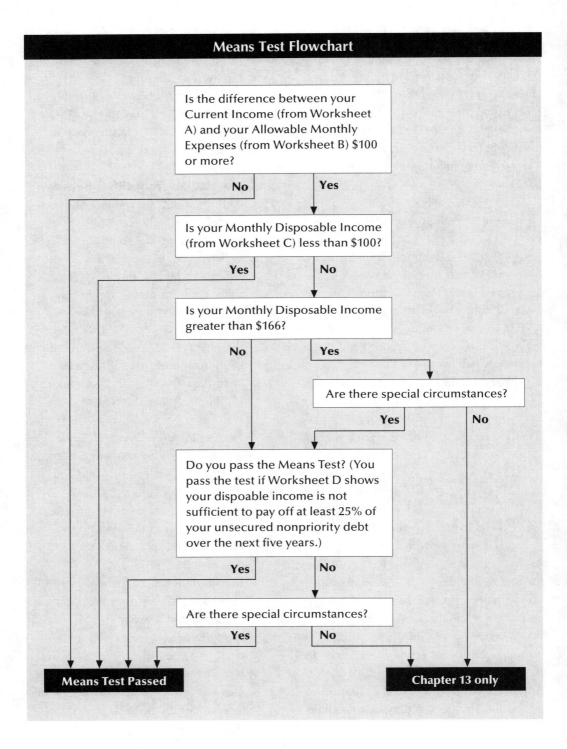

Means Test Flowchart

Is the difference between your Current Income (from Worksheet A) and your Allowable Monthly Expenses (from Worksheet B) $100 or more?

No → Yes →

Is your Monthly Disposable Income (from Worksheet C) less than $100?

Yes → No →

Is your Monthly Disposable Income greater than $166?

No → Yes →

Are there special circumstances?

Yes → No →

Do you pass the Means Test? (You pass the test if Worksheet D shows your dispoable income is not sufficient to pay off at least 25% of your unsecured nonpriority debt over the next five years.)

Yes → No →

Are there special circumstances?

Yes → No →

Means Test Passed

Chapter 13 only

to find out whether they have been updated).

- **Housing and utilities.** Use the local housing and utility expense standards for housing and utilities (you can find these at the U.S. Trustee's website at www.usdoj.gov/ust; click "Means Testing," then look under the heading "IRS Data"). If your actual home energy costs are higher than the IRS standards, you may deduct your actual costs instead.

- **Domestic violence.** Enter the expenses reasonably necessary to maintain your safety and the safety of your family from domestic violence.

- **Dependent care.** Enter the expenses reasonably necessary for the care and support of an elderly, chronically ill, or disabled family member (parent, grandparent, child, grandchild, dependent, spouse, or sibling).

- **Education.** You may enter up to $1,500 a year ($125 a month) per child for attendance at a public or private elementary or secondary school, if you can show that the amount is reasonable and isn't already covered by the IRS expense guidelines.

- **Taxes.** Enter the total average monthly expense that you actually incur for all federal, state, and local taxes, such as income taxes, self-employment taxes, Social Security taxes, and Medicare taxes. Do not include real estate or sales taxes.

- **Mandatory payroll deductions.** Enter the total average monthly payroll deductions that are required for your employment, such as mandatory retirement contributions, union dues, and uniform costs. Do not include discretionary amounts, such as voluntary 401(k) contributions.

- **Insurance.** Enter average monthly premiums that you actually pay for term life, dental, vision, long-term care, and other types of insurance that you didn't deduct elsewhere on the form.

- **Court-ordered payments.** Enter the total monthly amount that you are required to pay pursuant to court order, such as spousal or child support payments.

- **Charitable contributions.** Enter the total monthly amount you donate to charity.

- **Child care.** Enter the average monthly amount that you actually expend on child care. Do not include payments made for primary and secondary education.

- **Health care.** Enter the average monthly amount that you actually pay for health care expenses that are not reimbursed by insurance or paid by a health savings account.

- **Communications.** Enter the average monthly amount you actually pay for cell phones, pagers, call waiting, caller identification, and special long distance or Internet services necessary for the welfare of you or your dependents.

Worksheet B: Allowable Monthly Expenses

Use this worksheet to calculate the monthly expenses allowed by the IRS.

Calculate total allowable monthly expenses.

A. Food, clothing, and so on $ _____

B. Transportation   _____

C. Housing & utilities   _____

D. Domestic violence   _____

E. Dependent care   _____

F. Education   _____

G. Taxes   _____

H. Mandatory payroll deductions   _____

I. Insurance   _____

J. Court-ordered payments   _____

K. Charitable contributions   _____

L. Child care   _____

M. Health care   _____

N. Communications   _____

O. Business expenses   _____

P. Total allowable monthly expenses. Add lines A–N together $ _____

Current Monthly Income (from Worksheet A, Line 4B). $ _____

Total Allowable Monthly Expenses (from Line P above).   _____

Net monthly income $ _____

- If net monthly income is less than $100, you have passed the means test and you do not need to continue.

- If net monthly income is $100 or more, complete Worksheet C.

- **Business expenses.** Enter the average monthly expenses that are necessary to maintain and operate a business.

Subtract your total allowable monthly expenses from your current monthly income, which you calculated in Section B, above, using Worksheet A.

- If your net monthly income after subtracting these expenses is less than $100 a month, you can stop right here: You've passed the means test. You can consider filing a Chapter 7 bankruptcy without worrying that the court will try to push you into Chapter 13.
- If your net monthly income is $100 a month or more, continue to Step 2, below.

Step 2: Calculate Your Monthly Projected Disposable Income

If the total income left over after deducting the expenses in Step 1 is $100 or more, the next step is to figure out your monthly disposable income: how much money you would have left over each month, after paying certain mandatory debts, to devote to your unsecured, nonpriority debts. If your monthly disposable income is more than $100, then you must do a second set of calculations, to figure out whether you could pay 25% of your total unsecured, nonpriority debts over a five-year period.

The purpose of all this math is simple: to see whether you could feasibly complete a Chapter 13 repayment plan (and, therefore, whether you will be prohibited from filing for Chapter 7).

Use Worksheet C, *Monthly Disposable Income*, below (and in Appendix D), to calculate the figures described in this step.

Don't double dip. If you subtracted your car or mortgage payments with your IRS transportation expenses above, you shouldn't deduct them again here.

On Line 1, calculate the amount you will have to pay for all debts you owe under a contract for a secured debt (see Section 1, above). This typically includes payments on a mortgage, home equity loan, car note, or personal loan using any of your property as collateral. Add up all the payments you will be making on these debts during the next five years, then divide by 60 to figure out how much you would have to pay each month during that period to pay off these debts.

EXAMPLE: You are paying $1,500 a month on a mortgage that has ten years left on it. You pay $300 on a home equity loan that has three years left on it. And you have a car note for $200 a month that has two years left. First, multiply $1,500 by 60 to obtain the total amount you'll have to pay on the mortgage for the next five years ($90,000). Next multiply $300 by 36 to obtain the amount left on the home equity loan ($10,800). Finally, multiply $200 by 24 to obtain the amount left to pay on the car note over the next five years ($4,800). The total for a five-year period is $105,600, or $1,760 a month.

Worksheet C: Monthly Disposable Income

Use this worksheet to find out how much income you would have left over, after paying the IRS expenses calculated in Worksheet B, your secured and priority debts, any arrearages on your secured debts, and the administrative costs associated with a Chapter 13 bankruptcy, to devote to your unsecured, nonpriority debts.

Line 1. Figure out what you would have to pay each month over the next five years on your secured debts.

    A. Total amount due over the next five years for a mortgage or second deed of trust. $ _____

    B. Total amount due over the next five years on a car note.   _____

    C. Total amount due over the next five years on all other secured debts.   _____

    D. Add Lines A–C together to figure out the total amount you owe on all secured debts for the next five years.   _____

    E. Divide Line D by 60 to determine how much you would have to pay each month on these debts for the next five years.   _____

Line 2. Figure out what you would have to pay each month over the next five years to make up your arrearages (missed payments) on secured debts.

    A. Total arrearage on mortgage or second deed of trust.   _____

    B. Total arrearage on car note.   _____

    C. Total arrearage on all other secured debts.   _____

    D. Add Lines A–C together to figure out your total arrearage on secured debts.   _____

    E. Divide Line D by 60 to determine how much you would have to pay each month to pay off these arrearages over the next five years.

Line 3. Figure out how much you will owe on your priority debts for the next five years.

    A. Back child support and alimony you owe. $ _____

    B. Priority income taxes you owe.   _____

    C. Other priority debts you owe.   _____

    D. Add Lines A–C together to figure out the total priority debt you owe.   _____

    E. Divide Line D by 60 to determine how much you would have to pay each month to pay off these priority debts over the next five years.   _____

Line 4. Calculate the total amount you would have left over each month after paying allowable expenses and the debts you would have to pay in full in a Chapter 13 plan.

   A. Enter your current monthly income (from Line 4B on Worksheet A).

                                    _____

   B. Enter your allowable monthly expenses (from Line P on Worksheet B).

                                      _____

   C. Subtract Line B from Line A to calculate your net income, after allowable expenses.

                                      _____

   D. Enter your total monthly payments for secured debts, arrearages on secured debts, and priority debts (the sum of Lines 1E, 2E, and 3E, above).

                                      _____

   E. Subtract Line D from Line C to calculate how much you would have left over each month, after paying your allowable expenses and your monthly payments on the debts you would have to pay in full in a Chapter 13 plan.

                                      _____

Line 5. Calculate your monthly disposable income.

   A. Enter your leftover monthly income from Line 4E, above.

                                      _____

   B. Multiply Line A by the administrative expenses multiplier for your judicial district to calculate how much you would have to pay each month for administrative costs.

                                      _____

   C. MONTHLY DISPOSABLE INCOME. Subtract Line B from Line A.

                                   $ _____

- If your monthly disposable income (Line 5C) is less than $100, you have passed the means test and you do not need to continue.

- If your monthly disposable income (Line 5C) is $100 or more, complete Worksheet D.

On Line 2, calculate the total arrearages (missed payments) due on contractual secured debt described above, but only if the collateral is the primary family home, car, or other property necessary for the support of you and your family. This typically would include mortgage, home equity, and car note arrearages

> **EXAMPLE:** You are $4,000 behind on your mortgage, $1,500 behind on your car note, and $2,000 behind on a home equity loan. This adds up to a total arrearage of $7,500, or $125 a month.

On Line 3, calculate the total priority debts you owe, such as back child support and alimony, priority taxes, and wages you owe your employees. (See Section 1, above for more on priority debts).

On Line 4, add these amounts together, then subtract that total *and* the total from Worksheet B (your allowable IRS expenses) from the current monthly income you calculated in Section B, using Worksheet A. This is the total monthly amount you would have left over, after paying your allowable expenses and the debts you would have to pay in full in a Chapter 13 plan.

On Line 5, multiply your leftover monthly income from Line 4 by the "administrative expenses multiplier" for your judicial district. (You can find this percentage on the U.S. Trustee's website at www.usdoj.gov/ust; click "Bankruptcy Abuse Prevention and Consumer Protection Act of 2005," then "Administration Expenses Multiplier."). This represents the total monthly amount you would have to pay for administrative costs (primarily, the trustee's fee) if you filed for Chapter 13. Subtract that additional amount from your leftover monthly income. What's left is your monthly disposable income.

- If your monthly disposable income is less than $100 a month, you've passed the means test and can skip to Section C3, below, to see whether you meet the other eligibility requirements to file for Chapter 7.
- If your monthly disposable income is $100 or more a month, continue to Step 3, below.

Step 3: The Means Test

In this step, you have to figure out whether you have enough monthly disposable income to either:

- pay more than $10,000 towards your unsecured, nonpriority debt over a five-year period ($166.66 a month), or
- pay more than 25% of your unsecured, nonpriority debt over a five-year period.

Use *Worksheet D: The Means Test*, below (and in Appendix D), to do your calculations.

On Line 1, multiply your monthly disposable income (from Worksheet C) by 60. This is how much disposable income you will have over the next five years.

- If your five-year disposable income is more than $10,000 ($166.66 a month), you flunk the means test unless you can show special

Worksheet D: The Means Test

Use this worksheet to figure out whether you will be allowed to file for Chapter 7 bankruptcy, or whether you will be limited to Chapter 13.

Line 1. Figure out how much disposable income you will have over the next five years.

    A. Enter your monthly disposable income (from Line 5C of Worksheet C). $ _____

    B. Multiply Line A by 60 to calculate your monthly disposable income for the next five years.   _____

- If Line B is more than $10,000, you have failed the means test. Do not continue.

- If Line B is less than $6,000, you have passed the means test. Do not continue.

- If Line C is at least $6,000 but not more than $10,000, continue to Line 2.

Line 2. Add up your unsecured, nonpriority debts.

    A. Back rent   _____

    B. Medical bills   _____

    C. Alimony and child support   _____

    D. Student loans   _____

    E. Utility bills   _____

    F. Loans from friends or relatives   _____

    G. Health club dues   _____

    H. Lawyer and accountant bills   _____

    I. Union dues   _____

    J. Church or synagogue dues   _____

    K. Money judgments arising out of contract disputes   _____

    L. Money judgments arising out of negligent behavior   _____

M. Deficiency judgments from secured loans _____

N. Credit and charge card purchases and cash advances _____

O. Department store credit card purchases _____

P. Other _____

Q. TOTAL UNSECURED, NONPRIORITY DEBT.
Add Lines A–P. _____

R. Divide Line Q by four to calculate 25% of your total
unsecured priority debt. $ _____

- If Line 2R is larger than Line 1B, you have passed the means test and you do not need to continue.

- If Line 1B is equal to or larger than Line 2R, you have failed the means test unless you can prove special circumstances.

circumstances. (See "Proving Special Circumstances," below.)

- If your five-year disposable income is less than $6,000 ($100 a month), you pass the means test.
- If your five-year disposable is at least $6,000 but not more than $10,000, you must go on to Line 2.

On Line 2, add up all of your nonpriority, unsecured debts. Examples include credit card debt, student loans, and medical bills; use the categories in Worksheet D to make sure you don't forget anything.

On Line 3, figure out whether you could afford to pay 25% of your nonpriority, unsecured debts over the next five years by dividing the total on Line 2 by 4.

- If the total on Line 3 is more than Line 1, you won't be able to pay off 25% of your unsecured, nonpriority debt over five years. This means you have passed the means test, and can move on to Section C3, below.
- If the total on Line 3 is less than Line 1, you will be able to pay off at least 25% of your unsecured, nonpriority debt over five years. This means you have flunked the means test and will probably receive a motion to dismiss or convert from the U.S. Trustee. The motion will likely be granted unless you can establish that "special circumstances" change the result and let you pass the means test.

Proving Special Circumstances

If the U.S. Trustee seeks to dismiss or convert your Chapter 7 bankruptcy on the ground of presumed abuse, you can defend against that motion by showing that special circumstances apply in your case. These special circumstances must increase your expenses or decrease your income to bring your net monthly income down to a level that passes the means test. While the new bankruptcy law does not define the term "special circumstances," Congress cited as examples "a serious medical condition" or "a call or order to active duty in the Armed Forces."

For instance, assume you were activated from the reserves and faced a sharp drop in income as well as the costs of moving your family. If the judge agrees that these are special circumstances, and your changed economic picture gives you a net monthly income that passes the means test, you will be able to file a Chapter 7 bankruptcy. See Ch. 9, Section B, for more on using special circumstances to get you past the means test.

 You might be forced into Chapter 13 even if you pass the means test. The means test is a bright line to figure out whether you can afford a Chapter 13

repayment plan. If you flunk it, your Chapter 7 filing will be presumed abusive. But even if you pass the means test, a judge might push you into Chapter 13 or dismiss your case if all the circumstances in your case indicate that allowing you to file for Chapter 7 would be an abuse of the bankruptcy system. (See Ch. 9, Section B, for more on dismissals or conversions for abuse.)

3. You Must Be an Individual (or Married Couple) or a Small Business Owner

To file a *consumer* Chapter 7 bankruptcy case, you must be an individual (or a husband and wife filing jointly) or a sole proprietor filing with or without your spouse. As a sole proprietor, you can include all business debts on which you have personal liability. For example, if you operate your business as a sole proprietor, then you are personally liable for the debts of the business. For bankruptcy purposes, you and your business are one and the same. You can include all of the business debts in your consumer Chapter 7 bankruptcy case.

Similarly, if you are a member of a business partnership with people other than your spouse, you can file for Chapter 7 bankruptcy as a consumer and include all business debts on which you are personally liable. Your partners will remain fully liable for the debts you wipe out, however.

 If you are a member of a business partnership, consider consulting a small business lawyer before you file for bankruptcy. Your obligation to your partners may be governed by a buy-sell agreement that requires you to terminate your partnership interest before filing for bankruptcy. If you don't follow that agreement or any other understanding you and your partners have, you probably will be putting the partnership's property at risk. And your partners (or ex-partners) may ask the bankruptcy court to lift the automatic stay so they can file a lawsuit against you. A lawyer can help you assess your obligations and options.

You cannot file a consumer Chapter 7 bankruptcy case on behalf of a corporation, limited liability company, or partnership. In that situation, you must file a "business" Chapter 7 bankruptcy, which is beyond the scope of this book.

4. You Haven't Had a Previous Bankruptcy Discharge

You can't file for Chapter 7 bankruptcy if you previously had your debts discharged in:

- a Chapter 7 bankruptcy within the previous *eight* years, or
- a Chapter 13 bankruptcy within the previous *six* years.

These eight- and six-year periods run from the date you filed the earlier bankruptcy case, not the date of the discharge.

EXAMPLE: On June 14, 2000 you filed for Chapter 7 bankruptcy. You received your discharge on November 2, 2000. You've fallen on hard times again and are considering filing another Chapter 7 case. You cannot file before June 15, 2008. If the earlier case was a Chapter 13, you couldn't file before June 15, 2006. See Section D, below, for more on filing for Chapter 13.

5. You Aren't Barred by a Previous Bankruptcy Dismissal

You can't file for Chapter 7 bankruptcy if your previous bankruptcy case was dismissed within the past 180 days for any of the following reasons:

- You violated a court order.
- The court ruled that your filing was fraudulent or an abuse of the bankruptcy system.
- You requested the dismissal after a creditor asked the court to lift the automatic stay.

EXAMPLE: You filed for Chapter 7 bankruptcy on February 12, 2006 after your landlord started eviction proceedings. A week after you filed, your landlord filed a motion with the bankruptcy court to have the automatic stay lifted to continue the eviction proceedings. You dismissed your case. You've found a new place to live, but your debt problems haven't

gone away and you want to refile. You must wait at least 180 days before filing again—that is, until August 12, 2006.

6. You Have Not Been Dishonest With Your Creditors

Bankruptcy is intended for the honest debtor who got in too deep and needs the help of the bankruptcy court to get a fresh start. Your Chapter 7 bankruptcy case may be challenged or dismissed if you have tried to cheat your creditors or concealed assets so you could keep them for yourself.

Certain activities are red flags to trustees. If you have engaged in any of them during the past two years and are caught, your eligibility to file a Chapter 7 bankruptcy case is likely to be challenged. The most common no-no is unloading assets or cash to your friends or relatives to hide them from your creditors. Even if you undo such a transaction before you file for Chapter 7 bankruptcy, you may still get your bankruptcy dismissed if the trustee finds out about it (because it indicated a dishonest intent).

EXAMPLE: You want to file for Chapter 7 bankruptcy but you realize that you are listed on a deed as the co-owner of property where a friend is living—which was necessary to buy the property because your friend had bad credit. After learning that the trustee could take that property for the benefit of your unsecured creditors, you have yourself taken off the deed before filing. Assuming you wouldn't want to commit perjury in your bankruptcy papers, you would have to list that transaction, and your entire bankruptcy might go down the tubes.

You can also get into trouble if you:
- run up large debts for luxury items when you clearly are broke and have no way to pay the debts, or
- conceal property or money from your spouse during a divorce proceeding.

These activities cast a suspicion of fraud over your entire bankruptcy case.

7. You Can Produce a Tax Return, Wage Stubs, and a Credit Counseling Certificate

To file a Chapter 7 case, you must produce your most recent filed tax return. You'll also need a certificate showing that you completed a credit-counseling course (see Section A, above, for more on the credit counseling requirement) and wage stubs for the previous 60 days. (See Ch. 9, Section G, for more on these requirements.)

8. You Have Taken an Approved Personal Financial Management Course

Although you don't need to take a personal financial management course prior to filing for Chapter 7 bankruptcy,

you do need to take it before the court will discharge your debts. The agencies providing this service must be approved by the Office of the U.S. Trustee and must offer approximately two hours of required curriculum. Unlike the credit counseling agencies, personal financial management agencies don't have to be nonprofits, but they must offer in-person services on a sliding fee scale. For more information about the requirements for these agencies and how to find one in your area, visit the U.S. Trustee's website at www.usdoj.gov/ust; click "Credit Counseling and Debtor Education."

D. Chapter 13 Eligibility Requirements

Like Chapter 7 bankruptcy, Chapter 13 bankruptcy has several important eligibility requirements.

1. Prior Bankruptcy Discharges

You can't get a Chapter 13 discharge if you received a discharge in a previous Chapter 13 case in the last two years, or a discharge in a Chapter 7 case within the last four years. You aren't barred from filing a Chapter 13 in these circumstances, but you can't get a discharge until the requisite time has passed. For instance, you can file a Chapter 13 bankruptcy the instant you receive a Chapter 7 discharge (to handle liens that survived your Chapter 7 case or debts that weren't discharged in that case), but you won't get your Chapter 13 discharge until four years after the earlier Chapter 7 case was filed. (Filing for Chapter 7 after filing for Chapter 13 is known colloquially as a "Chapter 20 bankruptcy.")

2. Businesses Can't File for Chapter 13 Bankruptcy

To file a Chapter 13 bankruptcy case, you must be an individual (or a husband and wife filing jointly). If you own your own business as a sole proprietor or partner, you can include all business debts on which you have personal liability. You have to file your case in your name, however, and not in the name of the business, because a business cannot file for Chapter 13 bankruptcy. On your bankruptcy papers, you will need to list all fictitious business names or DBAs ("doing business as") that you've used as a sole proprietor or partnership.

As with Chapter 7 bankruptcy, if you operate your business as a sole proprietorship or in a partnership with your spouse or another party, you, or you and your partner, are personally liable for the debts of the business. For bankruptcy purposes, you and your business (or your share of a partnership) are one and the same. You can include all of the business debts in your Chapter 13 bankruptcy case. There is one exception: stockbrokers and commodity brokers cannot file a Chapter 13 bankruptcy case, even for personal (not business) debts.

You cannot file a Chapter 13 bankruptcy on behalf of a corporation, limited liability company (LLC), or partnership as such. If you want to file a reorganization bankruptcy in that situation, you must file a business Chapter 11 bankruptcy, which is beyond the scope of this book.

3. Your Debts Must Not Be Too High

You do not qualify for Chapter 13 bankruptcy if your secured debts exceed $922,975 or your unsecured debts are more than $307,675. If you need help figuring out which of your debts are secured and which are unsecured, see Section C1, above.

4. You Must be Current on Your Income Tax Filings

You will have to offer evidence that you have filed your federal and state income tax returns for the four tax years prior to your bankruptcy filing date. This evidence can be provided by the returns themselves or by transcripts of the returns obtained from the IRS. You have to provide this evidence no later than the date set for your first meeting of creditors (about a month after you file). The trustee can keep the creditors' meeting open for up to 120 days to give you time to file the returns, and the court can give you an additional 120 days. Ultimately, if you don't produce your returns or transcripts of the returns or transcripts for those four preceding years, your Chapter 13 will be dismissed.

5. Your Proposed Repayment Plan Must Satisfy Legal Requirements

Your eligibility for Chapter 13 bankruptcy depends on your ability to propose a plan that the court will approve of (confirm).

To determine whether a judge will confirm your plan, follow these steps (each is described in more detail below):

Step 1: Compute your disposable income.

Step 2: Compare your disposable income to the debts you would have to pay in full in a Chapter 13 case. If you don't have enough disposable income to pay off these debts in full within five years, you won't be able to propose a confirmable plan.

Step 3: If your plan will pay all required debts, it must commit all additional disposable income to repayment of your other debts within the appropriate time period. If not, your plan will not be confirmed.

Step 1: Compute Your Disposable Income

The starting point for computing your disposable income is the current monthly income figure you came up with in Section B, above, using Worksheet A. If your current monthly income is more than your state's family median income, you must commit all of your disposable income to a five-year plan, and your disposable income must be calculated on the basis of the IRS expense standards described in Section C2, above, as well as certain deductions specific to Chapter 13. If your current monthly income is less than your state's family median income, you can use your actual expenses to calculate your disposable income over a three-year period.

If your income is more than the state median, read Section C2, above, and use *Worksheet B: Allowable Monthly Expenses* in Appendix D to calculate available deductions from your current monthly income. If your income is less than the state median, then you can use your actual expenses (you'll probably still want to track the categories used in Worksheet B).

 Your plan might not be confirmed if your actual expenses look too low. If your current monthly income is less than your state's family median income, you can use your actual expenses to calculate how much you could devote to a Chapter 13 plan, provided those expenses are reasonable. Some people are tempted to decrease their stated expenses in order to increase their disposable income so they can qualify for Chapter 13. If it appears that your expenses are unreasonably low, however, the court may reject your plan as unreasonable.

Subtract your expenses (actual or IRS) from the current monthly income figure to arrive at your disposable income.

Step 2: Compare Your Disposable Income to the Debts That Must Be Paid in Full in a Chapter 13 Case

For this step, return to Section C2, Step 2. Use *Worksheet C: Monthly Disposable*

Income (in Appendix D) to compute your monthly average priority debt, your average monthly secured debt payments (mortgage, car note), and the average monthly payments on arrearages that you wish to make to hold on to collateral necessary for your family (all arrearages must be paid under your plan if you plan to hold on to the collateral). Calculate these amounts for a five-year period if you failed the means test, or a three-year period if you passed.

Deduct these expenses from your remaining income (your current monthly income minus your IRS or actual expenses). The result is your average monthly or "projected" disposable income.

Child Support and Alimony Owed to the Government

The general rule is that a Chapter 13 plan may be confirmed only if it provides for all priority debts to be paid in full over the life of the plan. However, if all of your disposable income is dedicated to repayment of debts over a five-year period, the plan may be confirmed even if you won't be able to fully repay back child support and alimony you owe to a governmental unit (such as a child support enforcement agency) during the five-year period. But, you will still be liable for the remaining back support after your Chapter 13 discharge.

If you still have enough income to pay all these debts, you have passed the first feasibility test for a Chapter 13 plan. If you don't, you'll have to go back to the drawing board to reexamine your expenses and income and file an amended plan if you can squeeze out enough disposable income after all to at least meet these debts.

 Get help calculating expenses in Chapter 13. If your disposable income falls short, it may be because you've deducted too many expenses or misinterpreted the meaning of a particular expense. There are many twists and turns to accurately computing the appropriate expenses in a Chapter 13 case, whether you are using the IRS expenses or actual expenses. A bankruptcy lawyer versed in the new law can be very helpful in this situation. You'll find additional guidance in *Chapter 13 Bankruptcy: Repay Your Debts*, by Robin Leonard (Nolo), 8th Edition and following.

Step 3: Does Your Plan Commit All Monthly Projected Disposable Income to Repayment of Your Other Debts?

In Step 2, you calculated your mandatory debts and deducted them from the income you had left after deducting your IRS or actual expenses in Step 1. If you have any remaining income after paying your mandatory debts, you will have to commit that income to paying your unsecured, nonpriority debts.

If your current monthly income is more than your state's median, you have to commit all of your projected disposable income to your plan for a five-year period. If your current monthly income is less than your state's median, you have to commit all of your disposable income to your plan for three years. Depending on which category you fit into, your plan will have to show what your projected disposable income can accomplish during the period in question.

For instance, if you are in the five-year category, will your projected disposable income cover all mandatory debts and necessary payments when spread out over 60 monthly payments? If there is anything left, does your plan apply that money to your unsecured, nonpriority debts? If so, then your plan should be confirmed by the court.

Similarly, if your current monthly income is less than the state's median, you need only commit to a three-year plan. So if you can make all required payments within 36 monthly payments, your plan will be confirmed provided that anything left over goes to your unsecured, nonpriority creditors.

By now, you should understand that it's possible to propose a confirmable Chapter 13 plan without paying anything to your unsecured nonpriority creditors—including credit card companies and hospital bills—assuming you have no nonexempt property. (See Section 6, below.)

Welcome to the New Math

Under the old law, a court would not confirm a Chapter 13 plan unless it was clear that the debtor's actual income could support a confirmable plan over three to five years. Under the new law, the court decides whether to confirm a plan based on a figure—your current monthly income—that does not necessarily reflect your actual income. Because your current monthly income is based on the six-month average prior to your filing date, your actual income may be much less. The result of this fiction is that many Chapter 13 plans that appear feasible under the new law will in fact be doomed to failure.

6. Your Proposed Payments Must Equal the Value of Your Nonexempt Assets

The total amount of payments to your unsecured creditors under your proposed plan must equal at least what those creditors would have received had you filed for Chapter 7 bankruptcy—that is, the value of your nonexempt property. (Exempt property is the property you are allowed to keep if you file a Chapter 7 case. The important topic of exempt property is discussed in Ch. 1 and explained in more detail in Chs. 4 and 5.)

As emphasized throughout this book, many bankruptcy filers have little or no nonexempt property and thus probably need not be concerned with this particular eligibility requirement. But if you do have valuable nonexempt property, you will have to pay your unsecured creditors at least that much in order for the judge to approve your plan.

To know for sure whether you have nonexempt property that might interfere with a Chapter 13 plan, you'll need to skip to Ch. 4. Find the exemptions that are available to you, compare your property with those exemptions, and then, if you do have nonexempt property, figure out whether its value would add to the amount you would have to pay your unsecured creditors.

7. You Have Taken an Approved Personal Financial Management Course

Although you don't need to take a personal financial management course prior to filing for Chapter 7 bankruptcy, you do need to take it before the court will discharge your debts. The agencies providing this service must be approved by the Office of the U.S. Trustee and must offer approximately two hours of required curriculum. Unlike the credit counseling agencies, personal financial management agencies don't have to be nonprofits, but they must offer in-person services on a sliding fee scale. For more information about the requirements for these agencies and how to find one in your area, visit the U.S. Trustee's website at www.usdoj.gov/ust; click "Credit Counseling and Debtor Education."

 Bankruptcy Rules in Ch. 2

- In order to file Chapter 7 or Chapter 13, you must complete a credit counseling course from an approved provider within 180 days preceding your bankruptcy filing. (11 U.S.C. § 111.)
- You must complete a form calculating your average monthly income over the six months prior to filing, called your "current monthly income." (11 U.S.C. § 101(10)(A).)

- If you file under Chapter 7 and your current monthly income is more than your state's median income for your family size, you must complete a form known as the "means test." (11 U.S.C. § 707(b)(2).)
- If you file under Chapter 7 but fail the means test, your filing will be presumed to be an abuse of the bankruptcy system and your case will be dismissed or, with your consent,

New Bankruptcy Rules in Ch. 2 (continued)

converted to Chapter 13. (11 U.S.C. § 707(b)(2).)

- If your current monthly income is less than your state's median income, or you passed the means test, your case can still be dismissed or converted to Chapter 13 if the court finds that it is abusive under the totality of the circumstances. (11 U.S.C. § 707(b)(3).)

- If your current monthly income is more than your state's median and you file for Chapter 13, you must commit all of your projected income to a five-year plan, and use the IRS expense standards when computing your projected disposable income. (11 U.S.C. § 1325(b)(3).)

- Your Chapter 13 plan needn't pay 100% of any support obligation owed to a government agency, even though it is a priority debt. (11 U.S.C. § 1322(a)(4).)

- When you file Chapter 13 bankruptcy, you must produce your federal and state tax returns for the previous four years. (11 U.S.C. § 1308.)

- You must participate in a budget management class before you can get your Chapter 7 or Chapter 13 discharge. (11 U.S.C. §§ 727(a)(11) and 1328(g)(2).)

- You must produce all tax returns filed while your Chapter 13 case is pending.

Upon request, your creditors may see these forms. (11 U.S.C. § 521(f).)

- You must remain current on support obligations while your Chapter 13 bankruptcy is pending. (11 U.S.C. § 1307(c)(11).)

- If your current monthly income is less than your state's median and you file for Chapter 13, you need only commit all your disposable income to a three-year plan and can use actual expenses (instead of the IRS expense standards) to calculate your disposable income. (11 U.S.C. § 1325(b)(4).)

- You can't receive a Chapter 7 discharge if you received a discharge in a previous Chapter 7 case that was filed within the last eight years, or a discharge in a previous Chapter 13 case that was filed within the last six years. (11 U.S.C. § 727(a)(8), (9).)

- You can't receive a Chapter 13 discharge if you received a discharge in a previous Chapter 13 case filed within the last two years, or a discharge in a Chapter 7 case within the last four years. (11 U.S.C. § 1328 (f).)

- You must include a credit counseling certificate, your most recent federal tax return, and wage stubs for the previous 60 days in your bankruptcy papers. (11 U.S.C. § 521(a), (b), and (e).)

How Bankruptcy Affects Your Debts

Most people consider bankruptcy because they want to get rid of debts—either immediately (in a Chapter 7 bankruptcy) or over time (in a Chapter 13 repayment plan bankruptcy). Most of your debts will, in fact, be wiped out in bankruptcy of either type. Some, however, will not—which means you will still be responsible for paying them.

If you successfully complete your bankruptcy, whether Chapter 7 or Chapter 13, you will receive a notice from the court discharging all debts that are legally dischargeable. Although the notice lists the types of debts that are dischargeable, it doesn't tell you which of your particular debts are discharged and which are not. This chapter explains what types of debts you might still owe after your bankruptcy case is over.

A. Debts That Will Be Discharged in Bankruptcy

Whether you file for Chapter 7 or Chapter 13 bankruptcy, certain types of debts will be discharged—that is, you will no longer be responsible for repaying them—at the end. In a Chapter 7 bankruptcy, you won't have to repay any portion of these debts directly: The bankruptcy trustee will divide your nonexempt assets (if you have any) among your creditors, then the court will discharge any amount that remains unpaid. In a Chapter 13 bankruptcy, your repayment plan will most likely provide for some portion of these debts to be paid back. If you complete your plan successfully, the remaining unpaid amount will be discharged.

1. Credit Card Debts

Without a doubt, the vast majority of those who file for bankruptcy are trying to get rid of credit card debts. Happily for these filers, the vast majority of bankruptcies succeed in this mission. With a few rare exceptions for cases involving fraud or luxury purchases immediately prior to your bankruptcy (outlined in Section B, below), you can expect to get rid of your credit card debt by filing for bankruptcy.

2. Medical Bills

Many people who file for bankruptcy got into financial trouble because of medical bills. Some 40 million Americans have no medical insurance or other access to affordable medical care and must rely on emergency rooms for their primary care. Many more millions of working Americans either have inadequate insurance from their employer or can't afford the plans that are available to them.

Luckily, bankruptcy provides an out: your medical bills will be discharged at the end of your bankruptcy case. In fact, billions of dollars in medical bills are discharged in bankruptcy every year.

3. Lawsuit Judgments

Most civil court cases are about money. If someone wins one of these lawsuits against you, the court issues a judgment ordering you to pay. If you don't come up with the money voluntarily, the judgment holder is entitled to collect on it by, for example, grabbing your bank account, levying your wages, or placing a lien on your home.

Money judgments are almost always dischargeable in bankruptcy, regardless of the facts that led to the lawsuit in the first place. There are a couple of exceptions (discussed in Section B, below), but in the vast majority of cases, money judgments are discharged. Even liens on your home arising from a court judgment can be cancelled if they interfere with your homestead exemption. (See "Are Secured Debts Dischargeable?" below.)

4. Obligations Under Leases and Contracts

Increasingly in our society, things are leased rather than owned. And most leases have severe penalty clauses if, for some reason, you are unable to make the monthly payment or do whatever else the lease requires you to do.

Some debtors also have obligations under a contract, such as a contract to sell real estate, buy a business, deliver merchandise, or perform in a play. The other party may want to force you to hold up your end of the deal, even if you don't want (or are unable) to, and sue you for breach of contract damages.

Obligations and liabilities under these types of agreements can also be discharged in bankruptcy. Almost always, filing for bankruptcy will convert your lease or contractual obligation into a dischargeable debt—unless the trustee believes the lease or contract will produce money to pay your unsecured creditors or the court finds that you've filed bankruptcy specifically for the purpose of getting out of a personal services contract (such as a recording contract).

5. Personal Loans and Promissory Notes

Money you borrow in exchange for a promissory note (or even a handshake and an oral promise to pay the money back) is almost always dischargeable in bankruptcy. As with any debt, however, the court may refuse to discharge a loan debt if the creditor can prove that you acted fraudulently. (See Section B3, below. But that almost never happens.

6. Other Obligations

The sections above outline the most common debts that are discharged in bankruptcy, but this isn't an exhaustive list. Any obligation or debt will be discharged (less any portion you pay through a Chapter 13 repayment plan) unless it fits within one of the exceptions discussed in Sections B and C, below.

B. Debts That Survive Chapter 7 Bankruptcy

Under bankruptcy law, there are several categories of debt that are "not dischargeable" in Chapter 7 (that is, you will still owe them after your bankruptcy is final):

- Some debts can't be discharged under any circumstances (see Section 1, below).
- Some will not be discharged unless you convince the court that the debt fits within a narrow exception to the rule (see Section 2, below).
- Some will not be discharged, but only if the creditor convinces the

court that they shouldn't be (see Section 3, below).

1. Debts Not Dischargeable Under Any Circumstances

There are certain debts that bankruptcy doesn't affect at all: You will continue to owe them just as if you had never filed.

a. Domestic Support Obligations

Obligations defined as "domestic support obligations" are not dischargeable. Domestic support obligations are child support, alimony, and any other debt that is *in the nature of* alimony, maintenance,

---

Are Secured Debts Dischargeable?

Some types of secured debts are contractually linked to specific items of property, called collateral. If you don't pay the debt, the creditor can take the collateral. The most common secured debts include loans for cars and homes.

If you have a debt secured by collateral, bankruptcy eliminates your personal liability for the underlying debt—that is, the creditor can't sue you to collect the debt itself. But bankruptcy doesn't eliminate the creditor's hold, or "lien," on the property that served as collateral under the contract.

Other types of secured debts arise involuntarily, often as a result of a lawsuit judgment or an enforcement action by

the IRS on taxes that are old enough to be discharged (see Section 2, below). In these cases too, bankruptcy gets rid of the underlying debt, but may not eliminate a lien placed on your property by the IRS or a judgment creditor.

Chapter 7 bankruptcy offers several options for dealing with secured debts, ranging from buying the property from the creditor for its replacement value, reaffirming the contract, surrendering the property, or (in some cases) getting rid of the debt while keeping the property and continuing to make payments as before. Secured debts and options for dealing with them in Chapter 7 bankruptcy are discussed in Ch. 6.

or support. For example, one spouse may have agreed to pay some of the other spouse's or the children's future living expenses (shelter, clothing, health insurance, and transportation) in exchange for a lower support obligation. The obligation to pay future living expenses may be treated as support owed to the other spouse (and considered nondischargeable), even though no court ordered it.

To be nondischargeable under this section, a domestic support obligation must have been established—or must be capable of becoming established—in

- a separation agreement, divorce decree, or property settlement agreement
- an order of a court that the law authorizes to impose support obligations, or
- a determination by a child support enforcement agency (or other government unit) that is legally authorized to impose support obligations.

A support obligation that has been assigned to a private entity for reasons other than collection (for example, as collateral for a loan) is dischargeable. This exception rarely applies, however: Almost all assignments of support to government or private entities are made for the purpose of collecting the support.

b. Other Debts Owed to a Spouse, Former Spouse, or Child

You can't discharge any debt you owe to a spouse, former spouse, or child that was incurred:

- in the course of a divorce or separation, or
- in connection with a separation agreement, divorce decree, or other court order.

Simply put, debts you owe because of a divorce are not dischargeable in Chapter 7. (However, they can be discharged in Chapter 13—see Section D, below.)

c. Fines, Penalties, and Restitution

You can't discharge fines, penalties, or restitution that a federal, state, or local government has imposed to punish you for violating a law. Examples include:

- fines or penalties imposed under federal election law
- fines for infractions, misdemeanors, or felonies
- fines imposed by a judge for contempt of court
- fines imposed by a government agency for violating agency regulations
- surcharges imposed by a court or agency for enforcement of a law, and
- restitution you are ordered to pay to victims in federal criminal cases.

d. Certain Tax Debts

Taxes are seldom dischargeable in bankruptcy. While regular income tax debts are dischargeable if they are old enough and meet the other requirements (see Section 2, below), other types of taxes may not be dischargeable. The specific rules depend on the type of tax.

Fraudulent income taxes. You cannot discharge debts for income taxes if you didn't file a return or you were intentionally avoiding your tax obligations.

Property taxes. Property taxes aren't dischargeable unless they became due more than a year before you file for bankruptcy. Even if your personal liability to pay the property tax is discharged, however, the tax lien on your property will remain. From a practical standpoint, this discharge is not meaningful, because you'll have to pay off the lien before you can transfer the property with clear title. In fact, you may even face a foreclosure action by the property tax creditor if you take too long to come up with the money.

Other taxes. Other types of taxes that aren't dischargeable are business related: payroll taxes, excise taxes, and customs duties. Sales, use, and poll taxes are also probably not dischargeable.

 Get help for business tax debts. If you owe any of these nondischargeable tax debts, see a bankruptcy attorney before you file.

e. Court Fees

If you are a prisoner, you can't discharge a fee imposed by a court for filing a case, motion, complaint, or appeal, or for other costs and expenses assessed for that court filing, even if you claimed that you were unable to afford the fees. (You can discharge these types of fees in Chapter 13—see Section D, below.)

f. Intoxicated Driving Debts

If you kill or injure someone while you are driving and are illegally intoxicated by alcohol or drugs, any debts resulting from the incident aren't dischargeable. Even if a judge or jury finds you liable but doesn't specifically find that you were intoxicated, the debt may still be nondischargeable. The judgment against you won't be discharged if the bankruptcy court (or a state court in a judgment collection action) determines that you were, in fact, intoxicated.

Note that this rule applies only to personal injuries: Debts for property damage resulting from your intoxicated driving are dischargeable.

g. Condominium, Cooperative, and Homeowners' Association Fees

You cannot discharge fees assessed after your bankruptcy filing date by a membership association for a condominium, housing cooperative, or lot in a homeownership association if you or the trustee have an ownership interest in the condominium, cooperative, or lot. As a practical matter, this means that any fees that become due after you file for Chapter 7 bankruptcy will survive the bankruptcy, but fees you owed prior to filing will be discharged. (You can discharge postfiling fees in Chapter 13—see Section D, below.)

h. Debts for Loans From a Retirement Plan

If you've borrowed from your 401(k) or other retirement plan that is qualified under IRS rules for tax-deferred status, you'll be stuck with that debt. (You can, however, discharge a loan from a retirement plan in Chapter 13—see Section D, below.)

i. Debts You Couldn't Discharge in a Previous Bankruptcy

If a bankruptcy court dismissed a previous bankruptcy case because of your fraud or other bad acts (misfeasance), you cannot discharge any debts that you tried to discharge in that earlier bankruptcy. (This rule doesn't affect debts incurred since the date you filed the earlier bankruptcy case.)

> **EXAMPLE:** You filed for Chapter 7 bankruptcy in 2001, during a really rough time in your life. You had received a Chapter 7 discharge in 1998, which made you ineligible to file for Chapter 7 again before 2004, so you used a phony Social Security number when you filed in 2001. The court quickly discovered your ruse and dismissed your case. Luckily for you, you were not prosecuted for fraud. You want to file a Chapter 7 case again. You can, because eight years have passed since you received your 1998 discharge. Because of your dishonesty, however, you won't be able to discharge any of the debts you listed in your 2001 case. But you can discharge those debts in a Chapter 13 bankruptcy. (See Section D, below.)

2. Debts Not Dischargeable Unless You Can Prove That an Exception Applies

Some debts cannot be discharged in Chapter 7 unless you show the bankruptcy court that the debt really is dischargeable because it falls within an exception.

a. Student Loans

Under the old law, student loans made by nonprofit organizations were not dischargeable unless the debtor could show undue hardship. Under the new law, this rule extends to all student loans, whether made by nonprofit or commercial entities.

To discharge your student loan on the basis of "undue hardship," you must file a separate action in the bankruptcy court and obtain a court ruling in your favor on this issue. An action to discharge a student loan debt typically requires the services of an attorney, although it's possible to do it yourself if you're willing to put in the time. (See Ch. 9 for general information about going to bankruptcy court.)

In determining undue hardship, most bankruptcy courts look at three factors (listed below). If you can show that all three factors are present, the court is likely to grant you an undue hardship discharge of your student loan. These factors are:

- **Poverty.** Based on your current income and expenses, you cannot maintain a minimal living standard and repay the loan.

- **Persistence of hardship.** Your current financial condition is likely to continue indefinitely—that is, your situation is hopeless or virtually hopeless. This factor is most likely to be present if you are elderly or have a disability that restricts your opportunities to earn a decent living.
- **Good faith.** You've made a good-faith effort to repay your debt. (You're not likely to be granted a hardship discharge if you file for bankruptcy immediately after getting out of school or if you haven't looked extensively for employment.)

Courts rarely allow student loans to be discharged. They take the position that Congress wants student loans to be repaid, absent exceptional circumstances. They also recognize that federal student loan regulations require a lot of flexibility on the creditor's part, including moratoriums on payments, temporary reductions in payments, and extensions of the repayment period that lowers the monthly payments to an affordable amount. These options give debtors other ways (short of filing for bankruptcy) to seek relief from student loan debt.

In some cases, courts have found that it would be an undue hardship to repay the entire loan and relieved the debtor of a portion of the debt. Other courts take the position that it's an all-or-nothing proposition—either the entire loan is discharged or none of it is discharged. Ask a local bankruptcy attorney how courts in your area handle student loans.

Special Rules for HEAL and PLUS Loans

The federal Health Education Assistance Loans (HEAL) Act, not bankruptcy law, governs HEAL loans. Under the HEAL Act, to discharge a loan, you must show that the loan became due more than seven years ago, and that repaying it would not merely be a hardship, but would impose an "unconscionable burden" on your life.

Parents can get Parental Loans for Students (PLUS Loans) to finance a child's education. Even though the parent does not receive the education, the loan is treated like any other student loan if the parent files for bankruptcy. The parents must meet the undue hardship test to discharge the loan.

---

b. Regular Income Taxes

People who are considering bankruptcy because of tax problems are almost always concerned about income taxes they owe to the IRS or the state equivalent. There is a myth afoot that income tax debts can never be discharged in bankruptcy. This is not true, however, if the debt is relatively old and you can meet several other conditions. Tax debts that qualify under these rules are technically discharged; however, you may have to go to court and have the judge order the IRS to honor the discharge. Here are the specifics.

You can discharge debts for income taxes in Chapter 7 bankruptcy only if you can meet all of these conditions:

- You filed a tax return for the tax year or years in question.
- The liability you wish to discharge is for a tax return that you actually filed at least two years before you filed for bankruptcy.
- The tax return for the tax debt you wish to discharge was due at least three years before you filed for bankruptcy.
- The taxing authority has not assessed your liability for the taxes within the 240 days (eight months) before you filed for bankruptcy (this time might be extended if the IRS suspended collection activity because of an offer in compromise or a previous bankruptcy filing).

EXAMPLE: Fred filed a tax return in August 2003 for the 2002 tax year. In March 2005, the IRS audited Fred's 2002 return and assesses a tax due of $8,000. In May 2006, Fred files for bankruptcy. The taxes that Fred wishes to discharge were for tax year 2002. The return for those taxes was due on April 15, 2003, more than three years prior to Fred's filing date. The tax return filed in August 2003 was at least two years prior to Fred's bankruptcy filing date, and the assessment date of March 2005 was well prior to 240 days of the filing date. Fred can discharge those taxes.

If you meet each of these four requirements, your personal liability for the taxes should be discharged. However, any lien placed on your property by the taxing authority will remain after your bankruptcy. The result is that the taxing authority can't go after your bank account or wages, but you'll have to pay off the lien before you can sell your real estate with a clear title.

 Debts incurred to pay nondischargeable taxes will also be nondischargeable. If you borrowed money or used your credit card to pay taxes that would otherwise not be discharged, you can't eliminate that loan or credit card debt in bankruptcy. In other words, you can't turn a nondischargeable tax debt into a dischargeable tax debt by paying it on your credit card. This is true for any type of nondischargeable tax owed to a governmental agency.

3. Debts Not Dischargeable in Bankruptcy If the Creditor Successfully Objects

Four types of debts may survive Chapter 7 bankruptcy if, and only if:

- the creditor files a formal objection—called a complaint to determine dischargeability—during the bankruptcy proceedings, and
- the creditor proves that the debt fits into one of the categories discussed below.

Creditors might not bother to object. Even though bankruptcy rules give creditors the right to object to the discharge of certain debts, many creditors—and their attorneys—don't fully understand this right. Even a creditor who knows the score might sensibly decide to write off the debt rather than contesting it. It can cost a lot to bring a "dischargeability action" (as this type of case is known). If you debt isn't huge, a cost benefit analysis might show that it will be cheaper to forgo collecting the debt than to fight about it in court.

a. Debts From Fraud

In order for a creditor to prove that one of your debts should survive bankruptcy because you incurred it through fraud, the debt must fit one of the categories below.

Debts from intentionally fraudulent behavior. If a creditor can show that a debt arose because of your dishonest act, and that the debt wouldn't have arisen had you been honest, the court probably will not let you discharge the debt. Here are some common examples:

- You wrote a check for something and stopped payment on it, even though you kept the item.
- You wrote a check against insufficient funds but assured the merchant that the check was good.
- You rented or borrowed an expensive item and claimed it was yours, in order to use it as collateral to get a loan.

- You got a loan by telling the lender you'd pay it back, when you had no intention of doing so.

For this type of debt to be nondischargeable, your deceit must be intentional, and the creditor must have relied on your deceit in extending credit. Again, these are facts that the creditor has to prove before the debt will be ruled nondischargeable by the court.

Debts from a false written statement about your financial condition. If a creditor proves that you incurred a debt by making a false written statement, the debt isn't dischargeable. Here are the rules:

- The false statement must be written—for instance, made in a credit application, rental application, or resume.
- The false statement must have been "material"—that is, it was a potentially significant factor in the creditor's decision to extend you credit. The two most common materially false statements are omitting debts and overstating income.
- The false statement must relate to your financial condition or the financial condition of an "insider"—a person close to you or a business entity with which you're associated.
- The creditor must have relied on the false statement, and the reliance must have been reasonable.
- You must have intended to deceive the creditor. This is extremely hard for the creditor to prove

based simply on your behavior. The creditor would have to show outrageous behavior on your part, such as adding a "0" to your income (claiming you make $180,000 rather than $18,000) on a credit application.

Recent debts for luxuries. If you run up more than $500 in debt to any one creditor for luxury goods or services within the 90 days before you file for bankruptcy, the law presumes that your intent was fraudulent regarding those charges; all the charges will survive your bankruptcy unless you prove that your intent wasn't fraudulent. The term "luxury goods and services" does not include things that are reasonably necessary for the support and maintenance of you and your dependents (what that means will be decided on a case-by-case basis).

Recent cash advances. If you get cash advances from any one creditor totaling more than $750 under an open-ended consumer credit plan within the 70 days before you file for bankruptcy, the debt is nondischargeable. "Open-ended" means there's no date when the debt must be repaid, but rather, as with most credit cards, you may take forever to repay the debt as long as you pay a minimum amount each month.

Additional information on credit card issuers' attempts to have credit card debt declared nondischargeable because of fraud is explained in Ch. 9, Section D.

b. Debts Arising From Debtor's Willful and Malicious Acts

If the act that caused the debt was willful *and* malicious (that is, you intended to inflict a specific injury to person or property), the debt isn't dischargeable if the creditor successfully objects. However, creditors don't often object in this situation.

Generally, crimes involving the intentional injury to people or damage to property are considered willful and malicious acts. Examples are assaults, rape, intentionally setting fire to a house (arson), or vandalism.

Your liability for the personal injury or property damage to the victim sustained in these types of cases will almost always be ruled nondischargeable—but only if the victim-creditor objects during your bankruptcy case. Other acts that would typically be considered to be willful and malicious include:

- kidnapping
- deliberately causing extreme anxiety, fear, or shock
- libel or slander, and
- illegal acts by a landlord to evict a tenant, such as removing a door or changing the locks.

The rules for Chapter 13 are different. In Chapter 7 bankruptcy, these debts are nondischargeable only if the underlying act is less willful and malicious. If you were simply careless (you should have taken more care, as is true of most automobile accidents), or even reckless (for example, you caused an injury by driving too fast), the

...discharged. Because creditors ...d time proving that a debt is both ...l malicious, these debts are often discharged. The new bankruptcy law creates a different rule for Chapter 13 bankruptcy: Under Chapter 13, the underlying act need only be willful or malicious. And debts for property damage, which can survive Chapter 7, can be discharged in Chapter 13. (See Section C1, below, for more on this important change.)

c. Debts From Embezzlement, Larceny, or Breach of Fiduciary Duty

A debt incurred as a result of embezzlement, larceny, or breach of fiduciary duty is not dischargeable if the creditor successfully objects to its discharge.

"Embezzlement" means taking property entrusted to you for another and using it for yourself. "Larceny" is another word for theft. "Breach of fiduciary duty" is the failure to live up to a duty of trust you owe someone, based on a relationship where you're required to manage property or money for another, or where your relationship is a close and confidential one. Common fiduciary relationships include those between:

- business partners
- attorney and client
- estate executor and beneficiary
- guardian and ward, and
- husband and wife.

d. Debts or Creditors You Don't List

Bankruptcy requires you to list all of your creditors on your bankruptcy papers and provide their most current addresses. This gives the court some assurance that everyone who needs to know about your bankruptcy will receive notice. As long as you do your part, the debt will be discharged (as long as it's otherwise dischargeable under the rules), even if the official notice fails to reach the creditor for some reason beyond your control—for example, because the post office errs, or the creditor moves without leaving a forwarding address.

Suppose, however, that you forget to list a creditor on your bankruptcy papers or carelessly misstated a creditor's identity or address. In that situation, the court's notice may not reach the creditor and the debt may not be discharged. Here are the rules:

- If the creditor knew or should have known of your bankruptcy through other means, such as a letter or phone call from you, the debt will be discharged even though the creditor wasn't listed. In this situation, the creditor should have taken steps to protect its interests, even though it didn't receive formal notice from the court.
- If all of your assets are exempt—that is, you have a "no-asset" case—the debt will be discharged unless the debt is nondischargeable in any circumstances (see Section B1, above). In this situation, the creditor wouldn't have benefited from receiving notice anyway, because there is no property to distribute. However, if the lack of notice deprives a creditor

of the opportunity to successfully object to the discharge by filing a complaint in the bankruptcy court (such as for a fraudulent debt), the debt may survive your bankruptcy.

If an Unknown Creditor Pops Up After Bankruptcy

If a creditor comes out of the wood-work after your bankruptcy case is closed, you can always reopen your case, name the creditor, and then seek an amended discharge. If it's the kind of debt that will be discharged anyway, many courts won't let you re-open because there is no need to. The debt is discharged by law and most creditors know this. However, if the creditor continues to try to collect the debt, you can haul the creditor into the bankruptcy court on a contempt charge.

C. Debts That Survive Chapter 13 Bankruptcy

In a Chapter 13 bankruptcy, you are supposed to pay off your debts over time, but few debtors pay back 100% of their debts. The typical Chapter 13 plan pays 100% of child support (except support owed to a government agency), back taxes, and other debts classified as priority debts, and some percentage of other unsecured debts, depending on the debtor's

disposable income and the value of the debtor's nonexempt property. (See Ch. 2, Section D, for more on Chapter 13 plans.) This section explains what happens to any remaining nonpriority, unsecured debt when your Chapter 13 plan is complete.

As in Chapter 7, several categories of debt may turn out to be "nondischargeable" in Chapter 13 bankruptcy:

- Some debts can't be discharged under any circumstance and you'll be stuck with them after your case is over.
- Student loans won't be discharged unless you convince the court that it would be an undue hardship to pay off the loan.
- Fraudulent debts won't be discharged, but only if the creditor convinces the court that they shouldn't be.

1. Debts Not Dischargeable Under Any Circumstances

Certain types of debts survive Chapter 13 bankruptcy, regardless of your income or circumstances.

a. Domestic Support Obligations

In both Chapter 7 and Chapter 13 bank-ruptcies, child support and alimony you owe directly to an ex-spouse or child are nondischargeable. (See Section B1, above, for more on these obligations.) Your Chapter 13 repayment plan must pro-vide for 100% repayment of these debts. Although you don't have to completely pay back support you owe to a child support collection agency during the life of your plan, any amount that is left over after you complete your plan is not dischargeable.

> **EXAMPLE:** In the final decree issued in his divorce, Fred was ordered to pay his ex-wife $500 a month for child support. Shortly after the divorce, Fred's ex-wife applied for welfare and assigned her child support rights to the county providing the welfare. Over time, Fred fell behind on his child support to the tune of $25,000 principal and interest. When Fred files for bankruptcy under Chapter 13, his plan—later confirmed by the court— required him to pay $15,000 of the $25,000 arrearage. When Fred receives his Chapter 13 discharge, he will still owe the $10,000 that won't be paid through his plan.

b. Criminal Penalties

Debts you owe on fines or restitution orders contained in the sentence for conviction of any crime (yes, even traffic tickets) may not be discharged in Chapter 13. If you read the newspapers, you'll often see accounts of whopping fines imposed on white-collar criminals for various reasons. These fines won't be affected by a Chapter 13 discharge.

c. Certain Taxes

Recent income tax debts—those that first became due within the three-year period prior to your filing date—are priority debts and have to be paid in full in any Chapter 13 plan (see Ch. 2, Section D). If your Chapter 13 ends prematurely for any reason, the tax debts you have not yet repaid will remain; you will either have to pay them outside of bankruptcy or convert your Chapter 13 to a Chapter 7 bankruptcy. (See Section B1, above, for information on which taxes are dischargeable.) If there is evidence in the tax records that you tried to avoid your duty to file an honest return or pay your taxes, the taxes will survive bankruptcy without exception. If you operated a business, you can't discharge taxes that you failed to withhold from an employee. And, in a departure from the old bankruptcy rules, tax debts for which you did not file returns are not dischargeable under any circumstances.

d. Intoxicated Driving Debts

If you operate a vehicle while illegally intoxicated by alcohol or drugs, and you kill or injure someone, any debt arising out of the injury is not dischargeable. But what if you are sued and the judge or jury finds you liable but doesn't specifically find that you were intoxicated? This may not help you: The judgment against you won't be discharged if the bankruptcy court (or a state court in a judgment collection action) determines that you were, in fact, intoxicated.

Note that this rule applies only to personal injuries: Debts for property damage resulting from your intoxicated driving are dischargeable.

e. Debts Arising From Your Willful or Malicious Actions

If a creditor obtains a judgment against you in civil court for personal injury or death caused by your willful or malicious act, the judgment will be nondischargeable. For example, O.J. Simpson, was acquitted of criminal charges but found liable, in a civil suit, for wrongful death—which fits the definition of a "willful or malicious act." Under this rule, O.J. could not discharge the debt in Chapter 13 bankruptcy.

Unlike the "willful and malicious" category of debts that may be nondischargeable in Chapter 7, a creditor in a Chapter 13 case need not go to court and prove that the debt should not be wiped out. Instead, these debts are automatically nondischargeable. Note that the act which gives rise to the debt need only be willful *or* malicious to be nondischargeable in Chapter 13, which greatly expands the types of debt that will survive discharge. For instance, a judgment for injury caused by your reckless driving would most likely survive Chapter 13 bankruptcy on the ground of "maliciousness," whereas it would be discharged in Chapter 7 because reckless driving, through malicious, is seldom considered willful.

Finally, unlike Chapter 7, which includes damage to property, this exception applies only to personal injury or death.

f. Debts or Creditors You Don't List

Bankruptcy requires you to list all your creditors on your bankruptcy papers and provide their most current addresses. That way, the court can mail out notice of your bankruptcy with the best chance of reaching them. If you do your part and the official notice fails to reach the creditor for some reason beyond your control—for example, because the post office errs, or the creditor moves without leaving a forwarding address—the debt will still be discharged (as long as it is otherwise dischargeable). Also, if the creditor knew or should have known of your bankruptcy through other means, such as a letter or phone call from you, the debt will be discharged.

Suppose, however, that you forget to list a creditor on your bankruptcy papers or carelessly misstate a creditor's identity or address. In that situation, the court won't notify the creditor and the debt almost always will survive your bankruptcy (unless the creditor wouldn't have received any payments under your plan, a very rare occurrence). The general rule is that debts not listed in a Chapter 13 case survive the bankruptcy. This means, of course, that you should be extra careful to list all of your creditors in a Chapter 13 case.

2. Student Loans

As in Chapter 7, a student loan cannot be discharged in Chapter 13 unless you show the bankruptcy court that paying the loan back would be a substantial hardship. See Section B2, above, for more on the rules for discharging student loans.

3. Fraudulent Debts

Under the new law, debts based on fraud, theft, or breach of fiduciary duty are not dischargeable in Chapter 13. (See Section B3, above, for a description of these types of debts.) And these debts appear to be automatically nondischargeable in Chapter 13—the creditor doesn't have to go to court to obtain a ruling, as it would if you filed for Chapter 7. As a practical matter, bankruptcy courts in Chapter 13 cases will most likely use the same procedure for determining the dischargeability of these debts as they use in Chapter 7 cases—that is, they will consider the debt to be discharged if the creditor doesn't establish fraud in the bankruptcy court.

D. Debts Discharged Only Under Chapter 13

Under previous law, debts owed for fraud, false financial statements, and injuries resulting from willful *and* malicious acts were discharged at the end of the Chapter 13 repayment plan, as part of what was called Chapter 13's "super discharge." Under the new law, those categories of debt will no longer be discharged. However, a new crop of debts that cannot be discharged in Chapter 7 will now be discharged in Chapter 13, giving rise to a new "super discharge" package. These debts are explained in more detail in Section B, above. They are:

- marital debts created in a divorce or settlement agreement

- debts incurred to pay a non-dischargeable debt
- court fees
- condominium, cooperative, and homeowners' association fees
- debts for loans from a retirement plan, and
- debts that couldn't be discharged in a previous bankruptcy.

E. How Joint Debts Are Handled

Debts for which you have a joint debtor—another person who owes the debt along with you—raise some tricky issues. Let's look at the different kinds of joint debtors and how your bankruptcy filing might affect them.

1. Cosigners and Guarantors

A cosigner or guarantor is someone who signs onto your debt in order to back up or guarantee your payment. If you don't pay, the cosigner or guarantor is legally responsible for payment. If you discharge a debt for which you have a cosigner or guarantor, your joint debtor will still owe the entire thing, even though you are no longer on the hook to repay it.

If you want to file for Chapter 7 bankruptcy but don't want to stick your cosigner or guarantor with the debt, you can make an agreement with the creditor to reaffirm the debt—that is, to continue to owe it after your bankruptcy ends.

If You Convert From One Chapter to Another

In most cases, bankruptcy filers may convert their cases from one chapter to another. If, for example, a court finds that a Chapter 7 filing is an abuse of the bankruptcy system under the new rules, the court can allow the filer to convert to Chapter 13 rather than dismissing the case altogether. Or, you may decide to convert—because a particular debt will only be discharged in Chapter 13, for example, or because you won't be able to complete a Chapter 13 repayment plan. Once you make the switch, you are subject to the dischargeability rules of the Chapter to which you converted, not the Chapter you started out using.

> **EXAMPLE:** Connie files for Chapter 13 bankruptcy because she owes a lot of debt from a divorce and has been told that those debts can be discharged in Chapter 13 but not in Chapter 7. Connie proposes a feasible Chapter 13 plan that pays only 25% of her divorce-related debt. Halfway through the plan, Connie loses her job and can't continue her payments. She converts to Chapter 7. Her Chapter 7 discharge won't include the divorce-related debts. However, Connie will receive a credit for the amounts she paid on those debts during her Chapter 13 case.

 It's usually better to reimburse the co-signer than to reaffirm the debt. For a variety of reasons, it's almost always a good idea to discharge the debt and agree to owe your cosigner for any potential liability, rather than to reaffirm it and continue to owe your original creditor. This approach gives you more flexibility regarding repayment than you'd have if you defaulted on your payments to the regular creditor under a reaffirmation agreement. Also, the creditor may decide not to try to collect from the cosigner, which means neither one of you would have to repay the debt. And finally, it's possible that the cosigner will also decide to file bankruptcy.

If you file for Chapter 13 bankruptcy, you can include the cosigned or guaranteed debt as part of your repayment plan, and your joint debtor will not be pursued during your bankruptcy case—typically, at least three years. If you can, you should pay the debt in full during your case. If you don't, you will be entitled to discharge whatever balance remains when your case is over, (assuming the debt is otherwise dischargeable in a Chapter 13 bankruptcy). But in that situation, the creditor can still go after the joint debtor for the balance.

2. Spousal Responsibility for Debts

Married people can file for bankruptcy jointly or separately. If they file jointly, all of their debt is subject to the rules explained above. If only one spouse files,

Bankruptcy and Preferences

If you file for Chapter 7 bankruptcy and have a joint debtor who is a relative, close friend, or business associate, the joint debtor may have to pay the bankruptcy trustee any amount that you pay the creditor on the loan. Here's how this works.

When you file for bankruptcy, the bankruptcy trustee will look to see whether you made any payments to creditors within the 90 days before you filed—or within one year of filing, if those payments were made to, or for the benefit of, a relative or close business associate. These payments are called "preferences" and they're not permitted. The idea is that you shouldn't be allowed to single out certain creditors for special treatment just before you file for bankruptcy. The bankruptcy trustee can demand that the creditor return the preferential payment so that it can be divided equally among your unsecured creditors. If the creditor pays up and the debt is discharged in bankruptcy, you won't owe anything, but your joint debtor will be on the hook for whatever remains of the original debt.

If the creditor can't or won't cough up the preference money you paid, the trustee could sue the creditor. But an easier route for the trustee may be to go after your joint debtor—who benefited from the preference because your payment wiped out or reduced his or her liability for the debt. In this scenario, believe it or not, the joint debtor would have to pay the trustee the amount of the preference. The joint debtor then continues to be liable for the debt, less the amount of the preference kept by the creditor.

Fraudulent transfers are closely related to preferences. If, in the two years before filing for bankruptcy, you transfer property to a friend, relative, or other insider without an exchange of equal value, the transfer may be considered fraudulent. Fraudulent transfers give the trustee the right to seize the transferred property for the benefit of your creditors. They may also result in the dismissal of your bankruptcy case.

state marital property rules determine which debts qualify for discharge.

a. Community Property Rules

Some states use what's called a "community property" system to determine who owns marital property, including debts. These states are Arizona, California, Idaho, Louisiana, Nevada, New Mexico, Texas, Washington, and Wisconsin. (Spouses in Alaska can elect to have their property treated as community property, if they make a written agreement to that effect.)

In community property states, both spouses owe debts incurred by either spouse during the marriage even if one spouse incurs a debt without the other spouse's knowledge. These are termed "community" debts. Debts incurred by a spouse prior to the marriage are considered separate debts, as are debts incurred after separation and divorce.

In bankruptcies filed in community property states, all community debts are subject to discharge even if only one spouse files—which means that the non-filing spouse will benefit from the filing spouse's discharge. However, the non-filing spouse's separate debts are not discharged and will survive the bankruptcy.

b. Common Law Property Rules

All states that don't use the community property system for dealing with marital debts are termed common law states. The rules for those states are bit simpler.

All debts either spouse incurs before the marriage are that spouse's separate debts. Debts incurred during the marriage might be either separate or joint: If the debt is jointly undertaken (for example, it was incurred from a joint account or the creditor considered the credit information of both spouses in deciding to extend the loan) or the debt benefits the marriage (for example, the debt was for necessary items, such as food, clothing, or child care), it is jointly owed by both spouses. Otherwise, a debt that one spouse incurs separately remains that spouse's separate debt.

When one spouse files for bankruptcy in a common law state, the only debts that come into play are that spouse's separate debts and any debts that can be classified as joint. The other spouse's separate debts continue unaffected by the bankruptcy filing.

3. Business Partners

As a general rule, all partners are responsible for partnership debts unless the partnership has special provisions limiting the liability of certain classes of partners (as in a limited partnership). If you are in a partnership and file for bankruptcy, you can get rid of your personal liability for partnership debts. However, the remaining partnership and individual partners (if there are any—often partnerships are dissolved if one partner leaves or declares bankruptcy) will still be on the hook.

Bankruptcy Rules in Ch. 3

- A credit card debt of more than $500 for luxuries that is incurred within 90 days of filing is presumed fraudulent and nondischargeable. (11 U.S.C. § 523(a)(2)(C).)

- Cash advances of more than $750 from an open-ended credit account, made within 70 days of filing, are presumed fraudulent and nondischargeable. (11 U.S.C. § 523(a)(2)(C).)

- In addition to support debts, any other type of debt or obligation arising from a divorce or separation decree or property settlement agreement is nondischargeable in Chapter 7, but dischargeable in Chapter 13. (11 U.S.C. §§ 523(a)(18) and 1328 (a)(2).)

- Loans owed to a pension or retirement fund are not dischargeable in Chapter 7, but are dischargeable in Chapter 13. (11 U.S.C. §§ 523(a)(18) and 1328(a)(2).)

- Absent a showing of hardship, loans from both nonprofit and commercial lenders are nondischargeable in Chapter 7 and Chapter 13. (11 U.S.C. §§ 523(a)(8)(B) and 1328(a)(2).)

- Debts incurred by fraud or embezzlement are nondischargeable in Chapter 13 as well as Chapter 7. (11 U.S.C. §§ 523(a)(2) and 1328(a)(2).)

- Taxes for which you did not file a return are no longer dischargeable in Chapter 13. (11.U.S.C. § 1328(a)(2).)

- Debts for death or personal injury arising from civil judgment involving willful *or* malicious acts are nondischargeable in Chapter 13. (11 U.S.C. § 1328(a)(4).)

- Debts incurred to pay any type of nondischargeable tax are nondischargeable in Chapter 7, but are dischargeable in Chapter 13. (11 U.S.C. §§ 523(a)(14)(A) and 1328(a)(2).)

Your Property and Bankruptcy

This chapter explains what happens to the property you own when you file for bankruptcy. It also covers exemptions—the rules that determine which property you can keep and which property you'll have to give up in Chapter 7 bankruptcy. If property is "exempt," you will probably be able to keep it; you may have to forfeit nonexempt property, or property that is worth more than the applicable exemption, to the bankruptcy trustee to pay off your creditors.

Exempt property can be taken to pay child support and alimony. This chapter explains the rules that protect certain types of property from being seized by creditors or the bankruptcy court to pay your debts. However, your exempt property is not protected if you owe money to a former spouse for child support or alimony: These obligations must be met, even if it means that you lose property that would otherwise be exempt.

Under the old law, most Chapter 7 filers emerged from bankruptcy with their property intact, because most of what they owned was exempt. The new law may change this, however. Now, all assets must be valued not at their resale value (what you could sell them for) as was true under the old law, but at their replacement cost (what you would have to pay to buy property of the same kind, age, and condition from a retail merchant). This means that assets will be valued higher and, as a result, more filers will be at risk of losing property in Chapter 7.

Chapter 13 filers also have to understand exemptions, even though they fund their repayment plans through their income rather than selling their property. Bankruptcy law requires your Chapter 13 plan to repay unsecured creditors at least as much as the value of your nonexempt property. So, even though Chapter 13 filers typically hang on to their nonexempt property (indeed, this is one of the main reasons people choose to file under Chapter 13), you need to know which exemption laws apply to you and how to use them to figure out the value of your nonexempt property.

 This chapter covers property you own outright. If you are making payments on your car or other personal property, or you have pledged property you own as collateral for a personal loan, see Ch. 6. For information on what happens to your house or apartment when you file for bankruptcy, see Ch. 5.

A. Your Bankruptcy Estate

The property you own on the day you file for bankruptcy is called your "bankruptcy estate." With very few exceptions (discussed in Section 2, below), property and income you acquire after you file for bankruptcy aren't included in your bankruptcy estate. When you file for bankruptcy, the forms you have to fill out require you to list all of the property in your bankruptcy estate.

1. What's in Your Bankruptcy Estate

Several broad categories of property make up your bankruptcy estate:

Property you own and possess. Everything in your possession that you own, whether or not you owe money on it—for example, a car, real estate, clothing, books, television, stereo system, furniture, tools, boat, artworks, or stock certificates—is included in your bankruptcy estate. Property that you have in your possession but belongs to someone else (such as the car your friend stores in your garage or the television you borrowed from your sister) is not part of your bankruptcy estate, because you don't have the right to sell it or give it away.

Property you own but don't possess. You can own something even if you don't have physical possession of it. For instance, you may own a car that someone else is using. Other examples include a deposit held by a stockbroker, a security deposit held by your landlord or a utility company, or a business in which you've invested money.

Property you are entitled to receive. Property that you have a legal right to receive but haven't gotten yet when you file for bankruptcy is included in your bankruptcy estate. Common examples include:

- wages, royalties, or commissions you have earned but have not yet been paid
- a tax refund legally due you
- vacation or termination pay you've earned

- property you've inherited but not yet received from someone who has died
- proceeds of an insurance policy, if the death, injury, or other event that gives rise to payment has already occurred, and
- money owed you for goods or services you've provided (often called "accounts receivable").

Community property. If you live in a community property state, all property either spouse acquires during the marriage is ordinarily considered "community property," owned jointly by both spouses. (The community property states are Arizona, California, Idaho, Louisiana, Nevada, New Mexico, Texas, Washington, and Wisconsin, and—if you have a written community property agreement or trust—Alaska.) Gifts and inheritances to only one spouse are the most common exceptions—these are the separate property of the spouse who receives them. If you're married and file jointly for bankruptcy, all the community property you and your spouse own, as well as all of both of your separate property, is considered part of your bankruptcy estate. If your spouse doesn't file, then your bankruptcy estate consists of all of the community property and all of your separate property—your spouse's separate property isn't included.

Marital property in a common law property state. If you are married and filing jointly, your bankruptcy estate includes all the property you and your spouse own, together and separately. If you are filing alone for bankruptcy in a common law property state (all states other than the community property states listed above), your bankruptcy estate includes:

- your separate property (property that has only your name on a title certificate or that was purchased, received as a gift, or inherited by you alone), and
- half of the property that is jointly owned by you and your spouse, unless you own the property as tenants by the entirety.

⚠️ **"Tenancy by the entirety" property often is handled differently in bankruptcy.** Property you and your spouse jointly own as "tenants by the entirety" usually receives special protection in bankruptcy if 1) it is located in Delaware, the District of Columbia, Florida, Hawaii, Illinois, Indiana, Maryland, Massachusetts, Michigan, Missouri, North Carolina, Pennsylvania, Tennessee, Vermont, Virginia, or Wyoming, and 2) only one spouse files for bankruptcy. In that event, the filing spouse's creditors (and therefore the bankruptcy court) typically cannot take property that both spouses own as tenants by the entirety. If both spouses file, however, this protection doesn't apply. If you have such property, consult a local bankruptcy lawyer before you file.

Certain property you receive within 180 days after filing for bankruptcy. Most property you acquire or become entitled to after you file for bankruptcy isn't included in your bankruptcy estate. But there are a few exceptions. If you acquire or become entitled to the following items within 180 days after you file, you must notify the trustee:

- an inheritance
- property you receive or have a right to receive from a marital settlement agreement or divorce decree, and
- death benefits or life insurance policy proceeds.

Property (revenue) generated by estate property. This type of property typically consists of the proceeds of contracts—such as those providing for rent, royalties, and commissions—that were in effect at the time of the bankruptcy filing, but which produced earnings after that date. For example, if you are a composer or author and receive royalties each year for a book that was written before you filed for bankruptcy, the trustee may collect those royalties as property of your estate. Proceeds from work you do after your filing date belong to you.

2. Property That's Not Part of Your Bankruptcy Estate

Property that is not in your bankruptcy estate is not subject to the bankruptcy court's jurisdiction, which means that the bankruptcy trustee can't take it to pay your creditors under any circumstances.

The most common examples of property that doesn't fall within your bankruptcy estate are:

- property you buy or receive after your filing date (with the few exceptions described in Section 1, above)

- pensions subject to the federal law known as ERISA (commonly, defined benefit pensions)
- property pledged as collateral for a loan where a licensed lender (pawnbroker) retains possession of the collateral
- property in your possession that belongs to someone else (for instance, property you are storing for someone), and
- wages that are withheld, and employer contributions that are made, for employee benefit and health insurance plans.

Your retirement plan may be exempt.
Even if a retirement plan is included in your bankruptcy estate, it may still be exempt, which will have the same effect as if it were not in your bankruptcy estate. For example, IRAs and 401(k) plans are exempt in all states. (See Section D, below, for more on exemptions.) To find out whether or not your pension is covered by ERISA, call the benefits coordinator on your job or the pension plan administrator.

Under the new bankruptcy law, funds placed in a qualified tuition program or Coverdell education savings account are also not part of your bankruptcy estate, as long as:

- you deposit the funds into the account at least one year before filing for bankruptcy, and

- the beneficiary of the account is your child, stepchild, grandchild, step-grandchild, or in some cases, foster child.

This exclusion applies only up to a $5,000 limit, and only to funds you place in the account within a one-year period beginning two years before you file for bankruptcy. This rule reflects Congress's intent to discourage filers from sheltering money by loading up an education account within the two years preceding their bankruptcy.

B. Inventory Your Property

If you decide to file for bankruptcy, you'll be required to list all property that belongs in your bankruptcy estate. Whether or not you can hold on to that property, or at least some of the property's value in dollar terms, depends on what the property is worth and which exemptions are available to you. The best way to start finding out what you'll be able to keep in Chapter 7—and get a jump on your filing paperwork—is to create an inventory (list) of your property.

The simplest strategy is to start with the property items that you are most interested in keeping—and worry about the rest of your property only if and when you actually file for bankruptcy. Or, you can be more systematic and make a list of every single thing in your bankruptcy estate. If you're married and would be filing jointly, enter all property owned by you and your

Worksheet E: Personal Property Checklist

Cash on hand (include sources)
- ☐ In your home
- ☐ In your wallet
- ☐ Under your mattress

Deposits of money (include sources)
- ☐ Bank account
- ☐ Brokerage account (with stockbroker)
- ☐ Certificates of deposit (CDs)
- ☐ Credit union deposit
- ☐ Escrow account
- ☐ Money market account
- ☐ Money in a safe deposit box
- ☐ Savings and loan deposit

Security deposits
- ☐ Electric
- ☐ Gas
- ☐ Heating oil
- ☐ Security deposit on a rental unit
- ☐ Prepaid rent
- ☐ Rented furniture or equipment
- ☐ Telephone
- ☐ Water

Household goods, supplies, and furnishings
- ☐ Antiques
- ☐ Appliances
- ☐ Carpentry tools
- ☐ China and crystal
- ☐ Clocks
- ☐ Dishes

- ☐ Food (total value)
- ☐ Furniture (list every item; go from room to room so you don't miss anything)
- ☐ Gardening tools
- ☐ Home computer (for personal use)
- ☐ Iron and ironing board
- ☐ Lamps
- ☐ Lawn mower or tractor
- ☐ Microwave oven
- ☐ Patio or outdoor furniture
- ☐ Radios
- ☐ Rugs
- ☐ Sewing machine
- ☐ Silverware and utensils
- ☐ Small appliances
- ☐ Snow blower
- ☐ Stereo system
- ☐ Telephone and answering machines
- ☐ Televisions
- ☐ Vacuum cleaner
- ☐ Video equipment (VCR, camcorder)

Books, pictures, and other art objects; stamp, coin, and other collections
- ☐ Art prints
- ☐ Bibles
- ☐ Books
- ☐ Coins
- ☐ Collectibles (such as political buttons, baseball cards)
- ☐ Family portraits

- ☐ Figurines
- ☐ Original artworks
- ☐ Photographs
- ☐ Records, CDs, audiotapes
- ☐ Stamps
- ☐ Videotapes

Apparel
- ☐ Clothing
- ☐ Furs

Jewelry
- ☐ Engagement and wedding rings
- ☐ Gems
- ☐ Precious metals
- ☐ Watches

Firearms, sports equipment, and other hobby equipment
- ☐ Board games
- ☐ Bicycle
- ☐ Camera equipment
- ☐ Electronic musical equipment
- ☐ Exercise machine
- ☐ Fishing gear
- ☐ Guns (rifles, pistols, shotguns, muskets)
- ☐ Model or remote-controlled cars or planes
- ☐ Musical instruments
- ☐ Scuba diving equipment
- ☐ Ski equipment
- ☐ Other sports equipment
- ☐ Other weapons (swords and knives)

Interests in insurance policies
- ☐ Credit insurance
- ☐ Disability insurance
- ☐ Health insurance
- ☐ Homeowners' or renters' insurance
- ☐ Term life insurance
- ☐ Whole life insurance

Annuities

Pension or profit sharing plans
- ☐ IRA
- ☐ Keogh
- ☐ Pension or retirement plan
- ☐ 401(k) plan

Stock and interests in incorporated and unincorporated companies

Interests in partnerships
- ☐ Limited partnership interest
- ☐ General partnership interest

Government and corporate bonds and other investment instruments
- ☐ Corporate bonds
- ☐ Municipal bonds
- ☐ Promissory notes
- ☐ U.S. savings bonds

Accounts receivable
- ☐ Accounts receivable from business
- ☐ Commissions already earned

Family support

☐ Alimony (spousal support, maintenance) due under court order

☐ Child support payments due under court order

☐ Payments due under divorce property settlement

Other debts for which the amount owed you is known and definite

☐ Disability benefits due

☐ Disability insurance due

☐ Judgments obtained against third parties you haven't yet collected

☐ Sick pay earned

☐ Social Security benefits due

☐ Tax refund due under returns already filed

☐ Vacation pay earned

☐ Wages due

☐ Workers' compensation due

Any special powers that you or another person can exercise for your benefit, other than those listed under "real estate"

☐ A right to receive, at some future time, cash, stock, or other personal property placed in an irrevocable trust

☐ Current payments of interest or principal from a trust

☐ General power of appointment over personal property

An interest in property due to another person's death

☐ Any interest as the beneficiary of a living trust, if the trustor has died

☐ Expected proceeds from a life insurance policy where the insured has died

☐ Inheritance from an existing estate in probate (the owner has died and the court is overseeing the distribution of the property), even if the final amount is not yet known

☐ Inheritance under a will that is contingent on one or more events occurring, but only if the owner has died

All other contingent claims and claims where the amount owed you is not known, including tax refunds, counterclaims, and rights to setoff claims (claims you think you have against a person, government, or corporation, but you haven't yet sued on)

☐ Claims against a corporation, government entity, or individual

☐ Potential tax refund on a return that is not yet filed

Patents, copyrights, and other intellectual property

☐ Copyrights

☐ Patents

☐ Trade secrets

☐ Trademarks

☐ Trade names

Licenses, franchises, and other general intangibles

☐ Building permits

☐ Cooperative association holdings

☐ Exclusive licenses

☐ Liquor licenses

- ☐ Nonexclusive licenses
- ☐ Patent licenses
- ☐ Professional licenses

Automobiles and other vehicles

- ☐ Car
- ☐ Minibike or motor scooter
- ☐ Mobile or motor home if on wheels
- ☐ Motorcycle
- ☐ Recreational vehicle (RV)
- ☐ Trailer
- ☐ Truck
- ☐ Van

Boats, motors, and accessories

- ☐ Boat (canoe, kayak, rowboat, shell, sailboat, pontoon, yacht)
- ☐ Boat radar, radio, or telephone
- ☐ Outboard motor

Aircraft and accessories

- ☐ Aircraft
- ☐ Aircraft radar, radio, and other accessories

Office equipment, furnishings, and supplies

- ☐ Artwork in your office
- ☐ Computers, software, modems, printers
- ☐ Copier
- ☐ Fax machine
- ☐ Furniture

- ☐ Rugs
- ☐ Supplies
- ☐ Telephones
- ☐ Typewriters

Machinery, fixtures, equipment, and supplies used in business

- ☐ Military uniforms and accoutrements
- ☐ Tools of your trade

Business inventory

Livestock, poultry, and other animals

- ☐ Birds
- ☐ Cats
- ☐ Dogs
- ☐ Fish and aquarium equipment
- ☐ Horses
- ☐ Other pets
- ☐ Livestock and poultry

Crops—growing or harvested

Farming equipment and implements

Farm supplies, chemicals, and feed

Other personal property of any kind not already listed

- ☐ Church pew
- ☐ Health aids (such as a wheelchair or crutches)
- ☐ Hot tub or portable spa
- ☐ Season tickets

spouse (or the property that you both care about). Use *Worksheet E: Personal Property Checklist,* above (and in Appendix D), to identify the property in your bankruptcy estate.

C. Value Your Property

Use *Worksheet F: Property Value Schedule,* below (and in Appendix D), to figure out what each item is worth. It's easy to enter a dollar amount for cash and most investments. If you own a car, start with the middle Kelley Blue Book price. If the car needs repair, reduce the value by what it would cost you to fix the car. You can find the Kelley Blue Book at a public library or online at www.kbb.com.

Under the new law, you need to compute the property's replacement value: what it would cost to buy that specific property—considering its age and condition—from a retail merchant. If you use the Internet, visit *ebay* (www.ebay.com) to get a fix on the going price for just about anything. Or briefly describe the item in *Google* (or your search engine of choice) and see what turns up. As long as your valuations are based on the going retail price for the item in question, you should use the lowest value you can find—that means you are more likely to be able to keep the property under your state's exemption laws.

If you are filing separately and own something jointly with someone (other than a spouse with whom you would file

for bankruptcy), reduce the value of the item to reflect only the portion you own. For example, you and your brother jointly bought a music synthesizer worth $10,000. Your ownership share is 40% and your brother's is 60%. You should list the value of the property you own as $4,000, not $10,000.

If you are married and filing separately in a community property state, include the total value of all the community property as well as the value of your separate property. (See Section A1, above.)

If you are married, you own the property with your spouse as tenants by the entirety, and you are filing separately, your ownership interest may not be 50% for purposes of computing your exemption. (Talk to a lawyer to find out what percentage of your tenancy by the entirety property you can claim as exempt.)

D. Understanding Exemptions

Bankruptcy is intended to give debtors a fresh start—not to leave them utterly destitute. You are entitled to keep certain property that the laws applicable to your bankruptcy categorize as exempt. Creditors cannot take exempt property as part of their collection efforts, and the bankruptcy trustee can't take it, either. Exempt property can literally range from "the shirt on your back" to a million-dollar estate, depending on which state's exemptions you use.

Worksheet F: Property Value Schedule

List the total replacement value of each item in your Personal Property Checklist.

Item	Replacement Value
1. Cash	$ _____
2. Bank accounts	_____
3. Security deposits	_____
4. Household goods & furniture	_____
5. Books, pictures, etc.	_____
6. Clothing	_____
7. Furs & jewelry	_____
8. Sports & hobby equipment	_____
9. Interest in insurance	_____
10. Annuities	_____
11. Pensions & profit sharing plans	_____
12. Stock & interest in business	_____
13. Interest in partnership & ventures	_____
14. Bonds	_____
15. Accounts receivable	_____
16. Alimony & family support	_____
17. Other liquidated debts, tax refund	_____
18. Future interests & life estates	_____
19. Interests due to another's death	_____
20. Other contingent claims	_____
21. Intellectual property rights	_____
22. Licenses & franchises	_____
23. Vehicles	_____
24. Boats, motors, & accessories	_____
25. Aircraft & accessories	_____
26. Office equipment, furniture, & supplies	_____
27. Machinery, fixtures etc.	_____
28. Inventory	_____
29. Animals	_____
30. Crops—growing or harvested	_____
31. Farm equipment	_____
32. Farm supplies, chemicals, & feed	_____
33. Anything not listed above	_____
TOTAL	$ _____

1. State Exemption Systems

Every state has its own fairly lengthy list of exempt property. (You can find these lists in Appendix A.) In addition, some states offer bankruptcy filers an alternative choice of exemptions—a list of exempt property found in the federal bankruptcy code. States that offer this choice are: Arkansas, Connecticut, Hawaii, Massachusetts, Michigan, Minnesota, New Hampshire, New Jersey, New Mexico, Pennsylvania, Rhode Island, Texas, Vermont, Washington, and Wisconsin. In these states, you must choose between the state exemption system and the federal exemption system.

Although California doesn't make the federal bankruptcy code exemptions available, it also has two separate exemption systems—but both are created by state law. Debtors who use the California exemptions must choose between System 1 (the regular exemptions available to debtors in and out of bankruptcy) and System 2 (available only in bankruptcy and very similar to the federal exemptions).

2. How Exemptions Work

Under both the federal and state exemption systems, some types of property are exempt regardless of value. For example, in some states, home furnishings, wedding rings, or clothing are exempt without regard to value. In Florida and Texas, homes are exempt regardless of their value or the value of the bankruptcy filer's ownership (equity) in the home.

Other kinds of property are exempt up to a limited value. For instance, cars are often exempt up to a certain amount—typically $2,500 to $3,000. The home equity exemption ranges from $5,000 in New York to $300,000 in Massachusetts. When there is a dollar limit on an exemption, any equity above the limit is considered nonexempt. (Your equity is the amount you would get to keep if you sold the property.) Even though a portion of your ownership in these items is exempt, the trustee can seize and sell property in which your equity exceeds the exemption limit, give you your exemption amount, and distribute the remainder to your unsecured creditors.

Many states offer a "wildcard" exemption—a dollar amount that you can apply to any property, in order to make it (or more of it) exempt. This type of exemption typically runs from a few hundred to several thousand dollars (but close to $20,000 in California's System 2 exemptions).

EXAMPLE: Fred and Susan are married and live in Virginia. They rent rather than own their home. Under the Virginia exemptions, equity in an automobile is limited to $2,000 ($4,000 for couples). However, Fred and Susan own $12,000 of equity in their cars. Fortunately for Fred and Susan, Virginia allows debtors to use the Virginia homestead exemption as a wildcard for their personal property, if they don't use it for a home. Because Fred and Susan rent, they can use this wildcard for their cars. The homestead exemption is $10,000 for couples. So, by adding $8,000 of the wildcard to their $4,000 car exemption, Fred and Susan can exempt all of their equity in their cars. They can use the other $2,000 of the wildcard exemption to keep property that isn't otherwise protected by the Virginia exemptions.

3. When the Trustee Takes Property

As a practical matter, the trustee won't take and sell property unless the value of the nonexempt portion, after the costs of storage and sale are deducted, is high enough to make it worth the trustee's while. For example, even if your used furniture exceeds the exemption limit in your state (assuming there is one), the trustee is unlikely to seize and sell the furniture unless it is quite valuable and could obviously be resold for an amount that will cover your exemption and leave enough for your unsecured creditors to generate a decent commission for the trustee. (See Ch. 1, Section C, for more on how trustees get paid.)

The kinds of property listed below are typically not exempt unless by application of a wildcard. If you are concerned about keeping any of these items, you should pay close attention to the exemptions that are available to you (see Section 4, below):

- interests in real estate other than your home (see Ch. 5 for more on residential property exemptions)
- substantial equity in a newer-model motor vehicle
- expensive musical instruments unrelated to your job or business
- stamp, coin, and other collections
- cash, deposit accounts, stocks, bonds, and other investments
- business assets
- valuable artwork
- expensive clothing and jewelry, or
- antiques.

4. Residency Requirements for Exemption Claims

Prior to the new bankruptcy law, filers used the exemptions available in the state where they filed for bankruptcy. Now, however, some filers may have to use the exemptions available in the state where they used to live. Congress was concerned about people gaming the system by moving to states with liberal exemptions just to file for bankruptcy. As a result, it passed residency requirements filers have to meet before claiming a state's exemptions. Here are the new rules:

- If you have lived in your current state for at least two years, you will file in that state and use that state's exemptions (subject to the homestead exception explained in Ch. 5).

- If you have lived in your current state for more than 91 days but less than two years, you will file in that state and use the exemptions of the state where you lived for the better part of the 180-day period immediately prior to the two-year period preceding your filing.
- If you have lived in your current state for fewer than 91 days, you'll need to wait until you have lived there for 91 days to file in that state (and then use whatever exemptions are available to you according to the rules set out above).
- If the state you are filing in offers the federal homestead exemption, you can use that exemption list regardless of how long you've been living in the state.
- If this system deprives you of the right to use any state's exemptions, you can use the federal exemptions. For example, some states allow their exemptions to be used only by current state residents, which might leave former residents who haven't lived in their new home for at least two years without any available state exemptions.

A longer residency requirement applies to homestead exemptions: If you acquired a home in your current state less than 40 months before your filing date, your homestead exemption may be subject to a $125,000 cap regardless of which state's exemption system you use. (Ch. 5 covers homestead exemptions in detail.)

These residency requirements may be declared unconstitutional. Some bankruptcy experts believe that using residency requirements to discourage bankruptcy filers from moving to seek more advantageous exemptions may impose an unconstitutional burden on filers' fundamental right to travel. Because this issue is sure to be raised early on by any attorney whose client is adversely affected by these residency requirements, you should check for updates at www.nolo.com before relying on the information in this section. If you are interested in reading the lead case on this issue, see *Shapiro v. Thompson*, 394 U.S. 618 (1969), available at www.oyez.org/oyez/resource/case/351.

EXAMPLE 1: Sammie Jo lives in South Carolina from July 2005 until January 2007, when she gets lucky at a casino, moves to Texas, and buys a car for $15,000. In March 2008, Sammie Jo files for bankruptcy in Texas. Because Sammie Jo has been living in Texas for only 14 months—not two years—before she files for bankruptcy, she can't use the Texas exemption for cars, which can be up to $30,000 depending on the value of other personal property claimed as exempt. Because Sammie Jo filed in March 2008, the two-year period begins in March 2006. And because Sammie Jo lived in South Carolina for nine months prior to March 2006, the South Carolina state exemptions are the only state exemptions available to her. As it turns out, the South Carolina exemption for cars is only $1,200, which means Sammie Jo will probably lose her car if she uses the South Carolina state exemptions.

As it turns out, however, Texas offers the federal exemptions as an alternative to its state exemptions. Under the new bankruptcy law, the state where a person files determines whether the federal exemptions are available, regardless of how long the person has lived in that state. This means that Sammie Jo can use the federal exemptions instead of the South Carolina state exemptions. Under the federal exemptions, Sammie Jo is entitled to exempt a motor vehicle up to $2,950—still not enough to cover her car, which is now worth $14,000. But wait. The federal exemptions also provide a wildcard of $975 plus $9,250 of unused homestead exemption. Sammie Jo rents rather than owns her home (and doesn't need a homestead exemption), so she can add the entire wildcard of $10,225 to her $2,950 vehicle exemption, for a total exemption applicable to her car of $13,175. While Sammie Jo's car still has $825 of nonexempt equity ($14,000 minus $13,175), the trustee will probably let her keep it. The cost of storing the car and selling it at auction would likely more than eat up that nonexempt equity, leaving little or nothing for Sammie Jo's unsecured creditors, let alone a decent commission for the trustee.

EXAMPLE 2: Julia lives in North Dakota for many years until she moves to Florida on January 15, 2007. She files for bankruptcy in Florida on November 30, 2008. Because she hasn't lived in Florida for two years (her two-year anniversary is January 14, 2009), Julia must use the exemptions from the state where she lived for the better part of the 180-day period preceding the two-year period—which is North Dakota. As it turns out, Julia's largest property item is a prepaid medical savings account deposit of $20,000. While this would be exempt under Florida law, North Dakota has no exemption for this item. Nor are the federal exemptions available in Florida. So the trustee will most likely seize the medical savings account and use it to pay Julia's creditors. Had Julia waited another month and a half to file, she would have been able to use Florida's exemptions and keep her medical savings account.

5. Using the Exemptions Appendix

You can find the exemptions for all 50 states in Appendix A. If you are considering filing for bankruptcy in one of the states listed below, you'll also want to look at the federal exemptions, which are listed right after Wyoming.

States That Offer the Federal Exemptions

Arkansas	New Mexico
Connecticut	Pennsylvania
Hawaii	Rhode Island
Massachusetts	Texas
Michigan	Vermont
Minnesota	Washington
New Hampshire	Wisconsin
New Jersey	

Use Appendix A to find the applicable exemptions for your property, using the residency rules set out in Section 4, above. Do this by comparing the type and value of your property, and the amount of equity you have in the property, with the exemptions. (You can find definitions of many of the terms in Appendix A in the Glossary at the back of this book.)

Remember, if you are filing in a state that offers the federal bankruptcy exemptions, you should also check the federal exemption chart (it comes right after Wyoming). Items that aren't exempt under the state exemptions available to you may be exempt under the federal system, and vice versa. However, you must pick one system or the other to use in your bankruptcy—you can't mix and match.

If you are married and filing jointly, you can double the federal exemptions and any state exemptions unless the chart says that you can't. This will be indicated either at the top of the chart for the particular state or next to a particular exemption.

If you have lived in California for more than two years when you file, you may choose System 1 (the regular state exemptions) or System 2, a state list that is derived from the federal exemptions but differs in important particulars. If you file in California but haven't lived there for two years, you can't use either California system—you'll have to use the residency rules set out in Section 4, above, to figure out which exemptions you can use.

Federal Nonbankruptcy Exemptions

If you are using the exemptions of particular state rather than the federal exemptions, you may also exempt property listed in Appendix A under Federal Nonbankruptcy Exemptions. Don't confuse those with the federal bankruptcy exemptions, which may be used only if a state allows, and only as an alternative to the state exemptions.

Bankruptcy Rules in Ch. 4

- Pensions that are not part of the bankruptcy estate are described in detail. (11 U.S.C. § 523(b)(4).)
- Funds that are placed in an education IRA more than one year prior to bankruptcy filing are not part of the bankruptcy estate, subject to certain restrictions. (11 U.S.C. § 541(a)(5).)
- Wages that are withheld, and employer contributions that are made, for employee benefit and health insurance plans are not part of the bankruptcy estate. (11 U.S.C. § 541(a)(8).)
- Pawned property is not part of the bankruptcy estate. (11 U.S.C. § 541(a)(9).)
- All assets must be valued at their replacement value. For property acquired for personal, family, or household purposes, replacement value means the price a retail merchant would charge for property of that kind considering the age and condition of the property at the time value is determined. (11 U.S.C. §§ 506(a)(2), 527(c), and 722.)
- You must be a resident of the state where you file for at least two years to claim that state's exemptions. (11 U.S.C. § 522(b)(3)(A).)
- If you have not lived for two years in the state where you file, you must claim the exemptions of the state where you lived during the greater part of the 180-day period immediately preceding the two-year period before your filing date. (11 U.S.C. § 522(b)(3)(A).)
- If the state where you file allows it, you can claim the federal bankruptcy exemptions under 11 U.S.C. § 523(d).
- If the residency requirement deprives you of the right to claim any exemption, you can claim the federal bankruptcy code exemptions in 523(d). (11 U.S.C. § 523(b)(3)(A).)
- Exempt property may be taken to pay debts for domestic support (child support or alimony). (11 U.S.C. § 522(c)(1).)

Your Home

One of the biggest worries you may face in deciding whether to file for bankruptcy is the possibility of losing your home, whether you own or rent. If so, you'll be relieved to know that the bankruptcy system is not designed to put you out on the street.

If you can get and stay current on your mortgage payments, and your equity in a home is fully protected by an available exemption, your chances of keeping a home you own look good. If, however, you are behind in your payments or your equity in the home is significantly more than the amount you are entitled to keep (called the "homestead exemption"), you might lose your home if your file under Chapter 7. In this situation, Chapter 13 bankruptcy will likely be a better option, assuming you qualify.

If you are a renter facing eviction, filing for bankruptcy is unlikely to improve your situation. If, however, you owe back rent but your landlord has not yet begun eviction proceedings, you can use bankruptcy to discharge the rent debt.

This chapter covers:

- issues facing homeowners who file under Chapter 7 (see Section A, below)
- issues facing homeowners who file under Chapter 13 (see Section B, below), and
- issues facing renters who file for bankruptcy under either Chapter.

A. Homeowners Filing for Bankruptcy Under Chapter 7

If you are current on your house payments, you can figure out how bankruptcy will affect your home ownership by doing some simple math:

- compute your equity in your home
- choose the appropriate homestead exemption, and
- compare your equity to the homestead exemption.

If your equity is less than the homestead exemption, your home is protected. If your equity is more than the homestead exemption, your home is at risk. (See Section 4, below, if you aren't current on your payments.)

1. Compute Your Equity

Your equity in your home is how much money you would end up with if you sold it. This is typically what it would cost you to sell the same property *less* what you will have to pay to others out of the sales price because of legal claims they have against the property (for example, your mortgage lender or the county tax collector). Don't include the costs of selling the house—such as closing costs or broker's fees—in your calculations. These costs will, however, be important in deciding later whether your home is safe from the trustee.

EXAMPLE: Your house will sell for $300,000. You have a mortgage for $200,000. There are no other debts that have to be paid out of the sales proceeds. Your equity is $100,000. If there is a lien on your home, you must subtract that as well. For example, if you didn't pay the contractor who remodeled your kitchen, and the contractor put a $20,000 lien on your home, your equity would be reduced by that lien amount, to $80,000.

a. Assess the Fair Market Value of Your Property

When computing your equity, you must first assess your home's fair market value. It is extremely important to get this right. One of the biggest mistakes that homeowners make when filing under Chapter 7 is to underestimate the value of their homes. This is especially true in markets where prices are rising rapidly. If your home is worth much more than you think, you risk losing it in bankruptcy— unless the homestead exemption you are using covers the increased equity.

In regions where prices are relatively stable, valuing homes is a fairly simple issue. Realtors in your area will know what similar homes have sold for and can give you a pretty accurate estimate of what they could get for your home. Although prices might rise by a few percentage points a year, you shouldn't have too much trouble valuing your home.

 Find sales prices for comparable homes in your area on the Internet. For a modest fee, you can get details on comparable houses—including neighborhood information, sales history, address, number of bedrooms and baths, square footage, and property tax information—from SmartHomeBuy, at www.smarthomebuy.com. Less detailed information (purchase price, sales date, and address) is available free from sites including www.homevalues.com, www.domania.com, www.homeradar.com , and http://list.realestate.yahoo.com/re/homevalues. Simply enter the home's address or zip code.

In some parts of the country, it is not as easy to find out what your home will sell for. This is because of what has come to be called "the housing bubble." As this book goes to press, home prices are going up by 50% a year in some cities. When housing prices are this volatile, it's hard to know what a house is worth from one day to the next, let alone over a six-month period. The house you bought for $150,000 five years ago might be worth $350,000 now. And your home may significantly increase in value between the time you have it appraised and the time you file for bankruptcy.

This rapid appreciation is good news but can be a real problem if you're filing for bankruptcy. The more equity you have in your home, the more likely you will have to forfeit it to pay your creditors (unless the available homestead exemption is large enough to cover your increased equity). And the harder it is to accurately predict your home value on the date you file for bankruptcy, the harder it will be to figure out whether your house will be safe in Chapter 7 or whether you should file for Chapter 13 instead. In hot real estate markets, you must make sure your appraisal occurs just before your filing date, so you can be sure your homestead exemption covers your equity.

b. Identify Liens on Your Property

When computing your equity, you must subtract any liens on the property. A lien is a legal claim on property that can only be removed voluntarily by the lienholder or by a court order. A mortgage, for example, is a debt that is secured by the property in the form of a lien.

Because a lien claims a right to some portion of the property's value, it "clouds" the owner's title to the property. Buyers don't want to buy property that is encumbered by liens—and insurance companies don't want to issue title insurance in this situation, either. As a practical matter, this means you will have to pay off liens in order to sell your house (unless you can get rid of the liens in your bankruptcy—as is often the case with liens arising from money judgments).

In addition to a mortgage, other typical liens arise from:

- second deeds of trust
- home equity loans
- money judgments issued by a court
- child support arrearages

- delinquent income or property taxes, and
- debts owed to people who improved the property but who weren't paid for some reason (these are called mechanic's and materialman's liens).

To compute your equity, deduct all liens on your home from its fair market value (what you could sell it for). If a debt is not secured by a lien on your home, you don't have to count it when computing your equity.

2. Choose Your Homestead Exemption

Your homestead exemption is the amount of equity in your home you are entitled to keep if you file for Chapter 7 bankruptcy. Every state has its own homestead exemption rules—and the exemption available to you will help determine whether you keep or lose your home. Because the new bankruptcy law imposes strict residency requirements, however, you may not qualify for the exemption you want to use. This section explains the various types of homestead exemptions available, and how to figure out which one to use.

a. Types of Homestead Exemptions

Homestead exemptions vary tremendously from state to state. In fact, in a few states, the homestead exemption isn't a monetary amount at all—it's based on your lot size. A handful of states have no homestead exemption at all. Some states are at the other extreme, and allow you to protect a very large or even unlimited amount of equity. In a few states, the homestead exemption is based on a combination of lot size and a monetary amount.

How Does Your State Calculate Its Homestead Exemption?	
Unlimited Homestead Exemption	District of Columbia
Homestead Exemption Based on Lot Size Only	Arkansas, Florida, Iowa, Kansas, Oklahoma, South Dakota, Texas
Homestead Exemption Based on Lot Size and Equity	Alabama, Hawaii, Louisiana, Michigan, Minnesota, Mississippi, Nebraska, Oregon
Homestead Exemption Based on Equity Only	Federal bankruptcy exemptions and: Alaska, Arizona, California, Colorado, Connecticut, Georgia, Idaho, Illinois, Indiana, Kentucky, Maine, Massachusetts, Missouri, Montana, Nevada, New Hampshire, New Mexico, New York, North Carolina, North Dakota, Ohio, Rhode Island, South Carolina, Tennessee, Utah, Vermont, Virginia, Washington, West Virginia, Wisconsin, Wyoming
No Homestead Exemption	Delaware, Maryland, New Jersey, Pennsylvania

b. Homestead Exemptions Protect Only Residences

With very few exceptions, you must reside in the home as your primary residence when you file for bankruptcy in order to claim a homestead exemption. Homestead exemption laws do not protect second homes, vacation homes, or other real estate in which you aren't living when you file. They do, however, typically apply to mobile homes and boats that you use as your primary residence.

c. Declared Homesteads

In California and many other states, the homestead exemption automatically kicks in when you file for bankruptcy. However, some states (listed below) require you to file a "Declaration of Homestead" with the county recorder in order to use the state's homestead exemption in bankruptcy. In rare cases, some states will allow you to claim an exemption for a declared homestead even if you aren't living in the home when you file.

States That Require a Declaration of Homestead	
Alabama	Texas
Idaho	Utah
Massachusetts	Virginia
Montana	Washington
Nevada	

d. States With Two Exemption Systems

In 15 states and the District of Columbia, you must choose between two different homestead amounts—one offered by the state and one offered under the federal Bankruptcy Code. California also offers a choice between two different amounts, but both amounts are offered under California state law. (See Ch. 4, Section D, for more on these dual systems.)

e. Wildcard Exemptions

In some states, you can increase the amount of your homestead exemption with a state "wildcard" exemption—that is, a dollar amount that your state allows you to apply to any property, in order to make it (or more of it) exempt. The exemptions under the federal bankruptcy code also include a wildcard exemption of $975. The chart below lists the state wildcard exemptions that you can apply to real estate; although other states have wildcard exemptions, they can by applied only to personal property.

> **EXAMPLE:** In Connecticut, the base homestead exemption is $75,000. In addition, Connecticut has a wildcard exemption of $1,000 applicable to any property. This means that if you don't use the wildcard exemption for other types of property, you can use it for your homestead, which would increase the exemption from $75,000 to $76,000.

State Wildcard Exemptions Applicable to Real Estate	
California, System 2	$1,000
Connecticut	1,000
Georgia	600
Indiana	4,000
Kentucky	1,000
Maine	400
Maryland (because Maryland has no homestead exemption, this is the only exemption you can use on your home)	5,500
Missouri	1,250
New Hampshire	8,000
Ohio	400
Pennsylvania	300
Vermont	400
Virginia (available only if you are a disabled veteran)	2,000
West Virginia	800
Federal	975

f. Tenancy by the Entirety

In 18 states, spouses are allowed to own property together in a form known as "tenancy by the entirety." If only one spouse files for bankruptcy, property the couple owns as tenants by the entirety is, generally, not part of the bankruptcy estate. In other words, the property is exempt in its entirety, regardless of its value. If, however, both spouses file, the property will be part of their bankruptcy estate and will be subject to the appropriate homestead exemption available to the couple under the rules discussed below.

States That Allow Spouses to Own Property in Tenancy by the Entirety

Delaware	Missouri
District of Columbia	North Carolina
Florida	Ohio
Hawaii	Pennsylvania
Illinois	Rhode Island
Indiana	Tennessee
Maryland	Vermont
Massachusetts	Virginia
Michigan	Wyoming

g. Choose the Appropriate Homestead Exemption

Prior to the new bankruptcy law, filers used the homestead exemption in the state where they filed for bankruptcy. The rules are more complicated now, however. As explained in Ch. 4, Section D, residency requirements now determine which exemptions filers can use. In addition to these general rules, Congress passed even stricter residency requirements for claiming a state's homestead law, to discourage people from moving to states with more generous homestead exemptions just to file for bankruptcy.

i. If You Acquired Your Current Home at Least 40 Months Before Filing

If you acquired your current home at least 40 months before filing, you can use your current state's homestead exemption without restriction.

> **EXAMPLE:** Mary and Peter live in Vermont. They have owned their home for five years. They file bankruptcy in Vermont and can use Vermont's homestead exemption (because they lived there for more than 40 months before filing). Because Vermont offers the federal exemption option, Mary and Peter can choose either the Vermont homestead exemption or the federal homestead exemption. As it turns out, the Vermont homestead exemption is $75,000 compared to a maximum federal homestead exemption of roughly $40,000 (for a couple filing together).

ii. If You Brought Your Home Within 40 Months of Filing, Using the Proceeds from the Sale of Another Home in the Same State

If you acquired your current home within 40 months of filing, but purchased it with the proceeds from the sale of another home in the same state that occurred at least 40 months earlier, you can use your current state's homestead exemption without restriction.

> **EXAMPLE:** Violet and Robin have lived in Montana for six years. When they

first moved there, they bought a home for $175,000. Three years later, they sold that home and bought another home for $250,000. Although they have lived in their current home for fewer than 40 months, they bought it with the proceeds of another Montana home that they purchased more than 40 months before filing. Violet and Robin can claim Montana's homestead exemption without restriction.

iii. If You Acquired Your Home Within 40 Months of Filing, and Have Lived in Your State Two Years or More

If you acquired your current home within the previous 40 months and have lived in your state for at least two years, you can use that state's homestead exemption, subject to a $125,000 cap.

> **EXAMPLE 1:** Three years ago, John and Susie moved from Massachusetts to Maine, where they bought a home. If they file for bankruptcy in Maine, they can claim the Maine homestead exemption because they have lived there longer than two years. Because they have lived in Maine for fewer than 40 months, however, they will be limited to a cap of $125,000. Maine's homestead allowance for joint filers who are over the age 60 is $140,000, so John and Susie (who are both 65 years old) will lose $15,000 worth of homestead exemption because of the residency cap ($140,000 minus $125,000=$15,000).

> **EXAMPLE 2:** Massachusetts provides a homestead exemption of $300,000. After moving from Vermont to Boston in 2006, Julius and his family buy a fine old Boston home in 2007 for $700,000. After borrowing heavily against the home because of financial reversals, Julius files for bankruptcy in early 2008. At the time Julius owns $250,000 equity in the house. Although the Massachusetts homestead exemption of $300,000 would easily cover Julius's equity, Julius may claim an exemption of only $125,000 because he moved to Massachusetts from another state within the previous 40 months.

iv. If You Have Lived in Your State for Less Than Two Years

If you moved to your current state within two years before filing, you must use the homestead exemption available in the state where you were living for the better part of the 180-day period prior to the two-year period, subject to a $125,000 cap. However if the state where you are filing offers the federal homestead exemption, you can use that exemption regardless of how long you've been living in that state or when you bought your home.

> **EXAMPLE 1:** Eighteen months ago, Fred moved from Florida to Nevada, where he purchased his current home with $400,000 he received from a recent inheritance. Fred files for bankruptcy in Nevada, his current state. Because Fred lived in Florida for two years

prior to moving to Nevada, he must use Florida's homestead exemption, subject to the $125,000 cap. The cap imposes an extreme penalty on Fred. Florida's homestead exemption is unlimited while Nevada's is $200,000. However, because Fred can protect only $125,000, most of his equity in his home is nonexempt, which means that the trustee will undoubtedly sell the home, give Fred his $125,000, and distribute the balance to Fred's unsecured creditors.

EXAMPLE 2: Joan moves from Delaware to Vermont, where she buys a home. Less than two years after moving to Vermont, Joan files for bankruptcy in that state. Because Joan was living in Delaware prior to the beginning of the two-year prebankruptcy filing period, she must either use Delaware's state homestead allowance or the federal homestead allowance if Vermont allows it—which it does. Delaware provides no homestead exemption at all, but the federal homestead exemption is approximately $20,000. Joan chooses to use the federal homestead allowance—a no-brainer.

 These residency requirements may be declared unconstitutional. Some bankruptcy experts believe that using residency requirements to discourage bankruptcy filers from seeking out more advantageous exemptions may impose an unconstitutional burden on filers'

fundamental right to travel. Because this issue is sure to be raised early on by any attorney whose client is adversely affected by these residency requirements, you should check for updates at www.nolo.com before relying on the information in this section. If you are interested in reading the lead case on this issue, see *Shapiro v. Thompson*, 394 U.S. 618 (1969), available at www.oyez.org/oyez/resource/case/351.

v. If You Have Committed Certain Crimes, Torts, or Deception Against Creditors

Even if you qualify for an "uncapped" homestead exemption under the rules explained above, your exemption might be limited if you have engaged in particular types of misconduct. If you have committed a felony, a securities act violation, or certain crimes or intentional torts that have led to death or serious bodily injury, your homestead exemption may be capped at $125,000, depending on how the court sees your circumstances. For instance, the court might decide to lift the cap if it finds that the homestead in question is reasonably necessary for you to support yourself and your dependents.

Even if you haven't committed a crime or tort, your homestead exemption might be limited if you have tried to cheat your creditors. If you have disposed of nonexempt property with the intent to hinder, delay, or defraud a creditor during the ten years before you file for bankruptcy, the value of your interest in your current home will be reduced by the value of the property you unloaded, which means you may be left with little or no homestead protection.

Watch for Developments on the $125,000 Cap

Because of the way the new law is written, the $125,000 cap on home-stead exemptions may apply only if:

- the exemption system available to the debtor offers a choice between federal and state exemption systems
- the debtor uses the state exemptions, and
- the state allows the debtor to exempt more than $125,000 for a homestead.

In other words, only Minnesota and Texas filers would have to worry about the cap. However, at least one court has interpreted the law differently, finding that the cap applies to filers in every state. (*In re Kaplan*, 331 B.R. 483 (S.D.Fla.2005).)

---

h. Find Your Homestead Exemption

Once you have decided which state's homestead exemption you can use, turn to Appendix A at the back of this book and look in the top box for that state.

If you are married and filing jointly with your spouse, check to see whether you can double your state's homestead amount.

If the chart for your state indicates that the federal exemptions are available, compare your state's exemption with the federal homestead exemption, which currently is $18,450 for a single filer and double that for a married couple filing jointly, plus a general purpose (wildcard) exemption of $975 for a single filer and double that for joint filers. So, under the federal exemptions, a married couple may exempt up to $36,900 plus $1,950, for a combined total homestead exemption of $38,850.

In California, the alternate exemption system (System 2) allows only $18,675 for a homestead, whether you file alone or jointly with a spouse. However, California's primary state exemption system (System 1) allows $50,000 for single filers, $75,000 for heads of households, and $150,000 for elderly and disabled filers, so people in California who have significant equity in their homes tend to choose System 1.

3. Compare Your Equity to the Homestead Exemption

Now that you've computed your equity and located the appropriate homestead exemption, it's time to put the two together. This comparison will tell you whether you can safely file for Chapter 7 bankruptcy and keep your home, or whether you should consider other options—such as filing under Chapter 13 (see Ch.2, Section D).

a. If You Have No Equity in Your Home

If the total amount of debt against your home is equal to or more than its market value, you have no equity and aren't at risk of losing the home as long as you keep current on your payments. This is true no matter how large or small the homestead exemption that's available to you. The trustee wouldn't get any money out of selling your home—all of the proceeds would go to the creditors who have liens on the property.

> **EXAMPLE:** Your home is worth $250,000. You owe $200,000 on your mortgage and the IRS has placed a $50,000 lien on the home for back taxes. If the trustee sold the home, the mortgage owner and IRS would have to be paid, which would leave no money at all for your creditors. In other words, even if you are living in a state that offers little or no homestead protection, you would still keep your home because the trustee can't profit from selling it.

b. If You Have Some Equity In Your Home

If the total amount of debt against your home is less than its market value, you will want to compare the difference—your equity—with the homestead exemption available to you. As long as the homestead exemption covers your equity, the trustee won't have any interest in selling your home; there wouldn't be any equity left over to pay your unsecured creditors, and the trustee wouldn't get any commission for the sale. Even if your equity is a little over the homestead limit, the trustee will have to figure in the costs of sale (about 10% of its selling price) before deciding whether it makes sense to sell the home.

> **EXAMPLE:** The real estate broker you used when you bought your home told you that it is currently worth $300,000. You owe your mortgage lender $200,000 and the IRS (which has issued a Notice of Federal Tax Lien) $35,000. The equity in your home is $65,000 ($300,000 minus $200,000 minus $35,000). If the trustee sells your $300,000 home, he or she will net approximately $270,000 because of the costs of sale and the trustee's commission. After paying the tax lien and the mortgage, the trustee would clear $35,000. If your homestead exemption is equal to or greater than $35,000, the trustee will gain nothing by selling the home. If a significant chunk of the $35,000 is unprotected by a homestead exemption, however, your home is in danger of being sold for the benefit of your unsecured creditors.

c. If Your Equity Is More Than Your Homestead Exemption

Until recently, the homestead exemptions in many states were adequate to cover all or most of a person's equity—primarily because people typically borrow against their home right up until the time they decide to file for bankruptcy (and therefore, have very little equity to protect).

In many parts of the country, however, this is no longer true. Housing prices have shot up so rapidly that people suddenly find themselves with lots of equity—and, therefore, a significant risk of losing their homes if they file for Chapter 7.

If you have nonexempt equity in your home (equity that isn't protected by your homestead exemption) and would lose it if you filed for Chapter 7 bankruptcy, you'll probably want to explore other options. For instance, if your home would sell for $300,000, the total liens are $100,000, and your state's homestead exemption is $100,000, you would have $100,000 of unprotected equity. The trustee would probably sell your home, pay off the $100,000 mortgage, pay you your $100,000 homestead exemption, and use the extra $100,000 (less costs of sale) to pay your unsecured creditors. If some of this money were left after your unsecured creditors were paid in full and the trustee took his or her cut, you would get that balance in addition to your homestead exemption.

If you have too much equity in your home, you may be able to use some of it to pay off your other debts and avoid bankruptcy altogether. If you still need to file for bankruptcy after paying down your equity, you may be able to save your house, although you will have to be extremely careful about when you file your bankruptcy. (See "Reducing Your Equity: Timing Is Key," below.)

If You Live on a Fixed Income

All too often, elderly people who live on a fixed income own much more equity in their homes than the homestead laws protect. They bought their homes when property could be had for a song and now they are land wealthy. If this is your situation, consider using a "reverse mortgage."

In a reverse mortgage, you borrow against your home equity and receive monthly payments that you can use to fix your home, pay down your debts, or pay them off altogether (if that's your preference). But you don't have to pay the loan back during your lifetime—instead, the loan is collected after your death, from your home equity. For more information on reverse mortgages, contact the FTC website at www.ftc.gov/bcp/conline/pubs/homes/rms.htm.

There are several ways to reduce your equity:

1. **Refinance your mortgage for more than you currently owe.** For example, let's say you owe $180,000 on your mortgage at a 9% interest rate. You have 22 years left on your mortgage, and your monthly payments are $1,568. Your house is worth $240,000, giving you $60,000 of equity, more than your state's homestead exemption of $30,000. If you refinance your mortgage, reducing your interest

rate to 7% and borrowing $215,000 ($180,000 to pay off your mortgage and $35,000 to pay off other debts), you could reduce your monthly payments to $1,430. In addition, your equity would be $25,000 ($240,000 minus $215,000), well within the homestead exemption.

2. **Take out a home equity loan or line of credit.** You may be able to use this money to pay off some high-interest debts, such as credit card bills, and avoid bankruptcy. Or you can pay off debts you wouldn't be able to discharge, such as child or spousal support, taxes, or a recent student loan, and still file for bankruptcy to deal with your other debts.

3. **Offer to substitute cash for the amount of nonexempt equity.** If you want to file for Chapter 7 bankruptcy but you're afraid you will lose your house because your equity exceeds the homestead amount, you might be able to save your house if you can pay the difference to the trustee. You may be able to raise the cash by selling exempt property or using income you earn after you file.

4. **File for Chapter 13 bankruptcy.** Chapter 13 bankruptcy lets you pay your debts out of your income, rather than by selling your property. Thus, if you file for Chapter 13 bankruptcy, you won't have to give up your home even if you have significant nonexempt equity. (See Section B, below, for more on Chapter 13.)

Reducing Your Equity: Timing Is Key

If you decide to take steps to reduce the equity in your house, keep an eye on the calendar. Most likely, you will have to wait at least 90 days after refinancing or making payments on an equity line of credit before you file for bankruptcy. If you pay $600 or more to a regular creditor in the 90 days before you file, the payment can be set aside as a forbidden "preferential payment to a creditor." There's an exception for payments made in the normal course of business (for example, payments by small business owners going into bankruptcy) or for necessities of life, such as housing, utilities, food, and the like.

If you pay $600 or more to a friend, relative, or close business associate during the year before you file for bankruptcy, these payments can also be set aside, unless they were made in the normal course of business. And any transfer you make for the purpose of putting your property beyond the reach of creditors during the **ten** years preceding your bankruptcy filing can deprive you of your homestead exemption altogether. See a bankruptcy lawyer if you wish to engage in this sort of planning.

d. If You Are on a Fixed Income

If you have excess equity in your home, you may be tempted to take out a loan and use it to pay your debts. However, if you are on fixed income because of retirement or disability, you may not be able to make the payments on a loan. In other words, by borrowing to pay your debts, you may end up defaulting on the loan and losing your home to the lender.

> **EXAMPLE:** Trudy bought her home in 1956 for $56,000. Over the years, the value of the house has increased to $400,000. Trudy owes $175,000 in credit card debt and is considering filing for bankruptcy. Trudy wants to borrow against her home and pay off the debt, but her sole income is $800 a month from Social Security. She won't be able to make the payments on the loan.

Although this is a difficult situation, Chapter 7 bankruptcy is not the answer— you would lose your home to the trustee. You might be able to buy a new home with the proceeds from your homestead exemption (the trustee would pay you that in cash), but for many, the loss of a home would be traumatic.

In Trudy's case, depending on her age, the best option may be a reverse mortgage that she can use to pay off the debt and augment her fixed income while remaining in her home for the rest of her life. The downside to this is that she won't own the home—and be able to pass it down to her kids or other heirs—when she dies.

4. If You Are Behind on Your Mortgage Payments

If you are behind on your mortgage payments when you file for Chapter 7 bankruptcy, you will almost certainly lose your home to foreclosure unless you can get current in a hurry. As a general rule, your mortgage lender will ask the bankruptcy court to lift the "automatic stay" (the court order that bars creditors from trying to collect their debts, discussed in Ch. 1, Section B), and the court will probably grant the request, allowing the mortgage lender to begin or resume foreclosure proceedings.

The only way Chapter 7 bankruptcy can help you is if you can stave off foreclosure for the length of your bankruptcy case. When the case is over, and your other debts are wiped out or reduced, you may have an easier time getting and remaining current on your mortgage payments, assuming the lender hasn't yet accelerated (called in) the loan.

a. Negotiating With the Lender

If you've missed only a few mortgage payments, your lender may be willing to negotiate. What the lender agrees to will depend on your credit history, the reason for your missed payments, and your financial prospects.

Here are the possible options your lender might agree to:

- Spread out the missed payments over a few months.

- Reduce or suspend your regular payments for a specified time and then add a portion of your overdue amount to your regular payments later on.
- Extend the length of your loan and add the missed payments at the end.
- Suspend the principal portion of your monthly payment for a while and have you pay only interest, taxes, and insurance.
- Refinance your loan to reduce future monthly payments.

b. If the Lender Starts to Foreclose

If your debt problems look severe or long-lasting, the lender may take steps toward foreclosure. In most cases, the lender will accelerate the loan before foreclosure actually occurs. This means you must pay the entire balance immediately. If you don't, the lender is entitled to foreclose.

There are two different kinds of foreclosure. One is called a "judicial" foreclosure, so named because the lender must file papers in court and obtain the court's approval before foreclosing. This kind of foreclosure can take as long as 18 to 36 months before you would ever lose your house. If you file for Chapter 7 bankruptcy, your bankruptcy may have little effect on this type of foreclosure. Your bankruptcy will probably start and end before much happens in the foreclosure case. (Remember, Chapter 7 bankruptcy typically takes only four to six months to complete.) The only real effect is that your lender will be barred from sending you foreclosure notices or proceeding with a court hearing unless it files a motion with the court to have the automatic stay lifted. And even if the stay is lifted, it won't affect your bankruptcy, because the judicial foreclosure process will likely be slower.

The other kind of foreclosure is called a "nonjudicial" foreclosure, so named because the lender does not have to go to court in order to foreclose. Instead, a third-party trustee (not the bankruptcy trustee) sells your property after sending you a series of notices. This trustee is the person or business named in the deed of trust that you signed (or their successors in interest) instead of, or in addition to, the traditional mortgage when you purchased or refinanced your property. Nonjudicial foreclosures can happen quickly, sometimes in as few as three or four months, the same amount of time you are likely to be in a Chapter 7 bankruptcy case.

c. When the Automatic Stay Will Be Lifted to Permit Foreclosure

If you file for bankruptcy and are behind on your payments, expect the mortgage lender to come to court and ask the judge to life the automatic stay. (See Ch. 1, Section B, for more on the automatic stay). If you have nonexempt equity in your home, the bankruptcy trustee is likely to successfully oppose the motion and sell the property for the benefit of your unsecured creditors (after the lender is paid off and you are paid the amount protected by the applicable exemption). If you have no equity, however, the trustee will probably not oppose the motion to lift the stay and will let the foreclosure go through.

During a foreclosure, you have several options (although if the creditor begins a nonjudicial foreclosure, some of them may not be available to you simply because of time constraints):

- Sell your house. If you don't get any offers that will cover what you owe your lender, the lender may agree to take less. This is called a "short sale."
- Get a new loan that pays off all or part of the first loan and puts you on a new schedule of monthly payments. If the original lender has accelerated the loan, you'll need to refinance the entire balance of the loan to prevent foreclosure.
- Reinstate the loan. If the lender hasn't accelerated the loan, you can prevent foreclosure simply by paying the missed payments, taxes, and insurance, plus interest.
- File for Chapter 13 bankruptcy. Section B, below, explains how Chapter 13 bankruptcy can save your home if you are behind on your mortgage.

B. Homeowners Filing for Bankruptcy Under Chapter 13

If you own your home and file for bankruptcy under Chapter 13, you won't face the same issues as you would under Chapter 7. Chapter 13 repayment plans are funded out of your projected disposable income, not your nonexempt property. As long as you can propose a legal plan out of your projected disposable income, you can keep your home no matter how much equity you have—or how large the homestead exemption available to you. As always, however, the devil is in the details.

Under the law governing Chapter 13, you must propose a repayment plan that pays your unsecured creditors at least as much as they would receive if you had filed for Chapter 7 bankruptcy. For example, if you have $100,000 worth of unprotected (nonexempt) equity in your home, you will have to pay your unsecured creditors at least $100,000 over the life of your plan. If you don't have adequate projected disposable income to pay that amount, the court will not confirm your plan and you'll find yourself in Chapter 7, or outside of bankruptcy if you choose to dismiss your Chapter 13 case. (See Ch. 2, Section D, for more on how projected disposable income is computed. You may be in for a surprise.)

1. Determining Which State's Exemptions Apply

The starting point is to figure out which exemptions are available to you. Section A2, above, helps you make that determination for homestead exemptions in a Chapter 7 case. The same rules apply in a Chapter 13 case for the purpose of deciding how much your unsecured creditors must be paid. These rules are:

- If you acquired your home at least 40 months before filing, you can use your state's homestead exemption without restriction.
- If you acquired your home less than 40 months ago but you have lived in your current state for at least 40 months and you purchased your current home with the proceeds from the sale a former home in your current state, you can use your current state's homestead exemption without restriction.
- If you have lived in your current state for at least two years but less than 40 months, you must use your current state's homestead exemption subject to a $125,000 cap.
- If you have lived in your current state for less than two years, you must use the homestead exemption of the state where you were living for the better part of the 180-day period prior to the two-year period, subject to the $125,000 cap.
- If the state you are filing in offers the federal homestead exemption, you can use that exemption regardless of how long you've been living in the state or when you bought your home.
- If you don't qualify for any state's homestead exemption, you can use the federal homestead exemption.

For a discussion and examples of these rules, review Section A2, above.

You must count all of your nonexempt property. In most cases, the equity you own in your home will be the big-ticket item that determines how much you must pay your unsecured creditors. However, if you own other valuable property that is nonexempt, you must add in the value of that property to determine how much your unsecured creditors must get under your repayment plan. Chs. 4 and 6 discuss exemptions for other kinds of property; residency requirements apply to those exemptions as well.

2. Selling or Refinancing Your Home to Increase Your Disposable Income

As discussed in Ch. 2, Section D, you qualify for Chapter 13 only if you have enough projected disposable income to remain current on certain obligations and pay 100% of any arrearages owed on them. For instance, your repayment plan must propose to pay:

- 100% of all support arrearages owed to a child or ex-spouse, as well as your current required payments on those obligations
- 100% of all arrearages on a mortgage as well as the current monthly payments (assuming you plan to keep your home), and
- an amount to your unsecured creditors equal to the value of your nonexempt property.

These and other requirements often make it difficult, if not impossible, to propose a viable Chapter 13 plan out of your projected disposable income. In this situation, you may wish to use some or all of the equity in your home to help fund your Chapter 13 plan—particularly if your equity, when added to your projected disposable income, is sufficient to make your plan confirmable, but isn't enough to make a serious dent in your debt load.

EXAMPLE: Ethan owes $125,000 in credit card debt and is contemplating bankruptcy. However, his projected disposable income is insufficient to propose a confirmable Chapter 13 plan (because he owes back child support and taxes that he must pay in full). Chapter 7 also isn't an attractive option for Ethan because he would lose nonexempt property that he really wants to keep: stock options and shares in a family corporation. Fortunately, Ethan owns a home that would produce $50,000 after costs of sale. If Ethan sells his home and devotes the proceeds to his plan, the plan will then become confirmable.

In order to use property to fund a Chapter 13 plan, you either must have:

- the proceeds in hand when you file your bankruptcy petition or shortly afterwards, or
- a feasible plan of sale that will convince the judge that you will sell the property and devote the proceeds to the plan.

Of course, if refinancing or borrowing against your home would pay off your debts outside of bankruptcy and still leave you with a manageable loan payment, this might be your best option.

3. If Your Mortgage Is in Arrears But Foreclosure Hasn't Started

If you are behind on your mortgage and want to keep your home, Chapter 13 will likely be your bankruptcy Chapter of choice. As discussed in Section B, above, filing for Chapter 7 bankruptcy usually won't prevent a lender from foreclosing on a mortgage default. But Chapter 13 is different. If you have enough disposable income to propose a plan that a) makes your regular payments on your mortgage and b) pays off your arrearage in a reasonable period of time, you will be allowed to keep your home as part of your Chapter 13 case.

EXAMPLE: Kenny and Zoe, a married couple, pay $2,000 a month on their mortgage. They have fallen five payments behind and owe an arrearage of $10,000. If they file for Chapter 7 bankruptcy, the lender will get the bankruptcy stay lifted and proceed to foreclose on the loan. Because they want to keep their home, Kenny and Zoe file a Chapter 13 bankruptcy and propose a repayment plan that will, among other things:

- pay their monthly mortgage of $2,000, and

- pay roughly $300 a month towards the arrearage, plus interest.

4. If Your Mortgage Is in Arrears And the Lender Has Started to Foreclose

If your lender has started to foreclose, you can file for Chapter 13 bankruptcy and make up your missed payments, reinstate the loan, and keep making the payments under the original contract. This is called "curing the default." Your right to cure the default depends on how far along the foreclosure proceeding is. If the lender has accelerated the loan or obtained a foreclosure judgment, you usually can still cure the default. If the foreclosure sale has already occurred, however, Chapter 13 usually won't help. Cases have held that the bankruptcy court has no jurisdiction to undo a sale regardless of what might be allowed under state law—such as the right of redemption prior to the recording of the new deed.

 Use Chapter 13 bankruptcy to buy time. If your lender has begun foreclosure proceedings, you can file for Chapter 13 bankruptcy to put the automatic stay in place to stop further foreclosure activity. During the time it takes for the lender to file a motion to have the stay lifted, for the court to schedule it, and for you to appear to argue it, you may be able to sell the house. You can then dismiss your case (unless, of course, you have other debts

you want to take care of through Chapter 13). If you do use Chapter 13 for this limited purpose, you can do it only once over a one-year period.

5. If Foreclosure Is Unavoidable

If it looks like foreclosure is inevitable, losing your home in bankruptcy is often better than losing it in a foreclosure sale.

If you have enough equity in your home to squeeze some money out for your unsecured creditors—after paying your homestead exemption, the costs of sale, and any liens against the property, the bankruptcy trustee will supervise a forced sale of your home for as much money as possible. Remember, the trustee's job is to generate as much money as possible for your unsecured creditors—and because the trustee earns a commission on the payments, he or she has a strong incentive to go for top dollar. On the other hand, in a foreclosure sale, the foreclosing creditor will try to get a price that's only high enough to cover the amount due on the mortgage. So you're more than likely going to lose any equity you have in the house.

 If your lender has sent you a foreclosure notice, it may be time to consult with a real estate attorney—quickly. You may have special legal options—and risks—in your state that are not discussed above. See "The Risk of Deficiency Judgments," below.

The Risk of Deficiency Judgments

In some states, and with certain property and types of loans, the lender can get a deficiency judgment following a foreclosure. A "deficiency judgment" is a judgment for the difference between what you owe and what the lender gets for the property at auction. The creditor can use this deficiency judgment to collect the rest of the debt by seizing your other available property.

The possibility of a deficiency judgment could affect your strategy when facing a foreclosure. For instance, if you are at risk of a deficiency judgment, you might try to deed the property back to the lender, in exchange for a release from liability (commonly called a "deed in lieu of foreclosure"). But if your state doesn't permit deficiency judgments, or your property is not subject to a deficiency judgment, you might benefit from fighting the foreclosure as long as possible without making any payments in the meantime.

These laws vary from state to state, which is one reason you may need to consult a real estate attorney if you get a notice of foreclosure.

C. Renters Filing for Bankruptcy

If you're current on your rent payments and you file for either Chapter 7 or Chapter 13 bankruptcy, your bankruptcy should have no effect on your tenancy. Although your landlord might not like the idea that you filed for bankruptcy, chances are good that he or she won't even find out about it. Because you are current on your rent, you don't have to list your landlord as a creditor entitled to notice of the proceeding. Although you have to list on your bankruptcy papers any security deposits held by your landlord, you will probably be able to claim those deposits as exempt. And even if you can't, it's a rare trustee who actually will go after that money.

1. If You Are Behind on Your Rent When You File

Back rent is dischargeable in both Chapter 7 and Chapter 13 bankruptcy. However, if you get very far behind on your rent, your landlord will likely file an action in court to evict you. If you file for bankruptcy before the court issues a judgment for possession (an eviction order), the automatic stay will prohibit your landlord from trying to evict you on the basis of your prefiling rent default during your bankruptcy—unless the landlord files a motion to lift the stay. However, if you don't stay current on your rent after you file, the landlord is free to seek your eviction on the basis of the postfiling rent default.

> **EXAMPLE:** Aldo owes two months back rent when he files for bankruptcy. At the time Aldo files, his landlord hasn't yet obtained a judgment of possession. The landlord can't evict him for this debt while the bankruptcy is pending unless he files a motion to lift the stay. However, if Aldo fails to pay rent on time after he files for bankruptcy, the landlord can give him a delinquency notice and file an eviction action in court if the rent isn't paid as required. Also, many states and localities give landlords the right to evict tenants for no reason at all, as long as the tenant receives adequate notice and the landlord strictly complies with the state's eviction procedures. So, even if Aldo faithfully pays his rent on time after his bankruptcy, he might still lose his apartment.

2. If Your Landlord Obtains a Judgment for Possession for Delinquent Rent Before You File

Under the old bankruptcy law, many people filed for Chapter 7 bankruptcy to stop the sheriff (or other local law enforcement official) from enforcing a judgment for possession. While landlords could come into court and ask the judge to lift the automatic stay (see Ch. 1) and let the eviction proceed, many landlords didn't know they had this right—and many others didn't have the wherewithal to hire an attorney (or the confidence to handle their own case). In other words, filing Chapter 7 bankruptcy often stopped court-ordered evictions dead in their tracks during the bankruptcy (typically, four to six months). Bankruptcy often gave potential evictees the time they needed to find a new home, and then some.

Under the new law, however, things are very different. Whether the landlord can proceed with the eviction without first moving to lift the stay depends on the reason for the eviction and when the landlord obtained a judgment of possession.

a. Judgment for Failure to Pay Rent

If your petition indicates that your landlord has already obtained a judgment of possession against you for failure to pay rent, the landlord may proceed with the eviction just as if you didn't file the bankruptcy, *unless* you take certain steps. (See "When the Automatic Stay Protects Against Evictions," below.) The steps are:

Step 1: When you file your bankruptcy petition, you must also file a certification (a statement under oath) that your state allows you to cure the rent delinquency after the judgment is obtained and remain on the premises. Very few states allow this. To find out whether yours is one of them, ask the sheriff or someone at legal aid (if you have legal aid in your area).

In addition, when you file the petition, you must deposit with the court clerk the amount of rent that will become due during the 30-day period after you file.

Once you file the certification and deposit the rent, you are protected from eviction for 30 days unless the landlord successfully objects to your initial certification before the 30-day period ends. If the landlord objects to your certification, the court must hold a hearing on the objection within ten days, so theoretically you could have less than 30 days of protection if the landlord files and serves the objection immediately.

Step 2: To keep the stay in effect beyond 30 days, you must, before the 30-day period runs out, file and serve a second certification showing that you have fully cured the default in the manner provided by your state's law. However, if the landlord successfully objects to this second certification, the stay will no longer be in effect and the landlord may proceed with the eviction. As in Step 1, the court must hold a hearing within ten days if the landlord objects.

b. Eviction for Endangering the Property or Illegal Use of Controlled Substances

Under the new bankruptcy law, a judgment for possession (other than for delinquent rent—see Subsection a, above) is stayed by your bankruptcy filing *unless* the judgment was obtained either because you were endangering the property or because you engaged in the "illegal use

of controlled substances" on the property. Your landlord may start an eviction action against you or continue with a pending eviction action *after* your filing date if the eviction is based on property endangerment or drug use.

To evict you on these grounds after you have filed for bankruptcy, your landlord must file and serve on you a certification showing that:

- the landlord has filed an eviction action against you based on property endangerment or illegal drug use on the property, or
- you have endangered the property or engaged in illegal drug use on the property during the 30-day period prior to the landlord's certification.

If your landlord files this certification, he or she can proceed with the eviction 15 days later unless, within that time, you file and serve on the landlord an objection to the truth of the statements in the certification. If you do that, the court must hold a hearing on your objection within ten days. If you prove that the statements in the certification aren't true or have been remedied, you will be protected from the eviction while your bankruptcy is pending. If the court denies your objection, the eviction may proceed immediately.

As a practical matter, you will have a very difficult time proving a negative—that is, that you weren't endangering the property or using drugs. Similarly, once allegations of property endangerment or drug use are made, it's hard to see how they would be "remedied."

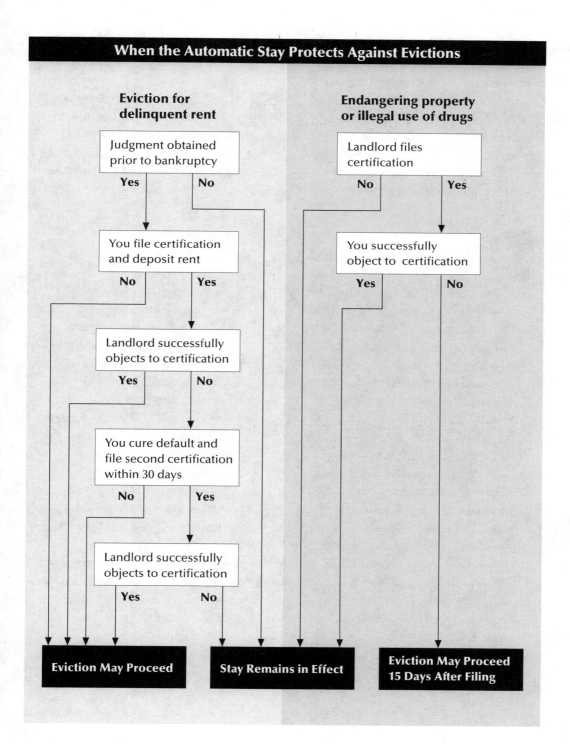

Landlords can always ask the court to lift the automatic stay to begin or continue an eviction on any grounds. Courts are usually inclined to lift a stay because most evictions will have no affect on the bankruptcy estate—that is, your tenancy isn't something that the trustee can turn into money to pay your creditors. As a general rule, bankruptcy courts are inclined to let landlords exercise their property rights regardless of the tenant's debt problems.

 Need help with your landlord? For more information on dealing with landlords—including landlords that are trying to evict you—see *Every Tenant's Legal Guide,* by Janet Portman and Marcia Stewart (Nolo).

New Bankruptcy Rules in Ch. 5

- You must have acquired your home at least 40 months before filing in order to use the homestead exemption in that state. (11 U.S.C. § 522(p).)
- If you have not lived in a state for at least 40 months, your homestead exemption is capped at $125,000. (11 U.S.C. § 522(q).)
- If you have been convicted of a felony securities law violation, or serious crimes or torts, your homestead exemption may be limited to $125,000 depending on the circumstances. (11 U.S.C. § 522(q).)
- Your homestead exemption may be reduced by the value of nonexempt property that you disposed of during the past ten years with the intent to hinder, delay, or defraud a creditor. (11 U.S.C. § 522(o).)
- You can claim a state's exemptions only if you have lived there for at least two years. (11 U.S.C. § 522(b)(3)(A).)

- If you haven't lived in a state for at least two years, you must claim the exemptions in the state where you lived for the better part of the 180 days preceding this two-year period. (11 U.S.C. § 522(b)(3)(A).)
- The automatic stay does not apply to a landlord who has obtained a judgment of eviction prior to the bankruptcy filing unless the tenant is able to make certain certifications and post a month's advance rent with the court. (11 U.S.C. §§ 362(b))(22) and 362(l).)
- The automatic stay lasts for 15 days after a landlord certifies that the tenant is being evicted for endangerment of, or use of controlled substances on, the property, unless the tenant files a successful objection. (11 U.S.C. §§ 362(b)(23 and 362(l).)

What Happens to Property That Secures a Loan

This chapter explains what happens to personal property you are making payments on when you file for bankruptcy—typically, a car or major household furnishings, such as living room or bedroom sets. It also covers other collateral: property you already owned that you pledged as security for a personal or business loan.

A. What Are Secured Debts?

Almost without exception, if you are making payments on property, you have agreed that the property will serve as collateral for repayment of the debt. This means that if you default on your payments, the creditor (or lender) can repossess the property, sell it, and obtain a court judgment against you (a deficiency judgment) for the difference between what you owe and what the property sold for. In bankruptcy, debts secured by collateral are called "secured debts."

B. How Secured Debts Are Handled in Chapter 7 Bankruptcy

Secured debts are treated differently in bankruptcy than other kinds of debts. Unlike a credit card debt or medical bills, a secured debt has a piece of property attached to it. Although the debt itself may be discharged in bankruptcy, the creditor may still have a right to take the property back.

A secured debt has two parts:

- **Personal liability.** You have personal liability for a secured debt just as you would for any other debt. This is what obligates you to pay the debt to the creditor. Chapter 7 bankruptcy wipes out this personal liability if the debt is otherwise dischargeable. Once your personal liability is eliminated, the creditor cannot sue you to collect the debt.

- **Security interest.** The second part of a secured debt is the creditor's legal claim (lien or security interest) on the property that serves as collateral for the debt. The lien gives the creditor the right to repossess the property or force its sale if you do not pay the debt. And liens are not affected by the bankruptcy discharge. In other words, you could still lose the property, even if the debt is discharged. (In some cases, however, you can ask the bankruptcy court to remove the lien.)

1. If You Are Current on Your Payments

If you are current on your payments for a secured debt when you file Chapter 7 bankruptcy, you can surrender the property and discharge the underlying debt (that is, you can walk away from the contract free and clear). Or, you can keep the property if:

- your equity in the property is protected by an applicable exemption (see Subsection a, below), and
- you are willing to take one of the two available options to secured debtors—reaffirmation or redemption (see Subsection b, below).

a. Does an Exemption Protect Your Equity in the Property?

You have equity in property serving as collateral if it could be sold for more than you owe. For instance, if you owe $3,000 on a car loan, and the car could be sold for $6,000, you have $3,000 worth of equity. This equity is part of your bankruptcy estate (see Ch. 4, Section A), which means the trustee can take it unless it's protected by an exemption. For instance, if you have $3,000 equity in your car, and the exemptions available to you allow only $1,000 for motor vehicles, the trustee could sell the car, pay your secured creditor the $3,000 you still owe, give you your $1,000 exemption in cash, and distribute the remaining $2,000 (less costs of sale) to your unsecured creditors.

Information for homeowners. See Ch. 5, Section A, for information on computing your equity in a home.

For personal property, debtors often owe more than the property is worth—which means they have no equity in it. The interest that is part of a secured loan typically makes your total payment much higher than it would be if you had paid cash for the property. Also, even though the value of the property decreases (depreciates) over time, your loan and accompanying interest is based on the value of the property when you bought it.

If you have no equity in the property, or if your equity is fully protected by an available exemption, the trustee will have no interest in the property. You can either surrender it to the secured creditor or take one of the actions explained in Subsection b, below, if you want to hold on to the property.

b. Redemption and Reaffirmation

Even if the trustee doesn't take your property (because there is insufficient equity to produce payments to your unsecured creditors), that doesn't necessarily mean that you get to keep it. The creditor still has that lien on the property, which means you might lose it to repossession unless you use one of the remedies explained in this section.

Of course, you always have the option of simply giving the secured property to the creditor. Surrendering the property completely frees you from the debt, quickly and easily: The lien is satisfied by your surrender of the property, and your personal liability is discharged by the bankruptcy. The downside, obviously, is that you lose the property.

If you want to hang on to secured property, you have two options: redemption or reaffirmation.

i. Redeem the Property

In Chapter 7 bankruptcy, you have the right to "redeem" property—that is, to buy it back from the creditor in a lump sum, rather than have the creditor take it and sell it to someone else. Under the new bankruptcy law, if the property is used for personal, family, or household purposes, you can redeem it by paying the replacement value—the price a retail merchant would charge for property of that kind, considering the age and condition of the property at the time you redeem it. This means, for example, that you can redeem a car for the retail price listed in the Kelley Blue Book (www.kbb.com) or similar car valuation systems such as www.edmunds.com.

At first glance, redemption doesn't seem like much of a remedy. After all, if you are filing for bankruptcy, how can you afford to buy the property outright? The answer is that all cash and other property you acquire after your bankruptcy filing date is yours to do with as you please (with the few exceptions explained in Ch. 4, Section A) and can be used to redeem property. For instance, you can sell some of your exempt property, get a loan from family or friends, or work overtime to raise the money.

Redemption is a great option if your debt exceeds the property's value. The creditor must accept the replacement value of the item as payment in full, even if you owe much more. However, you do have to come up with the replacement value of the property in a lump sum. If you can't afford to do that, you may be able to file a Chapter 13 case and pay off the property's replacement value over the life of your plan rather than through a lump sum payment. (See Section D, below, for more information on what happens to secured debts in Chapter 13 bankruptcy.)

You have the right to redeem property in a Chapter 7 bankruptcy only if all of the following are true:

- The debt is a consumer debt on goods used for personal or household purposes. This means you cannot redeem property that secures business debts.
- The property is tangible personal property. "Personal property" includes everything but real estate. "Tangible property" is property you can touch, such as a car or stereo system. (Examples of intangible personal property, for comparison purposes, include investments, like stocks and bonds, or intellectual property rights, like patents, trademarks, and copyrights.)
- You have claimed the property as exempt or the trustee has abandoned it.

ii. Reaffirm the Debt

When you "reaffirm" a debt, you and the creditor draw up a new agreement that sets out the amount you owe and the terms of the repayment. In essence, this creates a brand new debt, although you have a right to the same terms set out in the original contract. You might even be able to negotiate better terms. In return, you get to keep the property as long as you keep current on your payments under the new agreement. Both the creditor's lien on the collateral and your personal liability under the new contract survive bankruptcy intact.

Reaffirmation can be used when redemption is unavailable or impractical. It provides a sure way to keep property, as long as you abide by the terms of the reaffirmation agreement. But because reaffirmation leaves you personally liable, there is no way to walk away from the debt after your bankruptcy, even if the property becomes worthless or you simply decide you no longer want it. (Remember, you will have to wait eight years to file another Chapter 7 bankruptcy case.)

As a general rule, you should reaffirm a debt only if it is the sole way to keep property you can't be without, and you have good reason to believe you'll be able to pay off the balance. For example, many people use reaffirmation to keep a car, one of the few essential items of property in today's world.

Under the new bankruptcy law, the creditor must offer you a reaffirmation agreement that contains a number of disclosures about what you are getting

into by reaffirming the debt. If you are represented by an attorney, the agreement becomes effective upon its signing. If you are not represented by an attorney, the agreement will become effective only after it has been filed with the court and approved by the bankruptcy judge in a court hearing that you must attend.

c. The Statement of Intention

Under the new bankruptcy law, you are required to use a formal document called a "Statement of Intention" to tell your secured creditors what you plan to do with collateral. That is, you must tell them whether you plan to surrender the collateral, redeem it, or reaffirm the debt.

If you don't file the statement within 30 days after you file your bankruptcy petition, the automatic stay will be lifted, and you will be in default of your security agreement, which means your creditor can repossess the property in the manner permitted by state law. The stay will also be lifted and you will be in default of your agreement (and repossession may occur) if you fail to carry out your intentions within either 30 days after the date set for your first meeting of creditors or 45 days after the first meeting of creditors (the law appears to be contradictory as to this time limit).

Keeping Property Without Reaffirming or Redeeming

Under the old bankruptcy law, many bankruptcy courts allowed debtors to keep secured property as long as they remained current on their payments under the contract with the creditor. If the debtor fell behind, the creditor could take the property, but the debtor's personal liability for the debt was wiped out by the bankruptcy. This method was often referred to as the "retain and pay" option.

Under the new bankruptcy law, this remedy apparently is no longer available. However, if the law of your state forbids creditors from enforcing a lien on your property as long as you are current under the contract, your creditors may have to let you keep the property as long as you remain current, no matter what the new bankruptcy law says. Many creditors are perfectly happy with this arrangement; they would rather have a steady payment stream on the original contract than used property that has to be sold at auction.

2. If You Are Not Current on Your Payments

If you're behind on your payments to a secured creditor and don't have the wherewithal to get current, Chapter 7 bankruptcy probably won't prevent the creditor from repossessing the property. While your bankruptcy filing will initially stop any repossession activity, the creditor can ask the court to lift the automatic stay. If you are behind on your payments, most courts will lift the stay in order to let the creditor proceed with repossession. (For more on the automatic stay, see Ch. 1, Section B.) If you want to keep the property, you'll need to reinstate the loan outside of bankruptcy, by making up the missed payments and resuming your regular payments.

If your lender has already accelerated the loan (declared the entire balance due) and won't let you reinstate it, you can file for Chapter 13 bankruptcy (assuming you meet the eligibility requirements detailed in Ch. 2, Section C). You can make up the missed payments in your plan as long as you also make the regular payments called for under your original agreement. (See Ch. 2, Section D.) Also, in Chapter 13, you may be able to reduce the total amount of your payments to the property's actual value (See Section D, below.)

C. Eliminating Liens in Chapter 7 Bankruptcy

During your Chapter 7 bankruptcy case, you may be able to eliminate a lien on an item of secured property. If you can eliminate, or "avoid," a lien, you get to keep the property free and clear, without paying anything more to the creditor. To avoid a lien, you must be able to claim an exemption in the property that is impaired by the lien—that is, that the lien deprives you of your right to benefit from the exemption because you can't sell the property without paying off the lien. (See Ch. 4 for more on exemptions.)

For the purpose of lien avoidance, there are two types of liens: 1) judicial liens, and 2) liens you agree to have placed on property you already own in exchange for a personal loan. A judicial lien is one that was placed on your property to collect a court judgment for money. The second type of lien is called a nonpossessory, nonpurchase money lien because the lienholder doesn't possess the collateral (as would be the case if the lien were owned by a pawnbroker), and you didn't use the loan to buy the collateral.

A judicial lien may be "avoided" (wiped out) on any type of property, including real estate, to the extent the lien "impairs an exemption." A nonpossessory, non-purchase money lien, on the other hand, may be avoided only on certain types of property.

In most courts, lien avoidance actions are very simple. Most of the time, the lien owner doesn't contest the motion, so you'll just have to make sure you get the paperwork right. On occasion, however, a lien owner may object, which means you will have to participate in one or more court hearings, depending on the type of objection. (The procedural steps necessary for lien avoidance are described in more detail in Ch. 9.)

1. Avoiding Judicial Liens

Most judicial liens occur when:

- you've been sued for money and lost
- the judgment creditor (the winner of the lawsuit) obtains a judgment against you for a sum of money, and
- the judgment is recorded against your property in the form of a lien.

Most often, judicial liens are imposed on real estate. Judicial liens can also be imposed on business assets; almost all states provide a way to do this under the Uniform Commercial Code. However, liens are seldom, if ever, attached to personal property, both because there are no procedures for doing so and because ownership of personal property is rarely recorded in public documents.

If paying a judicial lien would deprive you of any part of the exemption you are entitled to claim on the property, you can get rid of the lien by following the process outlined in Ch. 9.

2. Avoiding Nonpossessory, Nonpurchase Money Liens

A nonpossessory, nonpurchase money security lien is almost always created when a consumer obtains a personal loan from Beneficial Finance or a credit union. These liens can be avoided only on the following types of property (and only if the property is exempt without regard to your equity in the property):

- household furnishings, household goods (see the list, below), clothing, appliances, books, musical instruments, or jewelry

- health aids professionally prescribed for you or a dependent
- the first $5,000 of a lien attaching to animals or crops held primarily for your personal, family, or household use, and
- the first $5,000 of a lien attaching to tools used in your trade.

Under the new bankruptcy law, the term "household goods" is limited to:

- clothing
- furniture
- appliances
- one radio
- one television
- one VCR
- linens
- china
- crockery
- kitchenware
- educational equipment and materials primarily for the use of your minor dependent children
- medical equipment and supplies
- furniture exclusively for the use of your minor children, or elderly or disabled dependents
- your personal effects (including the toys and hobby equipment of your minor dependent children and your wedding rings) and those of your dependents, and
- one personal computer and related equipment.

The following are not considered to be household goods, and you cannot avoid liens on them:

- works of art (unless they are by you or a relative)
- electronic entertainment equipment with a fair market value of more than $500 in the aggregate (excluding the one television, one radio, and one VCR listed above)
- items acquired as antiques with a fair market value of more than $500 in the aggregate
- jewelry with a fair market value of more than $500 in the aggregate (excluding wedding rings), and
- a computer (excluding the computer equipment listed above), motor vehicle (including a tractor or lawn tractor), boat, or a motorized recreational device, conveyance vehicle, watercraft, or aircraft.

To avoid a nonpossessory, nonpurchase money lien, you must have owned the property before the lien was "fixed" on it. This will almost always be the case with this type of lien. See Ch. 9 for more on lien avoidance.

D. How Secured Debts Are Handled in Chapter 13 Bankruptcy

Secured debts are handled completely differently in Chapter 13 than in Chapter 7. By filing for Chapter 13 bankruptcy, you can keep property subject to a secured debt even though you are behind on your payments when you file. Under your Chapter 13 plan, you can pay off the arrearage (the defaulted payments) over the course of the plan, as long as you remain current during that time.

1. Surrendering Property

If you don't want to keep property that is subject to a secured debt, you can surrender it to the creditor and schedule what you still owe on the contract as an unsecured debt. This means that you may have to pay a portion of the debt over the life of your plan, depending on the factors described in Ch. 2, Section D.

2. Reducing Secured Debt to the Property's Value (Cramdowns)

If you want to keep property that is worth less than what you still owe on it, you can propose a plan that pays off the replacement value of the property over the life of the plan (rather than what you owe on the contract). For example, if you owe $20,000 on the property and its replacement value is $10,000, you can propose a plan that pays only $10,000. If you complete your plan, then you'll own the property free and clear. This remedy of reducing a secured debt to the replacement value of the collateral

is known as a "cramdown," a most descriptive term. You can only cramdown personal property; it doesn't work for real estate.

Under the new bankruptcy law, you can't cramdown a debt you owe on your car if you purchased the car during the 30-month period before you filed for bankruptcy. You also can't cramdown a secured debt on other personal property you purchased within one year preceding your bankruptcy filing. The purpose of these restrictions is to prevent people from purchasing cars or other property with the intent to file for bankruptcy and use the cramdown remedy.

3. Continuing the Contract

If you want to continue the secured debt as before, all you have to do is provide in your proposed plan that you will remain current on the contract during the life of the plan. If you don't complete your Chapter 13 plan, but are still making payments on the secured debt, you can either convert to Chapter 7 and use one of the remedies mentioned in Section B, above, or continue making the payments outside of bankruptcy. If you are still in Chapter 13 and something happens to the collateral (for example, it is destroyed in an accident), it is usually possible to amend your plan and reschedule what you still owe as unsecured debt.

Bankruptcy Rules in Ch.6

- Cramdowns are not allowed for car purchases made within the 30 months prior to filing for bankruptcy. (11 U.S.C. § 1325(a)(9).)
- Cramdowns are not allowed for other personal property purchased within the year before filing for bankruptcy. (11 U.S.C. § 1325(a)(9).)
- You must use the replacement value of assets to determine how much you have to pay for a cramdown or redemption. (11 U.S.C. §§ 506(a)(2) and 722.)

- New standards have been imposed for reaffirmation hearings. (11 U.S.C. § 524(k).)
- The automatic stay will be lifted if you don't file a statement of intention within 30 days after filing for bankruptcy, or you don't follow through on your plan within 45 days after the meeting of creditors. (11 U.S.C. §§ 521(a)(2) and (6).)

Your Credit Cards

What will happen to your credit cards when you file for bankruptcy depends largely on the current status of your account, and to a lesser degree on the creditor. For this discussion, most credit cards fall into three possible categories:

- cards on which you have zero balance—that is, you're all paid up (see Section A, below)
- cards on which you have a balance but are current—that is, you make at least the minimum payment each month (see Section B, below), and
- cards on which you are in default— that is, you haven't made any payments in a while (see Section C, below).

A. If Your Balance Is Zero

On your bankruptcy papers, you'll have to list your creditors—all of the people and business to whom you currently owe money. If you have a balance of zero on a credit card, you don't currently owe the card issuer any money and you don't have to list it on your bankruptcy papers. This means you *might* come through bankruptcy —Chapter 7 or Chapter 13—still owning that credit card. But there are exceptions.

1. The Trustee May Take Your Card

It's possible that the bankruptcy trustee will confiscate your credit cards, ask you about the creditors with whom you have a zero balance, or demand that you write to them and tell them about your bankruptcy. This is much more likely to happen in a Chapter 13 case, where the trustee must supervise your finances for three to five years, than in a Chapter 7 case, where the trustee won't care about debts you incur after filing.

2. The Credit Card Issuer May Find Out About Your Bankruptcy

Most credit card companies constantly troll your credit reports for any sign of economic weakness. For example, credit card companies often raise interest rates on cards if the card holder makes a late payment on another card or to another creditor. Even if the credit card issuer in question doesn't check your credit report, other credit card companies may notify your company of your bankruptcy—a common practice. Either way, a credit card company with which you have a zero balance may find out about your bankruptcy.

> **EXAMPLE:** You file for bankruptcy and include the following debts, among others: BigBank Visa, MediumBank MasterCard, and LittleBank Visa. Your balance on your TinyBank MasterCard is $0, so you don't include that creditor on your bankruptcy papers. TinyBank learns of your bankruptcy anyway, from the credit bureaus it checks to monitor the creditworthiness of its customers.

3. Your Credit Card Issuer May Cancel Your Zero Balance Card

Once learning of your bankruptcy, the company that issued your credit card may decide to terminate your account, even though you don't owe that business a penny, on the ground that you are no longer a good credit risk. On the other hand, some credit card companies will be happy to continue doing business with you on the ground you are now an excellent credit risk because you won't be able to file a Chapter 7 bankruptcy again for eight years.

Even if you lose all your credit cards in your bankruptcy, don't get too worked up over it. Especially if you file for Chapter 7 bankruptcy, there are other ways to get a credit card, if you really think you need one. Although you may have trouble getting a card with a large credit balance, you will be able to obtain a check card that gives you all the advantages of a credit card, with one exception—the amount you can charge will be limited to the amount in your bank account.

4. The Trustee May Recover Recent Payments on Your Credit Card

It may not be wise to pay off a credit card just before you file bankruptcy. When you file for bankruptcy, you must indicate on your papers all of your recent financial transactions. For filers whose debts are primarily consumer debts, payments of more than $600 to any one creditor in the three months prior to filing may be retroactively cancelled. For filers whose debts are primarily business debts, payments of more than $5,000 to any one creditor in the three months prior to filing may be retroactively cancelled.

These "eve of bankruptcy" payments are called "preferences." The trustee can recover preferences from the creditor you paid and use the money for the benefit of all your creditors, not just the creditor who received the payment. There are exceptions to this rule for business debtors who make the payment in the normal course of their business, and for payments made for regular ongoing expenses like your mortgage or utilities (as opposed to one-time expenses, like paying off a delinquent bill).

So the bottom line is this: If you want to pay off a credit card balance before filing bankruptcy, your debts are primarily consumer debts, and the payments total $600 or more, you must wait at least 91 days after your last payment before filing. Of course, there is still no guarantee you will get to keep the card.

B. If You Owe Money but Are Current

If you owe money on a credit card but have managed to eke out at least a minimum payment each month, you will have to list this creditor on your bankruptcy papers even though you aren't behind. Your bankruptcy—Chapter 7 or

Chapter 13—may come as a great surprise to the creditor. In fact, credit card issuers have recently lamented the increase in "surprise" bankruptcies—cases filed by people not in default.

If you file for Chapter 7 bankruptcy and want to keep your credit card, you probably can do so by offering to sign a reaffirmation agreement with the credit card issuer. In a reaffirmation agreement, you agree to repay the balance in full, as if you never filed for bankruptcy. Under the new bankruptcy law, you will have to convince the court that reaffirming the debt is in your best interest. (See Ch. 6 for more on reaffirming debts.)

Before you reaffirm a credit card debt, ask yourself whether it really makes sense. For most people, it doesn't. The purpose of filing for bankruptcy is to get rid of debts, not to still owe money. Admittedly, some people choose to file, even though they know that they won't be able to eliminate certain debts. But even in that situation, it almost never makes sense to come out of bankruptcy owing a credit card balance you had before you filed. More likely, you will come out of bankruptcy still owing taxes or a student loan. If you want to have a credit card after bankruptcy, chances are very good that you'll be able to get one (but one that starts with a zero balance, not with the amount you owed before you filed). A check card will probably serve all of your needs—and won't get you back into debt.

The credit card issuer may ask you to sign a reaffirmation agreement when you file for Chapter 7 bankruptcy, even if you intend to wipe out the debt. The creditor may offer tempting terms—a reduction in the interest rate, a reduction of the balance you owe, or an increase in your line of credit. But you should resist. To sign a reaffirmation agreement would probably defeat a major, if not the sole, reason you filed—to get rid of your credit card debt. (If the creditor gets insistent or starts claiming that you incurred the credit card debt fraudulently, you still have options—see Ch. 9.)

If you file for Chapter 13 bankruptcy, your plan will propose to repay your unsecured creditors, including your credit card issuers, some percentage of what you owe. Chapter 13 plans are sometimes referred to by this percentage—for example, "this couple filed a 55% plan." (Remember that unlike credit card debts, some types of debts, including priority debts and secured debts, must be repaid in full, even in Chapter 13. For more on secured debts, see Ch. 6.) In most cases, if you propose to pay less than 100% of what you owe on a card, the creditor will cancel your account. And the trustee may confiscate your card anyway.

C. If You Are in Default

Now let's consider what might happen to your credit card if you are in default on your payments when you file for bankruptcy. The likely outcome is, in fact, fairly similar to the outcome for people who are current but owe a balance, as discussed in Section B, above—that is, you'll probably lose the card along with the debt. But there are two big differences.

First, your creditors won't be surprised that you file. With more than a million people filing for bankruptcy each year under the old law—discharging billions of dollars in credit card debts alone— bankruptcy filings have been a fact of life for credit card issuers. They may not have liked it, but they have had to deal with it. (In fact, they disliked it so much that they pretty much wrote the new bankruptcy law that pushes more filers in Chapter 13

bankruptcy, where they'll probably have to repay at least some portion of their credit card debt.)

This leads to the second difference. If you file for bankruptcy when you are in default on a credit card, the creditor may take aggressive steps to keep you from discharging the debt. The creditor will first ask you to voluntarily sign a reaffirmation agreement. If you don't agree—and you shouldn't—the creditor might really start playing hardball. (See Ch. 9, Section D, for more on what happens if a creditor wants to contest your ability to discharge a debt.)

■

Your Job, Freedom, and Self-Respect

For most people, the thought of filing for bankruptcy raises a number of troubling questions. Many of these have to do with eliminating debts. (Those are answered in Ch. 3.) Other questions concern the potential loss of property. (Those are addressed in Chs. 4, 5, and 6.)

But many of the questions go beyond debts and assets and hit at the core of what it means to be a member of our society— earning a living, bringing up your children, and keeping your freedom and self-respect.

A. Will You Lose Your Self-Respect?

Americans learn almost from birth that it's a good thing to buy all sorts of goods and services. A highly paid army of persuaders surrounds us with thousands of seductive messages each day that say "Buy, buy, buy." Easily available credit makes living beyond our means easy—and resisting the siren sounds of the advertisers difficult. But we're also told that if we fail to pay for it all right on time, we're miserable deadbeats. In short, much of American economic life is built on a contradiction.

Adding to this contradiction is the system of high interest and penalties employed by most credit card companies that cause our debt to soar beyond any reasonable expectation. In many cases, the interest rates are so high that the companies involved would have been prosecuted for loan sharking in the not-too-distant past—before the credit card industry systematically lobbied to do away with usury laws, or to create exceptions to those laws for credit card interest rates.

Credit card companies keep this system working by encouraging us to make the minimum payment, which stimulates us to make more credit purchases and eases us into debt loads far beyond our ability to ever pay them off. We now all owe our soul to the company store. To feel guilty about being caught in this deliberately contrived economic trap is nonsense. There's much more to life than an A+ credit rating, and bigger things to feel guilty about than the failure to pay bills on time—especially those owed to the credit card companies.

Fortunately, for thousands of years it's been recognized that debts can get the better of even the most conscientious among us. From Biblical times to the present, sane societies have discouraged debtors from falling on their swords and have provided sensible ways for debt-oppressed people to start new economic lives. In the United States, this is done through bankruptcy.

Until very recently, filing bankruptcy was a dignified way to achieve a fresh start in a world filled with economic uncertainty. The law presumed that bankruptcy filers were honest citizens seeking to get rid of their debt and start over, sadder but wiser. Unfortunately, thanks to provisions written primarily by the credit card industry, the new bankruptcy law turns this presumption on its head and views each debtor as a potential bankruptcy cheat.

While this change in attitude won't prevent you from achieving a bankruptcy discharge in most cases—because you, like most other filers, are in fact honest—it does have the potential to make you feel bad about yourself. But don't fall into this trap. Bankruptcy is a truly worthy part of our legal system, based as it is on forgiveness rather than retribution. Certainly, it gives people a fresh start in our increasingly volatile economy, helps keep families together, reduces suicide rates, and keeps the ranks of the homeless from growing even larger. So, don't let the word "bankruptcy" get you down.

What About Friendly Creditors?

While you may not care about discharging your credit card debts in bankruptcy, you may feel bad about doing the same to the debts you owe to friends, family, or business creditors in your community—such as a doctor, dentist, chiropractor, pharmacist, accountant, lawyer, contractor, or hardware store. While debts you owe to these creditors will most likely be discharged in your bankruptcy— because you have to list *all* debts you know of in your bankruptcy papers— there is nothing to prevent you from voluntarily paying the debts after you file. Communicating your intent to repay to these friendly creditors will make everybody involved feel a whole lot better about your bankruptcy.

B. Will You Lose Your Job?

No employer—government or private—may fire you because you filed for bankruptcy. Nor may an employer discriminate against you in other terms and conditions of employment—for example, by reducing your salary, demoting you, or taking away responsibilities—because of your bankruptcy.

1. Termination for Other Reasons

If there are other valid reasons for taking these actions, the fact that you filed for bankruptcy won't protect you. In other words, an employer who wants to take negative action against you can do so provided there are other valid reasons to explain the action—such as tardiness, dishonesty, or incompetence. But if you are fired shortly after your bankruptcy is brought to your employer's attention, you might have a case against the employer for illegal discrimination because of your bankruptcy.

2. How Employers Find Out About Bankruptcy Filings

In practice, employers rarely find out about a Chapter 7 bankruptcy filing. However, if a creditor has sued you, obtained a judgment, and started garnishing your wages, your employer will get the news. The bankruptcy will stop the wage garnishment, and your employer will be notified about it. In such a situation, your employer (or at least the payroll department) already knew you were having financial problems and will probably welcome the bankruptcy as a way for you to take affirmative steps to put your problems behind you.

If you file for Chapter 13 bankruptcy, your employer is likely to learn of your bankruptcy case. If you have a regular job with regular income, the bankruptcy judge may order your Chapter 13 payments to be automatically deducted from your wages and sent to the bankruptcy court. (This is called an "income deduction order.") In effect, your employer will be pressed into service as a sort of collection agency, to make sure you honor your Chapter 13 plan.

Income Deduction Orders Work

You may not like the idea of the income deduction order, but the bankruptcy court is likely to deny your Chapter 13 plan if you refuse to comply with it. And the order will probably make it easier for you to complete your plan. The success rate of Chapter 13 cases is higher for debtors with income deduction orders than for debtors who pay the trustee themselves, for the very obvious reason that it's hard to spend money you never lay hands on.

---

3. Security Clearances

Many jobs require a security clearance. If you are a member of the armed forces or an employee of the CIA, FBI, another government agency, or a private company that contracts with the government, you may have a security clearance. Do you risk losing your security clearance if you file for bankruptcy? Probably not—in fact, the opposite may be true. According to credit counselors for the military and the CIA, a person with financial problems—particularly someone with a lot of debt—is at high risk for being blackmailed. By filing for bankruptcy and getting rid of the debts, you substantially lower that risk. Bankruptcy usually works more in your favor than to your detriment.

C. Effect of Bankruptcy on Job Applicants

No federal, state, or local government agency may take your bankruptcy into consideration when deciding whether to hire you. There is no corresponding rule for private employers, however, and some people find that having a bankruptcy in their past comes back to haunt them, particularly when applying for jobs that require them to deal with money (book-keeping, accounting, payroll, and so on).

Many private employers conduct a credit check on job applicants as a matter of course, and will find out about your bankruptcy from the credit report. While employers need your permission to run a credit check, employers can also refuse to hire you if you don't consent. If you're asked to give this authorization, consider speaking candidly about what the employer will find in your file. Being honest up front about problems that are truly behind you may outweigh any negative effects of the bankruptcy filing itself.

D. Other Forms of Discrimination Because of Bankruptcy

Federal, state, and local governmental units can't legally discriminate against you because you filed for bankruptcy.

1. Discrimination by Government Agencies

Governmental units may not deny, revoke, suspend, or refuse to renew a license, permit, charter, franchise, or other similar grant on the basis of your bankruptcy. Judges interpreting this law have ruled that the government cannot:

- deny or terminate public benefits
- deny or evict you from public housing
- deny or refuse to renew your state liquor license
- exclude you from participating in a state home mortgage finance program

- withhold your college transcript
- deny you a driver's license
- deny you a contract, such as a contract for a construction project, or
- exclude you from participating in a government-guaranteed student loan program.

In general, once any government-related debt has been discharged, all acts against you that arise out of that debt must also end. If, for example, you lost your driver's license because you didn't pay a court judgment that resulted from a car accident, you must be granted a license once the debt is discharged. If the debt wasn't discharged, however, you can still be denied your license until you pay up.

2. Discrimination by Private Entities

Prohibitions against private discrimination aren't nearly as broad as prohibitions against government discrimination. As mentioned above, private employers may not fire you or punish you because you filed for bankruptcy. Other forms of discrimination in the private sector, however, such as denying you rental housing, a surety bond, or withholding a college transcript, are legal.

The best way to confront this type of discrimination is to build a solid credit history after bankruptcy. You can find sound strategies for getting back on your financial feet in *Credit Repair*, by Robin Leonard (Nolo).

If a potential landlord does a credit check, sees your bankruptcy, and refuses to rent to you, there's not much you can do except try to show that you'll pay your rent and be a responsible tenant. You probably will need to go apartment hunting with a "renter's résumé" that shows you in the best possible light. Be ready to offer a cosigner, find roommates, or pay several months rent up front in cash.

E. Effect of Bankruptcy on Child Custody

There are no reported cases from any state of a parent losing custody because he or she filed for bankruptcy. Bankruptcy and divorce (or separation) are so often related these days that one frequently follows the other. Bankruptcy judges are becoming experts on family law matters, and family law judges are becoming experts in bankruptcy. Don't worry about your bankruptcy affecting your custody status. Keep in mind, however, that bankruptcy does not relieve you of your child support and alimony obligations, past or present.

F. Effect of Bankruptcy on Your Freedoms

We Americans are used to some basic freedoms, and many people fear the loss of those freedoms if they file for bankruptcy. Relax. Except in some unusual cases, this is just not going to happen.

1. Consequences of Dishonesty

When you file for bankruptcy, you swear, under "penalty of perjury," that everything in your papers is true to the best of your knowledge. If you deliberately commit a dishonest act, such as failing to disclose property, omitting material information about your financial affairs, unloading nonexempt assets just before filing, or using a false Social Security number (to hide your identity as a prior filer), you can be criminally prosecuted for fraud.

While such prosecution has been rare in the past, the new bankruptcy law streamlines the process by which fraud-related cases can be referred to the U.S. Attorney's office for prosecution. Also, the new law requires the government to audit one out of every 250 bankruptcy cases, which means you are more likely to face an audit than bankruptcy filers in the past. More than ever, it is important to disclose all of your property and debts in your bankruptcy papers, provide accurate answers to the questions in the Statement of Financial Affairs (see Ch. 9, Section G), and not try to hide property from the trustee or your creditors prior to filing.

Examples of criminal prosecutions under the old law abound. A debtor in Massachusetts went to jail for failing to list on his bankruptcy papers his interest in a condominium and $26,000 worth of jewelry. Another Massachusetts debtor served time for listing her home on her bankruptcy papers as worth $70,000 when it had been appraised for $116,000. An Alaska debtor was jailed for failing to disclose buried cash and diamonds. A Pennsylvania debtor omitted from her papers $50,000 from a divorce settlement and was sentenced to some time in prison.

The message is simple: Bankruptcy is geared towards the honest debtor who inadvertently gets in too deep and needs the help of the bankruptcy court to get a fresh start. A bankruptcy judge will not help someone who has played fast and loose with creditors or tries to do so with the bankruptcy court. If you lie, hide, or cheat, it may come back to haunt you in ways much worse than your current debt crisis ever could.

2. Moving

You are free to change your residence after you file. Just be sure to send the trustee a change of address form if your case is still open. If your move involves selling your house and you've filed for Chapter 13 bankruptcy, the trustee may want to use proceeds of the sale to pay off your creditors (if your plan doesn't already propose full payment).

3. Changing Jobs

You can certainly change jobs while your bankruptcy case is pending, and after it ends. If you've filed a Chapter 13 case, be sure to tell the trustee so he or she can transfer the income deduction order.

4. Divorce

No one can force you to stay married, not even a bankruptcy judge. If you've filed for Chapter 7 bankruptcy and want to end your marriage, go ahead. Your bankruptcy case will probably end long before your divorce case does. However, it often makes sense to wait until a divorce is completed before filing for bankruptcy. Your property ownership and personal debt situation will be much clearer after your divorce becomes final—and your marital debts and property have been divided between you and your former spouse.

If you've filed a Chapter 13 case with your spouse, you may face some complications if you want to continue your case and get divorced. Bankruptcy law states that you must be a married couple to be eligible to file a joint case. If you divorce, you are no longer eligible to file (or maintain) a joint Chapter 13 case, at least in theory. The trustee could file a motion to dismiss your case. Some trustees have been known to ignore a divorce if both spouses want to keep the Chapter 13 going and continue to make the payments. Even so, you will probably want to ask the divorce court to handle your divorce in two stages ("bifurcate," in legalese) so that your marital status changes from married to divorced, but the final division of marital property and debts is postponed until your Chapter 13 case ends. You could simplify matters by separating, but not divorcing. In either situation, be sure to let the trustee know what's happening and where to reach you if you move.

 Who's going to know? It's highly unusual for anyone to find out about your bankruptcy other than your creditors, businesses that obtain a copy of your credit report, and the people you tell. Although your bankruptcy filing will be published in a local newspaper, these notices often appear in low-circulation papers, and few people sit around reading these notices anyway. Bankruptcy filings aren't broadcast on local television or radio.

■

Bankruptcy Forms and Procedures

Under the old law, filing for bankruptcy was a remarkably streamlined process. As long as you got your paperwork right, there were few disputes or reasons to appear before a judge. Unfortunately, the new law threatens to change that smooth procedure into a rocky journey that will more closely resemble the typical litigation process.

Even under the new law, however, Chapter 7 bankruptcy will still be a pretty straightforward process for some filers. You can look forward to a relatively simple bankruptcy proceeding if:

- your average income over the six-month period prior to filing is less than the median income for your state
- your income comes from employment or from Social Security or other government benefits
- you are current on your income tax filings
- you don't own your home
- you are current on your rent
- your debts consist primarily of credit card debts incurred at least 90 days before filing and/or medical bills
- you have lived in your current state for at least two years
- your income does not exceed your reasonable expenses by more than several hundred dollars
- you haven't given any property away during the previous two years
- any property you care about keeping is exempt (that is, the trustee can't take it under your state's laws or the federal exemption law), and

- you are current on your child support and alimony obligations.

If you meet all of these criteria, you will probably have only one encounter with the trustee, at the creditors' meeting, where you—not an attorney you might hire—must answer the trustee's questions. For this reason, if your case falls within these guidelines, you most likely won't need a lawyer to represent you (although you may want some telephonic legal advice).

As your case increases in complexity—which is much more likely under the new law—it may make sense to get some legal help in order to achieve the best possible results. Some brief descriptions of the Chapter 7 proceedings that might require some outside help are set out in Sections A through D, below. (Ch. 10 explains what type of help is available and how to find it.)

While many Chapter 7 filers have represented themselves in the past, most people who filed for Chapter 13 bankruptcy under the old law hired an attorney to represent them. Nothing about the new law indicates a different result. Chapter 13 bankruptcy is usually difficult for self-represented people to successfully complete without representation. Some of the trouble points are outlined in Section F.

If, after you file your bankruptcy, you want to change course and convert to another type of bankruptcy or get out of bankruptcy altogether, you'll need to know the rules covered in Section E. And, no matter what type of bankruptcy you file, you can look forward to completing plenty of paperwork. The basic forms required in both types of bankruptcy are explained in Section G.

A. The Means Test

Under the new bankruptcy law, a single dollar's difference between your income and expenses can have a huge impact on your bankruptcy plans. If your "current monthly income" (defined as described in Ch. 2) is one dollar less than your state's median income, you can:

- file for Chapter 7 bankruptcy without facing the means test
- use your actual expenses (rather than the IRS's expense standards, which are often lower) to compute your disposable income, and
- propose a three-year plan if you file for Chapter 13 bankruptcy (see Ch. 2, Section D).

On the other hand, if your "current monthly income" is even one dollar more than the state's median income, you must:

- pass the means test to file a Chapter 7 bankruptcy
- use the IRS standards to compute your disposable income, and
- propose a five-year plan if you file for Chapter 13 bankruptcy.

For many filers, this won't be a close call: It will be fairly easy to figure out where you stand. In fact, according to one comprehensive survey made just prior to the new law going into effect, only about 15% of bankruptcy filers would not have

passed the means test. But how should you proceed if a modest change in your income or expenses would put you below the median income or change the outcome of the means test?

In these situations, the stakes may well be worth the cost of a consultation with a bankruptcy attorney. The new bankruptcy law creates a number of new categories and definitions of income and expenses. In addition to appreciating the nuances contained within these changes, attorneys in close cases are sure to raise novel arguments on behalf of their clients. These arguments will result in court decisions that a bankruptcy attorney can use to suggest legal ways to decrease your income or increase your expenses to achieve a more desirable outcome.

B. Challenges for Abuse

Under the old law, your Chapter 7 bankruptcy filing could be challenged on the ground of "substantial abuse." Many courts held that substantial abuse existed if you had sufficient income to propose a feasible Chapter 13 plan.

The new law removes the word "substantial" and describes two kinds of abuse that can sink your Chapter 7 filing:

- failure to pass the means test (known as presumptive abuse because the trustee will presume that you aren't entitled to file under Chapter 7 if you flunk the means test—see Ch. 2, Section C), and

- abuse under the totality of the circumstances (general abuse).

If abuse is presumed because you fail the means test, you won't be allowed to proceed with your Chapter 7 bankruptcy unless you can rebut the presumption by showing special circumstances (see Section 4, below). If you are accused of abuse under the totality of the circumstances, however, the party bringing the charge has the burden of proving abuse. Needless to say, you are much more likely to be barred from Chapter 7 when abuse is presumed than when it must be proved.

 Abuse laws apply only to consumer debts. The new law on abuse, both general and presumed, applies only to filers with primarily consumer debts. Filers who have primarily business debts are not subject to abuse motions on either general or presumptive grounds. Your debts are primarily business debts if more than half of the total value of your debt arises from the operation of a business.

If you file under Chapter 7, you won't know for sure whether your bankruptcy filing will be challenged on abuse grounds until someone asks for a court hearing to dismiss or convert your case.

1. Presumed Abuse

If your bankruptcy paperwork (covered in Section G, below) demonstrates that you don't pass the means test, you can expect the U.S. Trustee to file a motion to dismiss your case or (with your consent) convert the case to Chapter 13. Under the new law, the regular trustee or any creditor can also file a motion to dismiss or convert your case on the grounds of abuse, but the U.S. Trustee will probably be the one bringing the motion: The U.S. Trustee is legally responsible for assessing your eligibility for Chapter 7 bankruptcy and otherwise seeing that the bankruptcy laws are complied with.

2. General Abuse

Even if you pass—or don't have to take—the means test, your Chapter 7 filing can still be challenged for general abuse.

a. If You Pass the Means Test

If you were subject to the means test but passed it on the face of your paperwork, the court, U.S. Trustee, regular trustee, or a creditor can still file a motion to dismiss your bankruptcy or convert it to Chapter 13 if the totality of the circumstances demonstrates abuse. For example, the new bankruptcy law indicates that you could be subject to an abuse motion if you seek to reject a personal services contract—a contract in which you've agreed to provide services to another person or business—without adequate financial justification. For instance, if you sign a three-year recording contract and then file for Chapter 7 bankruptcy just to get out of it, your case could be challenged on general abuse grounds.

b. If Your Income Is Less Than Your State's Median Income

If your average monthly income (calculated according to the formula explained in Ch. 2, Section B) is less than the state's median income, you aren't subject to the means test and your filing won't be presumed to be abusive. Your Chapter 7 filing can still be challenged on the ground of general abuse, but only if the judge or U.S. Trustee files the motion; no creditors allowed at this party. Again, absent the presumption, the court or U.S. Trustee must prove abuse.

The U.S. Trustee is likely to challenge your Chapter 7 bankruptcy filing on general abuse grounds if you could easily propose a feasible Chapter 13 plan, even though you weren't subject to the means test. For instance, if you otherwise qualify for Chapter 13 and can pay $166 or more a month towards a Chapter 13 plan—or you could pay at least 25% of your unsecured, nonpriority debt—you might be facing an abuse motion.

Some experts believe that if you pass the means test or don't have to take it, you can't be forced out of Chapter 7 bankruptcy just because you could propose a feasible Chapter 13 plan. Nothing in the new bankruptcy law says this explicitly, however, so only time will tell whether courts will agree with this interpretation.

Charitable Contributions

Under the new law, a court may not consider charitable contributions you have made or continue to make to any qualified religious or charitable entity or organizations. In other words, the trustee cannot argue that you should pay your money into a Chapter 13 repayment plan rather than to the charity of your choice.

EXAMPLE: You pass the means test but the U.S. Trustee files a motion to dismiss your case for abuse because you give 25% of your income to your church. The U.S. Trustee argues that if you only tithed (gave 10% of) your income, you could propose a feasible Chapter 13 repayment plan. Following this new law, the court dismisses the U.S. Trustee's motion and allows your Chapter 7 bankruptcy to proceed.

3. Court Procedures

If your income exceeds the state median, the U.S. Trustee must file a statement indicating whether your filing should be considered an abuse, either general or presumed, within ten days after your meeting of creditors. (See Ch. 1 for more on this meeting.) Five days after the U.S. Trustee's statement is filed, the court must send the notice to all of your creditors, to let them know about the U.S. Trustee's assessment and to give them an opportunity to file their own motion to dismiss or convert on abuse grounds, if they desire.

Within 30 days after filing this statement, the U.S. Trustee must either:

- file a motion to dismiss or convert your case on grounds of abuse, or
- explain why a motion to convert or dismiss isn't appropriate (for example, because you passed the means test).

If your income is below the state median income, the U.S. Trustee doesn't have to file either statement, because abuse will not be presumed. However, your filing can still be challenged for general abuse, as explained above.

Note that these duties and time limits apply only to the U.S. Trustee. If your income is more than the state median, your creditors can file a motion to dismiss or convert anytime after you file, but no later than 60 days after the first date set for your creditors meeting.

4. Defending a Motion to Dismiss or Convert

If the U.S. Trustee (or the trustee or a creditor in appropriate circumstances) files a motion to dismiss or convert your case, you are entitled to notice of the hearing at least 20 days in advance. You will receive papers in the mail explaining the grounds

for the motion and what you need to do to respond. If the motion to dismiss or convert is based on presumed abuse, the burden is on you to prove that your filing is not abusive (see Subsection a, below). If the motion is based on general abuse, you only have to show up at the hearing to argue that it should be denied. However, it's a good idea to also file an opposition to the motion, at least five days before the hearing (see Subsection b, below).

a. Presumed Abuse

If the motion to dismiss or convert is based on your failure to pass the means test, your only defense is to show "special circumstances." The special circumstances mentioned by the new law include a serious medical condition or a call or order to active duty in the armed forces. However, it's not enough to show that these circumstances exist: You must also show that they justify additional expenses or adjustments of current monthly income "for which there is no reasonable alternative."

In order to establish special circumstances, you must itemize each additional expense or adjustment of income and provide:

- documentation for the expense or adjustment, and
- a detailed explanation of the special circumstances that make the expense or adjustment necessary and reasonable.

You will win only if the additional expenses or adjustments to income enable you to pass the means test. (Ch. 2, Section C, explains how to make this calculation.)

EXAMPLE: Maureen and Ralph have a child (Sarah) with severe autism. Sarah is making remarkable progress in her private school, for which Maureen and Ralph pay $1,000 a month. No equivalent school is available at a lower tuition. Under the means test guidelines, Maureen and Ralph are entitled to deduct only $150 a month from their income for private school expenses. If Maureen and Ralph were allowed to deduct the full $1,000 monthly tuition, they would easily pass the means test. By documenting Sarah's condition, the necessity for the extra educational expense, and the fact that moving her to a less expensive school would greatly undermine her progress, Maureen and Ralph would have a good chance of convincing the court to allow the $1,000 expense, which would in turn rebut the presumption of abuse.

b. General Abuse

If your filing is challenged for general abuse, the party bringing the motion to dismiss or convert has the burden of proof. If the motion is based on your ability to fund a Chapter 13 plan (even though you passed the means test), you can raise any special expense you have— for example, necessary private tuition, extraordinary child care expenses, or legal fees associated with a continuing legal action—to demonstrate your inability to fund a Chapter 13 plan.

C. Valuation Hearings

There are two situations when you may need to ask the court to assign a value to a car or other personal property. In a Chapter 7 bankruptcy, you may need a valuation if you propose to redeem property that you are making payments on. (See Ch. 6 for more on redemption.) If the property's replacement value (what the property could be purchased for in a retail market) is less than the debt, you can pay the replacement value in a lump sum and own the property outright.

In a Chapter 13 bankruptcy, you may want the court to determine the replacement value of property that is collateral for a secured debt. If the replacement value is less than the debt, your repayment plan can pay the replacement value. This is called a "cramdown." For example, suppose you owe $13,000 on your car, and its replacement value is $8,000. You can propose to pay $8,000 in equal payments over the life of your plan and then own the car outright once you obtain a discharge. If you fail to complete your Chapter 13 plan, the cramdown is cancelled and you must pay the full balance of your debt before obtaining title.

There are two exceptions to the cramdown rule. You can't cramdown a debt owed on a motor vehicle purchased within 30 months of your filing date. Nor can you cramdown a debt owed on other personal property purchased within a year of your filing date.

Getting evidence of value. For cars, Kelley Blue Book appraisals are a good start (www.kbb.com). However, you and the creditor may disagree about the car's value because of its condition, something that the Blue Book can't shed much light on. In that case, a private appraisal would be persuasive.

To get a valuation hearing, you or a creditor must file a motion. These motions are handled in the same way as the other motions discussed in Section D below. If you or a creditor requests a valuation hearing in Chapter 13, the court will either postpone your confirmation hearing or hold the valuation hearing immediately before the confirmation hearing.

D. Common Chapter 7 Motions and Proceedings

In very simple Chapter 7 cases, you will probably have to attend only one official proceeding: the creditors' meeting, supervised by the trustee. But if your Chapter 7 case involves issues that must be decided by a bankruptcy judge—for example, if you are facing a motion to dismiss or convert for abuse—you, or someone helping you, must know the required court procedures. You will have to either take the time to learn how to represent yourself, or consult an attorney who already knows what needs to be done. You can also get help from bankruptcy petition preparers, but they are allowed only to fill in the bankruptcy forms in accordance with your instructions—they can't give you legal advice or appear for you in court. (See Ch. 10 for more information on bankruptcy petition preparers.)

This section briefly describes some of the more common court proceedings that might be required in a Chapter 7 bankruptcy (in addition to the abuse motion to dismiss or convert discussed in Section B, above). This will give you an idea of what you'll be facing if one of these issues pops up in your case.

 Use Nolo resources to help you through the litigation maze. Nolo's *How to File for Chapter 7 Bankruptcy*, by Stephen R. Elias, Albin Renauer, and Robin Leonard, provides guidance for some of these procedures. *Represent Yourself in Court*, by Paul Bergman and Sara J. Berman-Barrett (Nolo), also has an excellent chapter on litigating in bankruptcy court. For a plain-English guide to making your way through law books and other resources, see *Legal Research: How to Find & Understand the Law*, by Stephen R. Elias and Susan Levinkind (Nolo).

1. Hearing on Relief From Stay

A creditor who wants to collect from you directly may request relief from the automatic stay in order to do so. This is called a "relief from stay" hearing. (For more on the automatic stay, see Ch. 1, Section B.) This could come up, for example, if you are behind on your mortgage or car payments.

The creditor asks for this type of hearing by filing a motion in the bankruptcy case. The creditor doesn't need to file a separate lawsuit, as it would with some other types of disputes within a bankruptcy case (see Section 2, below). The work you have to do to oppose the request and get your side of the case heard in court is not all that difficult. However, you'll need to do a little legal research.

Always follow the new notice rules. When a debtor is required to give a creditor notice, the notice must contain the debtor's Social Security number and be sent to the contact address and account number that is listed on at least two written communications received from the creditor within the 180 days prior to the bankruptcy filing (or just the two most recent communications, if the debtor hasn't received two in the previous 180 days). If you don't provide notice in this way, the creditor may not be fined if it violates

---

Common Motion Procedures

There are many types of motions, but they all involve similar procedures. One party files the motion and sends notice of what is requested to the appropriate parties (this is called "serving" the parties). The notice is accompanied by a legal argument (points and authorities) and a declaration—a sworn statement that sets out the facts of the case under penalty of perjury.

The notice typically includes the date and time at which the court will hear the motion. Sometimes, the notice states that a hearing will be set only if the party served with the motion wants to oppose it. If a hearing is set, all parties must receive notice at least 20 days in advance. The party against whom the motion is brought typically can file a written opposition to the motion at any time up to five days before the hearing. Other parties in all bankruptcy motion

proceedings are the U.S. Trustee and the regular trustee.

The bankruptcy judge will hear argument on the motion and either rule right then and there (from the bench) or take the matter under submission (take it back to his or her chambers and think about it for a while). When the judge makes a decision, he or she typically issues a written memorandum of decision and orders the prevailing party to prepare a formal order.

Either party may appeal the motion to a U.S. District Court or a Bankruptcy Appellate Panel (if one has been established in the district where the case is heard). Notice of appeal must usually be filed with the bankruptcy court *within ten days* of the date the court's decision or order is "entered." If you don't file this notice on time, you will almost surely lose your right to appeal.

the automatic stay because it did not receive notice (see Ch. 1).

2. Dischargeability Hearing

Ch. 3 explains that some types of debts survive your bankruptcy only if the creditor comes into court and challenges the proposed discharge of the debt. In addition, student loans and certain other types of debts will be discharged only if you (the debtor) come into court and convince the judge that they should be discharged. These court procedures that determine whether debts survive a bankruptcy are called "dischargeability" actions.

Based on actions filed under the old law, debtors are most likely to bring a dischargeability action to discharge a student loan on the basis of hardship, or to cancel a tax debt on the basis that it meets the requirements for discharge under the bankruptcy code. Creditors are most likely to bring a dischargeability action alleging that a debtor incurred a debt through fraudulent means or caused personal injury through drunk driving or a willful and malicious act.

To start a dischargeability action, a creditor (or you, the debtor) must file a separate complaint in the bankruptcy court, formally serve the complaint on the other party, and move the case forward to trial before the bankruptcy judge. This requires considerable research and knowledge of court rules. You are likely to have one or two false starts, in which the clerk returns your paperwork or the court tells you to try again. Dealing with formal court procedures can be quite frustrating for self-represented people. On the other hand, if there is enough money at stake, it may be worth your while to spend the time and deal with the frustration that comes with formal court litigation.

Of course, you can hire a bankruptcy attorney just for this part of your case, if there is enough at stake to justify paying the attorney's fees and you are able to find an attorney willing to deliver piecemeal services. (See Ch. 10.)

3. Discharge Hearing

Years ago, before bankruptcy filings increased so dramatically, debtors were required to attend a discharge hearing at the end of their case. Today, most courts will require you to come to a discharge hearing only if you aren't represented by an attorney and have agreed with a creditor to "reaffirm" a debt (to recommit yourself to paying the debt, despite your bankruptcy discharge). At the hearing, the judge will warn you of the consequences of reaffirmation: You'll continue to owe the full debt, you may lose the collateral if you default on your payments, and in many states, the creditor can sue you for any balance due after the property is sold at auction. (For more on reaffirming a debt, see Ch. 6.)

4. Lien Avoidance Motions

Ch. 6 explains that certain types of liens can be removed from your property in a

Chapter 7 bankruptcy case. To do this, you need to file a motion to "avoid" the lien. As with other motions, you must mail the lienholder a written explanation of what you want (to avoid the lien) and why you are entitled to it. You must also provide the lien owner with a notice explaining what the lien owner must do to respond (in order to keep the lien). If there is no response, you can obtain an order to avoid the lien by default. If the creditor responds, you can set the matter for hearing. Sometimes, you set the matter for hearing in your initial notice—it all depends on the rules for your bankruptcy court's district. Lien avoidance motions are governed generally by Federal Bankruptcy Rule 9014.

E. Conversions From One Chapter to Another

The bankruptcy law allows you to change your bankruptcy from one Chapter to another. This process is called conversion. If you want to remain in bankruptcy and you convert, you won't have to pay another filing fee and your creditors are still prevented from taking action against you. In some cases, your case can even be converted against your wishes. Unless the court objects, you can always dismiss your case and file again (although you will have to pay a new filing fee and you will not be protected by the automatic stay in the interim).

1. Conversions From Chapter 7

You may voluntarily convert a Chapter 7 case into a Chapter 11 (usually only businesses do this), Chapter 12 (for farmers), or Chapter 13 bankruptcy *at any time*, unless you already converted to your Chapter 7 case from one of the other chapters. Some cases have held that a court may deny permission to convert if the conversion is made in bad faith, while other courts have upheld the plain language of the statute, which doesn't mention such a condition.

Upon a creditor's request, after notice and hearing, the court can convert a Chapter 7 case to a Chapter 11 case at any time. The court can convert your Chapter 7 case to a Chapter 13 case only if you consent. For example, as explained earlier, if you file for Chapter 7 and your filing is found to be abusive, the court can convert the case to Chapter 13 if you consent. If you don't consent, the court will dismiss your case outright.

Your case cannot be converted unless you qualify for relief under the new Chapter. For example, you can't convert to Chapter 13 unless you fall within the debt guidelines for that Chapter (secured debts not exceeding $922,975 and unsecured debts not exceeding $307,675).

2. Conversions From Chapter 13

Just like a Chapter 7 bankruptcy, you can convert your Chapter 13 case to another

Chapter, but only if you qualify for relief under that Chapter. And your Chapter 13 case can also be converted against your wishes, in some situations.

a. Voluntary Conversion

You may convert your Chapter 13 case into a Chapter 7 case at any time, as long as you qualify to file for Chapter 7 under the rules discussed in Ch. 2. Also, some courts might not allow the conversion if it appears to be in bad faith.

b. Involuntary Conversion

The U.S. Trustee, the trustee, or a creditor may request that the court, after notice and hearing, dismiss your Chapter 13 case or convert it to Chapter 7, whichever is in the best interest of your creditors. Your case might be converted to Chapter 7 rather than dismissed if you have valuable nonexempt property that the trustee could seize for the benefit of your creditors. If, on the other hand, you have no non-exempt property, the creditors would benefit more from an outright dismissal.

The court may order the dismissal of your Chapter 13 case, or convert it to Chapter 7, only for cause, such as your:

- unreasonable delay that is prejudicial to your creditors
- nonpayment of any court fees or charges
- failure to file a repayment plan in a timely manner
- failure to start making your plan payments on time
- failure to comply with your plan

- failure to file your bankruptcy papers on time
- failure to stay current on your alimony or child support payments after your filing date, or
- failure to file your state and federal tax returns with the court.

Any time prior to confirming the Chapter 13 plan, the court, after notice and hearing, may order your case converted to Chapter 11 or 12 upon request by the U.S. Trustee, the trustee, or a creditor. If you are a farmer, the court may not order a conversion to Chapters 7, 11, or 12 unless you request it. As with Chapter 7, no conversion may be ordered to another chapter unless you qualify for relief under that chapter.

c. Effect of Conversion From Chapter 13 to Chapter 7

One issue that often arises in the course of a conversion from Chapter 13 to Chapter 7 is how you treated your property between your filing date and your conversion date. As explained in Ch. 4, Section A, the trustee technically owns all of the property in your bankruptcy estate—which is essentially everything you own when you file, except pensions. If you start out in Chapter 13 and sell some of your nonexempt property, then convert to Chapter 7, what happens to the property you got rid of? Not a problem. When you convert from Chapter 13 to Chapter 7, the property of the estate is the property that remains in your possession or under your control on the date of conversion.

Under the new law, if you are able to cramdown a debt in Chapter 13, the lien remains on the property until you complete the plan or the claim is paid in full without regard to the cramdown. If you don't complete the plan, the cramdown becomes ineffective and you will still owe the entire debt with lien attached, less money you have paid to the creditor during your Chapter 13 plan.

F. Potential Problems in Chapter 13

As with Chapter 7 cases, there are some potential bumps in the road in Chapter 13 cases that you should understand. These typically come up in the context of the confirmation hearing, where the judge approves or rejects your proposed repayment plan.

1. Confirmation Hearing

Unlike Chapter 7, a Chapter 13 bankruptcy requires at least one appearance before a bankruptcy judge—the confirmation hearing. At the confirmation hearing, the court approves or rejects your proposed repayment plan. (Rejecting a plan is also called "denial of confirmation.")

Under the new law, the confirmation hearing must be held between 20 days and 45 days after your meeting of creditors. However, the hearing can be held earlier if no one objects.

Although a judge presides over the confirmation hearing, the trustee usually runs the show. If the trustee tells the judge that he or she has no objection to your plan, and no creditor shows up to convince the judge that your plan is unfair, the judge will most likely approve the plan without a further hearing. But if the trustee has some problems with your plan, or a creditor raises issues of fairness, the judge will most likely send you back to the drawing board and reschedule ("continue," in legalese) the confirmation hearing to another date, when you will have to submit a modified plan. Each time you submit a modified plan, you must notify all of your creditors (typically, by using the mailing matrix prepared by the court).

If it becomes obvious that Chapter 13 bankruptcy isn't realistic for you—for example, you earn very little money to pay into a plan—the judge will order that your case be dismissed unless you can convert it to Chapter 7 bankruptcy before the date set for the dismissal. (See Section E, above, for more on conversions.)

2. Objections to Your Plan

The trustee (or a creditor) may raise objections to your proposed plan, and this was fairly common under the previous law. It's uncertain which of these old objections will fly under the new law, which imposes a number of requirements and restrictions on the formulation of Chapter 13 plans. (See Ch. 2, Section D). It's still a good idea to be aware of these potential objections if you are thinking of filing a Chapter 13 bankruptcy.

Here are some objections you might face in Chapter 13:

The plan was not submitted in good faith. The new bankruptcy law explicitly requires you to file for Chapter 13 in good faith. This same requirement was implicitly recognized under the old law, so previous cases on this issue probably still apply. Following those cases, courts will look to see whether your proposed plan has any purpose other than sincerely trying for a fresh start. For example, one bankruptcy court ruled that a Chapter 13 filing was not in good faith because the debtor filed for the sole purpose of getting around a judge's decision in an ongoing state court case. If you are filing your papers with the honest intention of getting back on your feet, and you really can make the payments required by the plan, you probably will be able to overcome a "good faith" objection.

When a creditor or trustee pursued good faith objections under the old law, most bankruptcy courts looked at the following factors:

- How often you have filed for bankruptcy. Filing and then dismissing multiple bankruptcies does not, in itself, show bad faith. However, if you've filed and dismissed two or more other bankruptcy cases within one year, the court may find lack of good faith if there are inconsistencies in your papers or you can't show that your circumstances have changed since the previous dismissal.

- The accuracy of your bankruptcy papers and oral statements. The court is likely to find a lack of good faith if you misrepresent your income, debts, expenses, or assets, or if you lie at the creditors' meeting.

- Your efforts to repay your debts. If your plan will pay your unsecured creditors a small percentage of what you owe, or nothing at all, you may have to show the court that you are stretching as much as you can. The court will want to see that you are not living luxuriously and that you are making substantial efforts to pay your unsecured creditors, even if it means trading in your fancy new car for a used model.

The plan is not feasible. Probably the most common objection is that your plan is not feasible—that is, you won't be able to make the payments or comply with the other terms of the plan. To overcome this type of objection, your monthly income must exceed your monthly expenses by at least enough to allow you to make the payments required under Chapter 13 bankruptcy. For instance, a debtor who owes a $50,000 tax arrearage as well as $25,000 in credit card debts must propose a plan that, at a minimum pays the $50,000 in full over the life of the plan (because taxes are usually a priority debt and must be paid in full).

The trustee or a creditor might also question your job stability, the likelihood that you'll incur extraordinary expenses, and whether you have any outside sources of money. If your plan seems to reflect too much wishful thinking, and your sources of money are uncertain, the court will probably reject the plan on the ground that it isn't feasible. Possible scenarios leading the court to find that your plan isn't feasible include:

- You have a business that has been failing, but you've predicted a rebound and intend to use business income to make your plan payments.
- You propose making plan payments from the proceeds of the sale of certain property, but nothing points to the likelihood of a sale.
- Your plan includes a balloon payment (a large payment at the end), but you have not identified a source of money with which to make the payment.
- You've been convicted of a crime, and you haven't convinced the bankruptcy court that you will stay out of jail.

The plan fails to promote the "best interest" of the creditors. Under your Chapter 13 repayment plan, you must pay your unsecured creditors at least as much as they would have received had you filed for Chapter 7 bankruptcy—that is, the value of your nonexempt property. (Exemptions are discussed in Ch. 4.) This is called the "best interest of the creditors" test.

If the trustee or a creditor raises this objection, you will have to provide documents showing the values of the potentially nonexempt portions of your property, such as a recent appraisal of a home in which your equity is equal to or exceeds your state's homestead exemption, or a publication stating the value of an automobile of the same make, model, and year as yours.

The plan unfairly discriminates. Chapter 13 bankruptcy is intended to treat all unsecured creditors fairly, relative to each other. You might be inclined to pay some unsecured creditors more than others—for example, you might propose to pay 100% of a student loan (which isn't dischargeable anyway) but only 35% of your credit card debts (which are dischargeable). In this situation, the trustee or the credit card issuers are likely to object to your plan on the ground that they are unfairly being discriminated against.

The plan doesn't provide adequate protection for collateral. Under the new bankruptcy law, plans must provide that payments to secured creditors on property serving as collateral will be distributed in equal monthly amounts and will be sufficient to provide the creditor with adequate protection of its interest in the collateral. Because this is a new requirement, only time will tell how it affects Chapter 13 cases. Most likely, it will mean that you might have to do some heavy negotiating with a creditor to avoid an objection.

G. Filling Out the Bankruptcy Forms

The new bankruptcy law requires you to file many more documents than the old law did. You have several options for completing the forms. You can:

- get the forms on the Internet and fill them in yourself
- hire a bankruptcy petition preparer to complete the forms under your direction (see Ch. 10), or
- hire an attorney to handle everything.

If you use an attorney, the papers will be filed electronically in most courts. If you represent yourself, you will mail the forms to the court or file them in person.

1. Chapter 7 Documents

There are a number of documents you will have to file in a Chapter 7 case, particularly under the new law.

a. The Voluntary Petition

You start a Chapter 7 case by filing a "Voluntary Petition": the official court form that asks for some basic information, including:

- facts about yourself (name(s), address, and the last four digits of your Social Security number)
- whether you have lived, maintained a residence, maintained a business, or had assets in the district for the better part of 180 days prior to filing (this establishes your right to file in a particular district)

- the type of bankruptcy you are filing (Chapter 7, 11, 12, or 13)
- the type of debtor you are (individual, corporation, partnership, and so on)
- whether your debts are primarily consumer or business
- if you are a business debtor, the type of business
- how you will be paying your filing fee (at filing, in installments, or not at all because of a fee waiver)
- the estimated number of creditors
- the estimated amount of your debts
- the estimated value of your property
- whether you have nonexempt assets
- whether a judgment for eviction has been entered against you
- whether you are aware of some bankruptcy basics
- your history of bankruptcy filings, if any, and
- whether you have completed your debt counseling or obtained a waiver.

b. Additional Documents

Under the new law, a number of additional documents must be filed within 45 days after filing the petition. Others must be filed at the same time as the petition or within other time limits. Despite these differing deadlines, the best practice is to file all of these documents when you file your petition, to keep your case under control (and make sure you don't miss a deadline).

Here are the documents you must provide; those that have just been imposed as a requirement of the new bankruptcy law are marked "new":

- a list of all of your creditors, including their name, mailing address, and account number (this is called the "creditor matrix")
- lists of your assets (Schedules A (real property) and B (personal property))
- a schedule of liabilities (Schedules D (secured creditors), E (priority creditors), and F (unsecured creditors))
- a statement of your financial affairs for the two years prior to your filing date
- a schedule of your current income (Schedule I) and current expenditures (Schedule J)
- a certificate stating that you have received a notice explaining your duties under the bankruptcy law and the consequences of being untruthful or providing incomplete information (new)
- wage stubs for the 60 days prior to filing (new)
- a statement of your current monthly income and a means test calculation (new)
- a statement disclosing any reasonably anticipated increase in income and/ or expenditures in the year after you file the petition (new)
- a certificate showing that you received credit counseling from an authorized provider within the six months prior to filing (new)
- a copy of any debt repayment plan you developed during your mandatory credit counseling (new)
- a certificate showing that you received counseling in personal financial management from an authorized provider during the course of your bankruptcy case; this is due before you receive your discharge (new)
- a copy of your most recent tax return or a transcript of the return obtained from the IRS (new)
- a record of any interest you have in an education or individual retirement account or under a qualified state tuition program (new)
- a schedule indicating which assets you are claiming as exempt (Schedule C)
- a schedule of any executory contracts (contracts that are still in force and require action by one or both parties) and leases you have signed (Schedule G)
- a schedule of your codebtors, if any (Schedule H)
- a form called *Chapter 7 Individual Debtor's Statement of Intention,* in which you tell your secured creditors what you plan to do with your property listed as collateral for a secured loan (see Ch. 6)
- if you are being evicted and want your bankruptcy filing to hold the eviction off, the certification and rent described in Ch. 5, Section C (new), and

- a form setting out your full Social Security number.

2. Chapter 13 Documents

Almost all of the documents required for a Chapter 7 bankruptcy are also required in a Chapter 13 bankruptcy, with the exception of the *Chapter 7 Individual Debtor's Statement of Intention,* in which you tell your secured creditors what you plan to do with your property listed as collateral for a secured loan. In Chapter 13, you must provide this information in your proposed plan, which must be filed with your petition.

In addition to the documents mentioned in Section 1 (except the *Statement of Intention*), you must file a Chapter 13 Repayment Plan following the guidelines set out in Ch. 2, Section D, and a statement of your current monthly income and disposable income calculations.

Under the new law, you must also file tax returns (or transcripts from the IRS) for the previous four tax years, prior to the creditors' meeting. The trustee can keep the creditors' meeting open for 120 days after the first date for which it is scheduled to allow you extra time to obtain and file your returns. And the court can give you 30 additional days, if necessary.

While your Chapter 13 case is pending, you must also file with the court:

- any new tax returns and amendments that you file with the IRS

- a statement under oath of your income and expenditures for each tax year, and
- a statement of your monthly income that shows how income, expenditures, and monthly income are calculated.

These statements must show:

- the amount and sources of your income
- the identity of any person who is responsible (along with you) for the support of any of your dependents, and
- the identity of any person who contributed, and the amount contributed, to your household.

Upon request, you must provide these tax returns to your creditors, the U.S. Trustee, and the regular trustee.

3. Basic Requirements for Completing Bankruptcy Documents

Whether you file on your own or with the help of a professional, you have a duty to make sure that your papers meet these requirements:

- **You must be ridiculously thorough.** Always err on the side of giving too much information rather than too little.
- **You must respond to every question.** If a question doesn't apply to you, check the "none" box. If there isn't one, you will have to type "N/A" for "not applicable." Make sure to list and value all of your property, even

if you think it has no value. List the property, and either put zero for its value, or check the "unknown" box. Then be prepared to explain your answer at the creditors' meeting.

- **You must be willing to repeat yourself.** Sometimes different forms—or different questions on the same form—ask for the same or overlapping information. You will have to provide the same information multiple times.

- **You must be scrupulously honest.** You must swear, under penalty of perjury, that you've been truthful on your bankruptcy forms. The most likely consequence for failing to be scrupulously honest is a dismissal of your bankruptcy case, but you could be prosecuted for perjury if it's evident that you deliberately lied.

 Finding the forms. You can find samples of the basic forms described in this section in Appendix C. You can also view the current official forms online at www.uscourts.gov/bankform. For forms that you can download and fill in on your computer, go to the U.S. Trustee's website at www.usdoj.gov/ust; click "Data Enabled Form Standard" for pdf files of the official bankruptcy forms.

At first glance, you might think that there's no way you can deal with all of this paperwork. However, especially in Chapter 7 cases, it really isn't as difficult as it looks. Nolo publishes excellent, up-to-date, line-by-line guides for the forms, and you'll only need to complete the parts of the forms that apply to your personal situation. To paraphrase the old saying, just take it one document at a time.

Bankruptcy Rules in Ch.9

- Bankruptcy abuse is presumed if you fail the means test. (11 U.S.C. § 702(b)(2).)
- You must use the replacement value of assets in determining what they are worth. (11 U.S.C. §§ 527(c) and 506(a)(2).)
- Discharge hearings are more likely because of new reaffirmation requirements and legislation making reaffirmation and redemption the only ways to keep personal property collateral. (11 U.S.C. § 521(a)(6).)

- Hearings to avoid nonpossessory, nonpurchase money liens may be more frequent because the law limits what can be claimed as "household goods." (11 U.S.C. § 522(f)(4).)
- Your Chapter 7 case will be dismissed if certain papers are not filed within 45 days after you file your petition. (11 U.S.C. § 521(i)(1).) The court may extend the time by 45 days (11 U.S.C. § 521(i)(3), and the trustee may oppose dismissal if the debtor attempted to

New Bankruptcy Rules in Ch. 9 (continued)

file payment advices (wage stubs) on time. (11 U.S.C. § 521(i)(4).)

- A case may be converted from Chapter 7 to Chapter 13 only with the debtor's consent. (11 U.S.C. § 706(c).)
- If a debtor flunks the means test, the court will dismiss or, with the debtor's consent, convert the case to Chapter 13. (11 U.S.C. § 707(b)(2).)
- Failure to file prefiling tax returns with bankruptcy court can result in dismissal or conversion to Chapter 7, whichever is in creditors' best interest (11 U.S.C. § 1307 (e).)
- A case may be dismissed or converted if the debtor fails to stay current on domestic support obligations. (11 U.S.C. § 1307(c)(11).)
- Liens subject to cramdown in Chapter 13 remain on the property until the plan is completed or the claim is paid in full without regard to the cramdown. (11 U.S.C. §§ 348(f)(1)(C(ii) and 1325(a)(5).)

- The confirmation hearing must be held between 20 days and 45 days afteryour meeting of creditors (or earlier, if no one objects). (11 U.S.C. § 1324(b).)
- You are required to file your Chapter 13 bankruptcy in good faith. (13 U.S.C. § 1325(a)(7).)
- All documents filed, including tax returns, may be inspected by the U.S. Trustee, trustee and creditors upon request. (11 U.S.C. § 521(g)(2).)
- When debtors are required to provide notice, the notice must include the debtor's Social Security number and be sent to the contract address and account number contained in written communications from the creditor sent within 180 days of the bankruptcy filing. (11 U.S.C. § 342(c)(2).)
- The new law also creates a number of new forms and paperwork requirements, as discussed in Section G, above.

Getting Help With Your Bankruptcy

Under the old law, filing for bankruptcy—particularly Chapter 7 bankruptcy—was a lot like doing your taxes: While many could handle the process on their own, most sought some kind of professional help along the way. Because bankruptcy is a lot more complex under the new law, an even higher percentage of filers will benefit from lawyer representation. However, lawyers will also be more expensive under the new law (see Section B, below). Many who could afford a lawyer under the old law will now be priced out of the market and will have to represent themselves. This isn't as scary as it sounds, but it does mean that you'll have to line up your other available resources in order to get the most out of your bankruptcy.

You will have three sources of outside help if you wish to file for bankruptcy:

- a debt relief agency (as both lawyers and bankruptcy petition preparers are now called)
- a book that gives you step-by-step instructions on how to file for bankruptcy (such as those published by Nolo), or
- a combination of self-help bankruptcy books, Internet sites, lawyer consultants, and bankruptcy petition preparers (the best bang for your buck in many cases).

A. Debt Relief Agencies

Under the new bankruptcy law, any person or entity that you pay or otherwise compensate for help with your bankruptcy is considered a debt relief agency. The two main types of debt relief agencies are lawyers and bankruptcy petition preparers (BPPs). Credit counseling agencies and budget counseling agencies are not debt relief agencies. Nor are any of the following:

- employers or employees of debt relief agencies
- nonprofit organizations that have federal 501(c)(3) tax-exempt status
- any creditor who works with you to restructure your debt
- banks, credit unions, and other deposit institutions, or
- an author, publisher, distributor, or seller of works subject to copyright protection when acting in that capacity (in other words, Nolo Press and the stores that sell its books aren't debt relief agencies).

Lawyers and BPPs are covered separately in Sections B and C, below. This section explains what the new bankruptcy law requires of debt relief agencies generally, so you'll know what you can expect for your money.

1. Mandatory Contract

Within five days after a debt relief agency assists you, it (or he or she) must enter into a contract with you that explains, clearly and conspicuously:

- what services the agency will provide you
- what the agency will charge for the services, and

- the terms of payment.

The agency must give you a copy of the completed, signed, contract.

2. Mandatory Disclosures and Notices

The debt relief agency must inform you, in writing, that:

- All information you are required to provide in your bankruptcy papers must be complete, accurate, and truthful.
- You must completely and accurately disclose your assets and liabilities in the documents you file to begin your case.
- You must undertake a reasonable inquiry to establish the replacement value of any item you plan to keep, before you provide that value on your forms.
- Your current monthly income, the amounts you provide in the means test, and your computation of projected disposable income (in a Chapter 13 case), as stated in your bankruptcy papers, must be based on a reasonable inquiry into their accuracy.
- Your case may be audited, and your failure to cooperate in the audit may result in dismissal of your case or some other sanction, including a possible criminal penalty.

In addition to these stark warnings, a debt relief agency must also give you a general notice regarding some basic bankruptcy requirements and your options for help in filing and pursuing your case. The notice that you can expect to receive from any debt relief agency within three business days after the agency first offers to provide you with services is shown below. Failure to give you this notice can land the agency in big trouble.

3. Restrictions on Debt Relief Agencies

Under the new law a debt relief agency may not:

- fail to perform any service that the agency informed you it would perform in connection with your bankruptcy case
- counsel you to make any statement in a document that is untrue and misleading or that the agency should have known was untrue or misleading, or
- advise you to incur more debt in order to pay for the agency's services.

Any contract that doesn't comply with the new requirements on debt relief agencies may not be enforced against you. A debt relief agency is liable to you for costs and fees, including legal fees, if the agency negligently or intentionally:

- fails to comply with the new law's restrictions on debt relief agencies, or
- fails to file a document that results in dismissal of your case or conversion to another Chapter.

IMPORTANT INFORMATION ABOUT BANKRUPTCY ASSISTANCE SERVICES FROM AN ATTORNEY OR BANKRUPTCY PETITION PREPARER

If you decide to seek bankruptcy relief, you can represent yourself, you can hire an attorney to represent you, or you can get help in some localities from a bankruptcy petition preparer who is not an attorney. THE LAW REQUIRES AN ATTORNEY OR BANKRUPTCY PETITION PREPARER TO GIVE YOU A WRITTEN CONTRACT SPECIFYING WHAT THE ATTORNEY OR BANKRUPTCY PETITION PREPARER WILL DO FOR YOU AND HOW MUCH IT WILL COST. Ask to see the contract before you hire anyone.

The following information helps you understand what must be done in a routine bankruptcy case to help you evaluate how much service you need. Although bankruptcy can be complex, many cases are routine. Before filing a bankruptcy case, either you or your attorney should analyze your eligibility for different forms of debt relief available under the Bankruptcy Code and which form of relief is most likely to be beneficial for you. Be sure you understand the relief you can obtain and its limitations.

To file a bankruptcy case, documents called a Petition, Schedules and Statement of Financial Affairs, as well as in some cases a Statement of Intention need to be prepared correctly and filed with the bankruptcy court. You will have to pay a filing fee to the bankruptcy court. Once your case starts, you will have to attend the required first meeting of creditors where you may be questioned by your creditors.

If you choose to file a chapter 7 case, you may be asked by a creditor to reaffirm a debt. You may want help deciding whether to do so. A creditor is not permitted to coerce you into reaffirming your debts.

If you choose to file a chapter 13 case in which you repay your creditors what you can afford over 3 to 5 years, you may also want help with preparing your chapter 13 plan and with the confirmation hearing on your plan which will be before a bankruptcy judge.

If you select another type of relief under the Bankruptcy Code other than chapter 7 or chapter 13, you will want to find out what should be done from someone familiar with that type of relief.

Your bankruptcy case may also involve litigation. You are generally permitted to represent yourself in litigation in bankruptcy court, but only attorneys, not bankruptcy petition preparers, can give you legal advice.

In sum, debt relief agencies are on the hook if they are negligent in performing the services required by the bankruptcy law or other services they have agreed to provide.

B. Bankruptcy Lawyers

Bankruptcy lawyers (a type of debt relief agency under the new law) are regular lawyers who specialize in bankruptcy. Under the old law, it was usually possible to find an affordable bankruptcy lawyer who would provide at least a minimal level of representation. However, for the reasons discussed below, lawyers are charging a lot more for bankruptcies under the new law. Unfortunately, this means that many filers won't be able to afford legal representation.

If you aren't represented by a lawyer but want to file for bankruptcy, you will need to represent yourself. While this will involve a fair amount of work—much more than under the old law—it is certainly possible. And there is help available for you. In addition to books published by Nolo, you can use a combination of bankruptcy petition preparers and telephone legal advice to help you over the clerical and legal humps and get you through the process in reasonably good shape—for far less than regular lawyer representation will cost you. (See Sections C and D, below, for more information about the help available for people representing themselves.)

1. Lawyer Representation

You are represented by a lawyer if you contract with him or her to handle your entire bankruptcy case for you. When a bankruptcy lawyer signs up to represent you, he or she assumes responsibility—subject to a heightened standard of professional care applicable to lawyers—to obtain the best possible result in your bankruptcy. Under the new bankruptcy law, a lawyer who represents you is also responsible for the accuracy of the information that goes into your bankruptcy papers. Your need for lawyer representation will differ depending on whether you file a Chapter 7 or Chapter 13 bankruptcy.

a. Chapter 7 Bankruptcy

As explained in Ch. 9, you may be able to get by without lawyer representation in very simple Chapter 7 cases. The single most important determining factor is whether you will need to appear before the bankruptcy judge. You might also consider hiring a lawyer if you need to prepare custom-made court papers (for which there aren't any official forms) or to negotiate with creditors in situations where a lot is at stake and you don't have confidence in your own negotiating skills.

The only time you'll have to appear in court in a simple case is at the creditors' meeting, and lawyers don't play much of a role in these meetings. If this is the only reason you want to hire a lawyer, you really should think twice about the option of self-representation—with or without the help of a bankruptcy petition preparer (BPP).

If your case involves one of the more complicated procedures outlined in Ch. 9, then having a lawyer represent you can definitely be an advantage—especially if the creditor or trustee on the other side of the issue has a lawyer.

Unfortunately, lawyer representation doesn't come cheap. For bankruptcy lawyers, the new law creates new requirements and obligations—and you'll have to pay for the additional time the lawyer spends dealing with them. Because of these new requirements and the increased complexity of bankruptcy law, lawyers will be charging a lot more for their services. A poll of bankruptcy lawyers conducted by the American Bankruptcy Institute before the law took effect estimated that lawyer fees would at least double for routine bankruptcy cases, and increase even more for cases that required one or more appearances in a contested court action. You will most likely have to pay $1,500 to $2,000 for a lawyer to handle even a simple Chapter 7 case.

b. Chapter 13 Bankruptcy

Becoming knowledgeable about Chapter 13 bankruptcy will require some serious study. Under the new law, Chapter 13 bankruptcy is a fairly complex procedure, and there aren't any shortcuts. Most people who file for Chapter 13 bankruptcy will use an attorney right from the start, for several reasons:

- The lawyer's fee can be paid over time through the Chapter 13 plan (see Ch. 2, Section D).
- Chapter 13 bankruptcy often requires a lot of negotiating with creditors and with the bankruptcy trustee, often to reach agreement on an acceptable repayment plan.
- Chapter 13 bankruptcy requires at least one appearance in court before the bankruptcy judge (the confirmation hearing), and often several more.
- Chapter 13 cases can have many variables, such as valuation of property, reducing liens to the value of the collateral, creating a plan that doesn't discriminate among debtors and, often, requests for plan modifications or hardship discharges. An experienced lawyer can help you understand the specifics of your case, including the types of debts you have and the amount or percentage you must repay.

2. Alternative Roles for Lawyers

Traditionally, almost all people who filed bankruptcy were represented by lawyers. Since the advent of self-help law books in the early 1970s, however, more and more people have handled their own cases, often with the help of independent paralegals (now called bankruptcy petition preparers under the federal bankruptcy law). Since the 1990s, lawyers have been increasingly willing to offer their services on a piecemeal (unbundled) basis and provide legal advice over the telephone and Internet to help people helping themselves.

This combination of services—both professional and nonprofessional—has been a boon to people who can't afford full attorney representation. Even though a lawyer acting in an alternative role is considered a debt relief agency, the fees are far less than those associated with full representation, because the lawyer won't be taking on nearly as much responsibility.

a. Unbundled Services

When lawyers do specific jobs at a client's request but don't represent the client in the underlying case, they are said to be offering "unbundled" services. For example, you may be able to hire an attorney to handle a specific procedure— such as to defend against a motion for relief from stay, or to bring an action to determine the dischargeability of a particular debt—while you handle the main part of the bankruptcy yourself.

Some courts have held that attorneys can't ghostwrite legal documents for nonlawyers, but the issue has not been decided by most courts. Also, nothing prevents a lawyer from appearing for you in a limited capacity and putting his or her own name on associated documents.

As a general rule, you should bring an attorney into the case for an unbundled service whenever a dispute involves something of sufficient value to justify the attorney's fees. If a creditor objects to the discharge of a $500 debt, and it will cost you $400 to hire an attorney, you may be better off trying to handle the matter yourself, even though this increases the risk that the creditor will win. If, however, the dispute is worth $1,000 and the attorney will cost you $200, hiring the attorney makes better sense.

Unfortunately, many bankruptcy attorneys do not like to appear or do paperwork on a piecemeal basis. Justified or not, these attorneys believe that by doing a little work for you, they might be on the hook if something goes wrong in another part of your case—that is, if they are in for a penny, they are in for a pound. Also, the bar associations of many states frown on unbundled services on ethical grounds. On the other hand, a number of other state bar associations are starting to encourage their attorneys to offer unbundled services simply because so many people are unable to afford complete representation.

b. Legal Advice Over the Telephone and Internet

Under the old bankruptcy law, many people were able to represent themselves with a Nolo book as their main source of information. Bankruptcy under the new law is more complex, but in many cases, it's still just a matter of knowing what to put in the forms and what forms to file. (See Ch. 9, Section G). For many people, however, a book just won't do the trick, no matter how well written and complete. You want to talk to a human being. Because of unauthorized practice laws and restrictions in the bankruptcy law, however, there is only one kind of human being who is authorized to answer your questions about bankruptcy law and procedure—a lawyer.

Fortunately, there are lawyers and services that provide telephonic legal advice for a transaction fee (for example $39.95 flat rate) or a fee based on the amount of time your call takes (for example, $3 a minute). There are also free consultations offered by private attorneys and bar associations. Similar services—free and paid—are available on the Internet. To find a telephonic or online consultation service, go to Google or another search engine and look for "bankruptcy legal advice telephone or Internet."

Even if you use a BPP, you may need to talk to a lawyer to get the information you need to make your own choices and tell the BPP what you want in your papers. For instance, a BPP can't choose your exemptions for you, because that would be considered the practice of law—something only lawyers can do. However, a lawyer can help you decide which exemptions to pick so you can tell the BPP what to put in the form that lists your exemptions.

As with other debt relief agencies, lawyers offering telephonic services are considered debt relief agencies and will have to offer you a contract detailing their services and provide the other notices described in Section A, above.

3. How to Find a Bankruptcy Lawyer

Where there's a bankruptcy court, there are bankruptcy lawyers. They're listed in the Yellow Pages under "Attorneys," and often advertise in newspapers. You should use an experienced bankruptcy lawyer, not a general practitioner, to advise you or handle matters associated with bankruptcy.

There are several ways to find the best bankruptcy lawyer for your job:

- **Personal referrals.** This is your best approach. If you know someone who was pleased with the services of a bankruptcy lawyer, call that lawyer first.

- **Bankruptcy petition preparers.** If there's a BPP in your area, he or she may know some bankruptcy attorneys who are both competent and sympathetic to self-helpers. It is here that you are most likely to find a good referral to attorneys who are willing to deliver unbundled services or advice over the telephone.

- **Legal Aid.** Legal Aid offices are partially funded by the federal Legal Services Corporation and offer legal assistance in many areas. A few offices may do bankruptcies, although most do not. To qualify for Legal Aid, you must have a very low income.

- **Legal clinic.** Many law schools sponsor legal clinics and provide free legal advice to consumers. Some legal clinics have the same income requirements as Legal Aid; others offer free services to low-to-moderate-income people.

- **Group legal plans.** If you're a member of a plan that provides free or low-cost legal assistance and the plan covers bankruptcies, make that your first stop in looking for a lawyer.
- **Lawyer-referral panels.** Most county bar associations will give you the names of bankruptcy attorneys who practice in your area. But bar associations may not provide much screening. Take the time to check out the credentials and experience of the person to whom you're referred.

4. What to Look for in a Lawyer

No matter how you find a lawyer, these three suggestions will help you make sure you have the best possible working relationship.

First, fight any urge you may have to surrender to or be intimidated by the lawyer. You should be the one who decides what you feel comfortable doing about your legal and financial affairs. Keep in mind that you're hiring the lawyer to perform a service for you, so shop around if the price or personality isn't right.

Second, make sure you have good "chemistry" with any lawyer you hire. When making an appointment, ask to talk directly to the lawyer. If you can't, this may give you a hint as to how accessible he or she is. Of course, if you're told that

a paralegal will be handling the routine aspects of your case under the supervision of a lawyer, you may be satisfied with that arrangement. If you do talk directly, ask some specific questions. Do you get clear, concise answers? If not, try someone else. Also pay attention to how the lawyer responds to your knowledge. If you've read this book, you're already better informed than most clients (and some lawyers are threatened by clients who have done their homework).

Finally, once you find a lawyer you like, make an hour-long appointment to discuss your situation fully. The lawyer or a paralegal in the lawyer's office will tell you what to bring to the meeting, if anything (if not, be sure to ask ahead of time). Some lawyers will want to see a recent credit report while others will send you a questionnaire to complete prior to your visit. Depending on the circumstances, you may also be asked to bring your bills, tax returns, and documents pertaining to your home and other real estate you own. Some lawyers prefer not to deal with details during the first visit, and will simply ask you to come as you are.

Your main goal at the initial conference is to find out what the lawyer recommends in your particular case and how much it will cost. Go home and think about the lawyer's suggestions. If they don't make sense or you have other reservations, call someone else.

Look for a member of the National Association of Consumer Bankruptcy Attorneys. Because of the massive changes enacted by the new bankruptcy law, you will want to find an attorney who has a means of keeping up to date and communicating with other bankruptcy lawyers. Membership in the National Association of Consumer Bankruptcy Attorneys (NACBA) is a good sign that your lawyer will be tuned in to the nuances of the new law and the court interpretations of the law that are sure to come.

5. What Bankruptcy Lawyers Charge

As mentioned, fees charged by bankruptcy attorneys for a routine Chapter 7 bankruptcy will likely vary from about $1,500 to $2,500 (plus the nearly $300 filing fee). In most situations, you will have to pay the attorney in full before the attorney will file your case. The reason for this is that once you file your Chapter 7 bankruptcy, anything you owe the attorney is discharged along with your other dischargeable unsecured debts.

 You can pay a bankruptcy attorney without getting in trouble with the bankruptcy trustee. This kind of payment is generally not considered a "preference" payment that the trustee will try to undo. However, if the trustee thinks you've overpaid a lawyer or BPP, the amount of overpayment can be collected and returned to the bankruptcy estate.

For routine Chapter 13 cases, bankruptcy attorneys will likely charge about $2,500 to $3,500 (plus the $189 filing fee). The lawyer's fee is usually paid up front through the Chapter 13 plan.

On your bankruptcy papers, you must state the amount you are paying your bankruptcy lawyer. This is because every penny you pay to a bankruptcy lawyer is a penny not available to your creditors, at least in theory. The court has the legal authority to make the attorney justify the fee. This rarely happens, however, because attorneys know the range of fees generally allowed by local bankruptcy judges and set their fees accordingly. This means that you probably won't find much variation in the amounts charged by lawyers in your area (although it never hurts to shop around).

6. Extra Fees in Complicated Cases

If you hire an attorney to prepare and file your bankruptcy, the scope and range of services that the attorney promises you in return for your initial fee will be listed in what's called a Rule 2016 Attorney Fee Disclosure Form. This form is filed as part of your bankruptcy papers. In the typical Chapter 7 case, the attorney's fee will include counseling, form preparation, attendance at the creditors' meeting, and preparation of forms needed for reaffirmation. These are the routine tasks associated with bankruptcy. Any task not included in the Rule 2016 disclosure form is subject to a separate fee.

If your case requires more attorney time because you have to go through one or more of the types of procedures described in Ch. 9, you may—and probably will—be charged extra, according to the attorney's hourly fee or other criteria he or she uses. A typical bankruptcy attorney charges between $200 and $300 an hour (rural and urban) and would charge a minimum of roughly $400 to $600 for a court appearance. Because these fees are earned after your bankruptcy filing, they won't be discharged in your bankruptcy and the attorney need not collect them up front. Many attorneys will, however, insist on being paid in advance of the extra work. You are protected against fee gouging. An attorney must file a supplemental Rule 2016 form to cover any post-filing fees that he or she charges you and obtain permission from the court.

C. Bankruptcy Petition Preparers

You may decide that you want to represent yourself but that you can use help preparing your bankruptcy forms, to avoid all the typing and other basic organizational work that's involved. In that case, you may not need to use a lawyer. For this level of assistance, a bankruptcy petition preparer (BPP) can help you.

1. Available Services

BPPs are not lawyers, but they are familiar with the bankruptcy courts in your area. Their sole job is to use a computer or typewriter to complete your forms, using information that you provide about your debts, property, income, expenses, and economic transactions during the previous year or two (longer if you are a business).

Just like the old law, the new law prohibits a BPP from giving you legal advice, including a lot of the information in this book:

- whether to file a bankruptcy petition or which Chapter (7, 11, 12, or 13) is appropriate
- whether your debts will be discharged under a particular Chapter
- whether you will be able to hang on to your home or other property if you file under a particular Chapter (that is, what exemptions you should choose)
- information about the tax consequences of a case brought under a particular Chapter or whether tax claims in your case can be discharged
- whether you should offer to repay or agree to reaffirm a debt
- how to characterize the nature of your interest in property or debts, or
- information about bankruptcy procedures and rights.

Unless prohibited by a state's laws restricting who may give legal advice, every BPP must give you some plain English written information about basic bankruptcy tasks, such as how to deal with secured debts and choose exemptions. To file your own bankruptcy, however, you'll have to make your own decisions based on information from a book (such as a Nolo book), an Internet site, or a lawyer.

Teamwork Prevails Under the New Bankruptcy Law

Because lawyer fees have increased so dramatically under the new law, many people will have no choice but to use a BPP for help with their bankruptcy filing. However, BPPs are specifically prohibited from providing the very type of information their customers often need. For this reason, many BPPs make arrangements with lawyers who can provide this type of information directly to the customer over the phone, for a modest fee. And lawyers are more often willing to perform this role, recognizing that without it, people would be economically barred from the bankruptcy courts.

---

2. Fees

Under the old law, almost all bankruptcy courts could limit what BPPs might charge. The standard fee for most bankruptcies

was between $100 and $200, depending on the court and part of the country. Under the new law, there likely will be one fee (or regional fees) set by the administrative branch of the U.S. Supreme Court. Expect about $200–$250 in fees.

A BPP doesn't represent you. When you use a BPP, you are considered to be a self-represented debtor. This means that you are responsible for gathering the necessary legal information and making the appropriate decisions in your case. You might get the information and advice you need from a bankruptcy lawyer or from a self-help law resource, such as this book or the procedural bankruptcy guides published by Nolo. But you cannot, legally, pass this responsibility on to a BPP.

3. How Bankruptcy Petition Preparers Are Regulated

Bankruptcy petition preparers must put their name, address, telephone number, and Social Security number on every bankruptcy document they prepare. If you are representing yourself, the trustee will typically ask you questions at the creditors' meeting about how you got the information necessary to choose your exemptions or decide which Chapter to use. If you got that information from a BPP, the trustee will refer the case to the U.S. Trustee's office and the BPP will be hauled into court to explain why he or she violated the rules against giving legal advice. The BPP may be forced to return the fee you paid and may even be banned from practicing as a BPP, if it's not the first offense. None of this will have any effect on your case, however, other than the inconvenience about being dragged into court.

Under the new law, BPPs must submit a statement under oath with each petition they prepare stating how much you paid them in the previous 12 months and any fees that you owe them but haven't yet paid them.

If they charge you more than they are permitted, they will be ordered to return the excess fees to you. If they engage in any fraudulent act in regard to your case or fail to comply with the rules governing their behavior, they may be required to return your entire fee. And they may be fined $500 a pop for certain offenses.

4. How to Find Bankruptcy Petition Preparers

BPP services are springing up all over the country to help people who don't want or can't afford to hire a lawyer, but you're still more likely to find a BPP if you live on the West Coast. The best way to find a reputable BPP in your area is to get a recommendation from someone who has used a particular BPP and been satisfied with his or her work.

BPPs sometimes advertise in classified sections of local newspapers and in the Yellow Pages. You may have to look hard to spot their ads, however, because they go by different names in different states. In California, your best bet is to find a Legal Document Assistant (the official name given to independent paralegals in California) who also provide BPP services. In Arizona, hunt for a Legal Document Preparer. In other states, especially Florida, search for paralegals who directly serve the public (often termed independent paralegals or legal technicians). In many states, an independent paralegal franchise called We the People offers BPP services.

Attorneys and BPPs don't always play well together. Many bankruptcy attorneys have traditionally been unhappy with the competition from BPPs, often alleging that BPPs practice law without a license or are incompetent and even dangerous. While this attitude is sure to persist among some bankruptcy lawyers, many others will probably be more accepting as the new law makes the need to work together in order to assist low-income filers more evident.

D. Books and Internet Resources

This book is about bankruptcy under the new bankruptcy law. It gives you a good idea of what to expect if you file for Chapter 7 or Chapter 13 bankruptcy, whether you hire a bankruptcy lawyer or represent yourself. But if you do decide to handle your own case, you'll benefit from the great amount of information and tools available on the Internet, as well as a detailed, step-by-step guide to filing your own bankruptcy.

1. Using the Internet

If you are handling your own bankruptcy, you can expect to find all of the following on the internet:

- credit counseling agencies approved by the Office of the U.S. Trustee
- personal financial management courses approved by the Office of the U.S. Trustee
- services that will help you obtain your tax returns or transcripts and other documents you may need for filing (see Ch. 9, Section G)
- "calculators" that help you compute your "current monthly income" (Ch. 2, Section B)
- online programs that help you compare your current monthly income to your state's median income (Ch. 2, Section B), walk you through the means test (Ch. 2, Section C) if your current monthly income is above your state's median income, and locate the appropriate exemptions for your case (Ch. 4).
- bankruptcy-related print publication collections

- debt-relief agency websites offering a variety of services, and
- services that will help you obtain your credit report.

Finding these resources is easy, thanks to Google and similar search engines. Also visit Nolo's website, at www.nolo .com, to check for links that will be helpful in the use of this book. Finally, the National Bankruptcy Law Project (of which your author is a principal), at www .bankruptcylawproject.com, has links to a number of these services and can help you find the appropriate resources depending on your needs.

2. Books

You can expect to find many new books and guides to the new bankruptcy rules in bookstores in the coming months. *How to File for Chapter 7 Bankruptcy*, by Stephen Elias, Albin Renauer, and Robin Leonard (Nolo), has been around for 20 years; *Chapter 13 Bankruptcy*, by Robin Leonard and Stephen Elias, has been around for nearly ten years. Both will be fully updated to lead you step by step through the forms and procedures you'll need to navigate when doing your own Chapter 7 or Chapter 13 bankruptcy. For more information on Nolo and its large collection of self-help law books, visit www.nolo.com.

Bankruptcy Rules in Ch. 10

- The new law defines, and imposes many restrictions and obligations on, debt relief agencies, including bankruptcy lawyers. (11 U.S.C. §§ 101(12A), 526, 527, and 528.)

- In Chapter 7 cases, lawyers may be held responsible for the accuracy of the information included on the client's bankruptcy papers, especially if the result of the inaccuracy is that the petition is dismissed or converted to Chapter 13. (11 U.S.C. § 707(b)(4)(C-D).)

- Bankruptcy petition preparers are newly prohibited from engaging in certain activities, must make certain disclosures, file a fee statement with the petition, and disgorge fees in certain situations. (11 U.S.C. §§ 110 (b), (e), and (h)(3).)

- Bankruptcy petition preparers are subject to $500 fines for most violations of the code and three times that amount if the BPP engaged in deceptive activities. (11 U.S.C. § 110(l).)

Alternatives to Bankruptcy

After reading the previous ten chapters, you should have a pretty good idea of what filing a consumer Chapter 7 or a Chapter 13 bankruptcy will involve—and what you can hope to get out of it. Before you decide whether either type of bankruptcy is the right solution, however, consider the other options described in this chapter. Although bankruptcy is the only sensible remedy for some people with debt problems, an alternative course of action makes better sense for others. This chapter will explore these alternate courses of action, including:

- doing nothing (Section A)
- negotiating with your creditors (Section B)
- getting outside help with a repayment plan (Section C)
- filing for Chapter 11 bankruptcy (Section D), and
- filing for Chapter 12 bankruptcy (Section E).

If you own your home, see Ch. 5 for suggestions on alternatives to bankruptcy related to home ownership.

A. Do Nothing

Surprisingly, the best approach for some people who are deeply in debt is to take no action at all. You can't be thrown in jail for not paying your debts (except in the unusual situations described in Chapter 7), and your creditors can't collect money from you that you just don't have.

1. Creditors Must Sue to Collect

Except for taxing agencies and student loan creditors, creditors must first sue you in court and get a money judgment before they can go after your income and property. The big exception to this general rule is that a creditor can take back collateral—repossess a car or furniture, for example—when you default on a debt that's secured by that collateral. (If you're worried about foreclosure on a house, see Ch. 5.)

Under the typical security agreement (a contract involving collateral), the creditor can repossess the property without first going to court. But the creditor will not be able to go after your other property and income for any "deficiency" (the difference between what you owe and what the repossessed property fetches at auction) without first going to court for a money judgment.

2. Much of Your Property Is Protected

Even if creditors get a money judgment against you, they can't take away such essentials as:

- basic clothing
- ordinary household furnishings
- personal effects
- food
- Social Security or SSI payments
- unemployment benefits
- public assistance

- bank accounts with direct deposits from government benefit programs, and
- 75% of your wages (but child support judgments can grab a larger share).

The state exemptions described in Ch. 4 (and listed in Appendix A) apply whether or not you file for bankruptcy. Even creditors who get a money judgment against you can't take these protected items. (However, neither the federal bankruptcy exemptions nor the California System 2 exemptions described in Ch. 4 apply if a creditor sues you. Those are bankruptcy-only exemptions.)

3. What It Means to Be Judgment Proof

If all of the property you own is exempt, you are what is commonly referred to as "judgment proof." Whoever sues you and wins will be holding a useless piece of paper (at least temporarily), simply because you don't have anything that can legally be taken. While money judgments last a long time—typically ten years—and can be renewed, this won't make any difference unless your fortunes change for the better. If that happens, you might reconsider bankruptcy at that time.

If your creditors know that their chances of collecting a judgment from you any time soon are slim, they probably won't sue you in the first place. Instead, they'll simply write off your debt and treat it as a deductible business loss for income tax purposes. After some years have passed (usually between four and ten), the debt will become legally uncollectable, under state laws known as statutes of limitation.

Although statutes of limitation periods won't apply if the creditor sues you in time, lawsuits typically cost thousands of dollars in legal fees. If a creditor decides, on the basis of your economic profile, not to go to court at the present time, it is unlikely to seek a judgment down the line to extend its claims. In short, because creditors are reluctant to throw good money after bad, your poor economic circumstances might shield you from trouble.

Don't restart the clock. The statute of limitations can be renewed if you revive an old debt by, for example, admitting that you owe it or making a payment. As soon as you acknowledge a debt, the clock starts all over again. Savvy creditors are aware of this loophole and may try to trick you into admitting the debt so they can sue to collect it. Sometimes, it might be a good idea to try to repay a debt, particularly one to a local merchant with whom you wish to continue doing business. (See Section B, below, for more information.) But unless you are planning to make good on the debt or try to negotiate a new payment schedule, you should avoid any admissions. (See Section 4, below, for a sample letter that avoids admitting a debt.)

4. Stopping Bill Collector Harassment

Many people are moved to file for bankruptcy to stop their creditors from making harassing telephone calls and writing threatening letters. (See Ch. 1, Section B, for more on the automatic stay.) Fortunately, there is another way to get annoying creditors off your back. Federal law forbids collection agencies from threatening you, lying about what they can do to you, or invading your privacy. And many state laws prevent original creditors from taking similar actions.

Under the federal law, you can legally force collection agencies to stop phoning or writing you by simply demanding that they stop, even if you owe them a bundle and can't pay a cent. (The law is the federal Fair Debt Collections Practices Act, 15 U.S.C. §§ 1692 and following.) For more information, see *Solve Your Money Troubles*, by Robin Leonard (Nolo). Below is a sample letter asking a creditor to stop contacting the debtor.

B. Negotiate With Your Creditors

If you have some income, or you have assets you're willing to sell, you may be a lot better off negotiating with your creditors than filing for bankruptcy. Negotiation may buy you some time to

Sample Letter to Collection Agency

Sasnak Collection Service
49 Pirate Place
Topeka, Kansas 69000
November 11, 2005

Attn: Marc Mist

Re: Lee Anne Ito
    Account No. 88-90-92

Dear Mr. Mist:

For the past three months, I have received several phone calls and letters from you concerning an overdue Rich's Department Store account.

This is my formal notice to you under 15 U.S.C. § 1692c to cease all further communications with me except for the reasons specifically set forth in the federal law.

This letter is not meant in any way to be an acknowledgment that I owe this money.

Very truly yours,

Lee Anne Ito

Lee Anne Ito

get back on your feet, or you and your creditors may agree to settle your debts for less than the amount you owe.

Creditors hate it when debtors don't pay their debts. They don't like the hassle of instituting collection proceedings, or the fact that these proceedings tend to turn debt-owing customers into former customers. To avoid the collection process and to keep customers, creditors sometimes will reduce the debtor's expected payments, extend the time to pay, drop their demands for late fees, and make similar adjustments. They're most likely to be lenient if they believe you are making an honest effort to deal with your debt problems.

As soon as it becomes clear to you that you're going to have trouble paying a bill, write to the creditor. Explain the problem—whether it's an accident, job layoff, divorce, emergency expense for your child, unexpected tax bill, or something else. Mention any development that points to an improving financial condition, such as job prospects. Also, consider sending a token payment every month (the more the better of course). This tells the creditor that you are continuing to be serious about paying the full debt but just can't afford to right now.

Token payments make a big difference, especially to local creditors. And if you want to keep that credit or that business relationship, paying even a small amount might help. On the other hand, if it's been a long time since you've made any payments, you might want to hold off on your token payment until you've checked on the "statute of limitations" for that debt (the state time limit after which the debt goes away if no court action has been filed to collect it). Your payment might have the unfortunate effect of starting up a new limitations period.

Your success in getting creditors to give you time to pay will depend on the types of debts you have, how far behind you are, and the creditors' policies toward debts that are in arrears.

If you are not yet behind on your bills, be aware that a number of creditors have a ridiculous policy that requires you to default—and in some cases, become at least 90 days past due—before they will negotiate with you for better repayment terms. If any creditor makes this a condition of negotiating, find out from the creditor how you can keep the default out of your credit report.

In addition, increasing numbers of creditors simply refuse to negotiate with debtors. Despite the fact that creditors get at least something when they negotiate settlements, many ignore debtors' pleas for help, continue to make telephone calls demanding payment (unless you assert your right under federal law to not receive the calls—see "Stopping Bill Collector Harassment," above) and leave debtors with few options other than to file for bankruptcy. In fact, nearly one-third of the people who filed for bankruptcy during the mid-1990s stated that the final straw that sent them into bankruptcy was the unreasonableness of their creditors or the collection agencies hired by their creditors.

To help your creditors see the wisdom of settling with you on reasonable terms, it often won't hurt to mention the fact that you're thinking of filing for bankruptcy. Creditors know that they are very likely to get nothing in a bankruptcy case and may settle for a very few cents on the dollar. This being said, don't be surprised if a creditor tells you to "go ahead and file." More than a few creditors stand on what they take to be principle.

Legal Remedies for Unreasonable Creditor Actions

Creditors often violate federal laws preventing unfair collection practices— such as contacting you when you've made it clear you don't intend to repay a debt. These laws allow you to sue a law-breaking creditor in federal court and recover damages—including damages for emotional distress. If you become seriously irked by an overzealous collector and want to know whether a legal line has been crossed, take a look at *Solve Your Money Troubles,* by Robin Leonard (Nolo). You can also consult a consumer bankruptcy attorney, using your local Yellow Pages or the referral list on the National Association of Consumer Bankruptcy Attorneys website, at www.nacba.org.

C. Get Outside Help to Design a Repayment Plan

Prior to the new bankruptcy law, the combination of high consumer debt and easy access to information (especially on the Internet) led to an explosion in the number of credit and debt counseling agencies. Some provided limited services, such as budgeting and debt repayment, while others offered a range of services, from debt counseling to financial planning. Now, however, the advent of new requirements for credit counseling agencies under the new bankruptcy law (see Ch. 10), coupled with an aggressive auditing policy adopted by the IRS toward "non profit" counseling agencies, has significantly changed the credit counseling landscape.

1. Credit and Debt Counseling

Before you choose a credit counselor or debt management plan off the Web, be aware that while some of these agencies are legitimate, others may not be. How can you tell the difference? The key will be whether the agency has been approved by the Office of the U.S. Trustee for providing credit counseling to bankruptcy filers.

Prior to the new law, Money Management International and its family of Consumer Credit Counseling Services agencies had a good track record of providing consumers nationwide with financial education and credit counseling. And assuming they are approved by the Office of the U.S. Trustee, counseling will be available 24/7 by telephone (888-845-5669), on the Internet (www.moneymanagement.org), and in person at one of its more than 130 local branch offices. In addition to the U.S. Trustee requirements, guidelines for these credit counseling services are provided by the National Foundation for Credit Counseling (NFCC)™ at (www.nfcc.org), the trade organization that created the Consumer Credit Counseling Services (CCCS) network.

Credit Counseling Under the New Bankruptcy Law

The new bankruptcy law requires debtors to complete a credit counseling course before filing for bankruptcy. To implement this law, Congress has set out a number of requirements for credit counseling agencies and has designated the Office of the U.S. Trustee to approve and supervise credit counseling agencies. It's much safer to choose an agency that has been approved by the Office of the U.S. Trustee than an unapproved agency. You can find a list of approved agencies at the U.S. Trustee's website, www.usdoj.gov/ust (click "Credit Counseling and Debt Education").

---

2. How Debt Management Typically Works

To use a credit counseling agency to help you pay your debts, you must have some steady income. A counselor will contact your creditors to let them know that you've sought assistance and need more time to pay. Based on your income and debts, the counselor, with your creditors, will decide how much you must pay and for how long. You must then make one payment each month to the counseling agency, which in turn will pay your creditors. The agency will ask the creditors to return a small percentage of the money received to the agency office, in order to fund its work. This arrangement is generally referred to as a "debt management program."

Some creditors will make overtures to help you when you're participating in a debt management program such as reducing interest, waiving minimum payments, and forgiving late charges. But many creditors will not make interest concessions, such as waiving a portion of the accumulated interest to help you repay the principal portion of the debt. More likely, you'll get the late fees dropped and the opportunity to reinstate your credit if you successfully complete a debt management program.

3. Disadvantages of Debt Management

Participating in a credit counseling agency's debt management program is a little bit like filing for Chapter 13 bankruptcy. But working with a credit or debt counseling agency has one big advantage: No bankruptcy will appear on your credit record. On the other hand, a debt management program has two disadvantages when compared to Chapter 13 bankruptcy. First, if you miss a plan payment, Chapter 13 will often provide a way for you to make it up and continue to protect you from creditors who would otherwise start collection actions. A debt management program has no such protection, so any one creditor can pull the plug on your plan. Also, a debt management program plan usually requires you to pay your unsecured debts in full, over time. In Chapter 13, you often are only required to pay a small fraction of your nonpriority unsecured debts (if any), such as credit card and medical debts.

Critics of credit counseling agencies point out that the counselors tilt towards signing people up for a repayment plan in circumstances where bankruptcy would be in their best interest—so the agency will get a commission from the creditors that isn't available for cases that end up in bankruptcy. Under the new bankruptcy law, credit counseling agencies approved by the Office of the U.S. Trustee have a number of requirements placed on them to protect against undue influence by creditors and are required to make a number of disclosures that should prevent you from being ripped off. (See Ch. 2, Section A, for more on these rules.)

IRS Audits of Credit Counseling Agencies

As the new bankruptcy law went into effect, the IRS has been auditing dozens of credit counseling agencies that operate as federal nonprofits. In many of the cases, the IRS has found that the nonprofit agencies are really a front for profit-making enterprises and is revoking their federal tax-exempt status. This IRS activity, coupled with the new bankruptcy law requirements for credit counseling agency approval by the Office of the U.S. Trustee, is likely to reform the credit counseling industry for the better. Undoubtedly, some existing agencies will pass the IRS audits with flying colors and obtain U.S. Trustee approval, while others will be forced out of business. (For more on the problems that spurred the IRS investigation, see *Credit Counseling in Crisis*, a report by the National Consumer Law Center, at www.nclc.org.)

D. File for Chapter 11 Bankruptcy

Chapter 11 bankruptcy is ordinarily used by financially struggling businesses to reorganize their affairs. However, it is also available to individuals. Individuals who consider Chapter 11 bankruptcy usually have debts in excess of one or both of the

Chapter 13 bankruptcy limits—$307,675 of unsecured debts and $922,975 of secured debts—or substantial nonexempt assets, such as several pieces of real estate.

The initial filing fee is currently $839, compared to $274 for Chapter 7 or $189 for Chapter 13 bankruptcy. In addition, you must pay a quarterly fee, based on a percentage of the disbursements made to pay your debts. The fee runs from $250 a quarter when the disbursements total less than $15,000, to $10,000 a quarter when disbursements total $5,000,000 or more. The fee must be paid until your reorganization plan is either approved or dismissed, or your case is converted to Chapter 7 bankruptcy. Most attorneys require a minimum $7,500 retainer fee to handle a Chapter 11 bankruptcy case. Add to that the Chapter 11 bankruptcy court fees, which in one year could run from $1,000 to $10,000, and you can see that Chapter 11 isn't for everyone.

 Want to know more about Chapter 11 bankruptcy? Check out *A Feast for Lawyers: Chapter 11, An Expose*, by Sol Stein (Beard Books).

You'll need a lawyer to file for Chapter 11 bankruptcy. A Chapter 11 bankruptcy often turns into a long, expensive, lawyer-infested mess, and many Chapter 11 filings are converted to Chapter 7 once legal fees gobble up the business assets. The new bankruptcy law has made a Chapter 11 small business bankruptcy even more difficult by requiring all documents to be filed within 30 days of the filing of the petition. Even to file a "fast-track" Chapter 11 bankruptcy for small businesses with debts up to $2 million, you will need an attorney.

E. File for Chapter 12 Bankruptcy

Chapter 12 bankruptcy is almost identical to Chapter 13 bankruptcy. To be eligible for Chapter 12 bankruptcy, however, at least 80% of your debts must arise from the operation of a family farm. The fee for filing a Chapter 12 case is $230. Chapter 12 has its own rules and procedures, which aren't covered in this book. See a lawyer if you want to file for Chapter 12 bankruptcy.

Bankruptcy Rules in Ch. 11

- With some exceptions, you have to complete debt counseling within 180 days of filing bankruptcy. (11 U.S.C. § 109(h)(1).)

- The debt counseling requirement is waived if debt counseling services aren't reasonably available in your region. (11 U.S.C. § 109(h)(2).)

- The debt counseling requirement is waived if you have to make an emergency filing, but you must get counseling within 30 days after the bankruptcy filing (45 days if a court approves). (11 U.S.C. § 109(h)(3).)

- The debt counseling requirement is waived if you are prevented from participating because of incapacity or active military duty in a combat zone. (11 U.S.C. § 109(h)(4).)

- To meet the credit counseling requirement, a debtor must obtain a certificate of participation from a credit counseling agency approved by the U.S. Trustee, which requires all approved counseling agencies to meet certain standards. (11 U.S.C. §§ 111(a), (b), and (c).)

- Prior to receiving your discharge, you must complete a course in personal financial management and obtain a certificate from an agency approved for this purpose by the U.S. Trustee. (11 U.S.C. §§ 111(b) and (d).)

Glossary

341 meeting. *See* "meeting of creditors."

341 notice. A notice sent to the debtor and the debtor's creditors announcing the date, time, and place for the first meeting of creditors. The 341 notice is sent along with the notice of bankruptcy filing and information about important deadlines by which creditors have to take certain actions, such as filing objections.

342 notice. A notice that the court clerk is required to give to debtors pursuant to Section 342 of the Bankruptcy Code, to inform them of their obligations as a bankruptcy debtor and the consequences of not being completely honest in their bankruptcy case.

707(b) action. An action taken by the U.S. Trustee, the regular trustee, or any creditor, under authority of Section 707(b) of the Bankruptcy Code, to dismiss a debtor's Chapter 7 filing on the ground of abuse.

Abuse. Misuse of the Chapter 7 bankruptcy remedy. This term is typically applied to Chapter 7 bankruptcy filings that should have been filed under Chapter 13 because the debtor appears to have enough disposable income to fund a Chapter 13 repayment plan.

Accounts receivable. Money or other property that one person or business owes to another for goods or services. Accounts receivable most often refer to the debts owed to a business by its customers.

Administrative expenses. The trustee's fee, the debtor's attorney fee, and other costs of bringing a bankruptcy case that a debtor must pay in full in a Chapter 13 repayment plan. Administrative costs are typically 10% of the debtor's total payments under the plan.

Administrative Office of the United States Courts. The federal government agency that issues court rules and forms to be used by the federal courts, including bankruptcy courts.

Adversary action. Any lawsuit that begins with the filing of a formal complaint and formal service of process on the parties being sued. In a bankruptcy case, adversary actions are often brought to determine the dischargeability of a debt or to recover property transferred by the debtor shortly before filing for bankruptcy.

Affidavit. A written statement of facts, signed under oath in front of a notary public.

Allowed secured claim. A debt that is secured by collateral or a lien against the debtor's property, for which the creditor has filed a proof of claim with the bankruptcy court. The claim is secured only to the extent of the value of the property—for example, if a debtor owes $5,000 on a note for a car that is worth only $3,000, the remaining $2,000 is an unsecured claim.

Amendment. A document filed by the debtor that changes one or more documents previously filed with the court. A debtor often files an amendment because the trustee requires changes to the debtor's paperwork based on the testimony at the meeting of creditors.

Animals. An exemption category in many states. Some states specifically exempt pets or livestock and poultry. If your state simply allows you to exempt "animals," you may include livestock, poultry, or pets. Some states exempt only domestic animals, which are usually considered to be all animals except pets.

Annuity. A type of insurance policy that pays out during the life of the insured, unlike life insurance, which pays out at the insured's death. Once the insured reaches the age specified in the policy, he or she receives monthly payments until death.

Appliance. A household apparatus or machine, usually operated by electricity, gas, or propane. Examples include refrigerators, stoves, washing machines, dishwashers, vacuum cleaners, air conditioners, and toasters.

Arms and accoutrements. Arms are weapons (such as pistols, rifles, and swords); accoutrements are the furnishings of a soldier's outfit, such as a belt or pack, but not clothes or weapons.

Arms-length creditor. A creditor with whom the debtor deals in the normal course of business, as opposed to an insider (a friend, relative, or business partner).

Articles of adornment. *See* "jewelry."

Assessment benefits. *See* "stipulated insurance."

Assisted person. Any person contemplating or filing for bankruptcy who receives bankruptcy assistance, whose debts are primarily consumer debts, and whose nonexempt property is valued at less than $150,000. A person or entity that offers help to an assisted person is called a "debt relief agency."

Automatic stay. An injunction automatically issued by the bankruptcy court when a debtor files for bankruptcy. The automatic stay prohibits most creditor collection activities, such as filing or continuing lawsuits, making written requests for payment, or notifying credit reporting bureaus of an unpaid debt.

Avails. Any amount available to the owner of an insurance policy other than the actual proceeds of the policy. Avails include dividend payments, interest, cash or surrender value (the money you'd get if you sold your policy back to the insurance company), and loan value (the amount of cash you can borrow against the policy).

Bankruptcy Abuse Prevention and Reform Act of 2005. The formal name of the new bankruptcy law that took effect on October 17, 2005.

Bankruptcy administrator. The official responsible for supervising the administration of bankruptcy cases, estates, and trustees in Alabama and North Carolina, where there is no U.S. Trustee.

Bankruptcy Appellate Panel. A specialized court that hears appeals of bankruptcy court decisions (available only in some regions).

Bankruptcy assistance. Goods or services provided to an "assisted person" for the purpose of providing information, advice, counsel, document preparation or filing, or attendance at a creditors' meeting; appearing in a case or proceeding on behalf of another person; or providing legal representation.

Bankruptcy Code. The federal law that governs the creation and operation of the bankruptcy courts and establishes bankruptcy procedures. (You can find the Bankruptcy Code in Title 11 of the United States Code.)

Bankruptcy estate. All of the property you own when you file for bankruptcy, except for most pensions and educational trusts. The trustee technically takes control of your bankruptcy estate for the duration of your case.

Bankruptcy lawyer. A lawyer who specializes in bankruptcy and is licensed to practice law in the federal courts.

Bankruptcy petition preparer. Any non-lawyer who helps someone with his or her bankruptcy. Bankruptcy petition preparers (BPPs) are a special type of debt relief agency, regulated by the U.S. Trustee. Because they are not lawyers, BPPs can't represent anyone in bankruptcy court or provide legal advice.

Bankruptcy Petition Preparer Fee Declaration. An official form bankruptcy petition preparers must file with the bankruptcy court to disclose their fees.

Bankruptcy Petition Preparer Notice to Debtor. A written notice that bankruptcy petition preparers must provide to debtors who use their services. The Notice explains that bankruptcy petition preparers aren't attorneys and that they are permitted to perform only certain acts, such as entering information in the bankruptcy petition and schedules under the direction of their clients.

Benefit or benevolent society benefits. *See* "fraternal benefit society benefits."

Building materials. Items, such as lumber, brick, stone, iron, paint, and varnish, that are used to build or improve a structure.

Burial plot. A cemetery plot.

Business bankruptcy. A bankruptcy in which the debts arise primarily from the operation of a business, including bankruptcies filed by corporations, limited liability companies, and partnerships.

Certification. The act of signing a document under penalty of perjury. (The document that is signed is also called a certification.)

Chapter 7 bankruptcy. A liquidation bankruptcy, in which the trustee sells the debtor's nonexempt property and distributes the proceeds to the debtor's creditors. At the end of the case, the debtor receives a discharge of all remaining debts, except those that cannot legally be discharged.

Chapter 9 bankruptcy. A type of bankruptcy restricted to governmental units.

Chapter 11 bankruptcy. A type of bankruptcy intended to help businesses reorganize their debt load in order to remain in business. A Chapter 11 bankruptcy is typically much more expensive than a Chapter 7 or 13 bankruptcy because all of the lawyers must be paid out of the bankruptcy estate.

Chapter 12 bankruptcy. A type of bankruptcy designed to help small farmers reorganize their debts.

Chapter 13 bankruptcy. A type of consumer bankruptcy designed to help individuals reorganize their debts and pay all or a portion of them over three to five years.

Chapter 13 plan. A document filed in a Chapter 13 bankruptcy in which the debtor shows how all of his or her projected disposable income will be used over a three- to five-year period to pay all mandatory debts—for example, back child support, taxes, and mortgage arrearages—as well as some or all unsecured, nonpriority debts, such as medical and credit card bills.

Claim. A creditor's assertion that the bankruptcy filer owes it a debt or obligation.

Clothing. As an exemption category, the everyday clothes you and your family need for work, school, household use, and protection from the elements. In many states, luxury items and furs are not included in the clothing exemption category.

Codebtor. A person who assumes an equal responsibility, along with the debtor, to repay a debt or loan.

Collateral. Property pledged by a borrower as security for a loan.

Common law property states. States that don't use a community property system to classify marital property.

Community property. Certain property owned by married couples in Arizona, California, Idaho, Louisiana, New Mexico, Nevada, Texas, Washington, Wisconsin, and, if both spouses agree, Alaska. Very generally, all property acquired during the marriage is considered community property, belonging equally to both spouses, except for gifts and inheritances by one spouse. Similarly, all debts incurred during the marriage are considered community debts, owed equally by both spouses, with limited exceptions.

Complaint. A formal document that initiates a lawsuit.

Complaint to determine dischargeablity. A complaint initiating an adversary action in bankruptcy court that asks the court to decide whether a particular debt should be discharged at the end of the debtor's bankruptcy case.

Condominium. A building or complex in which separate units, such as townhouses or apartments, are owned by individuals, and the common areas (lobby, hallways, stairways, and so on) are jointly owned by the unit owners.

Confirmation. The bankruptcy judge's ruling approving a Chapter 13 plan.

Confirmation hearing. A court hearing conducted by a bankruptcy judge in which the judge decides whether a debtor's proposed Chapter 13 plan appears to be feasible and meets all applicable legal requirements.

Consumer bankruptcy. A bankruptcy in which a preponderance of the debt was incurred for personal, family, or household purposes.

Consumer debt. A debt incurred by an individual for personal, family, or household purposes.

Contingent debts. Debts that may be owed if certain events happen or conditions are satisfied.

Contingent interests in the estate of a decedent. The right to inherit property if one or more conditions to the inheritance are satisfied. For example, a debtor who will inherit property only if he survives his brother has a contingent interest.

Conversion. When a debtor who has filed one type of bankruptcy switches to another type—as when a Chapter 7 debtor converts to a Chapter 13 bankruptcy, or vice versa.

Cooperative housing. A building or other residential structure that is owned by a corporation formed by the residents. In exchange for purchasing stock in the corporation, the residents have the right to live in particular units.

Cooperative insurance. Compulsory employment benefits provided by a state or federal government, such as old age, survivors, disability, and health insurance, to assure a minimum standard of living for lower- and middle-income people. Also called social insurance.

Court clerk. The court employee who is responsible for accepting filings and other documents, and generally maintaining an accurate and efficient flow of paper and information in the court.

Cramdown. In a Chapter 13 bankruptcy, the act of reducing a secured debt to the replacement value of the collateral securing the debt.

Credit and debt counseling. Counseling that explores the possibility of repaying debts outside of bankruptcy and educates the debtor about credit, budgeting, and financial management. Under the new bankruptcy law, a debtor must undergo credit counseling with an approved provider before filing for bankruptcy.

Credit insurance. An insurance policy that covers a borrower for an outstanding loan. If the borrower dies or becomes disabled before paying off the loan, the policy will pay off the balance due.

Creditor. A person or institution to whom money is owed.

Creditor committee. In a Chapter 11 bankruptcy, a committee that represents the unsecured debtors in reorganization proceedings.

Creditor matrix. A specially formatted list of creditors that a debtor must file with the bankruptcy petition. The matrix helps the court notify creditors of the bankruptcy filing and the date and time set for the first meeting of creditors.

Creditors meeting. *See* "meeting of creditors."

Crops. Products of the soil or earth that are grown and raised annually and gathered in a single season. Thus, oranges (on the tree or harvested) are crops; an orange tree isn't.

Current market value. What property could be sold for. This is how a debtor's property was previously valued for purposes of determining whether the property is protected by an applicable exemption. Under the new bankruptcy law, property must be valued at its "replacement cost."

Current monthly income. As defined by the new bankruptcy law, a bankruptcy filer's total gross income (whether taxable or not), averaged over the six-month period immediately preceding the month in which the bankruptcy is filed. The current monthly income is used to determine whether the debtor can file for Chapter 7 bankruptcy, among other things.

Debt. An obligation of any type, including a loan, credit, or promise to perform a contract or lease.

Debt relief agency. An umbrella term for any person or agency—including lawyers and bankruptcy petition preparers, but excluding banks, non-profit and government agencies, and employees of debt relief agencies—that provides "bankruptcy assistance" to an "assisted person."

Debtor. Someone who owes money to another person or business. Also, the generic term used to refer to anyone who files for bankruptcy.

Declaration. A written statement that is made under oath but not witnessed by a notary public.

Declaration of homestead. A form filed with the county recorder's office to put on record your right to a homestead exemption. In most states, the homestead exemption is automatic—that is, you are not required to record a homestead declaration in order to claim the homestead exemption. A few states do require such a recording, however.

Disability benefits. Payments made under a disability insurance or retirement plan when the insured is unable to work (or retires early) because of disability, accident, or sickness.

Discharge. A court order, issued at the conclusion of a Chapter 7 or Chapter 13 bankruptcy case, which legally relieves the debtor of personal liability for debts that can be discharged in that type of bankruptcy.

Discharge exceptions. Debts that are not discharged in a bankruptcy case. The debtor continues to owe these debts even after the bankruptcy is concluded.

Discharge hearing. A hearing conducted by a bankruptcy court to explain the discharge, urge the debtor to stay out of debt, and review reaffirmation agreements to make sure they are feasible and fair.

Dischargeability action. An adversary action brought by a party who asks the court to determine whether a particular debt qualifies for discharge.

Dischargeable debt. A debt that is wiped out at the conclusion of a bankruptcy case, unless the judge decides that it should not be.

Dismissal. When the court orders a case to be closed without providing the relief available under the bankruptcy laws. For example, a Chapter 13 case might be dismissed because the debtor fails to propose a feasible plan; a Chapter 7 case might be dismissed for abuse.

Disposable income. The difference between a debtor's "current monthly income" and allowable expenses. This is the amount that the bankruptcy law deems available to pay into a Chapter 13 plan.

Domestic animals. *See* "animals."

Domestic support obligation. An obligation to pay alimony or child support to a spouse, child, or government entity pursuant to an order by a court or other governmental unit.

Doubling. The ability of married couples to double the amount of certain property exemptions when filing for bankruptcy together. The federal bankruptcy exemptions allow doubling. State laws vary—some permit doubling and some do not.

Education Individual Retirement Account. A type of account to which a person can contribute a certain amount of tax-deferred funds every year for the educational benefit of the debtor or certain relatives. Such an account is not part of the debtor's bankruptcy estate.

Emergency bankruptcy filing. An initial bankruptcy filing that includes only the petition and the creditor matrix, filed right away because the debtor needs the protection of the automatic stay to prevent a creditor from taking certain action, such as a foreclosure. An emergency filing case will be dismissed if the other required documents and forms are not filed in a timely manner.

Endowment insurance. An insurance policy that gives an insured who lives for a specified time (the endowment period) the right to receive the face value of the policy (the amount paid at death). If the insured dies sooner, the beneficiary named in the policy receives the proceeds.

Equity. The amount you get to keep if you sell property—typically the property's market value, less the costs of sale and the value of any liens on the property.

ERISA-qualified benefits. Pensions that meet the requirements of the Employee Retirement Income Security Act (ERISA), a federal law that sets minimum standards for such plans and requires beneficiaries to receive certain notices.

Executory contract. A contract in which one or both parties still have a duty to carry out one or more of the contract's terms.

Exempt property. Property described by state and federal laws (exemptions) that a debtor is entitled to keep in a Chapter 7 bankruptcy. Exempt property cannot be taken and sold by the trustee for the benefit of the debtor's unsecured creditors.

Exemptions. State and federal laws specifying the types of property creditors are not entitled to take to satisfy a debt, and the bankruptcy trustee is not entitled to take and sell for the benefit of the debtor's unsecured creditors.

Farm tools. Tools used by a person whose primary occupation is farming. Some states limit farm tools of the trade to items that can be held in the hand, such as hoes, axes, pitchforks, shovels, scythes, and the like. In other states, farm tools also include plows, harnesses, mowers, reapers, and so on.

Federal exemptions. A list of exemptions contained in the federal bankruptcy code. Some states give debtors the option of using the federal exemptions rather than the state exemptions.

Federal Rules of Bankruptcy Procedure. A set of rules issued by the Administrative Office of the United States Courts, which govern bankruptcy court procedures.

Filing date. The date a bankruptcy petition in a particular case is filed. With few exceptions, debts incurred after the filing date are not discharged. Similarly, property owned before the filing date is part of the bankruptcy estate, while property acquired after the filing date is not.

Fines, penalties, and restitution. Debts owed to a court or a victim as a result of a sentence in a criminal matter. These debts are generally not dischargeable in bankruptcy.

Foreclosure. The process by which a creditor with a lien on real estate forces a sale of the property in order to collect on the lien. Foreclosure typically occurs when a homeowner defaults on a mortgage.

Fraternal benefit society benefits. Benefits, often group life insurance, paid for by fraternal societies, such as the Elks, Masons, Knights of Columbus, or the Knights of Maccabees, for their members. Also called benefit society, benevolent society, or mutual aid association benefits.

Fraud. Generally, an act that is intended to mislead another for the purpose of financial gain. In a bankruptcy case, fraud is any writing or representation intended to mislead creditors for the purpose of obtaining a loan or credit, or any act intended to mislead the bankruptcy court or the trustee.

Fraudulent transfer. In a bankruptcy case, a transfer of property to another for less than the property's value for the purpose of hiding the property from the bankruptcy trustee—for instance, when a debtor signs a car over to a relative to keep it out of the bankruptcy estate. Fraudulently transferred property can be recovered and sold by the trustee for the benefit of the creditors.

Fraudulently concealed assets. Property that a bankruptcy debtor deliberately fails to disclose as required by the bankruptcy rules.

Furnishings. An exemption category recognized in many states, which includes furniture, fixtures in your home (such as a heating unit, furnace, or built-in lighting), and other items with which a home is furnished, such as carpets and drapes.

Good faith. In a Chapter 13 case, when a debtor files for bankruptcy with the sincere purpose of paying off debts over the period of time required by law rather than for manipulative purposes—such as to prevent a foreclosure that by all rights should be allowed to proceed.

Goods and chattels. *See* "personal property."

Group life or group health insurance. A single insurance policy covering individuals in a group (for example, employees) and their dependents.

Head of household. A person who supports and maintains, in one household, one or more people who are closely related to the person by blood, marriage, or adoption. Also referred to as "head of family."

Health aids. Items needed to maintain their owner's health, such as a wheelchair, crutches, prosthesis, or a hearing aid. Many states require that health aids be prescribed by a physician.

Health benefits. Benefits paid under health insurance plans, such as Blue Cross/ Blue Shield, to cover the costs of health care.

Heirloom. An item with special monetary or sentimental value, which is passed down from generation to generation.

Home equity loan. A loan made to a homeowner on the basis of the equity in the home—and secured by the home in the same manner as a mortgage.

Homestead. A state or federal exemption applicable to property where the debtor lives when he or she files bankruptcy— usually including boats and mobile homes.

Homestead declaration. *See* "declaration of homestead."

Household good. As an exemption category, an item of permanent nature (as opposed to items consumed, like food or cosmetics) used in or about the house. This includes linens, dinnerware, utensils, pots and pans, and small electronic equipment like radios. Many state laws specifically list the types of household goods that fall within this exemption, as do the federal bankruptcy laws.

Householder. A person who supports and maintains a household, with or without other people. Also called a "housekeeper."

Impairs an exemption. When a lien, in combination with any other liens on the property and the amount the debtor is entitled to claim as exempt, exceeds the value of the property the debtor could claim in the absence of any liens. For example, if property is worth $15,000, there are $5,000 worth of liens on the property, and the debtor is entitled to a $5,000 exemption in the property, a lien that exceeded $5,000 would impair the debtor's exemption. Certain types of liens that impair an exemption may be removed (avoided) by the debtor if the court so orders.

Implement. As an exemption category, an instrument, tool, or utensil used by a person to accomplish his or her job.

In lieu of homestead (or burial) exemption. Designates an exemption that is available only if you don't claim the homestead (or burial) exemption.

Individual Debtor's Statement of Intention. An official bankruptcy form that debtors with secured debts must file to indicate what they want to do with the property that secures the debt. For instance, a debtor with a car note must indicate whether he or she wants to keep the car and continue the debt (reaffirmation), pay off the car note at a reduced price (redemption), or give the car back to the creditor and cancel the debt.

Injunction. A court order prohibiting a person or entity from taking specified actions—for example, the automatic stay (in reality an automatic injunction), which prevents most creditors from trying to collect their debts.

Insider creditor. A creditor with whom the debtor has a personal relationship, such as a relative, friend, or business partner.

Intangible property. Property that cannot be physically touched, such as an ownership share in a corporation or a copyright. Documents—such as a stock certificate—may provide evidence of intangible property.

Involuntary dismissal. When a bankruptcy judge dismisses a case because the debtor fails to carry out his or her duties—such as filing papers in a timely manner and cooperating with the trustee—or because the debtor files the bankruptcy in bad faith or engages in abuse by wrongfully filing for Chapter 7 when he or she should have filed for Chapter 13.

Involuntary lien. A lien that is placed on the debtor's property without the debtor's consent—for instance, when the IRS places a lien on property for back taxes.

IRS expenses. A table of national and regional expense estimates published by the IRS. Debtors whose "current monthly income" is more than their state's "median family income" must use the IRS expenses to calculate their average net income in a Chapter 7 case, or their disposable income in a Chapter 13 case.

Jewelry. Items created for personal adornment; usually includes watches. Also called "articles of adornment."

Joint debtors. Married people who file for bankruptcy together and pay a single filing fee.

Judgment proof. A description of a person whose income and property are such that a creditor can't (or won't) seize them to enforce a money judgment—for example, a dwelling protected by a homestead exemption or a bank account containing only a few dollars.

Judicial lien. A lien created by the recording of a court money judgment against the debtor's property—usually real estate.

Lease. A contract that governs the relationship between an owner of property and a person who wishes to use the property for a specific period of time—as in car and real estate leases.

Lien. A legal claim against property that must be paid before title to the property can be transferred. Liens can also often be collected through repossession (personal property) or foreclosure (real estate), depending on the type of lien.

Lien avoidance. A bankruptcy procedure in which certain types of liens can be removed from certain types of property. Liens that are not avoided survive the bankruptcy even though the underlying debt may be cancelled—for instance, a lien remains on a car even if the debt evidenced by the car note is discharged in the bankruptcy.

Life estate. The right to live in, but not own, a specific home until your death.

Life insurance. A policy that provides for the payment of money to an individual (called the beneficiary) in the event of the death of another (called the insured). The policy matures (becomes payable) only when the insured dies.

Lifting the stay. When a bankruptcy court allows a creditor to continue with debt collection or other activities that are otherwise banned by the automatic stay. For instance, the court might allow a landlord to proceed with an eviction or a lender to repossess a car because the debtor has defaulted on the note.

Liquid assets. Cash or items that are easily convertible into cash, such as a money market account, stock, U.S. Treasury bill, or bank deposit.

Liquidated debt. An existing debt for a specified amount arising out of a contract or court judgment. In contrast, an unliquidated debt is a claim for an as-yet uncertain amount, such as for injuries suffered in a car accident before the case goes to court.

Lost future earnings. The portion of a lawsuit judgment intended to compensate an injured person for the money he or she won't be able to earn in the future because of the injury. Also called lost earnings payments or recoveries.

Luxuries. In bankruptcy, goods or services purchased by the debtor that a court decides were not appropriate in light of the debtor's insolvency. This might include vacations, jewelry, costly cars, or frequent meals at expensive restaurants.

Mailing matrix. *See* "creditor matrix."

Marital debts. Debts owed jointly by a married couple.

Marital property. Property owned jointly by a married couple.

Marital settlement agreement. An agreement between a divorcing couple that sets out who gets what percentage (or what specific items) of the marital property, who pays what marital debts, and who gets custody and pays child support if there are children of the marriage.

Materialmen's and mechanics' liens. Liens imposed by statute on real estate when suppliers of materials, labor, and contracting services used to improve the real estate are not properly compensated.

Matured life insurance benefits. Insurance benefits that are currently payable because the insured person has died.

Means test. A formula that uses predefined income and expense categories to determine whether a debtor whose income is more than the median family income for his or her state should be allowed to file a Chapter 7 bankruptcy.

Median family income. An annual income figure for which there are as many families with incomes below that level as there are above that level. The U.S. Census Bureau publishes median family income figures for each state and for different family sizes. In bankruptcy, the median family income is used as a basis for determining whether a debtor must pass the means test to file Chapter 7 bankruptcy, and whether a debtor filing a Chapter 13 bankruptcy must commit all his or her projected disposable income to a five-year repayment plan.

Meeting of creditors. A meeting that the debtor is required to attend in a bankruptcy case, at which the trustee and creditors may ask the debtor questions about his or her property, information in the documents and forms he or she filed, and his or her debts.

Mortgage. A contract in which a loan to purchase real estate is secured by the real estate as collateral. If the borrower defaults on loan payments, the lender can foreclose on the property.

Motion. A formal legal procedure in which the bankruptcy judge is asked to rule on a dispute in the bankruptcy case. To bring a motion, a party must file a document explaining what relief is requested, the facts of the dispute, and the legal reasons why the court should grant the relief. The party bringing the motion must mail these documents to all affected parties and let them know when the court will hear argument on the motion.

Motion to avoid judicial lien on real estate. A motion brought by a bankruptcy debtor that asks the bankruptcy court to remove a judicial lien on real estate because the lien impairs the debtor's homestead exemption.

Motion to lift stay. A motion in which a creditor asks the court for permission to continue a court action or collection activities in spite of the automatic stay.

Motor vehicle. A self-propelled vehicle suitable for use on a street or road. This includes a car, truck, motorcycle, van, and moped. *See also* "tools of the trade."

Musical instrument. An instrument having the capacity, when properly operated, to produce a musical sound. Pianos, guitars, drums, drum machines, synthesizers, and harmonicas are all musical instruments.

Mutual aid association benefits. *See* "fraternal benefit society benefits."

Mutual assessment or mutual life. *See* "stipulated insurance."

Necessities. Articles needed to sustain life, such as food, clothing, medical care, and shelter.

Newly discovered creditors. Creditors who the debtor discovers after the bankruptcy is filed. If the case is still open, the debtor can amend the list to include the creditor; if the case is closed, it usually can be reopened to accommodate the amendment.

Nonbankruptcy federal exemptions. Federal laws that allow a debtor who has not filed for bankruptcy to keep creditors away from certain property. The debtor can also use these exemptions in bankruptcy if the debtor is using a state exemption system.

Nondischargeable debt. Debt that survives bankruptcy, such as back child support and most student loans.

Nonexempt property. Property in the bankruptcy estate that is unprotected by the exemption system available to the debtor (this is typically—but not always—the exemption system in the state where the debtor files bankruptcy). In a Chapter 7 bankruptcy, the trustee may sell it for the benefit of the debtor's unsecured creditors. In a Chapter 13 bankruptcy, debtors must propose a plan that pays their unsecured creditors at least the value of their unsecured property.

Nonpossessory, nonpurchase money lien. A lien placed on property that is already owned by the debtor and is used as collateral for the loan without being possessed by the lender. In contrast, a nonpurchase money, possessory lien exists on collateral that is held by a pawnshop.

Nonpriority debt. A type of debt that is not entitled to be paid first in bankruptcy, as priority debts are. Nonpriority debts do not have to be paid in full in a Chapter 13 case.

Nonpriority, unsecured claim. A claim that is not for a priority debt (such as child support) and is not secured by collateral or other property. Typical examples include credit card debt, medical bills, and student loans. In a Chapter 13 repayment plan, nonpriority, unsecured claims are paid only after all other debts are paid.

Notice of appeal. A form that must be filed with a court when a party wishes to appeal a judgment or order issued by the court. Often, the notice of appeal must be filed within ten days of the date the order or judgment is entered in the court's records.

Objection. A document one party files to oppose a proposed action by another party—for instance, when a creditor or trustee files an objection to a bankruptcy debtor's claim of exemption.

Order for relief. The court's automatic injunction against certain collection and other activities that might negatively affect the bankruptcy estate. Another name for the "automatic stay."

Oversecured debt. A debt that is secured by collateral that is worth more than the amount of the debt.

PACER. An online, fee-based database containing bankruptcy court dockets (records of proceedings in bankruptcy cases) and federal court documents, such as court rules and recent appellate court decisions.

Pain and suffering damages. The portion of a court judgment intended to compensate for past, present, and future mental and physical pain, suffering, impairment of ability to work, and mental distress caused by an injury.

Partially secured debt. A debt secured by collateral that is worth less than the debt itself—for instance, when a person owes $15,000 on a car that is worth only $10,000.

Party in interest. Any person or entity that has a financial interest in the outcome of a bankruptcy case, including the trustee, the debtor, and all creditors.

Pension. A fund into which payments are made to provide an employee income after retirement. Typically, the beneficiary can't access the account without incurring a significant penalty, usually a tax. There are many types of pensions, including defined benefit pensions provided by many large corporations and individual pensions (such as 401(k) and IRA accounts). In bankruptcy, most pensions are not considered part of the bankruptcy estate and are therefore not affected by a bankruptcy filing.

Personal financial responsibility counseling. Under the new bankruptcy law, a two-hour class intended to teach good budget management. Every consumer bankruptcy filer must attend such a class in order to obtain a discharge in Chapter 7, Chapter 12, or Chapter 13 bankruptcy.

Personal injury cause of action. The right to seek compensation for physical and mental suffering, including injury to body, reputation, or both. For example, someone who is hit and injured by a car might have a personal injury cause of action against the driver.

Personal injury recovery. The portion of a lawsuit judgment or insurance settlement that is intended to compensate someone for physical and mental suffering, including physical injury, injury to reputation, or both. Bankruptcy exemptions usually do not apply to compensation for pain or suffering or punitive damages—in other words, that part of the recovery can be taken by the trustee in a Chapter 7 case.

Personal property. All property not classified as real property, including tangible items such as cars and jewelry, and intangible property such as stocks and pensions.

Petition. The document a debtor files to officially begin a bankruptcy case and ask for relief. Other documents and schedules must be filed to support the petition at the time it is filed, or shortly afterwards.

Pets. *See* "animals."

Preference. A payment made by a debtor to a creditor within a defined period prior to filing for bankruptcy—within three months for arms-length creditors (regular commercial creditors) and one year for insider creditors (friends, family, business associates). Because a preference gives that debtor an edge over other debtors in the bankruptcy case, the trustee can recover the preference and distribute it among all of the creditors.

Pre-petition. Any time prior to the moment the bankruptcy petition is filed.

Pre-petition counseling. Debt or credit counseling that occurs before the bankruptcy petition is filed—as opposed to personal financial management counseling, which occurs after the petition is filed.

Presumed abuse. In a Chapter 7 bankruptcy, when the debtor has a current monthly income in excess of the family median income for the state where the debtor lives, and has sufficient income to propose a Chapter 13 plan under the "means test." If abuse is presumed, the debtor has to prove that his or her Chapter 7 filing is not abusive in order to proceed further.

Primarily business debts. When the majority of debt owed by a bankruptcy debtor—in dollar terms—arises from debts incurred to operate a business.

Primarily consumer debts. When the majority of debt owed by a bankruptcy debtor—in dollar terms—arises from debts incurred for personal or family purposes.

Priority claim. *See* "priority debt."

Priority creditor. A creditor who has filed a Proof of Claim showing that the debtor owes it a priority debt.

Priority debt. A type of debt that is paid first if there are distributions to be made from the bankruptcy estate. Priority debts include alimony and child support, fees owed to the trustee and attorneys in the case, and wages owed to employees. With one exception (back child support obligations assigned to government entities), priority claims must be paid in full in a Chapter 13 bankruptcy.

Proceeds for damaged exempt property. Money received through insurance coverage, arbitration, mediation, settlement, or a lawsuit to pay for exempt property that has been damaged or destroyed. For example, if a debtor had the right to use a $30,000 homestead exemption, but his or her home was destroyed by fire, the debtor can instead exempt $30,000 of the insurance proceeds.

Projected disposable income. The amount of income a debtor will have left over each month, after deducting allowable expenses, payments on mandatory debts, and administrative expenses from his or her current monthly income. This is the amount the debtor must pay towards his or her unsecured nonpriority debts in a Chapter 13 plan.

Proof of Claim. A formal document filed by bankruptcy creditors in a bankruptcy case to assert their right to payments from the bankruptcy estate, if any payments are made.

Proof of service. A document signed under penalty of perjury by the person serving a document showing how the service was made, who made it, and when.

Property of the estate. *See* "bankruptcy estate."

Purchase money loans. Loans that are made to purchase specific property items, and that use the property as collateral to assure repayment, such as car loans and mortgages.

Purchase money security interest. A claim on property owned by the holder of a loan that was used to purchase the property and that is secured by the property (as collateral).

Reaffirmation. An agreement entered into after a bankruptcy filing (post-petition) between the debtor and a creditor in which the debtor agrees to repay all or part of a pre-petition debt after the bankruptcy is over. For instance, a debtor makes an agreement with the holder of a car note that the debtor can keep the car and must continue to pay the debt after bankruptcy.

Real property. Real estate (land and buildings on the land, usually including mobile homes attached to a foundation).

Reasonable investigation. A bankruptcy attorney's obligation, under the new bankruptcy law, to look into the information provided to them by their clients.

Redemption. In a Chapter 7 bankruptcy, when the debtor obtains legal title to collateral for a secured debt by paying the secured creditor the replacement value of the collateral in a lump sum. For example, a debtor may redeem a car note by paying the lender the replacement value of the car (what a retail vendor would charge for the car, considering its age and condition).

Reopen a case. To open a closed bankruptcy case—usually for the purpose of adding an overlooked creditor or filing a motion to avoid an overlooked lien. A debtor must request that the court reopen the case.

Repayment plan. An informal plan to repay creditors most or all of what they are owed outside of bankruptcy. Also refers to the plan proposed by a debtor in a Chapter 13 case.

Replacement cost. What it would cost to replace a particular item by buying it from a retail vendor, considering its age and condition—for instance, when buying a car from a used car dealer, furniture from a used furniture shop, or electronic equipment on eBay.

Repossession. When a secured creditor takes property used as collateral because the debtor has defaulted on the loan secured by the collateral.

Request to lift the stay. A written request filed in bankruptcy court by a creditor, which seeks permission to engage in debt collection activity otherwise prohibited by the automatic stay.

Schedule A. The official bankruptcy form a debtor must file to describe all of his or her real property

Schedule B. The official bankruptcy form a debtor must file to describe all personal property owned by the debtor, including tangible property such as jewelry and vehicles, and intangible property such as investments and accounts receivable.

Schedule C. The official bankruptcy form a debtor must file to describe the property the debtor is claiming as exempt, and the legal basis for the claims of exemption.

Schedule D. The official bankruptcy form a debtor must file to describe all secured debts owed by the debtor, such as car notes and mortgages.

Schedule E. The official bankruptcy form a debtor must file to describe all priority debts owed by the debtor, such as back child support and taxes.

Schedule F. The official bankruptcy form a debtor must file to describe all non-priority, unsecured debts owed by the debtor, such as most credit card and medical bills.

Schedule G. The official bankruptcy form a debtor must file to describe any leases and executory contracts (contracts under which one or both parties still have obligations) to which the debtor is a party.

Schedule H. The official bankruptcy form a debtor must file to describe all codebtors that might be affected by the bankruptcy.

Schedule I. The official bankruptcy form a debtor must file to describe the debtor's income.

Schedule J. The official bankruptcy form a debtor must file to describe the debtor's actual monthly expenses.

Schedules. Official bankruptcy forms a debtor must file, detailing the debtor's property, debts, income, and expenses.

Second deed of trust. A loan against real estate made after the original mortgage (or first deed of trust). Most home equity loans are second deeds of trust.

Secured claim. A debt secured by collateral under a written agreement (for instance, a mortgage or car note) or by operation of law—such as a tax lien.

Secured creditor. The owner of a secured claim.

Secured debt. A debt secured by collateral.

Secured interest. A claim to property used as collateral. For instance, a lender on a car note retains legal title to the car until the loan is paid off.

Secured property. Property that is collateral for a secured debt.

Serial bankruptcy filing. A practice used by some debtors to file and dismiss one bankruptcy after another to obtain the protection of the automatic stay, even though the bankruptcies themselves offer no debt relief—for instance, when a debtor files successive Chapter 13 cases to prevent foreclosure of his or her home even though there are no debts to repay.

Sickness benefits. *See* "disability benefits."

State exemptions. State laws that specify the types of property creditors are not entitled to take to satisfy a debt, and the bankruptcy trustee is not entitled to take and sell for the benefit of the debtor's unsecured creditors.

Statement of Affairs. The official bankruptcy form a debtor must file to describe the debtor's legal, economic, and business transactions for the several years prior to filing, including gifts, preferences, income, closing of deposit accounts, lawsuits, and other information that the trustee needs to assess the legitimacy of the bankruptcy and the true extent of the bankruptcy estate.

Statement of Current Monthly Income and Disposable Income Calculation. The official bankruptcy form a debtor must file in a Chapter 13 case, setting out the debtor's current monthly income and calculating the debtor's projected disposable income that will determine how much will be paid to the debtor's unsecured creditors.

Statement of Current Monthly Income and Means Test Calculation. The official bankruptcy form a debtor must file in a Chapter 7 filing that shows the debtor's current monthly income, calculates whether the debtor's income is higher than the state's median family income, and, if so, uses the means test to determine whether a Chapter 7 bankruptcy would constitute abuse.

Statement of Intention. The official bankruptcy form a debtor must file in a Chapter 7 case to tell the court and secured creditors how the debtor plans to treat his or her secured debts—that is, reaffirm the debt, redeem the debt, or surrender the property and discharge the debt.

Statement of Social Security Number. The official bankruptcy form a debtor must file to disclose the debtor's complete Social Security number.

Statutory lien. A lien imposed on property by law, such as tax liens and mechanics' liens, as opposed to voluntary liens (such as mortgages) and liens arising from court judgments (judicial liens).

Stay. *See* "automatic stay."

Stipulated insurance. An insurance policy that allows the insurance company to assess an amount on the insured, above the standard premium payments, if the company experiences losses worse than had been calculated into the standard premium. Also called assessment, mutual assessment, or mutual life insurance.

Stock options. A contract between a corporation and an employee that gives the employee the right to purchase corporate stock at a specific price mentioned in the contract (the strike price).

Strip down of lien. In a Chapter 13 bankruptcy, when the amount of a lien on collateral is reduced to the collateral's replacement value. *See* "cramdown."

Student loan. A type of loan made for educational purposes by nonprofit or commercial lenders with repayment and interest terms dictated by federal law. Student loans are not dischargeable in bankruptcy unless the debtor can show that repaying the loan would impose an "undue hardship."

Substantial abuse. Under the old bankruptcy law, filing a Chapter 7 bankruptcy when a Chapter 13 bankruptcy was feasible.

Suits, executions, garnishments, and attachments. Activities engaged in by creditors to enforce money judgments, typically involving the seizure of wages and bank accounts.

Summary of Schedules. The official bankruptcy form a debtor must file to summarize the property and debt information contained in a debtor's schedules

Surrender value. *See* "avails."

Surrendering collateral. In Chapter 7 bankruptcy, the act of returning collateral to a secured lender in order to discharge the underlying debt—for example, returning a car to discharge the car note.

Tangible personal property. *See* "tangible property" *and* "personal property."

Tangible property. Property that may be physically touched. Examples include money, furniture, cars, jewelry, artwork, and houses. *Compare* Intangible property.

Tax lien. A statutory lien imposed on property to secure payment of back taxes—typically income and property taxes.

Tenancy by the entirety. A way that married couples can hold title to property in about half of the states. When one spouse dies, the surviving spouse automatically owns 100% of the property. In most cases, this type of property is not part of the bankruptcy estate if only one spouse files.

To ____ acres. A limitation on the size of a homestead that may be exempted.

Tools of the trade. Items needed to perform a line of work that you are currently doing and relying on for support. For a mechanic, plumber, or carpenter, for example, tools of trade are the implements used to repair, build, and install. Traditionally, tools of the trade were limited to items that could be held in the hand. Most states, however, now embrace a broader definition, and a debtor may be able to fit many items under a tool of trade exemption.

Transcript of tax return. A summary of a debtor's tax return provided by the IRS upon the debtor's request, usually acceptable as a substitute for the return in the instances when a return must be filed under the new bankruptcy law.

Trustee. An official appointed by the bankruptcy court to carry out the administrative tasks associated with a bankruptcy and to seize and sell nonexempt property in the bankruptcy estate for the benefit of the debtor's unsecured creditors.

U.S. Trustee. An official employed by Office of the U.S. Trustee (a division of the U.S. Department of Justice) who is responsible for overseeing the bankruptcy trustees, regulating credit and personal financial management counselors, regulating bankruptcy petition preparers, auditing bankruptcy cases, ferreting out fraud, and generally making sure that the bankruptcy laws are obeyed.

Undersecured debt. A debt secured by collateral that is worth less than the debt.

Undue hardship. The conditions under which a debtor may discharge a student loan—for example, when the debtor has no income and little chance of earning enough to repay the loan in the future.

Unexpired lease. A lease that is still in effect.

Unmatured life insurance. A policy that is not yet payable because the insured is still alive.

Unscheduled debt. A debt that is not included in the schedules accompanying a bankruptcy filing, perhaps because it was overlooked or intentionally left out.

Unsecured priority claims. Priority claims that aren't secured by collateral, such as back child support or taxes for which no lien has been placed on the debtor's property.

Valuation of property. The act of determining the replacement value of property for the purpose of describing it in the bankruptcy schedules, determining whether it is protected by an applicable exemption, redeeming secured property, or cramming down a lien in Chapter 13 bankruptcy.

Voluntary dismissal. When a bankruptcy debtor dismisses his or her Chapter 7 or Chapter 13 case on his or her own, without coercion by the court.

Voluntary lien. A lien agreed to by the debtor, as when the debtor signs a mortgage, car note, or second deed of trust.

Weekly net earnings. The earnings a debtor has left after mandatory deductions, such as income tax, mandatory union dues, and Social Security contributions, have been subtracted from his or her gross income.

Wildcard exemption. A dollar value that the debtor can apply to any type of property to make it—or more of it—exempt. In some states, filers may use the unused portion of a homestead exemption as a wildcard exemption.

Willful and malicious act. An act done with the intent to cause harm. In a Chapter 7 bankruptcy, a debt arising from the debtor's willful and malicious act is not discharged if the victim proves to the bankruptcy court's satisfaction that the act occurred.

Willful or malicious act resulting in a civil judgment. A bad act that was careless or reckless, but was not necessarily intended to cause harm. In a Chapter 13 case, a debt arising from the debtor's act that was either willful or malicious is not discharged if it is part of a civil judgment.

Wrongful death cause of action. The right to seek compensation for having to live without a deceased person. Usually only the spouse and children of the deceased have a wrongful death cause of action.

Wrongful death recoveries. The portion of a lawsuit judgment intended to compensate a plaintiff for having to live without a deceased person. The compensation is intended to cover the earnings and the emotional comfort and support the deceased would have provided.

Federal and State Exemption Tables

Alabama

Federal Bankruptcy Exemptions not available. All law references are to Alabama Code.

ASSET	EXEMPTION	LAW
homestead	Real property or mobile home to $5,000; property cannot exceed 160 acres	6-10-2
	Must record homestead declaration before attempted sale of home	6-10-20
insurance	Annuity proceeds or avails to $250 per month	27-14-32
	Disability proceeds or avails to an average of $250 per month	27-14-31
	Fraternal benefit society benefits	27-34-27
	Life insurance proceeds or avails	6-10-8; 27-14-29
	Life insurance proceeds or avails if clause prohibits proceeds from being used to pay beneficiary's creditors	27-15-26
	Mutual aid association benefits	27-30-25
pensions	IRAs & other retirement accounts	19-3-1
	Judges (only payments being received)	12-18-10(a),(b)
	Law enforcement officers	36-21-77
	State employees	36-27-28
	Teachers	16-25-23
personal property	Books of debtor & family	6-10-6
	Burial place for self & family	6-10-5
	Church pew for self & family	6-10-5
	Clothing of debtor & family	6-10-6
	Family portraits or pictures	6-10-6
public benefits	Aid to blind, aged, disabled; & other public assistance	38-4-8
	Crime victims' compensation	15-23-15(e)
	Southeast Asian War POWs' benefits	31-7-2
	Unemployment compensation	25-4-140
	Workers' compensation	25-5-86(b)
tools of trade	Arms, uniforms, equipment that state military personnel are required to keep	31-2-78
wages	With respect to consumer loans, consumer credit sales, & consumer leases, 75% of weekly net earnings or 30 times the federal minimum hourly wage; all other cases, 75% of earned but unpaid wages; bankruptcy judge may authorize more for low-income debtors	5-19-15; 6-10-7
wildcard	$3,000 of any personal property, except wages	6-10-6

Alaska

Alaska law states that only the items found in Alaska Statutes §§ 9.38.010, 9.38.015(a), 9.38.017, 9.38.020, 9.38.025, and 9.38.030 may be exempted in bankruptcy. In *In re McNutt,* 87 B.R. 84 (9th Cir. 1988), however, an Alaskan debtor used the federal bankruptcy exemptions. All law references are to Alaska Statutes.

Alaska exemption amounts are adjusted regularly by administrative order. Current amounts are found at 8 Alaska Admin. Code tit. 8, § 95.030.

ASSET	EXEMPTION	LAW
homestead	$67,500 (joint owners may each claim a portion, but total can't exceed $67,500)	09.38.010(a)
insurance	Disability benefits	09.38.015(b); 09.38.030(e)(1),(5)

ASSET	EXEMPTION	LAW
insurance (continued)	Fraternal benefit society benefits	21.84.240
	Life insurance or annuity contracts, total aggregate cash surrender value to $12,500	09.38.025
	Medical, surgical, or hospital benefits	09.38.015(a)(3)
miscellaneous	Alimony, to extent wages exempt	09.38.030(e)(2)
	Child support payments made by collection agency	09.38.015(b)
	Liquor licenses	09.38.015(a)(7)
	Property of business partnership	09.38.100(b)
pensions	Elected public officers (only benefits building up)	09.38.015(b)
	ERISA-qualified benefits deposited more than 120 days before filing bankruptcy	09.38.017
	Judicial employees (only benefits building up)	09.38.015(b)
	Public employees (only benefits building up)	09.38.015(b); 39.35.505
	Roth & traditional IRAs, medical savings accounts	09.38.017(e)(3)
	Teachers (only benefits building up)	09.38.015(b)
	Other pensions, to extent wages exempt (only payments being received)	09.38.030(e)(5)
personal property	Books, musical instruments, clothing, family portraits, household goods, & heirlooms to $3,750 total	09.38.020(a)
	Building materials	34.35.105
	Burial plot	09.38.015(a)(1)
	Cash or other liquid assets to $1,750; for sole wage earner in household, $2,750 (restrictions apply—see *wages*)	09.38.030(b)
	Deposit in apartment or condo owners' association	09.38.010(e)
	Health aids needed	09.38.015(a)(2)
	Jewelry to $1,250	09.38.020(b)
	Motor vehicle to $3,750; vehicle's market value can't exceed $25,000	09.38.020(e)
	Personal injury recoveries, to extent wages exempt	09.38.030(e)(3)
	Pets to $1,250	09.38.020(d)
	Proceeds for lost, damaged, or destroyed exempt property	09.38.060
	Tuition credits under an advance college tuition payment contract	09.38.015(a)(8)
	Wrongful death recoveries, to extent wages exempt	09.38.030(e)(3)
public benefits	Adult assistance to elderly, blind, disabled	47.25.550
	Alaska longevity bonus	09.38.015(a)(5)
	Crime victims' compensation	09.38.015(a)(4)
	Federally exempt public benefits paid or due	09.38.015(a)(6)
	General relief assistance	47.25.210
	20% of permanent fund dividends	43.23.065
	Unemployment compensation	09.38.015(b); 23.20.405
	Workers' compensation	23.30.160
tools of trade	Implements, books, & tools of trade to $3,500	09.38.020(c)
wages	Weekly net earnings to $438; for sole wage earner in a household, $688; if you don't receive weekly or semimonthly pay, can claim $1,750 in cash or liquid assets paid any month; for sole wage earner in household, $2,750	9.38.030(a),(b); 9.38.050(b)
wildcard	None	

Arizona

Federal Bankruptcy Exemptions not available. All law references are to Arizona Revised Statutes unless otherwise noted.

ASSET	EXEMPTION	LAW
homestead	Real property, an apartment, or mobile home you occupy to $150,000; sale proceeds exempt 18 months after sale or until new home purchased, whichever occurs first (husband & wife may not double)	33-1101(A)
	May record homestead declaration to clarify which one of multiple eligible parcels is being claimed as homestead	33-1102
insurance	Fraternal benefit society benefits	20-877
	Group life insurance policy or proceeds	20-1132
	Health, accident, or disability benefits	33-1126(A)(4)
	Life insurance cash value or proceeds to $25,000 total if beneficiary is spouse or child & owned at least two years	33-1126(A)(6); 20-1131(D)
	Life insurance proceeds to $20,000 if beneficiary is spouse or child	33-1126(A)(1)
miscellaneous	Alimony, child support needed for support	33-1126(A)(3)
	Minor child's earnings, unless debt is for child	33-1126(A)(2)
pensions *see also wages*	Board of regents members, faculty & administrative officers under board's jurisdiction	15-1628(I)
	District employees	48-227
	ERISA-qualified benefits deposited over 120 days before filing	33-1126(C)
	IRAs & Roth IRAs	33-1126(c) *In re Herrscher*, 121 B.R. 29 (D. Ariz. 1989)
	Firefighters	9-968
	Police officers	9-931
	Rangers	41-955
	State employees retirement & disability	38-792; 38-797.11
personal property *husband & wife may double all personal property*	2 beds & bedding; 1 living room chair per person; 1 dresser, table, lamp; kitchen table; dining room table & 4 chairs (1 more per person); living room carpet or rug; couch; 3 lamps; 3 coffee or end tables; pictures, paintings, personal drawings, family portraits; refrigerator, stove, washer, dryer, vacuum cleaner; TV, radio, stereo, alarm clock to $4,000 total	33-1123
	Bank deposit to $150 in one account	33-1126(A)(8)
	Bible; bicycle; sewing machine; typewriter; burial plot; rifle, pistol, or shotgun to $500 total	33-1125
	Books to $250; clothing to $500; wedding & engagement rings to $1,000; watch to $100; pets, horses, milk cows, & poultry to $500; musical instruments to $250	33-1125
	Food & fuel to last 6 months	33-1124
	Funeral deposits to $5,000	32-1391.05(4)
	Health aids	33-1125(9)
	Motor vehicle to $5,000 ($10,000, if disabled)	33-1125(8)
	Prepaid rent or security deposit to $1,000 or 1-1/2 times your rent, whichever is less, in lieu of homestead	33-1126(D)
	Proceeds for sold or damaged exempt property	33-1126(A)(5),(7)
	Wrongful death awards	12-592
public benefits	Unemployment compensation	23-783(A)
	Welfare benefits	46-208
	Workers' compensation	23-1068(B)

ASSET	EXEMPTION	LAW
tools of trade *husband &* *wife may* *double*	Arms, uniforms, & accoutrements of profession or office required by law	33-1130(3)
	Farm machinery, utensils, seed, instruments of husbandry, feed, grain, & animals to $2,500 total	33-1130(2)
	Library & teaching aids of teacher	33-1127
	Tools, equipment, instruments, & books to $2,500	33-1130(1)
wages	75% of earned but unpaid weekly net earnings or 30 times the federal minimum hourly wage; 50% of wages for support orders; bankruptcy judge may authorize more for low-income debtors	33-1131
wildcard	None	

Arkansas

Federal Bankruptcy Exemptions available. All law references are to Arkansas Code Annotated unless otherwise noted.

Note: *In re Holt*, 894 F.2d 1005 (8th Cir. 1990) held that Arkansas residents are limited to exemptions in the Arkansas Constitution. Statutory exemptions can still be used within Arkansas for nonbankruptcy purposes, but they cannot be claimed in bankruptcy

ASSET	EXEMPTION	LAW
homestead *choose option* *1 or 2*	1. For married person or head of family: unlimited exemption on real or personal property used as residence to 1/4 acre in city, town, or village, or 80 acres elsewhere; if property is between 1/4–1 acre in city, town, or village, or 80-160 acres elsewhere, additional limit is $2,500; homestead may not exceed 1 acre in city, town, or village, or 160 acres elsewhere (husband & wife may not double)	Constitution 9-3; 9-4, 9-5; 16-66-210; 16-66-218(b)(3), (4) *In re Stevens*, 829 F.2d 693 (8th Cir. 1987)
	2. Real or personal property used as residence to $800 if single; $1,250 if married	16-66-218(a)(1)
insurance	Annuity contract	23-79-134
	Disability benefits	23-79-133
	Fraternal benefit society benefits	23-74-403
	Group life insurance	23-79-132
	Life, health, accident, or disability cash value or proceeds paid or due to $500	16-66-209; Constitution 9-1, 9-2; *In re Holt*, 894 F. 2d 1005 (7th Cir. 1990)
	Life insurance proceeds if clause prohibits proceeds from being used to pay beneficiary's creditors	23-79-131
	Life insurance proceeds or avails if beneficiary isn't the insured	23-79-131
	Mutual assessment life or disability benefits to $1,000	23-72-114
	Stipulated insurance premiums	23-71-112
miscellaneous	Property of business partnership (will be repealed in 2005)	4-42-502
pensions	Disabled firefighters	24-11-814
	Disabled police officers	24-11-417
	Firefighters	24-10-616
	IRA deposits to $20,000 if deposited over 1 year before filing for bankruptcy	16-66-218(b)(16)
	Police officers	24-10-616
	School employees	24-7-715
	State police officers	24-6-205; 24-6-223

ASSET	EXEMPTION	LAW
personal property	Burial plot to 5 acres, if choosing federal homestead exemption (option 2)	16-66-207; 16-66-218(a)(1)
	Clothing	Constitution 9-1, 9-2
	Motor vehicle to $1,200	16-66-218(a)(2)
	Prepaid funeral trusts	23-40-117
	Wedding rings	16-66-219
public benefits	Crime victims' compensation	16-90-716(e)
	Unemployment compensation	11-10-109
	Workers' compensation	11-9-110
tools of trade	Implements, books, & tools of trade to $750	16-66-218(a)(4)
wages	Earned but unpaid wages due for 60 days; in no event less than $25 per week	16-66-208; 16-66-218(b)(6)
wildcard	$500 of any personal property if married or head of family; $200 if not married	Constitution 9-1, 9-2; 16-66-218(b)(1),(2)

California—System 1

Federal Bankruptcy Exemptions not available. California has two systems; you must select one or the other. All law references are to California Code of Civil Procedure unless otherwise noted. Many exemptions do not apply to claims for child support.

Note: California's exemption amounts are no longer updated in the statutes themselves. California Code of Civil Procedure section 740.150 deputized the California Judicial Council to update the exemption amounts every three years. (The next revision will be in 2007.) As a result, the amounts listed in this chart will not match the amounts that appear in the cited statutes. The current exemption amounts can be found on the California Judicial Council website, www.courtinfo.ca.gov/forms/documents/exemptions.pdf.

ASSET	EXEMPTION	LAW
homestead	Real or personal property you occupy including mobile home, boat, stock cooperative, community apartment, planned development, or condo to $50,000 if single & not disabled; $75,000 for families if no other member has a homestead (if only one spouse files, may exempt one-half of amount if home held as community property & all of amount if home held as tenants in common); $150,000 if 65 or older, or physically or mentally disabled; $150,000 if 55 or older, single, & earn under $15,000 or married & earn under $20,000 & creditors seek to force the sale of your home; forced sale proceeds received exempt for 6 months after (husband & wife may not double.)	704.710; 704.720; 704.730 In re McFall, 112 B.R. 336 (9th Cir. B.A.P. 1990)
	May file homestead declaration to protect exemption amount from attachment of judicial liens and to protect proceeds of voluntary sale for 6 months	704.920
insurance	Disability or health benefits	704.130
	Fidelity bonds	Labor 404
	Fraternal benefit society benefits	704.170
	Fraternal unemployment benefits	704.120
	Homeowners' insurance proceeds for 6 months after received, to homestead exemption amount	704.720(b)
	Life insurance proceeds if clause prohibits proceeds from being used to pay beneficiary's creditors	Ins. 10132; Ins. 10170; Ins. 10171

ASSET	EXEMPTION	LAW
insurance (continued)	Matured life insurance benefits needed for support	704.100(c)
	Unmatured life insurance policy cash surrender value completely exempt. Loan value exempt to $9,700	704.100(b)
miscellaneous	Business or professional licenses	695.060
	Inmates' trust funds to $1,225 (husband & wife may not double)	704.090
	Property of business partnership	Corp. 16501-04
pensions	County employees	Gov't 31452
	County firefighters	Gov't 32210
	County peace officers	Gov't 31913
	Private retirement benefits, including IRAs & Keoghs	704.115
	Public employees	Gov't 21255
	Public retirement benefits	704.110
personal property	Appliances, furnishings, clothing, & food	704.020
	Bank deposits from Social Security Administration to $2,425 ($3,650 for husband & wife); unlimited if SS funds are not commingled with other funds Bank deposits of other public benefits to $1,225 ($1,825 for husband & wife)	704.080
	Building materials to repair or improve home to $2,425 (husband & wife may not double)	704.030
	Burial plot	704.200
	Funds held in escrow	Fin. 17410
	Health aids	704.050
	Jewelry, heirlooms, & art to $6,075 total (husband & wife may not double)	704.040
	Motor vehicles to $2,300, or $2,300 in auto insurance for loss or damages (husband & wife may not double)	704.010
	Personal injury & wrongful death causes of action	704.140(a); 704.150(a)
	Personal injury & wrongful death recoveries needed for support; if receiving installments, at least 75%	704.140(b),(c),(d); 704.150(b),(c)
public benefits	Aid to blind, aged, disabled; public assistance	704.170
	Financial aid to students	704.190
	Relocation benefits	704.180
	Unemployment benefits	704.120
	Union benefits due to labor dispute	704.120(b)(5)
	Workers' compensation	704.160
tools of trade	Tools, implements, materials, instruments, uniforms, books, furnishings, & equipment to $6,075 total ($12,150 total if used by both spouses in same occupation)	704.060
	Commercial vehicle (Vehicle Code § 260) to $4,850 ($9,700 total if used by both spouses in same occupation)	704.060
wages	Minimum 75% of wages paid within 30 days prior to filing	704.070
	Public employees' vacation credits; if receiving installments, at least 75%	704.113
wildcard	None	

California—System 2

Refer to the noes for California—System 1, above.

Note: Married couples may not double any exemptions. (*In re Talmadge*, 832 F.2d 1120 (9th Cir. 1987); *In re Baldwin*, 70 B.R. 612 (9th Cir. B.A.P. 1987).)

ASSET	EXEMPTION	LAW
homestead	Real or personal property, including co-op, used as residence to $18,675; unused portion of homestead may be applied to any property	703.140(b)(1)
insurance	Disability benefits	703.140(b)(10)(C)
	Life insurance proceeds needed for support of family	703.140(b)(11)(C)
	Unmatured life insurance contract accrued avails to $9,975	703.140(b)(8)
	Unmatured life insurance policy other than credit	703.140(b)(7)
miscellaneous	Alimony, child support needed for support	703.140(b)(10)(D)
pensions	ERISA-qualified benefits needed for support	703.140(b)(10)(E)
personal property	Animals, crops, appliances, furnishings, household goods, books, musical instruments, & clothing to $475 per item	703.140(b)(3)
	Burial plot to $18,675, in lieu of homestead	703.140(b)(1)
	Health aids	703.140(b)(9)
	Jewelry to $1,225	703.140(b)(4)
	Motor vehicle to $2,975	703.140(b)(2)
	Personal injury recoveries to $18,675 (not to include pain & suffering; pecuniary loss)	703.140(b)(11) (D),(E)
	Wrongful death recoveries needed for support	703.140(b)(11)(B)
public benefits	Crime victims' compensation	703.140(b)(11)(A)
	Public assistance	703.140(b)(10)(A)
	Social Security	703.140(b)(10)(A)
	Unemployment compensation	703.140(b)(10)(A)
	Veterans' benefits	703.140(b)(10)(B)
tools of trade	Implements, books, & tools of trade to $1,875	703.140(b)(6)
wages	None (use federal nonbankruptcy wage exemption)	
wildcard	$1,000 of any property	703.140(b)(5)
	Unused portion of homestead or burial exemption of any property	703.140(b)(5)

Colorado

Federal Bankruptcy Exemptions not available. All law references are to Colorado Revised Statutes.

ASSET	EXEMPTION	LAW
homestead	Real property, mobile home, manufactured home, or house trailer you occupy to $45,000; sale proceeds exempt 1 year after received	38-41-201; 38-41-201.6; 38-41-203; 38-41-207; *In re Pastrana*, 216 B.R. 948 (Colo., 1998)
	Spouse or child of deceased owner may claim homestead exemption	38-41-204
insurance	Disability benefits to $200 per month; if receive lump sum, entire amount exempt	10-16-212
	Fraternal benefit society benefits	10-14-403
	Group life insurance policy or proceeds	10-7-205

ASSET	EXEMPTION	LAW
insurance (continued)	Homeowners' insurance proceeds for 1 year after received, to homestead exemption amount	38-41-209
	Life insurance cash surrender value to $50,000, except contributions to policy within past 48 months	13-54-102(1)(l)
	Life insurance proceeds if clause prohibits proceeds from being used to pay beneficiary's creditors	10-7-106
miscellaneous	Child support	13-54-102.5
	Property of business partnership	7-60-125
pensions *see also wages*	ERISA-qualified benefits, including IRAs & Roth IRAs	13-54-102(1)(s)
	Firefighters & police officers	31-30.5-208; 31-31-203
	Public employees' pensions & defined contribution plans as of 2006	24-51-212
	Public employees' deferred compensation	24-52-105
	Teachers	22-64-120
	Veteran's pension for veteran, spouse, or dependents if veteran served in war or armed conflict	13-54-102(1)(h); 13-54-104
personal property	1 burial plot per family member	13-54-102(1)(d)
	Clothing to $1,500	13-54-102(1)(a)
	Food & fuel to $600	13-54-102(1)(f)
	Health aids	13-54-102(1)(p)
	Household goods to $3,000	13-54-102(1)(e)
	Jewelry & articles of adornment to $1,000	13-54-102(1)(b)
	Motor vehicles or bicycles used for work to $3,000; to $6,000 if used by a debtor or by a dependent who is disabled or 65 or over	13-54-102(j)(I), (II)
	Personal injury recoveries	13-54-102(1)(n)
	Family pictures & books to $1,500	13-54-102(1)(c)
	Proceeds for damaged exempt property	13-54-102(1)(m)
	Security deposits	13-54-102(1)(r)
public benefits	Aid to blind, aged, disabled; public assistance	26-2-131
	Crime victims' compensation	13-54-102(1)(q); 24-4.1-114
	Earned income tax credit	13-54-102(1)(o)
	Unemployment compensation	8-80-103
	Veteran's benefits for veteran, spouse, or child if veteran served in war or armed conflict	13-54-102(1)(h)
	Workers' compensation	8-42-124
tools of trade	Livestock or other animals, machinery, tools, equipment, & seed of person engaged in agriculture, to $25,000 total	13-54-102(1)(g)
	Professional's library to $3,000 (if not claimed under other tools of trade exemption)	13-54-102(1)(k)
	Stock in trade, supplies, fixtures, tools, machines, electronics, equipment, books, & other business materials, to $10,000 total	13-54-102(1)(i)
	Military equipment personally owned by members of the National Guard	13-54-102(1)(h.5)
wages	Minimum 75% of weekly net earnings or 30 times the federal minimum wage, whichever is greater, including pension & insurance payments	13-54-104
wildcard	None	

Connecticut

Federal Bankruptcy Exemptions available. All law references are to Connecticut General Statutes Annotated.

ASSET	EXEMPTION	LAW
homestead	Real property, including mobile or manufactured home, to $75,000; applies only to claims arising after 1993, but to $125,000 in the case of a money judgment arising out of services provided at a hospital	52-352a(e); 52-352b(t)
insurance	Disability benefits paid by association for its members	52-352b(p)
	Fraternal benefit society benefits	38a-637
	Health or disability benefits	52-352b(e)
	Life insurance proceeds if clause prohibits proceeds from being used to pay beneficiary's creditors	38a-454
	Life insurance proceeds or avails	38a-453
	Unmatured life insurance policy loan value to $4,000	52-352b(s)
miscellaneous	Alimony, to extent wages exempt	52-352b(n)
	Child support	52-352b(h)
	Farm partnership animals & livestock feed reasonably required to run farm where at least 50% of partners are members of same family	52-352d
pensions	ERISA-qualified benefits, including IRAs, Roth IRAs, & Keoghs, to extent wages exempt	52-321a; 52-352b(m)
	Medical savings account	52-321a
	Municipal employees	7-446
	State employees	5-171; 5-192w
	Teachers	10-183q
personal property	Appliances, food, clothing, furniture, bedding	52-352b(a)
	Burial plot	52-352b(c)
	Health aids needed	52-352b(f)
	Motor vehicle to $1,500	52-352b(j)
	Proceeds for damaged exempt property	52-352b(q)
	Residential utility & security deposits for 1 residence	52-3252b(l)
	Spendthrift trust funds required for support of debtor & family	52-321(d)
	Transfers to a nonprofit debt adjuster	52-352b(u)
	Wedding & engagement rings	52-352b(k)
public benefits	Crime victims' compensation	52-352b(o); 54-213
	Public assistance	52-352b(d)
	Social Security	52-352b(g)
	Unemployment compensation	31-272(c); 52-352b(g)
	Veterans' benefits	52-352b(g)
	Workers' compensation	52-352b(g)
tools of trade	Arms, military equipment, uniforms, musical instruments of military personnel	52-352b(i)
	Tools, books, instruments, & farm animals needed	52-352b(b)
wages	Minimum 75% of earned but unpaid weekly disposable earnings, or 40 times the state or federal hourly minimum wage, whichever is greater	52-361a(f)
wildcard	$1,000 of any property	52-352b(r)

Delaware

Federal Bankruptcy Exemptions not available. All law references are to Delaware Code Annotated (in the form title number–section number) unless otherwise noted.

Note: A single person may exempt no more than $5,000 total in all exemptions (not including retirement plans); a husband & wife may exempt no more than $10,000 total (10-4914).

ASSET	EXEMPTION	LAW
homestead	None; however, property held as tenancy by the entirety may be exempt against debts owed by only one spouse	*In re Kelley,* 289 B.R. 38 (Bankr. D. Del. 2003)
insurance	Annuity contract proceeds to $350 per month	18-2728
	Fraternal benefit society benefits	18-6218
	Group life insurance policy or proceeds	18-2727
	Health or disability benefits	18-2726
	Life insurance proceeds if clause prohibits proceeds from being used to pay beneficiary's creditors	18-2729
	Life insurance proceeds or avails	18-2725
pensions	IRAs, Roth IRAs, & any other retirement plans	*In re Yuhas,* 104 F.3d 612 (3rd Cir. 1997)
	Kent County employees	9-4316
	Police officers	11-8803
	State employees	29-5503
	Volunteer firefighters	16-6653
personal property	Bible, books, & family pictures	10-4902(a)
	Burial plot	10-4902(a)
	Church pew or any seat in public place of worship	10-4902(a)
	Clothing, includes jewelry	10-4902(a)
	College investment plan account (limit for year before filing is $5,000 or average of past two years' contribution, whichever is more)	10-4916
	Income from spendthrift trusts	12-3536
	Pianos & leased organs	10-4902(d)
	Sewing machines	10-4902(c)
public benefits	Aid to blind	31-2309
	Aid to aged, disabled, general assistance	31-513
	Crime victims' compensation	11-9011
	Unemployment compensation	19-3374
	Workers' compensation	19-2355
tools of trade	Tools, implements, & fixtures to $75 in New Castle & Sussex Counties; to $50 in Kent County	10-4902(b)
wages	85% of earned but unpaid wages	10-4913
wildcard	$500 of any personal property, except tools of trade, if head of family	10-4903

District of Columbia

Federal Bankruptcy Exemptions available. All law references are to District of Columbia Code unless otherwise noted.

ASSET	EXEMPTION	LAW
homestead	Any property used as a residence or co-op that debtor or debtor's dependent uses as a residence	15-501(a)(14)
	Property held as tenancy by the entirety may be exempt against debts owed by only one spouse	*Estate of Wall,* 440 F.2d 215 (D.C. Cir. 1971)
insurance	Disability benefits	15-501(a)(7)
	Fraternal benefit society benefits	31-5315
	Group life insurance policy or proceeds	31-4717
	Life insurance payments	15-501(a)(11)
	Life insurance proceeds if clause prohibits proceeds from being used to pay beneficiary's creditors	31-4719
	Life insurance proceeds or avails	31-4716
	Other insurance proceeds to $200 per month, maximum 2 months, for head of family; else $60 per month	15-503
	Unmatured life insurance contract other than credit life insurance	15-501(a)(5)
miscellaneous	Alimony or child support	15-501(a)(7)
pensions *see also wages*	ERISA-qualified benefits, IRAs, Keoghs, etc. to maximum deductible contribution	15-501(b)(9)
	Any stock bonus, annuity, pension, or profit-sharing plan	15-501(a)(7)
	Judges	11-1570(d)
	Public school teachers	38-2001.17; 38-2021.17
personal property	Appliances, books, clothing, household furnishings, goods, musical instruments, pets to $425 per item or $8,625 total	15-501(a)(2)
	Cemetery & burial funds	27-111
	Cooperative association holdings to $50	29-928
	Food for 3 months	15-501(a)(12)
	Health aids	15-501(a)(6)
	Higher education tuition savings account	47-4510
	Residential condominium deposit	42-1904.09
	All family pictures; & all the family library, to $400	15-501(a)(8)
	Motor vehicle to $2,575	15-501(a)(1)
	Payment including pain & suffering for loss of debtor or person depended on	15-501(a)(11)
	Uninsured motorist benefits	31-2408.01(h)
	Wrongful death damages	15-501(a)(11)
public benefits	Aid to blind, aged, disabled; general assistance	4-215.01
	Crime victims' compensation	15-501(a)(11)
	Social Security	15-501(a)(7)
	Unemployment compensation	51-118
	Veterans' benefits	15-501(a)(7)
	Workers' compensation	32-1517

ASSET	EXEMPTION	LAW
tools of trade	Library, furniture, tools of professional, or artist to $300	15-501(a)(13)
	Tools of trade or business to $1,625	15-501(a)(5)
	Mechanic's tools to $200	15-503(b)
	Seal & documents of notary public	1-1206
wages	Minimum 75% of earned but unpaid wages, pension payments; bankruptcy judge may authorize more for low-income debtors	16-572
	Nonwage (including pension & retirement) earnings to $200/mo for head of family; else $60/mo for a maximum of two months	15-503
	Payment for loss of future earnings	15-501(e)(11)
wildcard	Up to $850 in any property, plus up to $8,075 of unused homestead exemption	15-501(a)(3)

Florida

Federal Bankruptcy Exemptions not available. All law references are to Florida Statutes Annotated unless otherwise noted.

ASSET	EXEMPTION	LAW
homestead	Real or personal property including mobile or modular home to unlimited value; cannot exceed half acre in municipality or 160 acres elsewhere; spouse or child of deceased owner may claim homestead exemption	222.01; 222.02; 222.03; 222.05; Constitution 10-4 *In re Colwell*, 196 F.3d 1225 (11th Cir. 1999)
	May file homestead declaration	222.01
	Property held as tenancy by the entirety may be exempt against debts owed by only one spouse	*Havoco of America, Ltd. v. Hill*, 197 F.3d 1135 (11th Cir Fla.,1999)
insurance	Annuity contract proceeds; does not include lottery winnings	222.14; *In re Pizzi*, 153 B.R. 357 (S.D. Fla. 1993)
	Death benefits payable to a specific beneficiary, not the deceased's estate	222.13
	Disability or illness benefits	222.18
	Fraternal benefit society benefits	632.619
	Life insurance cash surrender value	222.14
miscellaneous	Alimony, child support needed for support	222.201
	Damages to employees for injuries in hazardous occupations	769.05
pensions *see also wages*	County officers, employees	122.15
	ERISA-qualified benefits, including IRAs & Roth IRAs	222.21(2)
	Firefighters	175.241
	Police officers	185.25
	State officers, employees	121.131
	Teachers	238.15

ASSET	EXEMPTION	LAW
personal property	Any personal property to $1,000 (husband & wife may double)	Constitution 10-4 *In re Hawkins*, 51 B.R. 348 (S.D. Fla. 1985)
	Federal income tax refund or credit	222.25
	Health aids	222.25
	Motor vehicle to $1,000	222.25
	Pre-need funeral contract deposits	497.413(8)
	Prepaid college education trust deposits	222.22(1)
	Prepaid medical savings account deposits	222.22(2)
public benefits	Crime victims' compensation, unless seeking to discharge debt for treatment of injury incurred during the crime	960.14
	Public assistance	222.201
	Social Security	222.201
	Unemployment compensation	222.201; 443.051(2),(3)
	Veterans' benefits	222.201; 744.626
	Workers' compensation	440.22
tools of trade	None	
wages	100% of wages for heads of family up to $500 per week either unpaid or paid & deposited into bank account for up to 6 months	222.11
	Federal government employees' pension payments needed for support & received 3 months prior	222.21
wildcard	See personal property	

Georgia

Federal Bankruptcy Exemptions not available. All law references are to the Official Code of Georgia Annotated, not to the Georgia Code Annotated.

ASSET	EXEMPTION	LAW
homestead	Real or personal property, including co-op, used as residence to $10,000; up to $5,000 of unused portion of homestead may be applied to any property	44-13-100(a)(1); 44-13-100(a)(6)
insurance	Annuity & endowment contract benefits	33-28-7
	Disability or health benefits to $250 per month	33-29-15
	Fraternal benefit society benefits	33-15-62
	Group insurance	33-30-10
	Proceeds & avails of life insurance	33-26-5; 33-25-11
	Life insurance proceeds if policy owned by someone you depended on, needed for support	44-13-100(a)(11)(C)
	Unmatured life insurance contract	44-13-100(a)(8)
	Unmatured life insurance dividends, interest, loan value, or cash value to $2,000 if beneficiary is you or someone you depend on	44-13-100(a)(9)
miscellaneous	Alimony, child support needed for support	44-13-100(a)(2)(D)
pensions	Employees of nonprofit corporations	44-13-100(a)(2.1)(B)
	ERISA-qualified benefits & IRAs	18-4-22

ASSET	EXEMPTION	LAW
pensions (continued)	Public employees	44-13-100(a)(2.1)(A); 47-2-332
	Payments from IRA necessary for support	44-13-100(a)(2)(F)
	Other pensions needed for support	18-4-22; 44-13-100(a)(2)(E); 44-13-100(a)(2.1)(C)
personal property	Animals, crops, clothing, appliances, books, furnishings, household goods, musical instruments to $300 per item, $5,000 total	44-13-100(a)(4)
	Burial plot, in lieu of homestead	44-13-100(a)(1)
	Compensation for lost future earnings needed for support to $7,500	44-13-100(a)(11)(E)
	Health aids	44-13-100(a)(10)
	Jewelry to $500	44-13-100(a)(5)
	Motor vehicles to $3,500	44-13-100(a)(3)
	Personal injury recoveries to $10,000	44-13-100(a)(11)(D)
	Wrongful death recoveries needed for support	44-13-100(a)(11)(B)
public benefits	Aid to blind	49-4-58
	Aid to disabled	49-4-84
	Crime victims' compensation	44-13-100(a)(11)(A)
	Local public assistance	44-13-100(a)(2)(A)
	Old age assistance	49-4-35
	Social Security	44-13-100(a)(2)(A)
	Unemployment compensation	44-13-100(a)(2)(A)
	Veterans' benefits	44-13-100(a)(2)(B)
	Workers' compensation	34-9-84
tools of trade	Implements, books, & tools of trade to $1,500	44-13-100(a)(7)
wages	Minimum 75% of earned but unpaid weekly disposable earnings, or 40 times the state or federal hourly minimum wage, whichever is greater, for private & federal workers; bankruptcy judge may authorize more for low-income debtors	18-4-20; 18-4-21
wildcard	$600 of any property	44-13-100(a)(6)
	Unused portion of homestead exemption to $5,000	44-13-100(a)(6)

Hawaii

Federal Bankruptcy Exemptions available. All law references are to Hawaii Revised Statutes unless otherwise noted.

ASSET	EXEMPTION	LAW
homestead	Head of family or over 65 to $30,000; all others to $20,000; property cannot exceed 1 acre; sale proceeds exempt for 6 months after sale (husband & wife may not double)	651-91; 651-92; 651-96
	Property held as tenancy by the entirety may be exempt against debts owed by only one spouse	*Security Pacific Bank v. Chang,* 818 F.Supp. 1343 (D. Haw. 1993)
insurance	Annuity contract or endowment policy proceeds if beneficiary is insured's spouse, child, or parent	431:10-232(b)
	Accident, health, or sickness benefits	431:10-231
	Fraternal benefit society benefits	432:2-403

ASSET	EXEMPTION	LAW
insurance (continued)	Group life insurance policy or proceeds	431:10-233
	Life insurance proceeds if clause prohibits proceeds from being used to pay beneficiary's creditors	431:10D-112
	Life or health insurance policy for spouse or child	431:10-234
miscellaneous	Property of business partnership	425-125
pensions	ERISA-qualified benefits deposited over 3 years before filing bankruptcy	651-124
	Firefighters	88-169
	Police officers	88-169
	Public officers & employees	88-91; 653-3
personal property	Appliances & furnishings	651-121(1)
	Books	651-121(1)
	Burial plot to 250 sq. ft. plus tombstones, monuments, & fencing	651-121(4)
	Clothing	651-121(1)
	Jewelry, watches, & articles of adornment to $1,000	651-121(1)
	Motor vehicle to wholesale value of $2,575	651-121(2)
	Proceeds for sold or damaged exempt property; sale proceeds exempt for 6 months after sale	651-121(5)
public benefits	Crime victims' compensation & special accounts created to limit commercial exploitation of crimes	351-66; 351-86
	Public assistance paid by Dept. of Health Services for work done in home or workshop	346-33
	Temporary disability benefits	392-29
	Unemployment compensation	383-163
	Unemployment work relief funds to $60 per month	653-4
	Workers' compensation	386-57
tools of trade	Tools, implements, books, instruments, uniforms, furnishings, fishing boat, nets, motor vehicle, & other property needed for livelihood	651-121(3)
wages	Prisoner's wages held by Dept. of Public Safety (except for restitution, child support, & other claims)	353-22.5
	Unpaid wages due for services of past 31 days	651-121(6)
wildcard	None	

Idaho

Federal Bankruptcy Exemptions not available. All law references are to Idaho Code.

ASSET	EXEMPTION	LAW
homestead	Real property or mobile home to $50,000; sale proceeds exempt for 6 months (husband & wife may not double)	55-1003; 55-1113
	Must record homestead exemption for property that is not yet occupied	55-1004
insurance	Annuity contract proceeds to $1,250 per month	41-1836
	Death or disability benefits	11-604(1)(a); 41-1834
	Fraternal benefit society benefits	41-3218
	Group life insurance benefits	41-1835
	Homeowners' insurance proceeds to amount of homestead exemption	55-1008

ASSET	EXEMPTION	LAW
insurance (continued)	Life insurance proceeds if clause prohibits proceeds from being used to pay beneficiary's creditors	41-1930
	Life insurance proceeds or avails for beneficiary other than the insured	11-604(d); 41-1833
	Medical, surgical, or hospital care benefits	11-603(5)
	Unmatured life insurance contract, other than credit life insurance, owned by debtor	11-605(8)
	Unmatured life insurance contract interest or dividends to $5,000 owned by debtor or person debtor depends on	11-605(9)
miscellaneous	Alimony, child support	11-604(1)(b)
	Liquor licenses	23-514
pension see also wages	ERISA-qualified benefits	55-1011
	Firefighters	72-1422
	Government & private pensions, retirement plans, IRAs, Roth IRAs, Keoghs, etc.	11-604A
	Police officers	50-1517
	Public employees	59-1317
personal property	Appliances, furnishings, books, clothing, pets, musical instruments, 1 firearm, family portraits, & sentimental heirlooms to $500 per item, $5,000 total	11-605(1)
	Building materials	45-514
	Burial plot	11-603(1)
	College savings program account	11-604A(4)(b)
	Crops cultivated on maximum of 50 acres, to $1,000; water rights to 160 inches	11-605(6)
	Health aids	11-603(2)
	Jewelry to $1,000	11-605(2)
	Motor vehicle to $3,000	11-605(3)
	Personal injury recoveries	11-604(1)(c)
	Proceeds for damaged exempt property for 3 months after proceeds received	11-606
	Wrongful death recoveries	11-604(1)(c)
public benefits	Aid to blind, aged, disabled	56-223
	Federal, state, & local public assistance	11-603(4)
	General assistance	56-223
	Social Security	11-603(3)
	Unemployment compensation	11-603(6)
	Veterans' benefits	11-603(3)
	Workers' compensation	72-802
tools of trade	Arms, uniforms, & accoutrements that peace officer, National Guard, or military personnel is required to keep	11-605(5)
	Implements, books, & tools of trade to $1,500	11-605(3)
wages	Minimum 75% of earned but unpaid weekly disposable earnings, or 30 times the federal hourly minimum wage, whichever is greater; pension payments; bankruptcy judge may authorize more for low-income debtors	11-207
wildcard	$800 in any tangible personal property	11-605(10)

Illinois

Federal Bankruptcy Exemptions not available. All law references are to Illinois Annotated Statutes.

ASSET	EXEMPTION	LAW
homestead	Real or personal property including a farm, lot, & buildings, condo, co-op, or mobile home to $7,500; sale proceeds exempt for 1 year	735-5/12-901; 735-5/12-906
	Spouse or child of deceased owner may claim homestead exemption	735-5/12-902
	Illinois recognizes tenancy by the entirety, with limitations	750-65/22; 765-1005/1c; *In re Gillissie*, 215 B.R. 370 (Bankr. N.D. Ill. 1998); *Great Southern Co. v. Allard*, 202 B.R. 938 (N.D. Ill. 1996).
insurance	Fraternal benefit society benefits	215-5/299.1a
	Health or disability benefits	735-5/12-1001(g)(3)
	Homeowners' proceeds if home destroyed, to $7,500	735-5/12-907
	Life insurance, annuity proceeds, or cash value if beneficiary is insured's child, parent, spouse, or other dependent	215-5/238; 735-5/12-1001(f)
	Life insurance proceeds to a spouse or dependent of debtor to extent needed for support	735-5/12-1001(f),(g)(3)
miscellaneous	Alimony, child support	735-5/12-1001(g)(4)
	Property of business partnership	805-205/25
pensions	Civil service employees	40-5/11-223
	County employees	40-5/9-228
	Disabled firefighters; widows & children of firefighters	40-5/22-230
	ERISA-qualified benefits	735-5/12-1006
	Firefighters	40-5/4-135; 40-5/6-213
	General assembly members	40-5/2-154
	House of correction employees	40-5/19-117
	Judges	40-5/18-161
	Municipal employees	40-5/7-217(a); 40-5/8-244
	Park employees	40-5/12-190
	Police officers	40-5/3-144.1; 40-5/5-218
	Public employees	735-5/12-1006
	Public library employees	40-5/19-218
	Sanitation district employees	40-5/13-805
	State employees	40-5/14-147
	State university employees	40-5/15-185
	Teachers	40-5/16-190; 40-5/17-151
personal property	Bible, family pictures, schoolbooks, & clothing	735-5/12-1001(a)
	Health aids	735-5/12-1001(e)
	Motor vehicle to $1,200	735-5/12-1001(c)
	Personal injury recoveries to $7,500	735-5/12-1001(h)(4)

ASSET	EXEMPTION	LAW
	Pre-need cemetery sales funds, care funds, & trust funds	235-5/6-1; 760-100/4; 815-390/16
	Prepaid tuition trust fund	110-979/45(g)
	Proceeds of sold exempt property	735-5/12-1001
	Wrongful death recoveries	735-5/12-1001(h)(2)
public benefits	Aid to aged, blind, disabled; public assistance	305-5/11-3
	Crime victims' compensation	735-5/12-1001(h)(1)
	Restitution payments on account of WWII relocation of Aleuts & Japanese Americans	735-5/12-1001(12)(h)(5)
	Social Security	735-5/12-1001(g)(1)
	Unemployment compensation	735-5/12-1001(g)(1),(3)
	Veterans' benefits	735-5/12-1001(g)(2)
	Workers' compensation	820-305/21
	Workers' occupational disease compensation	820-310/21
tools of trade	Implements, books, & tools of trade to $750	735-5/12-1001(d)
wages	Minimum 85% of earned but unpaid weekly wages or 45 times the federal minimum hourly wage; bankruptcy judge may authorize more for low-income debtors	740-170/4
wildcard	$2,000 of any personal property (does not include wages)	735-5/12-1001(b)

Indiana

Federal Bankruptcy Exemptions not available. All law references are to Indiana Statutes Annotated.

ASSET	EXEMPTION	LAW
homestead see also wildcard	Real or personal property used as residence to $7,500; homestead plus personal property—except health aids—can't exceed $10,000	34-55-10-2(b)(1); 34-55-10-2(c)
	Property held as tenancy by the entirety may be exempt against debts incurred by only one spouse	34-55-10-2(b)(5)
insurance	Employer's life insurance policy on employee	27-1-12-17.1
	Fraternal benefit society benefits	27-11-6-3
	Group life insurance policy	27-1-12-29
	Life insurance policy, proceeds, cash value, or avails if beneficiary is insured's spouse or dependent	27-1-12-14
	Life insurance proceeds if clause prohibits proceeds to be used to pay beneficiary's creditors	27-2-5-1
	Mutual life or accident proceeds	27-8-3-23
miscellaneous	Property of business partnership	23-4-1-25
pensions	Firefighters	36-8-7-22 36-8-8-17
	Police officers	36-8-8-17; 10-12-2-10
	Public employees	5-10.3-8-9
	Public or private retirement benefits & contributions	34-55-10-2(b)(6)
	Sheriffs	36-8-10-19
	State teachers	21-6.1-5-17

ASSET	EXEMPTION	LAW
personal property *see also wild card*	Health aids	34-55-10-2(b)(4)
	Money in medical care savings account	34-55-10-2(b)(7)
	Spendthrift trusts	30-4-3-2
	$100 of any intangible personal property, except money owed to you	34-55-10-2(b)(3)
public benefits	Crime victims' compensation, unless seeking to discharge the debts for which the victim was compensated	5-2-6.1-38
	Unemployment compensation	22-4-33-3
	Workers' compensation	22-3-2-17
tools of trade	National Guard uniforms, arms, & equipment	10-16-10-3
wages	Minimum 75% of earned but unpaid weekly disposable earnings, or 30 times the federal hourly minimum wage; bankruptcy judge may authorize more for low-income debtors	24-4.5-5-105
wildcard	$4,000 of any real estate or tangible personal property, but wildcard plus homestead cannot exceed $10,000	34-55-10-2(b)(2)

Iowa

Federal Bankruptcy Exemptions not available. All law references are to Iowa Code Annotated.

ASSET	EXEMPTION	LAW
homestead	May record homestead declaration	561.4
	Real property or an apartment to an unlimited value; property cannot exceed 1/2 acre in town or city, 40 acres elsewhere (husband & wife may not double)	499A.18; 561.2; 561.16
insurance	Accident, disability, health, illness, or life proceeds or avails	627.6(6)
	Disability or illness benefit	627.6(8)(c)
	Employee group insurance policy or proceeds	509.12
	Fraternal benefit society benefits	512B.18
	Life insurance proceeds if clause prohibits proceeds from being used to pay beneficiary's creditors	508.32
	Life insurance proceeds paid to spouse, child, or other dependent (limited to $10,000 if acquired within 2 years of filing for bankruptcy)	627.6(6)
	Upon death of insured, up to $15,000 total proceeds from all matured life, accident, health, or disability policies exempt from beneficiary's debts contracted before insured's death	627.6(6)
miscellaneous	Alimony, child support needed for support	627.6(8)(d)
	Liquor licenses	123.38
pensions *see also wages*	Disabled firefighters, police officers (only payments being received)	410.11
	Federal government pension	627.8
	Firefighters	411.13
	Other pensions, annuities, & contracts fully exempt; however, contributions made within 1 year prior to filing for bankruptcy not exempt to the extent they exceed normal & customary amounts	627.6(8)(e)
	Peace officers	97A.12
	Police officers	411.13
	Public employees	97B.39
	Retirement plans, Keoghs, IRAs, Roth IRAs, ERISA-qualified benefits	627.6(8)(f)

ASSET	EXEMPTION	LAW
personal property	Appliances, furnishings, & household goods to $2,000 total	627.6(5)
	Bibles, books, portraits, pictures, & paintings to $1,000 total	627.6(3)
	Burial plot to 1 acre	627.6(4)
	Clothing & its storage containers to $1,000	627.6(1)
	Health aids	627.6(7)
	Motor vehicle, musical instruments, tax refund, & accrued wages to $5,000 total; no more than $1,000 from tax refunds & accrued wages	627.6(9)
	Residential security or utility deposit, or advance rent, to $500	627.6(14)
	Rifle or musket; shotgun	627.6(2)
	Wedding or engagement rings	627.6(1)
public benefits	Adopted child assistance	627.19
	Aid to dependent children	239B.6
	Any public assistance benefit	627.6(8)(a)
	Social Security	627.6(8)(a)
	Unemployment compensation	627.6(8)(a)
	Veterans' benefits	627.6(8)(b)
	Workers' compensation	627.13
tools of trade	Farming equipment; includes livestock, feed to $10,000	627.6(11)
	Nonfarming equipment to $10,000	627.6(10)
wages	Expected annual earnings / Amount NOT exempt per year	642.21
	$0 to $12,000 — $250	
	$12,000 to $16,000 — $400	
	$16,000 to $24,000 — $800	
	$24,000 to $35,000 — $1,000	
	$35,000 to $50,000 — $2,000	
	More than $50,000 — 10%	
	Not exempt from spousal or child support	
	Wages or salary of a prisoner	356.29
wildcard	$100 of any personal property, including cash	627.6(13)

Kansas

Federal Bankruptcy Exemptions not available. All law references are to Kansas Statutes Annotated unless otherwise noted.

ASSET	EXEMPTION	LAW
homestead	Real property or mobile home you occupy or intend to occupy to unlimited value; property cannot exceed 1 acre in town or city, 160 acres on farm	60-2301; Constitution 15-9
insurance	Cash value of life insurance; not exempt if obtained within 1 year prior to bankruptcy with fraudulent intent.	60-2313(a)(7); 40-414(b)
	Disability & illness benefits	60-2313(a)(1)
	Fraternal life insurance benefits	60-2313(a)(8)
	Life insurance proceeds	40-414(a)
miscellaneous	Alimony, maintenance, & support	60-2312(b)
	Liquor licenses	60-2313(a)(6); 41-326

ASSET	EXEMPTION	LAW
pensions	Elected & appointed officials in cities with populations between 120,000 & 200,000	13-14a10
	ERISA-qualified benefits	60-2308(b)
	Federal government pension needed for support & paid within 3 months of filing for bankruptcy (only payments being received)	60-2308(a)
	Firefighters	12-5005(e); 14-10a10
	Judges	20-2618
	Police officers	12-5005(e); 13-14a10
	Public employees	74-4923; 74-49, 105
	State highway patrol officers	74-4978g
	State school employees	72-5526
	Payment under a stock bonus, pension, profit-sharing, annuity, or similar plan or contract on account of illness, disability, death, age, or length of service, to the extent reasonably necessary for support	60-2312(b)
personal property	Burial plot or crypt	60-2304(d)
	Clothing to last 1 year	60-2304(a)
	Food & fuel to last 1 year	60-2304(a)
	Funeral plan prepayments	60-2313(a)(10); 16-310(d)
	Furnishings & household equipment	60-2304(a)
	Jewelry & articles of adornment to $1,000	60-2304(b)
	Motor vehicle to $20,000; if designed or equipped for disabled person, no limit	60-2304(c)
public benefits	Crime victims' compensation	60-2313(a)(7); 74-7313(d)
	General assistance	39-717(c)
	Social Security	60-2312(b)
	Unemployment compensation	60-2313(a)(4); 44-718(c)
	Veterans' benefits	60-2312(b)
	Workers' compensation	60-2313(a)(3); 44-514
tools of trade	Books, documents, furniture, instruments, equipment, breeding stock, seed, grain, & stock to $7,500 total	60-2304(e)
	National Guard uniforms, arms, & equipment	48-245
wages	Minimum 75% of disposable weekly wages or 30 times the federal minimum hourly wage per week, whichever is greater; bankruptcy judge may authorize more for low-income debtors	60-2310
wildcard	None	

Kentucky

Federal Bankruptcy Exemptions not available. All law references are to Kentucky Revised Statutes.

ASSET	EXEMPTION	LAW
homestead	Real or personal property used as residence to $5,000; sale proceeds exempt	427.060; 427.090
insurance	Annuity contract proceeds to $350 per month	304.14-330
	Cooperative life or casualty insurance benefits	427.110(1)
	Fraternal benefit society benefits	427.110(2)
	Group life insurance proceeds	304.14-320
	Health or disability benefits	304.14-310
	Life insurance policy if beneficiary is a married woman	304.14-340
	Life insurance proceeds if clause prohibits proceeds from being used to pay beneficiary's creditors	304.14-350
	Life insurance proceeds or cash value if beneficiary is someone other than insured	304.14-300
miscellaneous	Alimony, child support needed for support	427.150(1)
	Property of business partnership	362.270
pensions	ERISA-qualified benefits, including IRAs, SEPs, & Keoghs deposited more than 120 days before filing	427.150
	Firefighters	67A.620; 95.878
	Police officers	427.120; 427.125
	State employees	61.690
	Teachers	161.700
	Urban county government employees	67A.350
personal property	Burial plot to $5,000, in lieu of homestead	427.060
	Clothing, jewelry, articles of adornment, & furnishings to $3,000 total	427.010(1)
	Health aids	427.010(1)
	Lost earnings payments needed for support	427.150(2)(d)
	Medical expenses paid & reparation benefits received under motor vehicle reparation law	304.39-260
	Motor vehicle to $2,500	427.010(1)
	Personal injury recoveries to $7,500 (not to include pain & suffering or pecuniary loss)	427.150(2)(c)
	Prepaid tuition payment fund account	164A.707(3)
	Wrongful death recoveries for person you depended on, needed for support	427.150(2)(b)
public benefits	Aid to blind, aged, disabled; public assistance	205.220(c)
	Crime victims' compensation	427.150(2)(a)
	Unemployment compensation	341.470(4)
	Workers' compensation	342.180
tools of trade	Library, office equipment, instruments, & furnishings of minister, attorney, physician, surgeon, chiropractor, veterinarian, or dentist to $1,000	427.040
	Motor vehicle of auto mechanic, mechanical, or electrical equipment servicer, minister, attorney, physician, surgeon, chiropractor, veterinarian, or dentist to $2,500	427.030
	Tools, equipment, livestock, & poultry of farmer to $3,000	427.010(1)
	Tools of nonfarmer to $300	427.030

ASSET	EXEMPTION	LAW
wages	Minimum 75% of disposable weekly earnings or 30 times the federal minimum hourly wage per week, whichever is greater; bankruptcy judge may authorize more for low-income debtors	427.010(2),(3)
wildcard	$1,000 of any property	427.160

Louisiana

Federal Bankruptcy Exemptions not available. All law references are to Louisiana Revised Statutes Annotated unless otherwise noted.

ASSET	EXEMPTION	LAW
homestead	Property you occupy to $25,000 (if debt is result of catastrophic or terminal illness or injury, limit is full value of property as of 1 year before filing); cannot exceed 5 acres in city or town, 200 acres elsewhere (husband & wife may not double)	20:1(A)(1),(2),(3)
	Spouse or child of deceased owner may claim homestead exemption; spouse given home in divorce gets homestead	20:1(B)
insurance	Annuity contract proceeds & avails	22:647
	Fraternal benefit society benefits	22:558
	Group insurance policies or proceeds	22:649
	Health, accident, or disability proceeds or avails	22:646
	Life insurance proceeds or avails; if policy issued within 9 months of filing, exempt only to $35,000	22:647
miscellaneous	Property of minor child	13:3881(A)(3); Civil Code Art. 223
pensions	Assessors	11:1403
	Court clerks	11:1526
	District attorneys	11:1583
	ERISA-qualified benefits, including IRAs, Roth IRAs, & Keoghs, if contributions made over 1 year before filing for bankruptcy	13:3881(D)(1); 20:33(1)
	Firefighters	11:2263
	Gift or bonus payments from employer to employee or heirs whenever paid	20:33(2)
	Judges	11:1378
	Louisiana University employees	11:952.3
	Municipal employees	11:1735
	Parochial employees	11:1905
	Police officers	11:3513
	School employees	11:1003
	Sheriffs	11:2182
	State employees	11:405
	Teachers	11:704
	Voting registrars	11:2033
personal property	Arms, military accoutrements; bedding; dishes, glassware, utensils, silverware (nonsterling); clothing, family portraits, musical instruments; bedroom, living room, & dining room furniture; poultry, 1 cow, household pets; heating & cooling equipment, refrigerator, freezer, stove, washer & dryer, iron, sewing machine	13:3881(A)(4)

ASSET	EXEMPTION	LAW
personal property (continued)	Cemetery plot, monuments	8:313
	Engagement & wedding rings to $5,000	13:3881(A)(5)
	Spendthrift trusts	9:2004
public benefits	Aid to blind, aged, disabled; public assistance	46:111
	Crime victims' compensation	46:1811
	Earned Income tax credit	13:3881 (A)(6)
	Unemployment compensation	23:1693
	Workers' compensation	23:1205
tools of trade	Tools, instruments, books, $7,500 of equity in a motor vehicle, one firearm to $500, needed to work	13:3881(A)(2)
wages	Minimum 75% of disposable weekly earnings or 30 times the federal minimum hourly wage per week, whichever is greater; bankruptcy judge may authorize more for low-income debtors	13:3881(A)(1)
wildcard	None	

Maine

Federal Bankruptcy Exemptions not available. All law references are to Maine Revised Statutes Annotated, in the form title number–section number.

ASSET	EXEMPTION	LAW
homestead	Real or personal property (including cooperative) used as residence to $35,000; if debtor has minor dependents in residence, to $70,000; if debtor over age 60 or physically or mentally disabled, $70,000; proceeds of sale exempt for six months	14-4422(1)
insurance	Annuity proceeds to $450 per month	24-A-2431
	Death benefit for police, fire, or emergency medical personnel who die in the line of duty	25-1612
	Disability or health proceeds, benefits, or avails	14-4422(13)(A), (C); 24-A-2429
	Fraternal benefit society benefits	24-A-4118
	Group health or life policy or proceeds	24-A-2430
	Life, endowment, annuity, or accident policy, proceeds or avails	14-4422(14)(C); 24-A-2428
	Life insurance policy, interest, loan value, or accrued dividends for policy from person you depended on, to $4,000	14-4422(11)
	Unmatured life insurance policy, except credit insurance policy	14-4422(10)
miscellaneous	Alimony & child support needed for support	14-4422(13)(D)
	Property of business partnership	31-305
pensions	ERISA-qualified benefits	14-4422(13)(E)
	Judges	4-1203
	Legislators	3-703
	State employees	5-17054
personal property	Animals, crops, musical instruments, books, clothing, furnishings, household goods, appliances to $200 per item	14-4422(3)
	Balance due on repossessed goods; total amount financed can't exceed $2,000	9-A-5-103
	Burial plot in lieu of homestead exemption	14-4422(1)

ASSET	EXEMPTION	LAW
personal property (continued)	Cooking stove; furnaces & stoves for heat	14-4422(6)(A),(B)
	Food to last 6 months	14-4422(7)(A)
	Fuel not to exceed 10 cords of wood, 5 tons of coal, or 1,000 gal. of heating oil	14-4422(6)(C)
	Health aids	14-4422(12)
	Jewelry to $750; no limit for one wedding & one engagement ring	14-4422(4)
	Lost earnings payments needed for support	14-4422(14)(E)
	Military clothes, arms, & equipment	37-B-262
	Motor vehicle to $5,000	14-4422(2)
	Personal injury recoveries to $12,500	14-4422(14)(D)
	Seeds, fertilizers, & feed to raise & harvest food for 1 season	14-4422(7)(B)
	Tools & equipment to raise & harvest food	14-4422(7)(C)
	Wrongful death recoveries needed for support	14-4422(14)(B)
public benefits	Maintenance under the Rehabilitation Act	26-1411-H
	Crime victims' compensation	14-4422(14)(A)
	Public assistance	22-3180, 22-3766
	Social Security	14-4422(13)(A)
	Unemployment compensation	14-4422(13)(A),(C)
	Veterans' benefits	14-4422(13)(B)
	Workers' compensation	39-A-106
tools of trade	Books, materials, & stock to $5,000	14-4422(5)
	Commercial fishing boat, 5-ton limit	14-4422(9)
	One of each farm implement (& its maintenance equipment needed to harvest & raise crops)	14-4422(8)
wages	None (use federal nonbankruptcy wage exemption)	
wildcard	Unused portion of exemption in homestead to $6,000; or unused exemption in animals, crops, musical instruments, books, clothing, furnishings, household goods, appliances, tools of the trade, & personal injury recoveries	14-4422(15)
	$400 of any property	14-4422(15)

Maryland

Federal Bankruptcy Exemptions not available. All law references are to Maryland Code of Courts & Judicial Proceedings unless otherwise noted.

ASSET	EXEMPTION	LAW
homestead	None; however, property held as tenancy by the entirety is exempt against debts owed by only one spouse	In re Birney, 200 F.3d 225 (4th Cir. 1999)
insurance	Disability or health benefits, including court awards, arbitrations, & settlements	11-504(b)(2)
	Fraternal benefit society benefits	Ins. 8-431; Estates & Trusts 8-115
	Life insurance or annuity contract proceeds or avails if beneficiary is insured's dependent, child, or spouse	Ins. 16-111(a); Estates & Trusts 8-115
	Medical insurance benefits deducted from wages plus medical insurance payments to $145 per week or 75% of disposable wages	Commercial Law 15-601.1(3)

ASSET	EXEMPTION	LAW
pensions	ERISA-qualified benefits, including IRAs, Roth IRAs, & Keoghs	11-504(h)(1), (4)
	State employees	State Pers. & Pen. 21-502
personal property	Appliances, furnishings, household goods, books, pets, & clothing to $1,000 total	11-504(b)(4)
	Burial plot	Bus. Reg. 5-503
	Health aids	11-504(b)(3)
	Perpetual care trust funds	Bus. Reg. 5-602
	Prepaid college trust funds	Educ. 18-1913
	Lost future earnings recoveries	11-504(b)(2)
public benefits	Baltimore Police death benefits	Code of 1957 art. 24, 16-103
	Crime victims' compensation	Crim. Proc. 11-816(b)
	General assistance	Code of 1957 88A-73
	Unemployment compensation	Labor & Employment 8-106
	Workers' compensation	Labor & Employment 9-732
tools of trade	Clothing, books, tools, instruments, & appliances to $5,000	11-504(b)(1)
wages	Earned but unpaid wages, the greater of 75% or $145 per week; in Kent, Caroline, & Queen Anne's of Worcester Counties, the greater of 75% or 30 times federal minimum hourly wage	Commercial Law 15-601.1
wildcard	$6,000 in cash or any property, if claimed within 30 days of attachment or levy	11-504(b)(5)
	An additional $5,000 in real or personal property	11-504(f)

Massachusetts

Federal Bankruptcy Exemptions available. All law references are to Massachusetts General Laws Annotated, in the form title number–section number.

ASSET	EXEMPTION	LAW
homestead	If statement of homestead is not in title to property, must record homestead declaration before filing bankruptcy	188-2
	Property held as tenancy by the entirety may be exempt against debt for nonnecessity owed by only one spouse.	209-1
	Property you occupy or intend to occupy (including mobile home) to $500,000; if over 65 or disabled, $300,000	188-1; 188-1A
	Spouse or children of deceased owner may claim homestead exemption	188-4
insurance	Disability benefits to $400 per week	175-110A
	Fraternal benefit society benefits	176-22
	Group annuity policy or proceeds	175-132C
	Group life insurance policy	175-135
	Life insurance or annuity contract proceeds if clause prohibits proceeds from being used to pay beneficiary's creditors	175-119A
	Life insurance policy if beneficiary is married woman	175-126

ASSET	EXEMPTION	LAW
insurance (continued)	Life or endowment policy, proceeds, or cash value	175-125
	Medical malpractice self-insurance	175F-15
miscellaneous	Property of business partnership	108A-25
pensions	Credit union employees	171-84
see also wages	ERISA-qualified benefits, including IRAs & Keoghs to specified limits.	235-34A; 246-28
	Private retirement benefits	32-41
	Public employees	32-19
	Savings bank employees	168-41; 168-44
personal property	Bank deposits to $125	235-34
	Beds & bedding; heating unit; clothing	235-34
	Bibles & books to $200 total; sewing machine to $200	235-34
	Burial plots, tombs, & church pew	235-34
	Cash for fuel, heat, water, or light to $75 per month	235-34
	Cash to $200/month for rent, in lieu of homestead	235-34
	Cooperative association shares to $100	235-34
	Food or cash for food to $300	235-34
	Furniture to $3,000; motor vehicle to $700	235-34
	Moving expenses for eminent domain	79-6A
	Trust company, bank, or credit union deposits to $500	246-28A
	2 cows, 12 sheep, 2 swine, 4 tons of hay	235-34
public benefits	Aid to families with dependent children	118-10
	Public assistance	235-34
	Unemployment compensation	151A-36
	Veterans' benefits	115-5
	Workers' compensation	152-47
tools of trade	Arms, accoutrements, & uniforms required	235-34
	Fishing boats, tackle, & nets to $500	235-34
	Materials you designed & procured to $500	235-34
	Tools, implements, & fixtures to $500 total	235-34
wages	Earned but unpaid wages to $125 per week	246-28
wildcard	None	

Michigan

Federal Bankruptcy Exemptions available. All law references are to Michigan Compiled Laws Annotated unless otherwise noted.

ASSET	EXEMPTION	LAW
homestead	Property held as tenancy by the entirety may be exempt against debts owed by only one spouse	*In re Smith*, 246 B.R. 540 (E.D. Mich., 2000); *In re Spears*, 313 B.R. 212 (W.D. Mich. 2004)
	Real property including condo to $3,500; property cannot exceed 1 lot in town, village, city, or 40 acres elsewhere; spouse or children of deceased owner may claim homestead exemption	559.214; 600.6023(1)(h),(i); 600.6023(3)

ASSET	EXEMPTION	LAW
insurance	Disability, mutual life, or health benefits	600.6023(1)(f)
	Employer-sponsored life insurance policy or trust fund	500.2210
	Fraternal benefit society benefits	500.8181
	Life, endowment, or annuity proceeds if clause prohibits proceeds from being used to pay beneficiary's creditors	500.4054
	Life insurance	500.2207
miscellaneous	Property of business partnership	449.25
pensions	ERISA-qualified benefits, except contributions within last 120 days	600.6023(1)(l)
	Firefighters, police officers	38.559(6); 38.1683
	IRAs & Roth IRAs, except contributions within last 120 days	600.6023(1)(k)
	Judges	38.2308; 38.1683
	Legislators	38.1057; 38.1683
	Probate judges	38.2308; 38.1683
	Public school employees	38.1346; 38.1683
	State employees	38.40; 38.1683
personal property	Appliances, utensils, books, furniture, & household goods to $1,000 total	600.6023(1)(b)
	Building & loan association shares to $1,000 par value, in lieu of homestead	600.6023(1)(g)
	Burial plots, cemeteries; church pew, slip, seat for entire family	600.6023(1)(c)
	Clothing; family pictures	600.6023(1)(a)
	Food & fuel to last family for 6 months	600.6023(1)(a)
	2 cows, 100 hens, 5 roosters, 10 sheep, 5 swine, & feed to last 6 months	600.6023(1)(d)
public benefits	Crime victims' compensation	18.362
	Social welfare benefits	400.63
	Unemployment compensation	421.30
	Veterans' benefits for Korean War veterans	35.977
	Veterans' benefits for Vietnam veterans	35.1027
	Veterans' benefits for WWII veterans	35.926
	Workers' compensation	418.821
tools of trade	Arms & accoutrements required	600.6023(1)(a)
	Tools, implements, materials, stock, apparatus, team, motor vehicle, horse, & harness to $1,000 total	600.6023(1)(e)
wages	Head of household may keep 60% of earned but unpaid wages (no less than $15/week), plus $2/week per nonspouse dependent; if not head of household may keep 40% (no less than $10/week)	600.5311
wildcard	None	

Minnesota

Federal Bankruptcy Exemptions available. All law references are to Minnesota Statutes Annotated.

NOTE: Section 550.37(4)(a) requires certain exemptions to be adjusted for inflation on July 1 of even-numbered years; this table includes all changes made through July 1, 2004. Exemptions are published in the May 1 issue of the Minnesota State Register, www.comm.media.state.mn.us/bookstore/stateregister.asp, or call the Minnesota Dept. of Commerce at 651-296-7977.

ASSET	EXEMPTION	LAW
homestead	Home & land on which it is situated to $200,000; if homestead is used for agricultural purposes, $500,000; cannot exceed 1/2 acre in city, 160 acres elsewhere (husband & wife may not double);	510.01; 510.02
	Manufactured home to an unlimited value	550.37 subd. 12
insurance	Accident or disability proceeds	550.39
	Fraternal benefit society benefits	64B.18
	Life insurance proceeds to $38,000, if beneficiary is spouse or child of insured, plus $9,500 per dependent	550.37 subd. 10
	Police, fire, or beneficiary association benefits	550.37 subd. 11
	Unmatured life insurance contract dividends, interest, or loan value to $7,600 if insured is debtor or person debtor depends on	550.37 subd. 23
miscellaneous	Earnings of minor child	550.37 subd. 15
pensions	ERISA-qualified benefits or needed for support, up to $57,000 in present value	550.37 subd. 24
	IRAs or Roth IRAs needed for support, up to $57,000 in present value	550.37 subd. 24
	Public employees	353.15
	State employees	352.96 subd. 6
	State troopers	352B.071
personal property	Appliances, furniture, jewelry, radio, phonographs, & TV to $8,550 total	550.37 subd. 4(b)
	Bible & books	550.37 subd. 2
	Burial plot; church pew or seat	550.37 subd. 3
	Clothing, one watch, food, & utensils for family	550.37 subd. 4(a)
	Motor vehicle to $3,800 (up to $38,000 if vehicle has been modified for disability)	550.37 subd. 12(a)
	Personal injury recoveries	550.37 subd. 22
	Proceeds for damaged exempt property	550.37 subds. 9, 16
	Wrongful death recoveries	550.37 subd. 22
public benefits	Crime victims' compensation	611A.60
	Public benefits	550.37 subd. 14
	Unemployment compensation	268.192 subd. 2
	Veterans' benefits	550.38
	Workers' compensation	176.175
tools of trade total (except teaching materials) can't exceed $13,000	Farm machines, implements, livestock, produce, & crops	550.37 subd. 5
	Teaching materials of college, university, public school, or public institution teacher	550.37 subd. 8
	Tools, machines, instruments, stock in trade, furniture, & library to $9,500 total	550.37 subd. 6
wages	Minimum 75% of weekly disposable earnings or 40 times federal minimum hourly wage, whichever is greater	571.922
	Wages deposited into bank accounts for 20 days after depositing	550.37 subd. 13
	Wages, paid within 6 mos. of returning to work, after receiving welfare or after incarceration; includes earnings deposited in a financial institution in the last 60 days	550.37 subd. 14
wildcard	None	

NOTE: In cases of suspected fraud, the Minnesota constitution permits courts to cap exemptions that would otherwise be unlimited. *In re Tveten*, 402 N.W.2d 551 (Minn. 1987); *In re Medill*, 119 B.R. 685 (Bankr. D. Minn. 1990); *In re Sholdan*, 217 F.3d 1006 (8th Cir. 2000).

Mississippi

Federal Bankruptcy Exemptions not available. All law references are to Mississippi Code.

ASSET	EXEMPTION	LAW
homestead	May file homestead declaration	85-3-27; 85-3-31
	Mobile home does not qualify as homestead unless you own land on which it is located (see personal property)	In re Cobbins, 234 B.R. 882 (S.D. Miss. 1999)
	Property you own & occupy to $75,000; if over 60 & married or widowed may claim a former residence; property cannot exceed 160 acres; sale proceeds exempt	85-3-1(b)(i); 85-3-21; 85-3-23
insurance	Disability benefits	85-3-1(b)(ii)
	Fraternal benefit society benefits	83-29-39
	Homeowners' insurance proceeds to $75,000	85-3-23
	Life insurance proceeds if clause prohibits proceeds from being used to pay beneficiary's creditors	83-7-5
miscellaneous	Property of business partnership	79-12-49
pensions	ERISA-qualified benefits, IRAs, Keoghs deposited over 1 yr. before filing bankruptcy	85-3-1(f)
	Firefighters (includes death benefits)	21-29-257; 45-2-1
	Highway patrol officers	25-13-31
	Law enforcement officers' death benefits	45-2-1
	Police officers (includes death benefits)	21-29-257; 45-2-1
	Private retirement benefits to extent tax-deferred	71-1-43
	Public employees retirement & disability benefits	25-11-129
	State employees	25-14-5
	Teachers	25-11-201(1)(d)
	Volunteer firefighters' death benefits	45-2-1
personal property	Mobile home to $20,000	85-3-1(e)
	Personal injury judgments to $10,000	85-3-17
	Sale or insurance proceeds for exempt property	85-3-1(b)(i)
	Tangible personal property to $10,000: any item worth less than $200; furniture, dishes, kitchenware, household goods, appliances, 1 radio & 1 TV, 1 firearm, 1 lawnmower, clothing, wedding rings, motor vehicles, tools of the trade, books, crops, health aids, domestic animals (does not include works of art, antiques, jewelry, or electronic entertainment equipment)	85-3-1(a)
public benefits	Assistance to aged	43-9-19
	Assistance to blind	43-3-71
	Assistance to disabled	43-29-15
	Crime victims' compensation	99-41-23(7)
	Social Security	25-11-129
	Unemployment compensation	71-5-539
	Workers' compensation	71-3-43
tools of trade	See personal property	
wages	Earned but unpaid wages owed for 30 days; after 30 days, minimum 75% of earned but unpaid weekly disposable earnings, or 30 times the federal hourly minimum wage, whichever is greater (bankruptcy judge may authorize more for low-income debtors)	85-3-4
wildcard	See personal property	

Missouri

Federal Bankruptcy Exemptions not available. All law references are to Annotated Missouri Statutes unless otherwise noted.

ASSET	EXEMPTION	LAW
homestead	Property held as tenancy by the entirety may be exempt against debts owed by only one spouse	In re Eads, 271 B.R. 371 (Bankr. W.D. Mo. 2002).
	Real property to $15,000 or mobile home to $5,000 (joint owners may not double)	513.430(6); 513.475 In re Smith, 254 B.R. 751 (Bank. W.D. Mo. 2000)
insurance	Assessment plan or life insurance proceeds	377.090
	Disability or illness benefits	513.430(10)(c)
	Fraternal benefit society benefits to $5,000, bought over 6 months before filing	513.430(8)
	Life insurance dividends, loan value, or interest to $150,000, bought over 6 months before filing	513.430(8)
	Life insurance proceeds if policy owned by a woman & insures her husband	376.530
	Life insurance proceeds if policy owned by unmarried woman & insures her father or brother	376.550
	Stipulated insurance premiums	377.330
	Unmatured life insurance policy	513.430(7)
miscellaneous	Alimony, child support to $750 per month	513.430(10)(d)
	Property of business partnership	358.250
pensions	Employee benefit spendthrift trust	456.072
	Employees of cities with 100,000 or more people	71.207
	ERISA-qualified benefits, IRAs, Roth IRAs, & other retirement accounts needed for support	513.430(10)(e), (f)
	Firefighters	87.090; 87.365; 87.485
	Highway & transportation employees	104.250
	Police department employees	86.190; 86.353; 86.493; 86.780
	Public officers & employees	70.695; 70.755
	State employees	104.540
	Teachers	169.090
personal property	Appliances, household goods, furnishings, clothing, books, crops, animals, & musical instruments to $3,000 total	513.430(1)
	Burial grounds to 1 acre or $100	214.190
	Health aids	513.430(9)
	Motor vehicle to $3,000	513.430(5)
	Personal injury causes of action	In re Mitchell, 73 B.R. 93 (Bankr. E.D. Mo. 1987)
	Wedding ring to $1,500, & other jewelry to $500	513.430(2)
	Wrongful death recoveries for person you depended on	513.430(11)

ASSET	EXEMPTION	LAW
public benefits	Crime victim's compensation	595.025
	Public assistance	513.430(10)(a)
	Social Security	513.430(10)(a)
	Unemployment compensation	288.380(10)(l); 513.430(10)(c)
	Veterans' benefits	513.430(10)(b)
	Workers' compensation	287.260
tools of trade	Implements, books, & tools of trade to $3,000	513.430(4)
wages	Minimum 75% of weekly earnings (90% of weekly earnings for head of family), or 30 times the federal minimum hourly wage, whichever is more; bankruptcy judge may authorize more for low-income debtors	525.030
	Wages of servant or common laborer to $90	513.470
wildcard	$1,250 of any property if head of family, else $600; head of family may claim additional $350 per child	513.430(3); 513.440

Montana

Federal Bankruptcy Exemptions not available. All law references are to Montana Code Annotated.

ASSET	EXEMPTION	LAW
homestead	Must record homestead declaration before filing for bankruptcy	70-32-105
	Real property or mobile home you occupy to $100,000; sale, condemnation, or insurance proceeds exempt for 18 months	70-32-104; 70-32-201; 70-32-213
insurance	Annuity contract proceeds to $350 per month	33-15-514
	Disability or illness proceeds, avails, or benefits	25-13-608(1)(d); 33-15-513
	Fraternal benefit society benefits	33-7-522
	Group life insurance policy or proceeds	33-15-512
	Hail insurance benefits	80-2-245
	Life insurance proceeds if clause prohibits proceeds from being used to pay beneficiary's creditors	33-20-120
	Medical, surgical, or hospital care benefits	25-13-608(1)(f)
	Unmatured life insurance contracts to $4,000	25-13-609(4)
miscellaneous	Alimony, child support	25-13-608(1)(g)
pensions	ERISA-qualified benefits deposited over 1 year before filing bankruptcy or up to 15% of debtor's gross annual income	31-2-106
	Firefighters	19-18-612(1)
	IRA & Roth IRA contributions & earnings made before judgment filed	25-13-608(1)(e)
	Police officers	19-19-504(1)
	Public employees	19-2-1004; 25-13-608(i)
	Teachers	19-20-706(2); 25-13-608(j)
	University system employees	19-21-212
personal property	Appliances, household furnishings, goods, animals with feed, crops, musical instruments, books, firearms, sporting goods, clothing, & jewelry to $600 per item, $4,500 total	25-13-609(1)
	Burial plot	25-13-608(1)(h)

ASSET	EXEMPTION	LAW
personal property (continued)	Cooperative association shares to $500 value	35-15-404
	Health aids	25-13-608(1)(a)
	Motor vehicle to $2,500	25-13-609(2)
	Proceeds from sale or for damage or loss of exempt property for 6 mos. after received	25-13-610
public benefits	Aid to aged, disabled needy persons	53-2-607
	Crime victims' compensation	53-9-129
	Local public assistance	25-13-608(1)(b)
	Silicosis benefits	39-73-110
	Social Security	25-13-608(1)(b)
	Subsidized adoption payments to needy persons	53-2-607
	Unemployment compensation	31-2-106(2); 39-51-3105
	Veterans' benefits	25-13-608(1)(c)
	Vocational rehabilitation to blind needy persons	53-2-607
	Workers' compensation	39-71-743
tools of trade	Implements, books, & tools of trade to $3,000	25-13-609(3)
	Uniforms, arms, accoutrements needed to carry out government functions	25-13-613(b)
wages	Minimum 75% of earned but unpaid weekly disposable earnings, or 30 times the federal hourly minimum wage, whichever is greater; bankruptcy judge may authorize more for low-income debtors	25-13-614
wildcard	None	

Nebraska

Federal Bankruptcy Exemptions not available. All law references are to Revised Statutes of Nebraska.

ASSET	EXEMPTION	LAW
homestead	$12,500 for married debtor or head of household; cannot exceed 2 lots in city or village, 160 acres elsewhere; sale proceeds exempt 6 months after sale (husband & wife may not double)	40-101; 40-111; 40-113
	May record homestead declaration	40-105
insurance	Fraternal benefit society benefits to $10,000 loan value unless beneficiary convicted of a crime related to benefits	44-1089
	Life insurance or annuity contract proceeds to $10,000 loan value	44-371
pensions see also wages	County employees	23-2322
	Deferred compensation of public employees	48-1401
	ERISA-qualified benefits including IRAs & Roth IRAs needed for support	25-1563.01
	Military disability benefits	25-1559
	School employees	79-948
	State employees	84-1324
personal property	Burial plot	12-517
	Clothing	25-1556(2)
	Crypts, lots, tombs, niches, vaults	12-605
	Furniture, household goods & appliances, household electronics, personal computers, books, & musical instruments to $1,500	25-1556(3)

ASSET	EXEMPTION	LAW
personal property (continued)	Health aids	25-1556(5)
	Perpetual care funds	12-511
	Personal injury recoveries	25-1563.02
	Personal possessions	25-1556
public benefits	Aid to disabled, blind, aged; public assistance	68-1013
	General assistance to poor persons	68-148
	Unemployment compensation	48-647
	Workers' compensation	48-149
tools of trade	Equipment or tools including a vehicle used in/or for commuting to principal place of business to $2,400 (husband & wife may double)	25-1556(4); *In re Keller*, 50 B.R. 23 (D. Neb. 1985)
wages	Minimum 85% of earned but unpaid weekly disposable earnings or pension payments for head of family; minimum 75% of earned but unpaid weekly disposable earnings, or 30 times the federal hourly minimum wage, whichever is greater, for all others; bankruptcy judge may authorize more for low-income debtors	25-1558
wildcard	$2,500 of any personal property, except wages, in lieu of homestead	25-1552

Nevada

Federal Bankruptcy Exemptions not available. All law references are to Nevada Revised Statutes Annotated.

ASSET	EXEMPTION	LAW
homestead	Must record homestead declaration before filing for bankruptcy	115.020
	Real property or mobile home to $200,000	115.010; 21.090(1)(m)
insurance	Annuity contract proceeds to $350 per month	687B.290
	Fraternal benefit society benefits	695A.220
	Group life or health policy or proceeds	687B.280
	Health proceeds or avails	687B.270
	Life insurance policy or proceeds if annual premiums not over $1,000	21.090(1)(k); *In re Bower*, 234 B.R. 109 (Nev. 1999)
	Life insurance proceeds if you're not the insured	687B.260
miscellaneous	Alimony & child support	21.090(1)(r)
	Property of business partnership	87.250
pensions	ERISA-qualified benefits, deferred compensation, SEP IRA, or IRAs to $500,000	21.090(1)(q)
	Public employees	286.670
personal property	Appliances, household goods, furniture, home & yard equipment to $10,000 total	21.090(1)(b)
	Books to $1,500	21.090(1)(a)
	Burial plot purchase money held in trust	689.700
	Funeral service contract money held in trust	689.700
	Health aids	21.090(1)(p)
	Keepsakes & pictures	21.090(1)(a)

ASSET	EXEMPTION	LAW
personal property (continued)	Metal-bearing ores, geological specimens, art curiosities, or paleontological remains; must be arranged, classified, catalogued, & numbered in reference books	21.100
	Mortgage impound accounts	645B.180
	Motor vehicle to $15,000; no limit on vehicle equipped for disabled person	21.090(1)(f),(o)
	One gun	21.090(1)(i)
	Personal injury compensation to $16,500	21.090(t)
	Restitution received for criminal act	21.090(w)
	Wrongful death awards to survivors	21.090(u)
public benefits	Aid to blind, aged, disabled; public assistance	422.291
	Crime victim's compensation	21.090
	Industrial insurance (workers' compensation)	616C.205
	Public assistance for children	432.036
	Unemployment compensation	612.710
	Vocational rehabilitation benefits	615.270
tools of trade	Arms, uniforms, & accoutrements you're required to keep	21.090(1)(j)
	Cabin or dwelling of miner or prospector; mining claim, cars, implements, & appliances to $4,500 total (for working claim only)	21.090(1)(e)
	Farm trucks, stock, tools, equipment, & seed to $4,500	21.090(1)(c)
	Library, equipment, supplies, tools, & materials to $4,500	21.090(1)(d)
wages	Minimum 75% of disposable weekly earnings or 30 times the federal minimum hourly wage per week, whichever is more; bankruptcy judge may authorize more for low-income debtors	21.090(1)(g)
wildcard	None	

New Hampshire

Federal Bankruptcy Exemptions available. All law references are to New Hampshire Revised Statutes Annotated.

ASSET	EXEMPTION	LAW
homestead	Real property or manufactured housing (& the land it's on if you own it) to $100,000	480:1
insurance	Firefighters' aid insurance	402:69
	Fraternal benefit society benefits	418:17
	Homeowners' insurance proceeds to $5,000	512:21(VIII)
miscellaneous	Jury, witness fees	512:21(VI)
	Property of business partnership	304-A:25
	Wages of minor child	512:21(III)
pensions	ERISA-qualified retirement accounts including IRAs & Roth IRAs	512:2 (XIX)
	Federally created pension (only benefits building up)	512:21(IV)
	Firefighters	102:23
	Police officers	103:18
	Public employees	100-A:26
personal property	Beds, bedding, & cooking utensils	511:2(II)
	Bibles & books to $800	511:2(VIII)
	Burial plot, lot	511:2(XIV)
	Church pew	511:2(XV)

ASSET	EXEMPTION	LAW
personal property (continued)	Clothing	511:2(I)
	Cooking & heating stoves, refrigerator	511:2(IV)
	Domestic fowl to $300	511:2(XIII)
	Food & fuel to $400	511:2(VI)
	Furniture to $3,500	511:2(III)
	Jewelry to $500	511:2(XVII)
	Motor vehicle to $4,000	511:2(XVI)
	Proceeds for lost or destroyed exempt property	512:21(VIII)
	Sewing machine	511:2(V)
	1 cow, 6 sheep & their fleece, 4 tons of hay	511:2(XI); (XII)
	1 hog or pig or its meat (if slaughtered)	511:2(X)
public benefits	Aid to blind, aged, disabled; public assistance	167:25
	Unemployment compensation	282-A:159
	Workers' compensation	281-A:52
tools of trade	Tools of your occupation to $5,000	511:2(IX)
	Uniforms, arms, & equipment of military member	511:2(VII)
	Yoke of oxen or horse needed for farming or teaming	511:2(XII)
wages	50 times the federal minimum hourly wage per week	512:21(II)
	Deposits in any account designated a payroll account	512:21(XI)
	Earned but unpaid wages of spouse	512:21(III)
wildcard	$1,000 of any property	511:2(XVIII)
	Unused portion of exemptions for bibles & books, food & fuel, furniture, jewelry, motor vehicle, & tools of trade exemptions to $7,000	511:2(XVIII)

New Jersey

Federal Bankruptcy Exemptions available. All law references are to New Jersey Statutes Annotated.

ASSET	EXEMPTION	LAW
homestead	None, but survivorship interest of a spouse in property held as tenancy by the entirety is exempt from creditors of a single spouse	*Freda v. Commercial Trust Co. of New Jersey*, 570 A.2d 409 (N.J.,1990)
insurance	Annuity contract proceeds to $500 per month	17B:24-7
	Disability benefits	17:18-12
	Disability, death, medical, or hospital benefits for civil defense workers	App. A:9-57.6
	Disability or death benefits for military member	38A:4-8
	Group life or health policy or proceeds	17B:24-9
	Health or disability benefits	17:18-12; 17B:24-8
	Life insurance proceeds if clause prohibits proceeds from being used to pay beneficiary's creditors	17B:24-10
	Life insurance proceeds or avails if you're not the insured	17B:24-6b
pensions	Alcohol beverage control officers	43:8A-20
	City boards of health employees	43:18-12
	Civil defense workers	App. A:9-57.6
	County employees	43:10-57; 43:10-105
	ERISA-qualified benefits for city employees	43:13-9
	Firefighters, police officers, traffic officers	43:16-7; 43:16A-17

ASSET	EXEMPTION	LAW
pensions (continued)	IRAs	*In re Yuhas,* 104 F.3d 612 (3rd Cir. 1997)
	Judges	43:6A-41
	Municipal employees	43:13-44
	Prison employees	43:7-13
	Public employees	43:15A-53
	School district employees	18A:66-116
	State police	53:5A-45
	Street & water department employees	43:19-17
	Teachers	18A:66-51
	Trust containing personal property created pursuant to federal tax law, including 401(k) plans, IRAs, Roth IRAs, & higher education (529) savings plans	25:2-1; *In re Yuhas,* 104 F.3d 612 (3d Cir. 1997)
personal property	Burial plots	45:27-21
	Clothing	2A:17-19
	Furniture & household goods to $1,000	2A:26-4
	Personal property & possessions of any kind, stock or interest in corporations to $1,000 total	2A:17-19
public benefits	Old age, permanent disability assistance	44:7-35
	Unemployment compensation	43:21-53
	Workers' compensation	34:15-29
tools of trade	None	
wages	90% of earned but unpaid wages if annual income under $7,500; if annual income over $7,500, judge decides amount that is exempt	2A:17-56
	Wages or allowances received by military personnel	38A:4-8
wildcard	None	

New Mexico

Federal Bankruptcy Exemptions available. All law references are to New Mexico Statutes Annotated.

ASSET	EXEMPTION	LAW
homestead	$30,000	42-10-9
insurance	Benevolent association benefits to $5,000	42-10-4
	Fraternal benefit society benefits	59A-44-18
	Life, accident, health, or annuity benefits, withdrawal or cash value, if beneficiary is a New Mexico resident	42-10-3
	Life insurance proceeds	42-10-5
miscellaneous	Ownership interest in unincorporated association	53-10-2
	Property of business partnership	54-1A-501
pensions	Pension or retirement benefits	42-10-1; 42-10-2
	Public school employees	22-11-42A
personal property	Books & furniture	42-10-1; 42-10-2
	Building materials	48-2-15
	Clothing	42-10-1; 42-10-2
	Cooperative association shares, minimum amount needed to be member	53-4-28

ASSET	EXEMPTION	LAW
personal property (continued)	Health aids	42-10-1; 42-10-2
	Jewelry to $2,500	42-10-1; 42-10-2
	Materials, tools, & machinery to dig, drill, complete, operate, or repair oil line, gas well, or pipeline	70-4-12
	Motor vehicle to $4,000	42-10-1; 42-10-2
public benefits	Crime victims' compensation (will be repealed in 2006)	31-22-15
	General assistance	27-2-21
	Occupational disease disablement benefits	52-3-37
	Unemployment compensation	51-1-37
	Workers' compensation	52-1-52
tools of trade	$1,500	42-10-1; 42-10-2
wages	Minimum 75% of disposable earnings or 40 times the federal hourly minimum wage, whichever is more; bankruptcy judge may authorize more for low-income debtors	35-12-7
wildcard	$500 of any personal property	42-10-1
	$2,000 of any real or personal property, in lieu of homestead	42-10-10

New York

Federal Bankruptcy Exemptions not available. Law references to Consolidated Laws of New York; Civil Practice Law & Rules are abbreviated C.P.L.R.

ASSET	EXEMPTION	LAW
homestead	Real property including co-op, condo, or mobile home, to $10,000	C.P.L.R. 5206(a); In re Pearl, 723 F.2d 193 (2nd Cir. 1983)
insurance	Annuity contract benefits due the debtor, if debtor paid for the contract; $5,000 limit if purchased within 6 mos. prior to filing & not tax-deferred	Ins. 3212(d); Debt. & Cred. 283(1)
	Disability or illness benefits to $400/month	Ins. 3212(c)
	Life insurance proceeds & avails if the beneficiary is not the debtor, or if debtor's spouse has taken out policy	Ins. 3212(b)
	Life insurance proceeds left at death with the insurance company, if clause prohibits proceeds from being used to pay beneficiary's creditors	Est. Powers & Trusts 7-1.5(a)(2)
miscellaneous	Alimony, child support	C.P.L.R. 5205 (d)(3); Debt. & Cred. 282(2)(d)
	Property of business partnership	Partnership 51
pensions	ERISA-qualified benefits, IRAs, Roth IRAs, & Keoghs & income needed for support	C.P.L.R. 5205(c); Debt. & Cred. 282(2)(e)
	Public retirement benefits	Ins. 4607
	State employees	Ret. & Soc. Sec. 10
	Teachers	Educ. 524
	Village police officers	Unconsolidated 5711-o
	Volunteer ambulance workers' benefits	Vol. Amb. Wkr. Ben. 23
	Volunteer firefighters' benefits	Vol. Firefighter Ben. 23

ASSET	EXEMPTION	LAW
personal property	Bible, schoolbooks, other books to $50; pictures; clothing; church pew or seat; sewing machine, refrigerator, TV, radio; furniture, cooking utensils & tableware, dishes; food to last 60 days; stoves with fuel to last 60 days; domestic animal with food to last 60 days, to $450; wedding ring; watch to $35; exemptions may not exceed $5,000 total (including tools of trade & limited annuity)	C.P.L.R. 5205(a)(1)-(6); Debt. & Cred. 283(1)
	Burial plot without structure to 1/4 acre	C.P.L.R. 5206(f)
	Cash (including savings bonds, tax refunds, bank & credit union deposits) to $2,500, or to $5,000 after exemptions for personal property taken, whichever amount is less (for debtors who do not claim homestead)	Debt. & Cred. 283(2)
	College tuition savings program trust fund	C.P.L.R. 5205(j)
	Health aids, including service animals with food	C.P.L.R. 5205(h)
	Lost future earnings recoveries needed for support	Debt. & Cred. 282(3)(iv)
	Motor vehicle to $2,400	Debt. & Cred. 282(1); *In re Miller,* 167 B.R. 782 (S.D. N.Y. 1994)
	Personal injury recoveries up to 1 year after receiving	Debt. & Cred. 282(3)(iii)
	Recovery for injury to exempt property up to 1 year after receiving	C.P.L.R. 5205(b)
	Savings & loan savings to $600	Banking 407
	Security deposit to landlord, utility company	C.P.L.R. 5205(g)
	Spendthrift trust fund principal, 90% of income if not created by debtor	C.P.L.R. 5205(c),(d)
	Wrongful death recoveries for person you depended on	Debt. & Cred. 282(3)(ii)
public benefits	Aid to blind, aged, disabled	Debt. & Cred. 282(2)(c)
	Crime victims' compensation	Debt. & Cred. 282(3)(i)
	Home relief, local public assistance	Debt. & Cred. 282(2)(a)
	Public assistance	Soc. Serv. 137
	Social Security	Debt. & Cred. 282(2)(a)
	Unemployment compensation	Debt. & Cred. 282(2)(a)
	Veterans' benefits	Debt. & Cred. 282(2)(b)
	Workers' compensation	Debt. & Cred. 282(2)(c); Work. Comp. 33, 218
tools of trade	Farm machinery, team, & food for 60 days; professional furniture, books, & instruments to $600 total	C.P.L.R. 5205(a),(b)
	Uniforms, medal, emblem, equipment, horse, arms, & sword of member of military	C.P.L.R. 5205(e)
wages	90% of earned but unpaid wages received within 60 days before & anytime after filing	C.P.L.R. 5205(d)

ASSET	EXEMPTION	LAW
wages (continued)	90% of earnings from dairy farmer's sales to milk dealers	C.P.L.R. 5205(f)
	100% of pay of noncommissioned officer, private, or musician in U.S. or N.Y. state armed forces	C.P.L.R. 5205(e)
wildcard	None	

North Carolina

Federal Bankruptcy Exemptions not available. All law references are to General Statutes of North Carolina unless otherwise noted.

ASSET	EXEMPTION	LAW
homestead	Property held as tenancy by the entirety may be exempt against debts owed by only one spouse	In re Chandler, 148 B.R. 13 (E.D. N.C., 1992)
	Real or personal property, including co-op, used as residence to $10,000; up to $3,500 of unused portion of homestead may be applied to any property	1C-1601(a)(1),(2)
insurance	Employee group life policy or proceeds	58-58-165
	Fraternal benefit society benefits	58-24-85
	Life insurance on spouse or children	1C-1601(a)(6); Const. Art. X § 5
miscellaneous	Property of business partnership	59-55
	Support received by a surviving spouse for 1 year, up to $10,000	30-15
pensions	Firefighters & rescue squad workers	58-86-90
	IRAs	1C-1601(a)(9)
	Law enforcement officers	143-166.30(g)
	Legislators	120-4.29
	Municipal, city, & county employees	128-31
	Teachers & state employees	135-9; 135-95
personal property	Animals, crops, musical instruments, books, clothing, appliances, household goods & furnishings to $3,500 total; may add $750 per dependent, up to $3,000 total additional (all property must have been purchased at least 90 days before filing)	1C-1601(a)(4),(d)
	Burial plot to $10,000, in lieu of homestead	1C-1601(a)(1)
	Health aids	1C-1601(a)(7)
	Motor vehicle to $1,500	1C-1601(a)(3)
	Personal injury & wrongful death recoveries for person you depended on	1C-1601(a)(8)
public benefits	Aid to blind	111-18
	Crime victims' compensation	15B-17
	Public adult assistance under work first program	108A-36
	Unemployment compensation	96-17
	Workers' compensation	97-21
tools of trade	Implements, books, & tools of trade to $750	1C-1601(a)(5)
wages	Earned but unpaid wages received 60 days before filing for bankruptcy, needed for support	1-362
wildcard	$3,500 less any amount claimed for homestead or burial exemption, of any property	1C-1601(a)(2)
	$500 of any personal property	Constitution Art. X § 1

North Dakota

Federal Bankruptcy Exemptions not available. All law references are to North Dakota Century Code.

ASSET	EXEMPTION	LAW
homestead	Real property, house trailer, or mobile home to $80,000 (husband & wife may not double)	28-22-02(10); 47-18-01
insurance	Fraternal benefit society benefits	26.1-15.1-18; 26.1-33-40
	Life insurance proceeds payable to deceased's estate, not to a specific beneficiary	26.1-33-40
	Life insurance surrender value to $100,000 per policy, if beneficiary is insured's dependent & policy was owned over 1 year before filing for bankruptcy; limit does not apply if more needed for support	28-22-03.1(3)
miscellaneous	Child support payments	14-09-09.31
pensions	Disabled veterans' benefits, except military retirement pay	28-22-03.1(4)(d)
	ERISA-qualified benefits, IRAs, Roth IRAs, & Keoghs to $100,000 per plan; no limit if more needed for support; total exemption (with life insurance surrender value) cannot exceed $200,000	28-22-03.1(3)
	Public employees deferred compensation	54-52.2-06
	Public employees pensions	28-22-19(1)
personal property	1. All debtors may exempt:	
	Bible, schoolbooks; other books to $100	28-22-02(4)
	Burial plots, church pew	28-22-02(2),(3)
	Clothing & family pictures	28-22-02(1),(5)
	Crops or grain raised by debtor on 160 acres where debtor resides	28-22-02(8)
	Food & fuel to last 1 year	28-22-02(6)
	Insurance proceeds for exempt property	28-22-02(9)
	Motor vehicle to $1,200 (or $32,000 for vehicle that has been modified to accommodate owner's disability)	28-22-03.1(2)
	Personal injury recoveries to $7,500	28-22-03.1(4)(b)
	Wrongful death recoveries to $7,500	28-22-03.1(4)(a)
	2. Head of household not claiming crops or grain may claim $5,000 of any personal property or:	28-22-03
	Books & musical instruments to $1,500	28-22-04(1)
	Household & kitchen furniture, beds & bedding, to $1,000	28-22-04(2)
	Library & tools of professional, tools of mechanic, & stock in trade, to $1,000	28-22-04(4)
	Livestock & farm implements to $4,500	28-22-04(3)
	3. Non-head of household not claiming crops or grain may claim $2,500 of any personal property	28-22-05
public benefits	Crime victims' compensation	28-22-19(2)
	Old age & survivor insurance program benefits	52-09-22
	Public assistance	28-22-19(3)
	Social Security	28-22-03.1(4)(c)
	Unemployment compensation	52-06-30
	Workers' compensation	65-05-29
tools of trade	See personal property, option 2	
wages	Minimum 75% of disposable weekly earnings or 40 times the federal minimum wage, whichever is more; bankruptcy judge may authorize more for low-income debtors	32-09.1-03
wildcard	$7,500 of any property in lieu of homestead	28-22-03.1(1)

Ohio

Federal Bankruptcy Exemptions not available. All law references are to Ohio Revised Code unless otherwise noted.

ASSET	EXEMPTION	LAW
homestead	Property held as tenancy by the entirety may be exempt against debts owed by only one spouse	*In re Pernus*, 143 B.R. 856 (N.D. Ohio, 1992)
	Real or personal property used as residence to $5,000	2329.66(A)(1)(b)
insurance	Benevolent society benefits to $5,000	2329.63; 2329.66(A)(6)(a)
	Disability benefits to $600 per month	2329.66(A)(6)(e); 3923.19
	Fraternal benefit society benefits	2329.66(A)(6)(d); 3921.18
	Group life insurance policy or proceeds	2329.66(A)(6)(c); 3917.05
	Life, endowment, or annuity contract avails for your spouse, child, or dependent	2329.66(A)(6)(b); 3911.10
	Life insurance proceeds for a spouse	3911.12
	Life insurance proceeds if clause prohibits proceeds from being used to pay beneficiary's creditors	3911.14
miscellaneous	Alimony, child support needed for support	2329.66(A)(11)
	Property of business partnership	1775.24; 2329.66(A)(14)
pensions	ERISA-qualified benefits needed for support	2329.66(A)(10)(b)
	Firefighters, police officers	742.47
	IRAs, Roth IRAs, & Keoghs needed for support	2329.66(A)(10)(c), (a)
	Public employees	145.56
	Public safety officers' death benefit	2329.66(A)(10)(a)
	Public school employees	3309.66
	State highway patrol employees	5505.22
	Volunteer firefighters' dependents	146.13
personal property	Animals, crops, books, musical instruments, appliances, household goods, furnishings, firearms, hunting & fishing equipment to $200 per item; jewelry to $400 for 1 item, $200 for all others; $1,500 total ($2,000 if no homestead exemption claimed)	2329.66(A)(4)(b), (c),(d); *In re Szydlowski*, 186 B.R. 907 (N.D. Ohio 1995)
	Beds, bedding, clothing to $200 per item	2329.66(A)(3)
	Burial plot	517.09; 2329.66(A)(8)
	Cash, money due within 90 days, tax refund, bank, security, & utility deposits to $400 total	2329.66(A)(4)(a); *In re Szydlowski*, 186 B.R. 907 (N.D. Ohio 1995)
	Compensation for lost future earnings needed for support, received during 12 months before filing	2329.66(A)(12)(d)
	Cooking unit & refrigerator to $300 each	2329.66(A)(3)
	Health aids (professionally prescribed)	2329.66(A)(7)
	Motor vehicle to $1,000	2329.66(A)(2)(b)
	Personal injury recoveries to $5,000, received during 12 months before filing	2329.66(A)(12)(c)

ASSET	EXEMPTION	LAW
personal property (continued)	Tuition credit or payment	2329.66(A)(16)
	Wrongful death recoveries for person debtor depended on, needed for support, received during 12 months before filing	2329.66(A)(12)(b)
public benefits	Crime victim's compensation, received during 12 months before filing	2329.66(A)(12)(a); 2743.66(D)
	Disability assistance payments	2329.66(A)(9)(f); 5115.07
	Public assistance	2329.66(A)(9)(d); 5107.12, 5108.08
	Unemployment compensation	2329.66(A)(9)(c); 4141.32
	Vocational rehabilitation benefits	2329.66(A)(9)(a); 3304.19
	Workers' compensation	2329.66(A)(9)(b); 4123.67
tools of trade	Implements, books, & tools of trade to $750	2329.66(A)(5)
wages	Minimum 75% of disposable weekly earnings or 30 times the federal hourly minimum wage, whichever is higher; bankruptcy judge may authorize more for low-income debtors	2329.66(A)(13)
wildcard	$400 of any property	2329.66(A)(18)

Oklahoma

Federal Bankruptcy Exemptions not available. All law references are to Oklahoma Statutes Annotated, in the form title number–section number.

ASSET	EXEMPTION	LAW
homestead	Real property or manufactured home to unlimited value; property cannot exceed 1 acre in city, town, or village, or 160 acres elsewhere; $5,000 limit if more than 25% of total sq. ft. area used for business purposes; okay to rent homestead as long as no other residence is acquired	31-1(A)(1); 31-1(A)(2); 31-2
insurance	Annuity benefits & cash value	36-3631.1
	Assessment or mutual benefits	36-2410
	Fraternal benefit society benefits	36-2718.1
	Funeral benefits prepaid & placed in trust	36-6125
	Group life policy or proceeds	36-3632
	Life, health, accident, & mutual benefit insurance proceeds & cash value, if clause prohibits proceeds from being used to pay beneficiary's creditors	36-3631.1
	Limited stock insurance benefits	36-2510
miscellaneous	Alimony, child support	31-1(A)(19)
	Beneficiary's interest in a statutory support trust	6-3010
	Liquor license	37-532
	Property of business partnership	54-1-504
pensions	County employees	19-959
	Disabled veterans	31-7
	ERISA-qualified benefits, IRAs, Roth IRAs, Education IRAs, & Keoghs	31-1(A)(20),(23),(24)
	Firefighters	11-49-126
	Judges	20-1111

ASSET	EXEMPTION	LAW
pensions (continued)	Law enforcement employees	47-2-303.3
	Police officers	11-50-124
	Public employees	74-923
	Tax-exempt benefits	60-328
	Teachers	70-17-109
personal property	Books, portraits, & pictures	31-1(A)-7
	Burial plots	31-1(A)(4); 8-7
	Clothing to $4,000	31-1(A)(8)
	College savings plan interest	31-1(24)
	Deposits in an IDA (Individual Development Account)	31-1(22)
	Federal earned income tax credit	31-1(A)(25)
	Food & seed for growing to last 1 year	31-1(A)(17)
	Health aids (professionally prescribed)	31-1(A)(9)
	Household & kitchen furniture	31-1(A)(3)
	Livestock for personal or family use: 5 dairy cows & calves under 6 months; 100 chickens; 20 sheep; 10 hogs; 2 horses, bridles, & saddles; forage & feed to last 1 year	31-1(A)(10),(11), (12),(15),(16),(17)
	Motor vehicle to $3,000	31-1(A)(13)
	Personal injury & wrongful death recoveries to $50,000	31-1(A)(21)
	Prepaid funeral benefits	36-6125(H)
	War bond payroll savings account	51-42
	1 gun	31-1(A)(14)
public benefits	Crime victims' compensation	21-142.13
	Public assistance	56-173
	Social Security	56-173
	Unemployment compensation	40-2-303
	Workers' compensation	85-48
tools of trade	Implements needed to farm homestead, tools, books, & apparatus to $5,000 total	31-1(A)(5),(6); 31-1(C)
wages	75% of wages earned in 90 days before filing bankruptcy; bankruptcy judge may allow more if you show hardship	12-1171.1; 31-1(A)(18); 31-1.1
wildcard	None	

Oregon

Federal Bankruptcy Exemptions not available. All law references are to Oregon Revised Statutes.

ASSET	EXEMPTION	LAW
homestead	Prepaid rent & security deposit for renters dwelling	*In re Casserino*, 379 F.3d 1069 (9th Cir. 2004)
	Real property of a soldier or sailor during time of war	408.440
	Real property you occupy or intend to occupy to $25,000 ($33,000 for joint owners); mobile home on property you own or houseboat to $23,000 ($30,000 for joint owners); mobile home not on your land to $20,000 ($27,000 for joint owners); property cannot exceed 1 block in town or city or 160 acres elsewhere; sale proceeds exempt 1 year from sale, if you intend to purchase another home	18.428; 18.395; 18.402
	Tenancy by entirety not exempt, but subject to survivorship rights of nondebtor spouse	*In re Pletz*, 225 B.R. 206 (D. Or., 1997)

ASSET	EXEMPTION	LAW
insurance	Annuity contract benefits to $500 per month	743.049
	Fraternal benefit society benefits to $7,500	748.207; 18.348
	Group life policy or proceeds not payable to insured	743.047
	Health or disability proceeds or avails	743.050
	Life insurance proceeds or cash value if you are not the insured	743.046, 743.047
miscellaneous	Alimony, child support needed for support	18.345(1)(i)
	Liquor licenses	471.292 (1)
pensions	ERISA-qualified benefits, including IRAs & SEPs; & payments to $7,500	18.358; 18.348
	Public officers, employees pension payments to $7,500	237.980; 238.445; 18.348 (2)
personal property	Bank deposits to $7,500; cash for sold exempt property	18.348; 18.345(2)
	Books, pictures, & musical instruments to $600 total	18.345(1)(a)
	Building materials for construction of an improvement	87.075
	Burial plot	65.870
	Clothing, jewelry, & other personal items to $1,800 total	18.345(1)(b)
	Compensation for lost earnings payments for debtor or someone debtor depended on, to extent needed	18.345(1)(L),(3)
	Domestic animals, poultry, & pets to $1,000 plus food to last 60 days	18.345(1)(e)
	Federal earned income tax credit	18.345(1)(n)
	Food & fuel to last 60 days if debtor is householder	18.345(1)(f)
	Furniture, household items, utensils, radios, & TVs to $3,000 total	18.345(1)(f)
	Health aids	18.345(1)(h)
	Higher education savings account to $7,500	348.863; 18.348(1)
	Motor vehicle to $1,700	18.345(1)(d),(3)
	Personal injury recoveries to $10,000	18.345(1)(k),(3)
	Pistol; rifle or shotgun (owned by person over 16) to $1,000	18.362
public benefits	Aid to blind to $7,500	412.115; 18.348
	Aid to disabled to $7,500	412.610; 18.348
	Civil defense & disaster relief to $7,500	401.405; 18.348
	Crime victims' compensation	18.345(1)(j)(A),(3); 147.325
	General assistance to $7,500	411.760; 18.348
	Injured inmates' benefits to $7,500	655.530; 18.348
	Medical assistance to $7,500	414.095; 18.348
	Old-age assistance to $7,500	413.130; 18.348
	Unemployment compensation to $7,500	657.855; 18.348
	Veterans' benefits & proceeds of Veterans' loans	407.125; 407.595; 18.348(m)
	Vocational rehabilitation to $7,500	344.580; 18.348
	Workers' compensation to $7,500	656.234; 18.348
tools of trade	Tools, library, team with food to last 60 days, to $3,000	18.345(1)(c),(3)
wages	75% of disposable wages or $170 per week, whichever is greater; bankruptcy judge may authorize more for low-income debtors	18.385
	Wages withheld in state employee's bond savings accounts	292.070
wildcard	$400 of any personal property not already covered by existing exemption	18.348(1)(o)

Pennsylvania

Federal Bankruptcy Exemptions available. All law references are to Pennsylvania Consolidated Statutes Annotated.

ASSET	EXEMPTION	LAW
homestead	None; however, property held as tenancy by the entirety may be exempt against debts owed by only one spouse	*In re Martin*, 259 B.R. 119 (M.D. Pa. 2001)
insurance	Accident or disability benefits	42-8124(c)(7)
	Fraternal benefit society benefits	42-8124(c)(1),(8)
	Group life policy or proceeds	42-8124(c)(5)
	Insurance policy or annuity contract payments, where insured is the beneficiary, cash value or proceeds to $100 per month	42-8124(c)(3)
	Life insurance & annuity proceeds if clause prohibits proceeds from being used to pay beneficiary's creditors	42-8214(c)(4)
	Life insurance annuity policy cash value or proceeds if beneficiary is insured's dependent, child or spouse	42-8124(c)(6)
	No-fault automobile insurance proceeds	42-8124(c)(9)
miscellaneous	Property of business partnership	15-8342
pensions	City employees	53-13445; 53-23572; 53-39383; 42-8124(b)(1)(iv)
	County employees	16-4716
	Municipal employees	53-881.115; 42-8124(b)(1)(vi)
	Police officers	53-764; 53-776; 53-23666; 42-8124(b)(1)(iii)
	Private retirement benefits to extent tax-deferred, if clause prohibits proceeds from being used to pay beneficiary's creditors; exemption limited to deposits of $15,000 per year made at least 1 year before filing (limit does not apply to rollovers from other exempt funds or accounts)	42-8124(b)(1)(vii), (viii),(ix)
	Public school employees	24-8533; 42-8124(b)(1)(i)
	State employees	71-5953; 42-8124(b)(1)(ii)
personal property	Bibles & schoolbooks	42-8124(a)(2)
	Clothing	42-8124(a)(1)
	Military uniforms & accoutrements	42-8124(a)(4); 51-4103
	Sewing machines	42-8124(a)(3)
public benefits	Crime victims' compensation	18-11.708
	Korean conflict veterans' benefits	51-20098
	Unemployment compensation	42-8124(a)(10); 43-863
	Veterans' benefits	51-20012; 20048; 20098; 20127
	Workers' compensation	42-8124(c)(2)
tools of trade	Seamstress's sewing machine	42-8124(a)(3)
wages	Earned but unpaid wages	42-8127
	Prison inmates' wages	61-1054
	Wages of victims of abuse	42-8127(f)
wildcard	$300 of any property, including cash, real property, securities, or proceeds from sale of exempt property	42-8123

Rhode Island

Federal Bankruptcy Exemptions available. All law references are to General Laws of Rhode Island.

ASSET	EXEMPTION	LAW
homestead	$200,000 in land & buildings you occupy or intend to occupy as a principal residence (husband & wife may not double)	9-26-4.1
insurance	Accident or sickness proceeds, avails, or benefits	27-18-24
	Fraternal benefit society benefits	27-25-18
	Life insurance proceeds if clause prohibits proceeds from being used to pay beneficiary's creditors	27-4-12
	Temporary disability insurance	28-41-32
miscellaneous	Earnings of a minor child	9-26-4(9)
	Property of business partnership	7-12-36
pensions	ERISA-qualified benefits	9-26-4(12)
	Firefighters	9-26-5
	IRAs & Roth IRAs	9-26-4(11)
	Police officers	9-26-5
	Private employees	28-17-4
	State & municipal employees	36-10-34
personal property	Beds, bedding, furniture, household goods, & supplies, to $8,600 total (husband & wife may not double)	9-26-4(3); *In re Petrozella*, 247 B.R. 591 (R.I. 2000)
	Bibles & books to $300	9-26-4(4)
	Burial plot	9-26-4(5)
	Clothing	9-26-4(1)
	Consumer cooperative association holdings to $50	7-8-25
	Debt secured by promissory note or bill of exchange	9-26-4(7)
	Jewelry to $1,000	9-26-4 (14)
	Motor vehicles to $10,000	9-26-4 (13)
	Prepaid tuition program or tuition savings account	9-26-4 (15)
public benefits	Aid to blind, aged, disabled; general assistance	40-6-14
	Crime victims' compensation	12-25.1-3(b)(2)
	Family assistance benefits	40-5.1-15
	State disability benefits	28-41-32
	Unemployment compensation	28-44-58
	Veterans' disability or survivors' death benefits	30-7-9
	Workers' compensation	28-33-27
tools of trade	Library of practicing professional	9-26-4(2)
	Working tools to $1,200	9-26-4(2)
wages	Earned but unpaid wages due military member on active duty	30-7-9
	Earned but unpaid wages due seaman	9-26-4(6)
	Earned but unpaid wages to $50	9-26-4(8)(iii)
	Wages of any person who had been receiving public assistance are exempt for 1 year after going off of relief	9-26-4(8)(ii)
	Wages of spouse & minor children	9-26-4(9)
	Wages paid by charitable organization or fund providing relief to the poor	9-26-4(8)(i)
wildcard	None	

South Carolina

Federal Bankruptcy Exemptions not available. All law references are to Code of Laws of South Carolina.

ASSET	EXEMPTION	LAW
homestead	Real property, including co-op, to $5,000	15-41-30(1)
insurance	Accident & disability benefits	38-63-40(D)
	Benefits accruing under life insurance policy after death of insured, where proceeds left with insurance company pursuant to agreement; benefits not exempt from action to recover necessaries if parties agree	38-63-50
	Disability or illness benefits	15-41-30(10)(C)
	Fraternal benefit society benefits	38-38-330
	Group life insurance proceeds; cash value to $50,000	38-63-40(C); 38-65-90
	Life insurance avails from policy for person you depended on to $4,000	15-41-30(8)
	Life insurance proceeds from policy for person you depended on, needed for support	15-41-30(11)(C)
	Proceeds & cash surrender value of life insurance payable to beneficiary other than insured's estate & for the express benefit of insured's spouse, children, or dependents (must be purchased 2 years before filing)	38-63-40(A)
	Proceeds of life insurance or annuity contract	38-63-40(B)
	Unmatured life insurance contract, except credit insurance policy	15-41-30(7)
miscellaneous	Alimony, child support	15-41-30(10)(D)
	Property of business partnership	33-41-720
pensions	ERISA-qualified benefits; your share of the pension plan fund	15-41-30(10)(E),(13)
	Firefighters	9-13-230
	General assembly members	9-9-180
	IRAs & Roth IRAs needed for support	15-41-30(12)
	Judges, solicitors	9-8-190
	Police officers	9-11-270
	Public employees	9-1-1680
personal property	Animals, crops, appliances, books, clothing, household goods, furnishings, musical instruments to $2,500 total	15-41-30(3)
	Burial plot to $5,000, in lieu of homestead	15-41-30(1)
	Cash & other liquid assets to $1,000, in lieu of burial or homestead exemption	15-41-30(5)
	College investment program trust fund	59-2-140
	Health aids	15-41-30(9)
	Jewelry to $500	15-41-30(4)
	Motor vehicle to $1,200	15-41-30(2)
	Personal injury & wrongful death recoveries for person you depended on for support	15-41-30(11)(B)
public benefits	Crime victims' compensation	15-41-30(11)(A); 16-3-1300
	General relief; aid to aged, blind, disabled	43-5-190
	Local public assistance	15-41-30(10)(A)
	Social Security	15-41-30(10)(A)

ASSET	EXEMPTION	LAW
public benefits (continued)	Unemployment compensation	15-41-30(10)(A)
	Veterans' benefits	15-41-30(10)(B)
	Workers' compensation	42-9-360
tools of trade	Implements, books, & tools of trade to $750	15-41-30(6)
wages	None (use federal nonbankruptcy wage exemption)	
wildcard	None	

South Dakota

Federal Bankruptcy Exemptions not available. All law references are to South Dakota Codified Laws.

ASSET	EXEMPTION	LAW
homestead	Gold or silver mine, mill, or smelter not exempt	43-31-5
	May file homestead declaration	43-31-6
	Real property to unlimited value or mobile home (larger than 240 sq. ft. at its base & registered in state at least 6 months before filing) to unlimited value; property cannot exceed 1 acre in town or 160 acres elsewhere; sale proceeds to $30,000 ($170,000 if over age 70 or widow or widower who hasn't remarried) exempt for 1 year after sale (husband & wife may not double)	43-31-1; 43-31-2; 43-31-3; 43-31-4 43-45-3
	Spouse or child of deceased owner may claim homestead exemption	43-31-13
insurance	Annuity contract proceeds to $250 per month	58-12-6; 58-12-8
	Endowment, life insurance, policy proceeds to $20,000; if policy issued by mutual aid or benevolent society, cash value to $20,000	58-12-4
	Fraternal benefit society benefits	58-37A-18
	Health benefits to $20,000	58-12-4
	Life insurance proceeds, if clause prohibits proceeds from being used to pay beneficiary's creditors	58-15-70
	Life insurance proceeds to $10,000, if beneficiary is surviving spouse or child	43-45-6
pensions	City employees	9-16-47
	ERISA-qualified benefits, limited to income & distribution on $250,000	43-45-16
	Public employees	3-12-115
personal property	Bible, schoolbooks; other books to $200	43-45-2(4)
	Burial plots, church pew	43-45-2(2),(3)
	Cemetery association property	47-29-25
	Clothing	43-45-2(5)
	Family pictures	43-45-2(1)
	Food & fuel to last 1 year	43-45-2(6)
public benefits	Crime victim's compensation	23A-28B-24
	Public assistance	28-7A-18
	Unemployment compensation	61-6-28
	Workers' compensation	62-4-42
tools of trade	None	
wages	Earned wages owed 60 days before filing bankruptcy, needed for support of family	15-20-12
	Wages of prisoners in work programs	24-8-10
wildcard	Head of family may claim $6,000, or non-head of family may claim $4,000 of any personal property	43-45-4

Tennessee

Federal Bankruptcy Exemptions not available. All law references are to Tennessee Code Annotated unless otherwise noted.

ASSET	EXEMPTION	LAW
homestead	$5,000; $7,500 for joint owners (if 62 or older, $12,500 if single; $20,000 if married; $25,000 if spouse is also 62 or older)	26-2-301
	2–15 year lease	26-2-303
	Life estate	26-2-302
	Property held as tenancy by the entirety may be exempt against debts owed by only one spouse, but survivorship right is not exempt	*In re Arango,* 136 B.R. 740, aff'd, 992 F.2d 611 (6th Cir. 1993); *In re Arwood,* 289 B.R. 889 (Bankr. E.D. Tenn. 2003)
	Spouse or child of deceased owner may claim homestead exemption	26-2-301
insurance	Accident, health, or disability benefits for resident & citizen of Tennessee	26-2-110
	Disability or illness benefits	26-2-111(1)(C)
	Fraternal benefit society benefits	56-25-1403
	Life insurance or annuity	56-7-203
miscellaneous	Alimony, child support owed for 30 days before filing for bankruptcy	26-2-111(1)(E)
	Educational scholarship trust funds & prepayment plans	49-4-108; 49-7-822
pensions	ERISA-qualified benefits, IRAs, & Roth IRAs	26-2-111(1)(D)
	Public employees	8-36-111
	State & local government employees	26-2-105
	Teachers	49-5-909
personal property	Bible, schoolbooks, family pictures, & portraits	26-2-104
	Burial plot to 1 acre	26-2-305; 46-2-102
	Clothing & storage containers	26-2-104
	Health aids	26-2-111(5)
	Lost future earnings payments for you or person you depended on	26-2-111(3)
	Personal injury recoveries to $7,500; wrongful death recoveries to $10,000 ($15,000 total for personal injury, wrongful death, & crime victims' compensation)	26-2-111(2)(B),(C)
	Wages of debtor deserting family, in hands of family	26-2-109
public benefits	Aid to blind	71-4-117
	Aid to disabled	71-4-1112
	Crime victims' compensation to $5,000 (*see personal property*)	26-2-111(2)(A); 29-13-111
	Local public assistance	26-2-111(1)(A)
	Old-age assistance	71-2-216
	Relocation assistance payments	13-11-115
	Social Security	26-2-111(1)(A)
	Unemployment compensation	26-2-111(1)(A)
	Veterans' benefits	26-2-111(1)(B)
	Workers' compensation	50-6-223

ASSET	EXEMPTION	LAW
tools of trade	Implements, books, & tools of trade to $1,900	26-2-111(4)
wages	Minimum 75% of disposable weekly earnings or 30 times the federal minimum hourly wage, whichever is more, plus $2.50 per week per child; bankruptcy judge may authorize more for low-income debtors	26-2-106,107
wildcard	$4,000 of any personal property including deposits on account with any bank or financial institution	26-2-103

Texas

Federal Bankruptcy Exemptions available. All law references are to Texas Revised Civil Statutes Annotated unless otherwise noted.

ASSET	EXEMPTION	LAW
homestead	Unlimited; property cannot exceed 10 acres in town, village, city or 100 acres (200 for families) elsewhere; sale proceeds exempt for 6 months after sale (renting okay if another home not acquired, Prop. 41.003)	Prop. 41.001; 41.002; Const. Art. 16 §§ 50, 51
	Must file homestead declaration, or court will file it for you & charge you for doing so	Prop. 41.005(f); 41.021 to 41.023
insurance	Church benefit plan benefits	1407a (6)
	Fraternal benefit society benefits	Ins. 885.316
	Life, health, accident, or annuity benefits, monies, policy proceeds, & cash values due or paid to beneficiary or insured	Ins. 1108.051
	Texas employee uniform group insurance	Ins. 1551.011
	Texas public school employees group insurance	Ins. 1575.006
	Texas state college or university employee benefits	Ins. 1601.008
miscellaneous	Alimony & child support	Prop. 42.001(b)(3)
	Higher education savings plan trust account	Educ. 54.709(e)
	Liquor licenses & permits	Alco.Bev.Code 11.03
	Prepaid tuition plans	Educ. 54.639
	Property of business partnership	6132b-5.01
pensions	County & district employees	Gov't. 811.006
	ERISA-qualified government or church benefits, including Keoghs & IRAs	Prop. 42.0021
	Firefighters	6243e(5); 6243a-1(8.03); 6243b(15); 6243e(5); 6243e.1(1.04)
	Judges	Gov't. 831.004
	Law enforcement officers, firefighters, emergency medical personnel survivors	Gov't. 615.005
	Municipal employees & elected officials, state employees	6243h(22); Gov't. 811.005
	Police officers	6243d-1(17); 6243j(20); 6243a-1(8.03); 6243b(15); 6243d-1(17)
	Retirement benefits to extent tax-deferred	Prop. 42.0021
	Teachers	Gov't. 821.005

ASSET	EXEMPTION	LAW
personal property to $60,000 total for family, $30,000 for single adult (see also tools of trade)	Athletic & sporting equipment, including bicycles	Prop. 42.002(a)(8)
	Burial plots (exempt from total)	Prop. 41.001
	Clothing & food	Prop. 42.002(a)(2),(5)
	Health aids (exempt from total)	Prop. 42.001(b)(2)
	Home furnishings including family heirlooms	Prop. 42.002(a)(1)
	Jewelry (limited to 25% of total exemption)	Prop. 42.002(a)(6)
	Pets & domestic animals plus their food: 2 horses, mules, or donkeys & tack; 12 head of cattle; 60 head of other livestock; 120 fowl	Prop. 42.002(a)(10),(11)
	1 two-, three-, or four-wheeled motor vehicle per family member or per single adult who holds a driver's license; or, if not licensed, who relies on someone else to operate vehicle	Prop. 42.002(a)(9)
	2 firearms	Prop. 42.002(a)(7)
public benefits	Crime victims' compensation	Crim. Proc. 56.49
	Medical assistance	Hum. Res. 32.036
	Public assistance	Hum. Res. 31.040
	Unemployment compensation	Labor 207.075
	Workers' compensation	Labor 408.201
tools of trade included in aggregate dollar limits for personal property	Farming or ranching vehicles & implements	Prop. 42.002(a)(3)
	Tools, equipment (includes boat & motor vehicles used in trade), & books	Prop. 42.002(a)(4)
wages	Earned but unpaid wages	Prop. 42.001(b)(1)
	Unpaid commissions not to exceed 25% of total personal property exemptions	Prop. 42.001(d)
wildcard	None	

Utah

Federal Bankruptcy Exemptions not available. All law references are to Utah Code.

ASSET	EXEMPTION	LAW
homestead	Must file homestead declaration before attempted sale of home	78-23-4
	Real property, mobile home, or water rights to $20,000 if primary residence; $5,000 if not primary residence	78-23-3(1),(2),(4)
	Sale proceeds exempt for 1 year	78-23-3(5)(b)
insurance	Disability, illness, medical, or hospital benefits	78-23-5(1)(a)(iii)
	Fraternal benefit society benefits	31A-9-603
	Life insurance policy cash surrender value to $5,000	78-23-7
	Life insurance proceeds if beneficiary is insured's spouse or dependent, as needed for support	78-23-6(2)
	Medical, surgical, & hospital benefits	78-23-5(1)(a)(iv)
miscellaneous	Alimony needed for support	78-23-5(1)(a)(vi); 78-23-6(1)
	Child support	78-23-5(1)(f),(k)
	Property of business partnership	48-1-22

ASSET	EXEMPTION	LAW
pensions	ERISA-qualified benefits, IRAs, Roth IRAs, & Keoghs (benefits that have accrued & contributions that have been made at least 1 year prior to filing)	78-23-5(1)(a)(x)
	Other pensions & annuities needed for support	78-23-6(3)
	Public employees	49-11-612
personal property	Animals, books, & musical instruments to $500	78-23-8(1)(c)
	Artwork depicting, or done by, a family member	78-23-5(1)(a)(viii)
	Bed, bedding, carpets	78-23-5(1)(a)(vii)
	Burial plot	78-23-5(1)(a)(i)
	Clothing (cannot claim furs or jewelry)	78-23-5(1)(a)(vii)
	Dining & kitchen tables & chairs to $500	78-23-8(1)(b)
	Food to last 12 months	78-23-5(1)(a)(vii)
	Health aids	78-23-5(1)(a)(ii)
	Heirlooms to $500	78-23-8(1)(d)
	Motor vehicle to $2,500	78-23-8(3)
	Personal injury, wrongful death recoveries for you or person you depended on	78-23-5(1)(a)(ix)
	Proceeds for sold, lost, or damaged exempt property	78-23-9
	Refrigerator, freezer, microwave, stove, sewing machine, washer & dryer	78-23-5(1)(a)(vii)
	Sofas, chairs, & related furnishings to $500	78-23-8(1)(a)
public benefits	Crime victims' compensation	63-25a-421(4)
	General assistance	35A-3-112
	Occupational disease disability benefits	34A-3-107
	Unemployment compensation	35A-4-103(4)(b)
	Veterans' benefits	78-23-5(1)(a)(v)
	Workers' compensation	34A-2-422
tools of trade	Implements, books, & tools of trade to $3,500	78-23-8(2)
	Military property of National Guard member	39-1-47
wages	Minimum 75% of disposable weekly earnings or 30 times the federal hourly minimum wage, whichever is more; bankruptcy judge may authorize more for low-income debtors	70C-7-103
wildcard	None	

Vermont

Federal Bankruptcy Exemptions available. All law references are to Vermont Statutes Annotated unless otherwise noted.

ASSET	EXEMPTION	LAW
homestead	Property held as tenancy by the entirety may be exempt against debts owed by only one spouse	In re McQueen, 21 B.R. 736 (D. Ver. 1982)
	Real property or mobile home to $75,000; may also claim rents, issues, profits, & outbuildings	27-101
	Spouse of deceased owner may claim homestead exemption	27-105

ASSET	EXEMPTION	LAW
insurance	Annuity contract benefits to $350 per month	8-3709
	Disability benefits that supplement life insurance or annuity contract	8-3707
	Disability or illness benefits needed for support	12-2740(19)(C)
	Fraternal benefit society benefits	8-4478
	Group life or health benefits	8-3708
	Health benefits to $200 per month	8-4086
	Life insurance proceeds for person you depended on	12-2740(19)(H)
	Life insurance proceeds if clause prohibits proceeds from being used to pay beneficiary's creditors	8-3705
	Life insurance proceeds if beneficiary is not the insured	8-3706
	Unmatured life insurance contract other than credit	12-2740(18)
miscellaneous	Alimony, child support	12-2740(19)(D)
pensions	Municipal employees	24-5066
	Other pensions	12-2740(19)(J)
	Self-directed accounts (IRAs, Roth IRAs, Keoghs); contributions must be made 1 year before filing	12-2740(16)
	State employees	3-476
	Teachers	16-1946
personal property	Appliances, furnishings, goods, clothing, books, crops, animals, musical instruments to $2,500 total	12-2740(5)
	Bank deposits to $700	12-2740(15)
	Cow, 2 goats, 10 sheep, 10 chickens, & feed to last 1 winter; 3 swarms of bees plus honey; 5 tons coal or 500 gal. heating oil, 10 cords of firewood; 500 gal. bottled gas; growing crops to $5,000; yoke of oxen or steers, plow & ox yoke; 2 horses with harnesses, halters, & chains	12-2740(6), (9)-(14)
	Health aids	12-2740(17)
	Jewelry to $500; wedding ring unlimited	12-2740(3),(4)
	Motor vehicles to $2,500	12-2740(1)
	Personal injury, lost future earnings, wrongful death recoveries for you or person you depended on	12-2740(19)(F), (G),(I)
	Stove, heating unit, refrigerator, freezer, water heater, & sewing machines	12-2740(8)
public benefits	Aid to blind, aged, disabled; general assistance	33-124
	Crime victims' compensation needed for support	12-2740(19)(E)
	Social Security needed for support	12-2740(19)(A)
	Unemployment compensation	21-1367
	Veterans' benefits needed for support	12-2740(19)(B)
	Workers' compensation	21-681
tools of trade	Books & tools of trade to $5,000	12-2740(2)
wages	Entire wages, if you received welfare during 2 months before filing	12-3170
	Minimum 75% of weekly disposable earnings or 30 times the federal minimum hourly wage, whichever is greater; bankruptcy judge may authorize more for low-income debtors	12-3170
wildcard	Unused exemptions for motor vehicle, tools of trade, jewelry, household furniture, appliances, clothing, & crops to $7,000	12-2740(7)
	$400 of any property	12-2740(7)

Virginia

Federal Bankruptcy Exemptions not available. All law references are to Code of Virginia unless otherwise noted.

ASSET	EXEMPTION	LAW
homestead	$5,000 plus $500 per dependent; rents & profits; sale proceeds exempt to $5,000 (unused portion of homestead may be applied to any personal property)	*Cheeseman v. Nachman,* 656 F.2d 60 (4th Cir. 1981); 34-4; 34-18; 34-20
	May include mobile home	*In re Goad,* 161 B.R. 161 (W.D. Va. 1993)
	Must file homestead declaration before filing for bankruptcy	34-6
	Property held as tenancy by the entirety may be exempt against debts owed by only one spouse	*In re Bunker,* 312 F.3d 145 (4th Cir., 2002)
	Surviving spouse may claim $15,000; if no surviving spouse, minor children may claim exemption	64.1-151.3
insurance	Accident or sickness benefits	38.2-3406
	Burial society benefits	38.2-4021
	Cooperative life insurance benefits	38.2-3811
	Fraternal benefit society benefits	38.2-4118
	Group life or accident insurance for government officials	51.1-510
	Group life insurance policy or proceeds	38.2-3339
	Industrial sick benefits	38.2-3549
	Life insurance proceeds	38.2-3122
miscellaneous	Property of business partnership	50-73.108
pensions *see also wages*	City, town, & county employees	51.1-802
	ERISA-qualified benefits to $17,500	34-34
	Judges	51.1-300
	State employees	51.1-124.4(A)
	State police officers	51.1-200
personal property	Bible	34-26(1)
	Burial plot	34-26(3)
	Clothing to $1,000	34-26(4)
	Family portraits & heirlooms to $5,000 total	34-26(2)
	Health aids	34-26(6)
	Household furnishings to $5,000	34-26(4a)
	Motor vehicle to $2,000	34-26(8)
	Personal injury causes of action & recoveries	34-28.1
	Pets	34-26(5)
	Prepaid tuition contracts	23-38.81(E)
	Spendthrift trusts not created by debtor	55-19
	Wedding & engagement rings	34-26(1a)

ASSET	EXEMPTION	LAW
public benefits	Aid to blind, aged, disabled; general relief	63.2-506
	Crime victims' compensation unless seeking to discharge debt for treatment of injury incurred during crime	19.2-368.12
	Payments to tobacco farmers	3.1-1111.1
	Unemployment compensation	60.2-600
	Workers' compensation	65.2-531
tools of trade	For farmer, pair of horses, or mules with gear; one wagon or cart, one tractor to $3,000; 2 plows & wedges; one drag, harvest cradle, pitchfork, rake; fertilizer to $1,000	34-27
	Tools, books, & instruments of trade, including motor vehicles, to $10,000, needed in your occupation or education	34-26(7)
	Uniforms, arms, equipment of military member	44-96
wages	Minimum 75% of weekly disposable earnings or 30 times the federal minimum hourly wage, whichever is greater; bankruptcy judge may authorize more for low-income debtors	34-29
wildcard	Unused portion of homestead or personal property exemption	34-13
	$2,000 of any property for disabled veterans	34-4.1

Washington

Federal Bankruptcy Exemptions available. All law references are to Revised Code of Washington Annotated.

ASSET	EXEMPTION	LAW
homestead	Must record homestead declaration before sale of home if property unimproved or home unoccupied	6.15.040
	Real property or mobile home to $40,000; unimproved property intended for residence to $15,000 (husband & wife may not double)	6.13.010; 6.13.030
insurance	Annuity contract proceeds to $250 per month	48.18.430
	Disability proceeds, avails, or benefits	48.36A.180
	Fraternal benefit society benefits	48.18.400
	Group life insurance policy or proceeds	48.18.420
	Life insurance proceeds or avails if beneficiary is not the insured	48.18.410
miscellaneous	Child support payments	6.15.010(3)(d)
pensions	City employees	41.28.200; 41.44.240
	ERISA-qualified benefits, IRAs, Roth IRAs, & Keoghs	6.15.020
	Judges	2.10.180; 2.12.090
	Law enforcement officials & firefighters	41.26.053
	Police officers	41.20.180
	Public & state employees	41.40.052
	State patrol officers	43.43.310
	Teachers	41.32.052
	Volunteer firefighters	41.24.240
personal property	Appliances, furniture, household goods, home & yard equipment to $2,700 total for individual ($5,400 for community)	6.15.010(3)(a)
	Books to $1,500	6.15.010(2)
	Burial ground	68.24.220

ASSET	EXEMPTION	LAW
personal property (continued)	Burial plots sold by nonprofit cemetery association	68.20.120
	Clothing, no more than $1,000 in furs, jewelry, ornaments	6.15.010(1)
	Fire insurance proceeds for lost, stolen, or destroyed exempt property	6.15.030
	Food & fuel for comfortable maintenance	6.15.010(3)(a)
	Health aids prescribed	6.15.010(3)(e)
	Keepsakes & family pictures	6.15.010(2)
	Motor vehicle to $2,500 total for individual (two vehicles to $5,000 for community)	6.15.010(3)(c)
	Personal injury recoveries to $16,150	6.15.010(3)(f)
public benefits	Child welfare	74.13.070
	Crime victims' compensation	7.68.070(10)
	General assistance	74.04.280
	Industrial insurance (workers' compensation)	51.32.040
	Old-age assistance	74.08.210
	Unemployment compensation	50.40.020
tools of trade	Farmer's trucks, stock, tools, seed, equipment, & supplies to $5,000 total	6.15.010(4)(a)
	Library, office furniture, office equipment, & supplies of physician, surgeon, attorney, clergy, or other professional to $5,000 total	6.15.010(4)(b)
	Tools & materials used in any other trade to $5,000	6.15.010(4)(c)
wages	Minimum 75% of weekly disposable earnings or 30 times the federal minimum hourly wage, whichever is greater; bankruptcy judge may authorize more for low-income debtors	6.27.150
wildcard	$2,000 of any personal property (no more than $200 in cash, bank deposits, bonds, stocks, & securities)	6.15.010(3)(b)

West Virginia

Federal Bankruptcy Exemptions not available. All law references are to West Virginia Code.

ASSET	EXEMPTION	LAW
homestead	Real or personal property used as residence to $25,000; unused portion of homestead may be applied to any property	38-10-4(a)
insurance	Fraternal benefit society benefits	33-23-21
	Group life insurance policy or proceeds	33-6-28
	Health or disability benefits	38-10-4(j)(3)
	Life insurance payments from policy for person you depended on, needed for support	38-10-4(k)(3)
	Unmatured life insurance contract, except credit insurance policy	38-10-4(g)
	Unmatured life insurance contract's accrued dividend, interest, or loan value to $8,000, if debtor owns contract & insured is either debtor or a person on whom debtor is dependent	38-10-4(h)
miscellaneous	Alimony, child support needed for support	38-10-4(j)(4)
pensions	ERISA-qualified benefits, IRAs needed for support	38-10-4(j)(5)
	Public employees	5-10-46
	Teachers	18-7A-30
personal property	Animals, crops, clothing, appliances, books, household goods, furnishings, musical instruments to $400 per item, $8,000 total	38-10-4(c)
	Burial plot to $25,000, in lieu of homestead	38-10-4(a)

ASSET	EXEMPTION	LAW
personal property (continued)	Health aids	38-10-4(i)
	Jewelry to $1,000	38-10-4(d)
	Lost earnings payments needed for support	38-10-4(k)(5)
	Motor vehicle to $2,400	38-10-4(b)
	Personal injury recoveries to $15,000	38-10-4(k)(4)
	Prepaid higher education tuition trust fund & savings plan payments	38-10-4(k)(6)
	Wrongful death recoveries for person you depended on, needed for support	38-10-4(k)(2)
public benefits	Aid to blind, aged, disabled; general assistance	9-5-1
	Crime victims' compensation	38-10-4(k)(1)
	Social Security	38-10-4(j)(1)
	Unemployment compensation	38-10-4(j)(1)
	Veterans' benefits	38-10-4(j)(2)
	Workers' compensation	23-4-18
tools of trade	Implements, books, & tools of trade to $1,500	38-10-4(f)
wages	Minimum 30 times the federal minimum hourly wage per week; bankruptcy judge may authorize more for low-income debtors	38-5A-3
wildcard	$800 plus unused portion of homestead or burial exemption, of any property	38-10-4(e)

Wisconsin

Federal Bankruptcy Exemptions available. All law references are to Wisconsin Statutes Annotated.

ASSET	EXEMPTION	LAW
homestead	Property you occupy or intend to occupy to $40,000; sale proceeds exempt for 2 years if you intend to purchase another home (husband & wife may not double)	815.20
insurance	Federal disability insurance benefits	815.18(3)(ds)
	Fraternal benefit society benefits	614.96
	Life insurance proceeds for someone debtor depended on, needed for support	815.18(3)(i)(a)
	Life insurance proceeds held in trust by insurer, if clause prohibits proceeds from being used to pay beneficiary's creditors	632.42
	Unmatured life insurance contract (except credit insurance contract) if debtor owns contract & insured is debtor or dependents, or someone debtor is dependent on	815.18(3)(f)
	Unmatured life insurance contract's accrued dividends, interest, or loan value to $4,000 total, if debtor owns contract & insured is debtor or dependents, or someone debtor is dependent on	815.18(3)(f)
miscellaneous	Alimony, child support needed for support	815.18(3)(c)
	Property of business partnership	178.21(3)(c)
pensions	Certain municipal employees	62.63(4)
	Firefighters, police officers who worked in city with population over 100,000	815.18(3)(ef)
	Military pensions	815.18(3)(n)
	Private or public retirement benefits	815.18(3)(j)
	Public employees	40.08(1)

ASSET	EXEMPTION	LAW
personal property	Burial plot, tombstone, coffin	815.18(3)(a)
	College savings account or tuition trust fund	14.64(7); 14.63(8)
	Deposit accounts to $1,000	815.18(3)(k)
	Fire & casualty proceeds for destroyed exempt property for 2 years from receiving	815.18(3)(e)
	Household goods & furnishings, clothing, keepsakes, jewelry, appliances, books, musical instruments, firearms, sporting goods, animals, & other tangible personal property to $5,000 total	815.18(3)(d)
	Lost future earnings recoveries, needed for support	815.18(3)(i)(d)
	Motor vehicles to $1,200; unused portion of $5,000 personal property exemption may be added	815.18(3)(g)
	Personal injury recoveries to $25,000	815.18(3)(i)(c)
	Tenant's lease or stock interest in housing co-op, to homestead amount	182.004(6)
	Wages used to purchase savings bonds	20.921(1)(e)
	Wrongful death recoveries, needed for support	815.18(3)(i)(b)
public benefits	Crime victims' compensation	949.07
	Social services payments	49.96
	Unemployment compensation	108.13
	Veterans' benefits	45.35(8)(b)
	Workers' compensation	102.27
tools of trade	Equipment, inventory, farm products, books, & tools of trade to $7,500 total	815.18(3)(b)
wages	75% of weekly net income or 30 times the greater of the federal or state minimum hourly wage; bankruptcy judge may authorize more for low-income debtors	815.18(3)(h)
	Wages of county jail prisoners	303.08(3)
	Wages of county work camp prisoners	303.10(7)
	Wages of inmates under work-release plan	303.065(4)(b)
wildcard	None	

Wyoming

Federal Bankruptcy Exemptions not available. All law references are to Wyoming Statutes Annotated unless otherwise noted.

ASSET	EXEMPTION	LAW
homestead	Property held as tenancy by the entirety may be exempt against debts owed by only one spouse	*In re Anselmi*, 52 B.R. 479 (D. Wy. 1985)
	Real property you occupy to $10,000 or house trailer you occupy to $6,000	1-20-101; 102; 104
	Spouse or child of deceased owner may claim homestead exemption	1-20-103
insurance	Annuity contract proceeds to $350 per month	26-15-132
	Disability benefits if clause prohibits proceeds from being used to pay beneficiary's creditors	26-15-130
	Fraternal benefit society benefits	26-29-218

ASSET	EXEMPTION	LAW
insurance (continued)	Group life or disability policy or proceeds, cash surrender & loan values, premiums waived, & dividends	26-15-131
	Individual life insurance policy proceeds, cash surrender & loan values, premiums waived, & dividends	26-15-129
	Life insurance proceeds held by insurer, if clause prohibits proceeds from being used to pay beneficiary's creditors	26-15-133
miscellaneous	Liquor licenses & malt beverage permits	12-4-604
pensions	Criminal investigators, highway officers	9-3-620
	Firefighters' death benefits	15-5-209
	Game & fish wardens	9-3-620
	Police officers	15-5-313(c)
	Private or public retirement funds & accounts	1-20-110
	Public employees	9-3-426
personal property	Bedding, furniture, household articles, & food to $2,000 per person in the home	1-20-106(a)(iii)
	Bible, schoolbooks, & pictures	1-20-106(a)(i)
	Burial plot	1-20-106(a)(ii)
	Clothing & wedding rings to $1,000	1-20-105
	Medical savings account contributions	1-20-111
	Motor vehicle to $2,400	1-20-106(a)(iv)
	Prepaid funeral contracts	26-32-102
public benefits	Crime victims' compensation	1-40-113
	General assistance	42-2-113(b)
	Unemployment compensation	27-3-319
	Workers' compensation	27-14-702
tools of trade	Library & implements of profession to $2,000 or tools, motor vehicle, implements, team & stock in trade to $2,000	1-20-106(b)
wages	Earnings of National Guard members	19-9-401
	Minimum 75% of disposable weekly earnings or 30 times the federal hourly minimum wage, whichever is more	1-15-511
	Wages of inmates in adult community corrections program	7-18-114
	Wages of inmates in correctional industries program	25-13-107
	Wages of inmates on work release	7-16-308
wildcard	None	

Federal Bankruptcy Exemptions

Married couples filing jointly may double all exemptions. All references are to 11 U.S.C. § 522. These exemptions were last adjusted in 2004. Every three years ending on April 1, these amounts will be adjusted to reflect changes in the Consumer Price Index. Debtors in the following states may select the Federal Bankruptcy Exemptions:

Arkansas	Massachusetts	New Jersey	Texas
Connecticut		New Mexico	Vermont
District of Columbia	Minnesota	Pennsylvania	Washington
Hawaii	New Hampshire	Rhode Island	Wisconsin

ASSET	EXEMPTION	SUBSECTION
homestead	Real property, including co-op or mobile home, or burial plot to $18,450; unused portion of homestead to $9,250 may be applied to any property	(d)(1)
insurance	Disability, illness, or unemployment benefits	(d)(10)(C)
	Life insurance payments for person you depended on, needed for support	(d)(11)(C)
	Life insurance policy with loan value, in accrued dividends or interest, to $9,850	(d)(8)
	Unmatured life insurance contract, except credit insurance policy	(d)(7)
miscellaneous	Alimony, child support needed for support	(d)(10)(D)
pensions	ERISA-qualified benefits needed for support; includes IRA	(d)(10)(E); *Rousey v. Jacoway*, No. 03-1407 (April 4, 2005). 347 F.3d 689 (8th Cir. 2003), *cert. granted*, 73 U.S.L.W. 3204 (U.S. Sept. 28, 2004) (No. 03-1407)
personal property	Animals, crops, clothing, appliances, books, furnishings, household goods, musical instruments to $475 per item, $9,850 total	(d)(3)
	Health aids	(d)(9)
	Jewelry to $1,225	(d)(4)
	Lost earnings payments	(d)(11)(E)
	Motor vehicle to $2,950	(d)(2)
	Personal injury recoveries to $17,425 (not to include pain & suffering or pecuniary loss)	(d)(11)(D)
	Wrongful death recoveries for person you depended on	(d)(11)(B)
public benefits	Crime victims' compensation	(d)(11)(A)
	Public assistance	(d)(10)(A)
	Social Security	(d)(10)(A)
	Unemployment compensation	(d)(10)(A)
	Veterans' benefits	(d)(10)(A)
tools of trade	Implements, books, & tools of trade to $1,850	(d)(6)
wages	None	
wildcard	$975 of any property	(d)(5)
	Up to $9,250 of unused homestead exemption amount, for any property	(d)(5)

Federal Nonbankruptcy Exemptions

These exemptions are available only if you select your state exemptions. You may use them for any exemptions in addition to those allowed by your state, but they cannot be claimed if you file using federal bankruptcy exemptions. All law references are to the United States Code.

ASSET	EXEMPTION	LAW
death & disability benefits	Government employees	5 § 8130
	Longshoremen & harbor workers	33 § 916
	War risk, hazard, death, or injury compensation	42 § 1717
retirement	Civil service employees	5 § 8346
	Foreign Service employees	22 § 4060
	Military Medal of Honor roll pensions	38 § 1562(c)
	Military service employees	10 § 1440
	Railroad workers	45 § 231m
	Social Security	42 § 407
	Veterans' benefits	38 § 5301
survivor's benefits	Judges, U.S. court & judicial center directors, administrative assistants to U.S. Supreme Court Chief Justice	28 § 376
	Lighthouse workers	33 § 775
	Military service	10 § 1450
miscellaneous	Indian lands or homestead sales or lease proceeds	25 § 410
	Klamath Indians tribe benefits for Indians residing in Oregon	25 §§ 543; 545
	Military deposits in savings accounts while on permanent duty outside U.S.	10 §§ 1035
	Military group life insurance	38 § 1970(g)
	Railroad workers' unemployment insurance	45 § 352(e)
	Seamen's clothing	46 § 11110
	Seamen's wages (while on a voyage) pursuant to a written contract	46 § 11109
	Minimum 75% of disposable weekly earnings or 30 times the federal minimum hourly wage, whichever is more; bankruptcy judge may authorize more for low-income debtors	15 § 1673

Charts

···

Median Family Income

For the most recent figures, go to the U.S. Trustee's website at www.usdoj.gov/ust, and click "Means Testing Information."

State	Median Income	State	Median Income	State	Median Income
Alabama		**Delaware**		**Indiana**	
2-person families	$39,755	2-person families	$51,955	2-person families	$46,603
3-person families	$48,957	3-person families	$61,508	3-person families	$50,804
4-person families	$54,338	4-person families	$72,003	4-person families	$63,276
Alaska		**District of Columbia**		**Iowa**	
2-person families	$59,980	2-person families	$62,167	2-person families	$46,518
3-person families	$68,140	3-person families	$42,137	3-person families	$54,099
4-person families	$76,369	4-person families	$51,510	4-person families	$61,951
Arizona		**Florida**		**Kansas**	
2-person families	$46,429	2-person families	$44,831	2-person families	$48,610
3-person families	$51,348	3-person families	$49,612	3-person families	$54,537
4-person families	$58,187	4-person families	$59,798	4-person families	$59,498
Arkansas		**Georgia**		**Kentucky**	
2-person families	$37,178	2-person families	$45,775	2-person families	$37,932
3-person families	$41,231	3-person families	$49,855	3-person families	$46,383
4-person families	$49,790	4-person families	$58,060	4-person families	$55,001
California		**Hawaii**		**Louisiana**	
2-person families	$53,506	2-person families	$54,534	2-person families	$38,017
3-person families	$59,633	3-person families	$64,554	3-person families	$45,732
4-person families	$68,310	4-person families	$75,785	4-person families	$51,402
Colorado		**Idaho**		**Maine**	
2-person families	$54,187	2-person families	$42,990	2-person families	$46,340
3-person families	$58,565	3-person families	$47,288	3-person families	$52,432
4-person families	$66,664	4-person families	$55,914	4-person families	$64,083
Connecticut		**Illinois**		**Maryland**	
2-person families	$61,374	2-person families	$51,572	2-person families	$58,556
3-person families	$76,506	3-person families	$62,178	3-person families	$70,043
4-person families	$88,276	4-person families	$70,357	4-person families	$85,554

State	Median Income	State	Median Income	State	Median Income
Massachusetts		**New Hampshire**		**Oregon**	
2-person families	$55,291	2-person families	$57,784	2-person families	$47,080
3-person families	$71,416	3-person families	$68,360	3-person families	$52,842
4-person families	$85,157	4-person families	$82,134	4-person families	$59,202
Michigan		**New Jersey**		**Pennsylvania**	
2-person families	$47,444	2-person families	$58,547	2-person families	$44,361
3-person families	$60,431	3-person families	$75,470	3-person families	$58,986
4-person families	$68,563	4-person families	$88,401	4-person families	$66,569
Minnesota		**New Mexico**		**Rhode Island**	
2-person families	$54,598	2-person families	$39,876	2-person families	$51,334
3-person families	$64,851	3-person families	$41,420	3-person families	$57,967
4-person families	$73,498	4-person families	$47,256	4-person families	$69,029
Mississippi		**New York**		**South Carolina**	
2-person families	$35,729	2-person families	$48,492	2-person families	$43,263
3-person families	$37,794	3-person families	$57,430	3-person families	$48,557
4-person families	$49,893	4-person families	$67,564	4-person families	$59,694
Missouri		**North Carolina**		**South Dakota**	
2-person families	$44,631	2-person families	$42,105	2-person families	$42,014
3-person families	$49,925	3-person families	$49,206	3-person families	$51,678
4-person families	$62,265	4-person families	$55,117	4-person families	$59,479
Montana		**North Dakota**		**Tennessee**	
2-person families	$41,984	2-person families	$45,821	2-person families	$41,468
3-person families	$44,732	3-person families	$53,580	3-person families	$49,017
4-person families	$50,666	4-person families	$58,298	4-person families	$55,907
Nebraska		**Ohio**		**Texas**	
2-person families	$45,541	2-person families	$44,734	2-person families	$46,454
3-person families	$54,248	3-person families	$55,390	3-person families	$48,755
4-person families	$59,979	4-person families	$62,991	4-person families	$56,246
Nevada		**Oklahoma**		**Utah**	
2-person families	$50,387	2-person families	$41,058	2-person families	$45,374
3-person families	$51,645	3-person families	$47,703	3-person families	$51,219
4-person families	$52,750	4-person families	$49,881	4-person families	$57,916

State	Median Income
Vermont	
2-person families	$49,503
3-person families	$59,259
4-person families	$65,833
Virginia	
2-person families	$54,604
3-person families	$61,106
4-person families	$71,948

State	Median Income
Washington	
2-person families	$52,272
3-person families	$57,773
4-person families	$70,857
West Virginia	
2-person families	$35,183
3-person families	$45,629
4-person families	$51,795

State	Median Income
Wisconsin	
2-person families	$48,281
3-person families	$58,135
4-person families	$67,869
Wyoming	
2-person families	$50,957
3-person families	$52,181
4-person families	$62,014

National Standards for Allowable Living Expenses

Collection Financial Standards for food, clothing, and other Items. Due to their unique geographic cirumstances and higher costs of living, separate standards have been established for Alaska and Hawaii. The Alaska and Hawaii charts follow the ones for the 48 contiguous states.

One Person National Standards for the 48 Contiguous States
Based on Gross Monthly Income

Item	less than $833	$834 to $1,249	$1,250 to $1,666	$1,667 to $2,499	$2,500 to $3,333	$3,334 to $4,166	$4,167 to $5,833	$5,834 and over
Food	197	215	231	258	300	339	369	543
Housekeeping supplies	19	20	25	26	29	36	37	51
Apparel & services	60	61	70	75	100	124	134	207
Personal care products & services	19	24	26	27	40	42	43	44
Miscellaneous	108	108	108	108	108	108	108	108
Total	$403	$428	$460	$494	$577	$649	$691	$953

Two Persons National Standards for the 48 Contiguous States
Based on Gross Monthly Income

Item	less than $833	$834 to $1,249	$1,250 to $1,666	$1,667 to $2,499	$2,500 to $3,333	$3,334 to $4,166	$4,167 to $5,833	$5,834 and over
Food	336	337	338	424	439	487	559	691
Housekeeping supplies	36	37	38	48	52	53	107	108
Apparel & services	81	88	91	95	125	132	164	276
Personal care products & services	33	34	35	43	44	51	56	71
Miscellaneous	134	134	134	134	134	134	134	134
Total	$620	$630	$636	$744	$794	$857	$1,020	$1,280

Three Persons National Standards for the 48 Contiguous States
Based on Gross Monthly Income

Item	less than $833	$834 to $1,249	$1,250 to $1,666	$1,667 to $2,499	$2,500 to $3,333	$3,334 to $4,166	$4,167 to $5,833	$5,834 and over
Food	467	468	469	470	490	546	622	778
Housekeeping supplies	41	42	43	49	53	55	108	109
Apparel & services	132	144	157	158	159	188	204	303
Personal care products & services	34	36	37	44	45	52	61	79
Miscellaneous	161	161	161	161	161	161	161	161
Total	$835	$851	$867	$882	$908	$1,002	$1,156	$1,430

Four Persons National Standards for the 48 Contiguous States
Based on Gross Monthly Income

Item	less than $833	$834 to $1,249	$1,250 to $1,666	$1,667 to $2,499	$2,500 to $3,333	$3,334 to $4,166	$4,167 to $5,833	$5,834 and over
Food	468	525	526	527	528	640	722	868
Housekeeping supplies	42	43	44	50	54	61	109	110
Apparel & services	146	169	170	171	174	189	217	317
Personal care products & services	37	42	43	45	46	53	62	81
Miscellaneous	188	188	188	188	188	188	188	188
Total	$881	$967	$971	$981	$990	$1,131	$1,298	$1,564

More Than Four Persons National Standards for the 48 Contiguous States
Based on Gross Monthly Income

Item	less than $833	$834 to $1,249	$1,250 to $1,666	$1,667 to $2,499	$2,500 to $3,333	$3,334 to $4,166	$4,167 to $5,833	$5,834 and over
For each additional person, add to four-person total allowance:	$134	$145	$155	$166	$177	$188	$199	$209

Effective January 1, 2005

Alaska National Standards for Allowable Living Expenses

One Person National Standards for Alaska
Based on Gross Monthly Income

Item	less than $833	$834 to $1,249	$1,250 to $1,666	$1,667 to $2,499	$2,500 to $3,333	$3,334 to $4,166	$4,167 to $5,833	$5,834 and over
Food	229	249	268	299	348	393	428	630
Housekeeping supplies	22	23	29	30	34	42	43	59
Apparel & services	70	71	81	87	116	144	155	240
Personal care products & services	22	28	30	31	46	49	50	51
Miscellaneous	125	125	125	125	125	125	125	125
Total	$468	$496	$533	$572	$669	$753	$801	$1,105

Two Persons National Standards for Alaska
Based on Gross Monthly Income

Item	less than $833	$834 to $1,249	$1,250 to $1,666	$1,667 to $2,499	$2,500 to $3,333	$3,334 to $4,166	$4,167 to $5,833	$5,834 and over
Food	390	391	392	492	509	565	648	802
Housekeeping supplies	42	43	44	56	60	61	124	125
Apparel & services	94	102	106	110	145	153	190	320
Personal care products & services	38	39	41	50	51	59	65	82
Miscellaneous	155	155	155	155	155	155	155	155
Total	$719	$730	$738	$863	$920	$993	$1,182	$1,484

Three Persons National Standards for Alaska
Based on Gross Monthly Income

Item	less than $833	$834 to $1,249	$1,250 to $1,666	$1,667 to $2,499	$2,500 to $3,333	$3,334 to $4,166	$4,167 to $5,833	$5,834 and over
Food	542	543	544	545	568	633	722	902
Housekeeping supplies	48	49	50	57	61	64	125	126
Apparel & services	153	167	182	183	184	218	237	351
Personal care products & services	39	42	43	51	52	60	71	92
Miscellaneous	187	187	187	187	187	187	187	187
Total	**$969**	**$988**	**$1,006**	**$1,023**	**$1,052**	**$1,162**	**$1,342**	**$1,658**

Four Persons National Standards for Alaska
Based on Gross Monthly Income

Item	less than $833	$834 to $1,249	$1,250 to $1,666	$1,667 to $2,499	$2,500 to $3,333	$3,334 to $4,166	$4,167 to $5,833	$5,834 and over
Food	543	609	610	611	612	742	838	1,007
Housekeeping supplies	49	50	51	58	63	71	126	128
Apparel & services	169	196	197	198	202	219	252	368
Personal care products & services	43	49	50	52	53	61	72	94
Miscellaneous	218	218	218	218	218	218	218	218
Total	**$1,022**	**$1,122**	**$1,126**	**$1,137**	**$1,148**	**$1,311**	**$1,506**	**$1,815**

More Than Four Persons National Standards for Alaska
Based on Gross Monthly Income

Item	less than $833	$834 to $1,249	$1,250 to $1,666	$1,667 to $2,499	$2,500 to $3,333	$3,334 to $4,166	$4,167 to $5,833	$5,834 and over
For each additional person, add to four-person total allowance:	$155	$168	$180	$193	$205	$218	$231	$242

Effective January 1, 2005

Hawaii National Standards for Allowable Living Expenses

One Person National Standards for Hawaii
Based on Gross Monthly Income

Item	less than $833	$834 to $1,249	$1,250 to $1,666	$1,667 to $2,499	$2,500 to $3,333	$3,334 to $4,166	$4,167 to $5,833	$5,834 and over
Food	199	217	233	261	303	342	373	548
Housekeeping supplies	19	20	25	26	29	36	37	52
Apparel & services	61	62	71	76	101	125	135	209
Personal care products & services	19	24	26	27	40	42	43	44
Miscellaneous	109	109	109	109	109	109	109	109
Total	$407	$432	$464	$499	$582	$654	$697	$962

Two Persons National Standards for Hawaii
Based on Gross Monthly Income

Item	less than $833	$834 to $1,249	$1,250 to $1,666	$1,667 to $2,499	$2,500 to $3,333	$3,334 to $4,166	$4,167 to $5,833	$5,834 and over
Food	339	340	341	428	443	492	565	698
Housekeeping supplies	36	37	38	48	53	54	108	109
Apparel & services	82	89	92	96	126	133	166	279
Personal care products & services	33	34	35	43	44	52	57	72
Miscellaneous	135	135	135	135	135	135	135	135
Total	$625	$635	$641	$750	$801	$866	$1,031	$1,293

Three Persons National Standards for Hawaii
Based on Gross Monthly Income

Item	less than $833	$834 to $1,249	$1,250 to $1,666	$1,667 to $2,499	$2,500 to $3,333	$3,334 to $4,166	$4,167 to $5,833	$5,834 and over
Food	472	473	474	475	495	551	628	786
Housekeeping supplies	41	42	43	49	54	56	109	110
Apparel & services	133	145	159	160	161	190	206	306
Personal care products & services	34	36	37	44	45	53	62	80
Miscellaneous	163	163	163	163	163	163	163	163
Total	**$843**	**$859**	**$876**	**$891**	**$918**	**$1,013**	**$1,168**	**$1,445**

Four Persons National Standards for Hawaii
Based on Gross Monthly Income

Item	less than $833	$834 to $1,249	$1,250 to $1,666	$1,667 to $2,499	$2,500 to $3,333	$3,334 to $4,166	$4,167 to $5,833	$5,834 and over
Food	473	530	531	532	533	646	729	877
Housekeeping supplies	42	43	44	51	55	62	110	111
Apparel & services	147	171	172	173	176	191	219	320
Personal care products & services	37	42	43	45	46	54	63	82
Miscellaneous	190	190	190	190	190	190	190	190
Total	**$889**	**$976**	**$980**	**$991**	**$1,000**	**$1,143**	**$1,311**	**$1,580**

More Than Four Persons National Standards for Hawaii
Based on Gross Monthly Income

Item	less than $833	$834 to $1,249	$1,250 to $1,666	$1,667 to $2,499	$2,500 to $3,333	$3,334 to $4,166	$4,167 to $5,833	$5,834 and over
For each additional person, add to four person total allowance:	$135	$146	$157	$168	$179	$190	$201	$211

Effective January 1, 2005

Allowable Living Expenses for Transportation

Ownership Costs

	First Car	Second Car
National	$475	$338

Operating Costs & Public Transportation Costs

	No Car	One Car	Two Cars
Northeast Region	$230	$298	$393
New York	$302	$384	$479
Philadelphia	$236	$298	$392
Boston	$259	$284	$380
Pittsburgh	$161	$286	$380
Midwest Region	$194	$251	$345
Chicago	$257	$329	$422
Detroit	$312	$376	$469
Milwaukee	$212	$247	$341
Minneapolis-St. Paul	$276	$303	$397
Cleveland	$198	$293	$387
Cincinnati	$222	$272	$365
St. Louis	$203	$287	$383
Kansas City	$246	$291	$384
South Region	$197	$242	$336
Washington, DC	$289	$313	$407
Baltimore	$225	$240	$334
Atlanta	$283	$258	$351
Miami	$284	$344	$439
Tampa	$255	$265	$359
Dallas-Ft. Worth	$309	$332	$425
Houston	$281	$367	$462
West Region	$246	$305	$399
Los Angeles	$275	$353	$448
San Francisco	$317	$373	$466
San Diego	$311	$318	$415
Portland	$189	$246	$339
Seattle	$258	$335	$427
Honolulu	$295	$314	$409
Anchorage	$312	$336	$431
Phoenix	$273	$326	$420
Denver	$302	$351	$442

Does not include personal property taxes. (Effective January 1, 2005)

For Use With Allowable Transportation Expenses Table

The Operating Costs and Public Transportation Costs sections of the Transportation Standards are provided by Census Region and Metropolitan Statistical Area (MSA). The following table lists the states that make up each Census Region. Once the taxpayer's Census Region has been ascertained, to determine if an MSA standard is applicable, use the definitions below to see if the taxpayer lives within an MSA (MSAs are defined by county and city, where applicable). If the taxpayer does not reside in an MSA, use the regional standard.

Northeast Census Region

Maine, New Hampshire, Vermont, Massachusetts, Rhode Island, Connecticut, Pennsylvania, New York, New Jersey

MSA	Counties	
New York	in NY:	Bronx, Dutchess, Kings, Nassau, New York, Orange, Putnam, Queens, Richmond, Rockland, Suffolk, Westchester
	in NJ:	Bergen, Essex, Hudson, Hunterdon, Mercer, Middlesex, Monmouth, Morris, Ocean, Passaic, Somerset, Sussex, Union, Warren
	in CT:	Fairfield, Litchfield, Middlesex, New Haven
	in PA:	Pike
Philadelphia	in PA:	Bucks, Chester, Delaware, Montgomery, Philadelphia
	in NJ:	Atlantic, Burlington, Camden, Cape May, Cumberland, Gloucester, Salem
	in DE:	New Castle
	in MD:	Cecil
Boston	in MA:	Bristol, Essex, Hampden, Middlesex, Norfolk, Plymouth, Suffolk, Worcester
	in NH:	Hillsborough, Merrimack, Rockingham, Strafford
	in CT:	Windham
	in ME:	York
Pittsburgh	in PA:	Allegheny, Beaver, Butler, Fayette, Washington, Westmoreland

Midwest Census Region

North Dakota, South Dakota, Nebraska, Kansas, Missouri, Illinois, Indiana, Ohio, Michigan, Wisconsin, Minnesota, Iowa

MSA	Counties (unless otherwise specified)	
Chicago	in IL:	Cook, DeKalb, DuPage, Grundy, Kane, Kankakee, Kendall, Lake, McHenry, Will
	in IN:	Lake, Porter
	in WI:	Kenosha
Detroit	in MI:	Genesee, Lapeer, Lenawee, Livingston, Macomb, Monroe, Oakland, St. Clair, Washtenaw, Wayne
Milwaukee	in WI:	Milwaukee, Ozaukee, Racine, Washington, Waukesha
Minneapolis-St. Paul	in MN:	Anoka, Carver, Chisago, Dakota, Hennepin, Isanti, Ramsey, Scott, Sherburne, Washington, Wright
	in WI:	Pierce, St. Croix
Cleveland	in OH:	Ashtabula, Cuyahoga, Geauga, Lake, Lorain, Medina, Portage, Summit
Cincinnati	in OH:	Brown, Butler, Clermont, Hamilton, Warren
	in KY:	Boone, Campbell, Gallatin, Grant, Kenton, Pendleton
	in IN:	Dearborn, Ohio
St. Louis	in MO:	Crawford, Franklin, Jefferson, Lincoln, St. Charles, St. Louis, Warren, St. Louis city
	in IL:	Clinton, Jersey, Madison, Monroe, St.Clair
Kansas City	in MO:	Cass, Clay, Clinton, Jackson, Lafayette, Platte, Ray
	in KS:	Johnson, Leavenworth, Miami, Wyandotte

South Census Region

Texas, Oklahoma, Arkansas, Louisiana, Mississippi, Tennessee, Kentucky, West Virginia, Virginia, Maryland, District of Columbia, Delaware, North Carolina, South Carolina, Georgia, Florida, Alabama

MSA		Counties (unless otherwise specified)
Washington, DC	in DC	District of Columbia
	in MD:	Calvert, Charles, Frederick, Montgomery, Prince George's, Washington
	in VA:	Arlington, Clarke, Culpepper, Fairfax, Fauquier, King George, Loudoun, Prince William, Spotsylvania, Stafford, Warren, Alexandria city, Fairfax city, Falls Church city, Fredericksburg city, Manassas city, Manassas Park city
	in WV:	Berkeley, Jefferson
Baltimore	in MD:	Anne Arundel, Baltimore, Carroll, Harford, Howard, Queen Anne's, Baltimore city
Atlanta	in GA:	Barrow, Bartow, Carroll, Cherokee, Clayton, Cobb, Coweta, DeKalb, Douglas, Fayette, Forsyth, Fulton, Gwinnett, Henry, Newton, Paulding, Pickens, Rockdale, Spalding, Walton
Miami	in FL:	Broward, Miami-Dade
Tampa	in FL:	Hernando, Hillsborough, Pasco, Pinellas
Dallas-Ft. Worth	in TX:	Collin, Dallas, Denton, Ellis, Henderson, Hood, Hunt, Johnson, Kaufman, Parker, Rockwall, Tarrant
Houston	in TX:	Brazoria, Chambers, Fort Bend, Galveston, Harris, Liberty, Montgomery, Waller

West Census Region:

New Mexico, Arizona, Colorado, Wyoming, Montana, Nevada, Utah, Washington, Oregon, Idaho, California, Alaska, Hawaii

MSA	Counties (unless otherwise specified)	
Los Angeles	in CA:	Los Angeles, Orange, Riverside, San Bernadino, Ventura
San Francisco	in CA:	Alameda, Contra Costa, Marin, Napa, San Francisco, San Mateo, Santa Clara, Santa Cruz, Solano, Sonoma
San Diego	in CA:	San Diego
Portland	in OR:	Clackamas, Columbia, Marion, Multnomah, Polk, Washington, Yamhill
	in WA:	Clark
Seattle	in WA:	Island, King, Kitsap, Pierce, Snohomish, Thurston
Honolulu	in HI:	Honolulu
Anchorage	in AK:	Anchorage borough
Phoenix	in AZ:	Maricopa, Pinal
Denver	in CO:	Adams, Arapahoe, Boulder, Denver, Douglas, Jefferson, Weld

■

Sample Bankruptcy Forms

(Official Form 1) (10/05)

United States Bankruptcy Court Northern District of California	Voluntary Petition

Name of Debtor (if individual, enter Last, First, Middle): Edwards, Carrie Anne	Name of Joint Debtor (Spouse) (Last, First, Middle):
All Other Names used by the Debtor in the last 8 years (include married, maiden, and trade names):	All Other Names used by the Joint Debtor in the last 8 years (include married, maiden, and trade names):
Last four digits of Soc. Sec./Complete EIN or other Tax ID No. (if more than one, state all) xxx-xx-6287	Last four digits of Soc. Sec./Complete EIN or other Tax ID No. (if more than one, state all)
Street Address of Debtor (No. & Street, City, and State): 3045 Berwick St Lakeport, CA ZIP Code 95453	Street Address of Joint Debtor (No. & Street, City, and State): ZIP Code
County of Residence or of the Principal Place of Business: Lake	County of Residence or of the Principal Place of Business:
Mailing Address of Debtor (if different from street address): PO Box 1437 Lakeport, CA ZIP Code 95453	Mailing Address of Joint Debtor (if different from street address): ZIP Code

Location of Principal Assets of Business Debtor
(if different from street address above):

Type of Debtor (Form of Organization) (Check one box)
- ■ Individual (includes Joint Debtors)
- ☐ Corporation (includes LLC and LLP)
- ☐ Partnership
- ☐ Other (If debtor is not one of the above entities, check this box and provide the information requested below.) State type of entity:

Nature of Business (Check all applicable boxes.)
- ☐ Health Care Business
- ☐ Single Asset Real Estate as defined in 11 U.S.C. § 101 (51B)
- ☐ Railroad
- ☐ Stockbroker
- ☐ Commodity Broker
- ☐ Clearing Bank
- ☐ Nonprofit Organization qualified under 15 U.S.C. § 501(c)(3)

Chapter of Bankruptcy Code Under Which the Petition is Filed (Check one box)
- ■ Chapter 7   ☐ Chapter 11   ☐ Chapter 15 Petition for Recognition of a Foreign Main Proceeding
- ☐ Chapter 9   ☐ Chapter 12   ☐ Chapter 15 Petition for Recognition of a Foreign Nonmain Proceeding
- ☐ Chapter 13

Nature of Debts (Check one box)
- ■ Consumer/Non-Business   ☐ Business

Filing Fee (Check one box)
- ■ Full Filing Fee attached
- ☐ Filing Fee to be paid in installments (Applicable to individuals only) Must attach signed application for the court's consideration certifying that the debtor is unable to pay fee except in installments. Rule 1006(b). See Official Form 3A.
- ☐ Filing Fee waiver requested (Applicable to chapter 7 individuals only). Must attach signed application for the court's consideration. See Official Form 3B.

Chapter 11 Debtors
Check one box:
- ☐ Debtor is a small business debtor as defined in 11 U.S.C. § 101(51D).
- ☐ Debtor is not a small business debtor as defined in 11 U.S.C. § 101(51D).

Check if:
- ☐ Debtor's aggregate noncontingent liquidated debts owed to non-insiders or affiliates are less than $2 million.

Statistical/Administrative Information
- ☐ Debtor estimates that funds will be available for distribution to unsecured creditors.
- ■ Debtor estimates that, after any exempt property is excluded and administrative expenses paid, there will be no funds available for distribution to unsecured creditors.

THIS SPACE IS FOR COURT USE ONLY

Estimated Number of Creditors

1-49	50-99	100-199	200-999	1000-5,000	5001-10,000	10,001-25,000	25,001-50,000	50,001-100,000	OVER 100,000
■	☐	☐	☐	☐	☐	☐	☐	☐	☐

Estimated Assets

$0 to $50,000	$50,001 to $100,000	$100,001 to $500,000	$500,001 to $1 million	$1,000,001 to $10 million	$10,000,001 to $50 million	$50,000,001 to $100 million	More than $100 million
☐	☐	■	☐	☐	☐	☐	☐

Estimated Debts

$0 to $50,000	$50,001 to $100,000	$100,001 to $500,000	$500,001 to $1 million	$1,000,001 to $10 million	$10,000,001 to $50 million	$50,000,001 to $100 million	More than $100 million
☐	☐	■	☐	☐	☐	☐	☐

(Official Form 1) (10/05)   FORM B1, Page 2

Voluntary Petition

(This page must be completed and filed in every case)

| Name of Debtor(s): |
| Edwards, Carrie Anne |

Prior Bankruptcy Case Filed Within Last 8 Years (If more than one, attach additional sheet)

Location Where Filed: - None -	Case Number:	Date Filed:

Pending Bankruptcy Case Filed by any Spouse, Partner, or Affiliate of this Debtor (If more than one, attach additional sheet)

Name of Debtor: - None -	Case Number:	Date Filed:
District:	Relationship:	Judge:

Exhibit A	**Exhibit B**
(To be completed if debtor is required to file periodic reports (e.g., forms 10K and 10Q) with the Securities and Exchange Commission pursuant to Section 13 or 15(d) of the Securities Exchange Act of 1934 and is requesting relief under chapter 11.) ☐ Exhibit A is attached and made a part of this petition.	(To be completed if debtor is an individual whose debts are primarily consumer debts.) I, the attorney for the petitioner named in the foregoing petition, declare that I have informed the petitioner that [he or she] may proceed under chapter 7, 11, 12, or 13 of title 11, United States Code, and have explained the relief available under each such chapter. I further certify that I delivered to the debtor the notice required by §342(b) of the Bankruptcy Code. X _____ Signature of Attorney for Debtor(s) Date

Exhibit C	**Certification Concerning Debt Counseling by Individual/Joint Debtor(s)**
Does the debtor own or have possession of any property that poses or is alleged to pose a threat of imminent and identifiable harm to public health or safety? ☐ Yes, and Exhibit C is attached and made a part of this petition. ■ No	■ I/we have received approved budget and credit counseling during the 180-day period preceding the filing of this petition. ☐ I/we request a waiver of the requirement to obtain budget and credit counseling prior to filing based on exigent circumstances. (Must attach certification describing.)

Information Regarding the Debtor (Check the Applicable Boxes)

Venue (Check any applicable box)

■   Debtor has been domiciled or has had a residence, principal place of business, or principal assets in this District for 180 days immediately preceding the date of this petition or for a longer part of such 180 days than in any other District.

☐   There is a bankruptcy case concerning debtor's affiliate, general partner, or partnership pending in this District.

☐   Debtor is a debtor in a foreign proceeding and has its principal place of business or principal assets in the United States in this District, or has no principal place of business or assets in the United States but is a defendant in an action or proceeding [in a federal or state court] in this District, or the interests of the parties will be served in regard to the relief sought in this District.

Statement by a Debtor Who Resides as a Tenant of Residential Property
Check all applicable boxes.

☐   Landlord has a judgment against the debtor for possession of debtor's residence. (If box checked, complete the following.)

_____
(Name of landlord that obtained judgment)

_____
(Address of landlord)

☐   Debtor claims that under applicable nonbankruptcy law, there are circumstances under which the debtor would be permitted to cure the entire monetary default that gave rise to the judgment for possession, after the judgment for possession was entered, and

☐   Debtor has included in this petition the deposit with the court of any rent that would become due during the 30-day period after the filing of the petition.

(Official Form 1) (10/05)   **FORM B1**, Page 3

Voluntary Petition

(This page must be completed and filed in every case)

Name of Debtor(s):
Edwards, Carrie Anne

Signatures

Signature(s) of Debtor(s) (Individual/Joint)	**Signature of a Foreign Representative**

Signature(s) of Debtor(s) (Individual/Joint)

I declare under penalty of perjury that the information provided in this petition is true and correct.
[If petitioner is an individual whose debts are primarily consumer debts and has chosen to file under chapter 7] I am aware that I may proceed under chapter 7, 11, 12, or 13 of title 11, United States Code, understand the relief available under each such chapter, and choose to proceed under chapter 7.
[If no attorney represents me and no bankruptcy petition preparer signs the petition] I have obtained and read the notice required by §342(b) of the Bankruptcy Code.

I request relief in accordance with the chapter of title 11, United States Code, specified in this petition.

X _____
  Signature of Debtor

X _____
  Signature of Joint Debtor

_____
Telephone Number (If not represented by attorney)

_____
Date

Signature of a Foreign Representative

I declare under penalty of perjury that the information provided in this petition is true and correct, that I am the foreign representative of a debtor in a foreign proceeding, and that I am authorized to file this petition.

(Check only one box.)

☐ I request relief in accordance with chapter 15 of title 11. United States Code. Certified copies of the documents required by §1515 of title 11 are attached.

☐ Pursuant to §1511 of title 11, United States Code, I request relief in accordance with the chapter of title 11 specified in this petition. A certified copy of the order granting recognition of the foreign main proceeding is attached.

X _____
  Signature of Foreign Representative

_____
Printed Name of Foreign Representative

_____
Date

Signature of Attorney

X Debtor not represented by attorney
  Signature of Attorney for Debtor(s)

_____
Printed Name of Attorney for Debtor(s)

_____
Firm Name

_____
Address

_____
Telephone Number

_____
Date

Signature of Non-Attorney Bankruptcy Petition Preparer

I declare under penalty of perjury that: (1) I am a bankruptcy petition preparer as defined in 11 U.S.C. § 110; (2) I prepared this document for compensation and have provided the debtor with a copy of this document and the notices and information required under 11 U.S.C. §§ 110(b), 110(h), and 342(b); and, (3) if rules or guidelines have been promulgated pursuant to 11 U.S.C. § 110(h) setting a maximum fee for services chargeable by bankruptcy petition preparers, I have given the debtor notice of the maximum amount before preparing any document for filing for a debtor or accepting any fee from the debtor, as required in that section. Official Form 19B is attached.

_____
Printed Name and title, if any, of Bankruptcy Petition Preparer

_____
Social Security number (If the bankrutpcy petition preparer is not an individual, state the Social Security number of the officer, principal, responsible person or partner of the bankruptcy petition preparer.)(Required by 11 U.S.C. § 110.)

_____
Address

X _____

_____
Date

Signature of Bankruptcy Petition Preparer or officer, principal, responsible person,or partner whose social security number is provided above.

Names and Social Security numbers of all other individuals who prepared or assisted in preparing this document unless the bankruptcy petition preparer is not an individual:

If more than one person prepared this document, attach additional sheets conforming to the appropriate official form for each person.

A bankruptcy petition preparer's failure to comply with the provisions of title 11 and the Federal Rules of Bankruptcy Procedure may result in fines or imprisonment or both 11 U.S.C. §110; 18 U.S.C. §156.

Signature of Debtor (Corporation/Partnership)

I declare under penalty of perjury that the information provided in this petition is true and correct, and that I have been authorized to file this petition on behalf of the debtor.

The debtor requests relief in accordance with the chapter of title 11, United States Code, specified in this petition.

X _____
  Signature of Authorized Individual

_____
Printed Name of Authorized Individual

_____
Title of Authorized Individual

_____
Date

Form 6-Summary
(10/05)

United States Bankruptcy Court
Northern District of California

In re   Carrie Anne Edwards   ,   Case No. _____

                                         Debtor

                                                    Chapter_____ 7 _____

SUMMARY OF SCHEDULES

Indicate as to each schedule whether that schedule is attached and state the number of pages in each. Report the totals from Schedules A, B, D, E, F, I, and J in the boxes provided. Add the amounts from Schedules A and B to determine the total amount of the debtor's assets. Add the amounts of all claims from Schedules D, E, and F to determine the total amount of the debtor's liabilities. Individual debtors must also complete the "Statistical Summary of Certain Liabilities."

NAME OF SCHEDULE	ATTACHED (YES/NO)	NO. OF SHEETS	AMOUNTS SCHEDULED		
			ASSETS	LIABILITIES	OTHER
A - Real Property	Yes	1	140,000.00		
B - Personal Property	Yes	4	25,325.00		
C - Property Claimed as Exempt	Yes	2			
D - Creditors Holding Secured Claims	Yes	1		141,000.00	
E - Creditors Holding Unsecured Priority Claims	Yes	3		5,500.00	
F - Creditors Holding Unsecured Nonpriority Claims	Yes	3		147,150.00	
G - Executory Contracts and Unexpired Leases	Yes	1			
H - Codebtors	Yes	1			
I - Current Income of Individual Debtor(s)	Yes	1			3,991.66
J - Current Expenditures of Individual Debtor(s)	Yes	2			3,945.00
Total Number of Sheets of ALL Schedules		19			
Total Assets			165,325.00		
Total Liabilities				293,650.00	

Form 6-Summ2
(10/05)

United States Bankruptcy Court
Northern District of California

In re   Carrie Anne Edwards   ,
                                   Debtor

Case No. _____

Chapter _____ 7 _____

STATISTICAL SUMMARY OF CERTAIN LIABILITIES (28 U.S.C. § 159)
[Individual Debtors Only]

Summarize the following types of liabilities, as reported in the Schedules, and total them.

Type of Liability	Amount
Domestic Support Obligations (from Schedule E)	2,500.00
Taxes and Certain Other Debts Owed to Governmental Units (from Schedule E)	3,000.00
Claims for Death or Personal Injury While Debtor Was Intoxicated (from Schedule E)	0.00
Student Loan Obligations (from Schedule F)	0.00
Domestic Support, Separation Agreement, and Divorce Decree Obligations Not Reported on Schedule E	0.00
Obligations to Pension or Profit-Sharing, and Other Similar Obligations (from Schedule F)	0.00
TOTAL	5,500.00

The foregoing information is for statistical purposes only under 28 U.S.C § 159.

Form B6A
(10/05)

In re Carrie Anne Edwards   Case No. _____
_____,
                              Debtor

SCHEDULE A. REAL PROPERTY

Except as directed below, list all real property in which the debtor has any legal, equitable, or future interest, including all property owned as a cotenant, community property, or in which the debtor has a life estate. Include any property in which the debtor holds rights and powers exercisable for the debtor's own benefit. If the debtor is married, state whether husband, wife, or both own the property by placing an "H," "W," "J," or "C" in the column labeled "Husband, Wife, Joint, or Community." If the debtor holds no interest in real property, write "None" under "Description and Location of Property."

Do not include interests in executory contracts and unexpired leases on this schedule. List them in Schedule G - Executory Contracts and Unexpired Leases.

If an entity claims to have a lien or hold a secured interest in any property, state the amount of the secured claim. See Schedule D. If no entity claims to hold a secured interest in the property, write "None" in the column labeled "Amount of Secured Claim."

If the debtor is an individual or if a joint petition is filed, state the amount of any exemption claimed in the property only in Schedule C - Property Claimed as Exempt.

Description and Location of Property	Nature of Debtor's Interest in Property	Husband, Wife, Joint, or Community	Current Value of Debtor's Interest in Property, without Deducting any Secured Claim or Exemption	Amount of Secured Claim
Residence Location: 3045 Berwick St, Lakeport CA		-	140,000.00	140,000.00

	Sub-Total >	140,000.00	(Total of this page)
	Total >	140,000.00	

 0   continuation sheets attached to the Schedule of Real Property

(Report also on Summary of Schedules)

Form B6B
(10/05)

In re   Carrie Anne Edwards   ,   Case No. _____

Debtor

SCHEDULE B. PERSONAL PROPERTY

Except as directed below, list all personal property of the debtor of whatever kind. If the debtor has no property in one or more of the categories, place an "x" in the appropriate position in the column labeled "None." If additional space is needed in any category, attach a separate sheet properly identified with the case name, case number, and the number of the category. If the debtor is married, state whether husband, wife, or both own the property by placing an "H," "W," "J," or "C" in the column labeled "Husband, Wife, Joint, or Community." If the debtor is an individual or a joint petition is filed, state the amount of any exemptions claimed only in Schedule C - Property Claimed as Exempt.

Do not list interests in executory contracts and unexpired leases on this schedule. List them in Schedule G - Executory Contracts and Unexpired Leases.

If the property is being held for the debtor by someone else, state that person's name and address under "Description and Location of Property." In providing the information requested in this schedule, do not include the name or address of a minor child. Simply state "a minor child."

Type of Property	N O N E	Description and Location of Property	Husband, Wife, Joint, or Community	Current Value of Debtor's Interest in Property, without Deducting any Secured Claim or Exemption
1. Cash on hand		Cash in wallet	–	50.00
2. Checking, savings or other financial accounts, certificates of deposit, or shares in banks, savings and loan, thrift, building and loan, and homestead associations, or credit unions, brokerage houses, or cooperatives.		Bank of America Checking Account #12345 Lakeport California from wages WestAmerica Bank, Lakeport CA Savings Account	– –	150.00 300.00
3. Security deposits with public utilities, telephone companies, landlords, and others.	X			
4. Household goods and furnishings, including audio, video, and computer equipment.		All items at replacement value Stereo system ($300), washer dryer set (200), refrigerator (400), electric stove (250), misc furniture (couch, 2 chairs, 2 end tables) (500), minor appliances (blender, toaster, mixer) (125), roll top desk (700), vacuum (50), bed and bedding (650), 20 inch tv (75), lawnmower (200), swing set, childrens toys (240), snowblower (160), oriental rug (2500) Location: 3045 Berwick St, Lakeport CA	–	6,350.00
5. Books, pictures and other art objects, antiques, stamp, coin, record, tape, compact disc, and other collections or collectibles.		250 books at used book store prices Location: 3045 Berwick St, Lakeport CA stamp collection at stamp dealer price Location: 3045 Berwick St, Lakeport CA	– –	1,250.00 2,500.00

Sub-Total >   10,600.00
(Total of this page)

  3   continuation sheets attached to the Schedule of Personal Property

Form B6B
(10/05)

In re   Carrie Anne Edwards   Case No. _____
                                          ,
                              Debtor

SCHEDULE B. PERSONAL PROPERTY
(Continuation Sheet)

Type of Property	N O N E	Description and Location of Property	Husband, Wife, Joint, or Community	Current Value of Debtor's Interest in Property, without Deducting any Secured Claim or Exemption
6. Wearing apparel.		normal clothing at used clothing store prices Location: 3045 Berwick St, Lakeport CA	–	800.00
7. Furs and jewelry.		diamond necklace at used jewelry store price (800), watch at flea market price (75) Location: 3045 Berwick St, Lakeport CA	–	875.00
8. Firearms and sports, photographic, and other hobby equipment.		Mountain bike at used bicycle store price (250), Digital camera priced at ebay (200), sword collection priced at antique store Location: 3045 Berwick St, Lakeport CA	–	1,250.00
9. Interests in insurance policies. Name insurance company of each policy and itemize surrender or refund value of each.	X			
10. Annuities. Itemize and name each issuer.	X			
11. Interests in an education IRA as defined in 26 U.S.C. § 530(b)(1) or under a qualified State tuition plan as defined in 26 U.S.C. § 529(b)(1). Give particulars. (File separately the record(s) of any such interest(s). 11 U.S.C. § 521(c); Rule 1007(b)).	X			
12. Interests in IRA, ERISA, Keogh, or other pension or profit sharing plans. Give particulars.		TIAA/CREF (ERISA Qualified Pension), not in bankruptcy estate	–	0.00
		IRA, Bank of America, Lakeport CA (25,000), not in bankruptcy estate	–	0.00
13. Stock and interests in incorporated and unincorporated businesses. Itemize.		5,000 shares in BLP Bankruptcy Services, Inc, a close corporation Location of certificates: 3045 Berwick St, Lakeport CA (valued at $.10 a share	–	500.00
14. Interests in partnerships or joint ventures. Itemize.	X			

Sub-Total >   3,425.00
(Total of this page)

Sheet _1_ of _3_ continuation sheets attached
to the Schedule of Personal Property

Form B6B
(10/05)

In re   Carrie Anne Edwards   Case No. _____
_____,
                          Debtor

SCHEDULE B. PERSONAL PROPERTY
(Continuation Sheet)

Type of Property	N O N E	Description and Location of Property	Husband, Wife, Joint, or Community	Current Value of Debtor's Interest in Property, without Deducting any Secured Claim or Exemption
15. Government and corporate bonds and other negotiable and nonnegotiable instruments.		U.S. Savings Bonds, all certificates at Ameritrust, 10 Financial Way, Cleveland Heights OH 41118	-	1,000.00
		Negotiable promissory note from Jonathan Edwards, Carrie's brother, dated 11/3/XX Location: 3045 Berwick St, Lakeport CA	-	500.00
16. Accounts receivable.	X			
17. Alimony, maintenance, support, and property settlements to which the debtor is or may be entitled. Give particulars.	X			
18. Other liquidated debts owing debtor including tax refunds. Give particulars.		Wages for 6/1/XX to 8/1/XX from ABC Typing Services	-	500.00
19. Equitable or future interests, life estates, and rights or powers exercisable for the benefit of the debtor other than those listed in Schedule A - Real Property.	X			
20. Contingent and noncontingent interests in estate of a decedent, death benefit plan, life insurance policy, or trust.	X			
21. Other contingent and unliquidated claims of every nature, including tax refunds, counterclaims of the debtor, and rights to setoff claims. Give estimated value of each.	X			
22. Patents, copyrights, and other intellectual property. Give particulars.		Copyright in book published by Nolo Press (Independent Paralegal's Handbook)	-	Unknown
23. Licenses, franchises, and other general intangibles. Give particulars.	X			

Sub-Total >   2,000.00
(Total of this page)

Sheet __2__ of __3__ continuation sheets attached
to the Schedule of Personal Property

Form B6B
(10/05)

In re   Carrie Anne Edwards   ,   Case No. _____

                          Debtor

SCHEDULE B. PERSONAL PROPERTY
(Continuation Sheet)

Type of Property	N O N E	Description and Location of Property	Husband, Wife, Joint, or Community	Current Value of Debtor's Interest in Property, without Deducting any Secured Claim or Exemption
24. Customer lists or other compilations containing personally identifiable information (as defined in 11 U.S.C. § 101(41A)) provided to the debtor by individuals in connection with obtaining a product or service from the debtor primarily for personal, family, or household purposes.	X			
25. Automobiles, trucks, trailers, and other vehicles and accessories.		2002 Buick LeSabre fully loaded in good condition (replacement value from nada.com)	–	8,500.00
26. Boats, motors, and accessories.	X			
27. Aircraft and accessories.	X			
28. Office equipment, furnishings, and supplies.		Used computer valued at Ebay price, used in business	–	800.00
		Copier (used Xerox) no known market for replacement value	–	Unknown
29. Machinery, fixtures, equipment, and supplies used in business.	X			
30. Inventory.	X			
31. Animals.	X			
32. Crops - growing or harvested. Give particulars.	X			
33. Farming equipment and implements.	X			
34. Farm supplies, chemicals, and feed.	X			
35. Other personal property of any kind not already listed. Itemize.	X			

Sub-Total > (Total of this page)	9,300.00
Total >	25,325.00

Sheet __3__ of __3__ continuation sheets attached
to the Schedule of Personal Property

(Report also on Summary of Schedules)

Form B6C
(10/05)

In re   Carrie Anne Edwards   ,   Case No. _____
                          Debtor

SCHEDULE C. PROPERTY CLAIMED AS EXEMPT

Debtor elects the exemptions to which debtor is entitled under: ☐ Check if debtor claims a homestead exemption that exceeds
(Check one box) $125,000.
☐ 11 U.S.C. §522(b)(2)
■ 11 U.S.C. §522(b)(3)

Description of Property	Specify Law Providing Each Exemption	Value of Claimed Exemption	Current Value of Property Without Deducting Exemption
Real Property Residence Location: 3045 Berwick St, Lakeport CA	C.C.P. § 703.140(b)(1)	0.00	140,000.00
Cash on Hand Cash in wallet	C.C.P. § 703.140(b)(5)	50.00	50.00
Checking, Savings, or Other Financial Accounts, Certificates of Deposit Bank of America Checking Account #12345 Lakeport California from wages	C.C.P. § 703.140(b)(5)	150.00	150.00
WestAmerica Bank, Lakeport CA Savings Account	C.C.P. § 703.140(b)(5)	300.00	300.00
Household Goods and Furnishings All items at replacement value Stereo system ($300), washer dryer set (200), refrigerator (400), electric stove (250), misc furniture (couch, 2 chairs, 2 end tables) (500), minor appliances (blender, toaster, mixer) (125), roll top desk (700), vacuum (50), bed and bedding (650), 20 inch tv (75), lawnmower (200), swing set, childrens toys (240), snowblower (160), oriental rug (2500) Location: 3045 Berwick St, Lakeport CA	C.C.P. § 703.140(b)(3)	6,350.00	6,350.00
Books, Pictures and Other Art Objects; Collectibles 250 books at used book store prices Location: 3045 Berwick St, Lakeport CA	C.C.P. § 703.140(b)(5)	1,250.00	1,250.00
stamp collection at stamp dealer price Location: 3045 Berwick St, Lakeport CA	C.C.P. § 703.140(b)(5)	2,500.00	2,500.00
Wearing Apparel normal clothing at used clothing store prices Location: 3045 Berwick St, Lakeport CA	C.C.P. § 703.140(b)(3)	800.00	800.00

___1___ continuation sheets attached to Schedule of Property Claimed as Exempt

Form B6C
(10/05)

In re   Carrie Anne Edwards   ,   Case No. _____

Debtor

SCHEDULE C. PROPERTY CLAIMED AS EXEMPT
(Continuation Sheet)

Description of Property	Specify Law Providing Each Exemption	Value of Claimed Exemption	Current Value of Property Without Deducting Exemption
Furs and Jewelry diamond necklace at used jewelry store price (800), watch at flea market price (75) Location: 3045 Berwick St, Lakeport CA	C.C.P. § 703.140(b)(4)	875.00	875.00
Firearms and Sports, Photographic and Other Hobby Equipment Mountain bike at used bicycle store price (250), Digital camera priced at ebay (200), sword collection priced at antique store Location: 3045 Berwick St, Lakeport CA	C.C.P. § 703.140(b)(5)	1,250.00	1,250.00
Stock and Interests in Businesses 5,000 shares in BLP Bankruptcy Services, Inc, a close corporation Location of certificates: 3045 Berwick St, Lakeport CA (valued at $.10 a share	C.C.P. § 703.140(b)(5)	500.00	500.00
Government & Corporate Bonds, Other Negotiable & Non-negotiable Inst. U.S. Savings Bonds, all certificates at Ameritrust, 10 Financial Way, Cleveland Heights OH 41118	C.C.P. § 703.140(b)(5)	1,000.00	1,000.00
Negotiable promissory note from Jonathan Edwards, Carrie's brother, dated 11/3/XX Location: 3045 Berwick St, Lakeport CA	C.C.P. § 703.140(b)(5)	500.00	500.00
Other Liquidated Debts Owing Debtor Including Tax Refund Wages for 6/1/XX to 8/1/XX from ABC Typing Services	C.C.P. § 703.140(b)(5)	500.00	500.00
Automobiles, Trucks, Trailers, and Other Vehicles 2002 Buick LeSabre fully loaded in good condition (replacement value from nada.com)	C.C.P. § 703.140(b)(2) C.C.P. § 703.140(b)(5)	2,975.00 5,525.00	8,500.00
Office Equipment, Furnishings and Supplies Used computer valued at Ebay price, used in business	C.C.P. § 703.140(b)(6)	800.00	800.00

Sheet __1__ of __1__ continuation sheets attached to the Schedule of Property Claimed as Exempt

Form B6D
(10/05)

In re   Carrie Anne Edwards   Case No. _____
_____,
                           Debtor

SCHEDULE D. CREDITORS HOLDING SECURED CLAIMS

State the name, mailing address, including zip code, and last four digits of any account number of all entities holding claims secured by property of the debtor as of the date of filing of the petition. The complete account number of any account the debtor has with the creditor is useful to the trustee and the creditor and may be provided if the debtor chooses to do so. List creditors holding all types of secured interests such as judgment liens, garnishments, statutory liens, mortgages, deeds of trust, and other security interests.

List creditors in alphabetical order to the extent practicable. If a minor child is a creditor, indicate that by stating "a minor child" and do not disclose the child's name. See 11 U.S.C§112; Fed.R.Bankr.P. 1007(m). If all secured creditors will not fit on this page, use the continuation sheet provided.

If any entity other than a spouse in a joint case may be jointly liable on a claim, place an "X" in the column labeled "Codebtor", include the entity on the appropriate schedule of creditors, and complete Schedule H-Codebtors. If a joint petition is filed, state whether husband, wife, both of them, or the marital community may be liable on each claim by placing an "H", "W", "J", or "C" in the column labeled "Husband, Wife, Joint, or Community." If the claim is contingent, place an "X" in the column labeled "Contingent". If the claim is unliquidated, place an "X" in the column labeled "Unliquidated". If the claim is disputed, place an "X" in the column labeled "Disputed." (You may need to place an "X" in more than one of these three columns.)

Report the total of all claims listed on this schedule in the box labeled "Total" on the last sheet of the completed schedule. Report this total also on the Summary of Schedules.

☐   Check this box if debtor has no creditors holding secured claims to report on this Schedule D.

CREDITOR'S NAME AND MAILING ADDRESS INCLUDING ZIP CODE, AND ACCOUNT NUMBER (See instructions above.)	CODEBTOR	Husband, Wife, Joint, or Community				DATE CLAIM WAS INCURRED, NATURE OF LIEN, AND DESCRIPTION AND VALUE OF PROPERTY SUBJECT TO LIEN	CONTINGENT	UNLIQUIDATED	DISPUTED	AMOUNT OF CLAIM WITHOUT DEDUCTING VALUE OF COLLATERAL	UNSECURED PORTION, IF ANY
		H	W	J	C						
Account No. 444555666777 GMAC PO Box 23567 Duchesne, UT 84021						November, 2002 Purchase Money Security 2002 Buick LeSabre fully loaded in good condition (replacement value from nada.com)					
						Value $ 8,500.00				1,000.00	0.00
Account No. 64-112-1861 Grand Junction Mortgage 3456 Eight St. Clearlake, CA 95422						5/2005 First Mortgage Residence Location: 3045 Berwick St, Lakeport CA					
						Value $ 140,000.00				135,000.00	0.00
Account No. 55555555555 Lending Tree PO Box 3333 Palo Alto, CA 94310						12/xx Second Mortgage Residence Location: 3045 Berwick St, Lakeport CA					
						Value $ 140,000.00				5,000.00	0.00
Account No. 4454444432333 Loantree PO Box 305 Lucerne, CA 95458						12/XX Second Mortgage home equity loan on home					
						Value $ 5,000.00				0.00	0.00

_0_   continuation sheets attached

	Subtotal (Total of this page)	141,000.00
	Total (Report on Summary of Schedules)	141,000.00

Form B6E
(10/05)

In re ___Carrie Anne Edwards_____,   Case No. _____
                                    Debtor

SCHEDULE E. CREDITORS HOLDING UNSECURED PRIORITY CLAIMS

A complete list of claims entitled to priority, listed separately by type of priority, is to be set forth on the sheets provided. Only holders of unsecured claims entitled to priority should be listed in this schedule. In the boxes provided on the attached sheets, state the name, mailing address, including zip code, and last four digits of the account number, if any, of all entities holding priority claims against the debtor or the property of the debtor, as of the date of the filing of the petition. Use a separate continuation sheet for each type of priority and label each with the type of priority.

The complete account number of any account the debtor has with the creditor is useful to the trustee and the creditor and may be provided if the debtor chooses to do so. If a minor child is a creditor, indicate that by stating "a minor child" and do not disclose the child's name. See 11 U.S.C.§112; Fed.R.Bankr.P. 1007(m).

If any entity other than a spouse in a joint case may be jointly liable on a claim, place an "X" in the column labeled "Codebtor", include the entity on the appropriate schedule of creditors, and complete Schedule H-Codebtors. If a joint petition is filed, state whether husband, wife, both of them or the marital community may be liable on each claim by placing an "H", "W", "J", or "C" in the column labeled "Husband, Wife, Joint, or Community". If the claim is contingent, place an "X" in the column labeled "Contingent". If the claim is unliquidated, place an "X" in the column labeled "Unliquidated". If the claim is disputed, place an "X" in the column labeled "Disputed". (You may need to place an "X" in more than one of these three columns.)

Report the total of claims listed on each sheet in the box labeled "Subtotal" on each sheet. Report the total of all claims listed on this Schedule E in the box labeled "Total" on the last sheet of the completed schedule. Report this total also on the Summary of Schedules.

Report the total of amounts entitled to priority listed on each sheet in the box labeled "Subtotal" on each sheet. Report the total of all amounts entitled to priority listed on this Schedule E in the box labeled "Total" on the last sheet of the completed schedule. If applicable, also report this total on the Means Test form.

☐ Check this box if debtor has no creditors holding unsecured priority claims to report on this Schedule E.

TYPES OF PRIORITY CLAIMS (Check the appropriate box(es) below if claims in that category are listed on the attached sheets.)

■ **Domestic support obligations**

Claims for domestic support that are owed to or recoverable by a spouse, former spouse, or child of the debtor, or the parent, legal guardian, or responsible relative of such a child, or a governmental unit to whom such a domestic support claim has been assigned to the extent provided in 11 U.S.C. § 507(a)(1).

☐ **Extensions of credit in an involuntary case**

Claims arising in the ordinary course of the debtor's business or financial affairs after the commencement of the case but before the earlier of the appointment of a trustee or the order for relief. 11 U.S.C. § 507(a)(3).

☐ **Wages, salaries, and commissions**

Wages, salaries, and commissions, including vacation, severance, and sick leave pay owing to employees and commissions owing to qualifying independent sales representatives up to $10,000* per person earned within 180 days immediately preceding the filing of the original petition, or the cessation of business, which ever occurred first, to the extent provided in 11 U.S.C. § 507 (a)(4).

☐ **Contributions to employee benefit plans**

Money owed to employee benefit plans for services rendered within 180 days immediately preceding the filing of the original petition, or the cessation of business, whichever occurred first, to the extent provided in 11 U.S.C. § 507(a)(5).

☐ **Certain farmers and fishermen**

Claims of certain farmers and fishermen, up to $4,925* per farmer or fisherman, against the debtor, as provided in 11 U.S.C. § 507(a)(6).

☐ **Deposits by individuals**

Claims of individuals up to $2,225* for deposits for the purchase, lease, or rental of property or services for personal, family, or household use, that were not delivered or provided. 11 U.S.C. § 507(a)(7).

■ **Taxes and certain other debts owed to governmental units**

Taxes, customs duties, and penalties owing to federal, state, and local governmental units as set forth in 11 U.S.C § 507(a)(8).

☐ **Commitments to maintain the capital of an insured depository institution**

Claims based on commitments to the FDIC, RTC, Director of the Office of Thrift Supervision, Comptroller of the Currency, or Board of Governors of the Federal Reserve System, or their predecessors or successors, to maintain the capital of an insured depository institution. 11 U.S.C. § 507(a)(9).

☐ **Claims for death or personal injury while debtor was intoxicated**

Claims for death or personal injury resulting from the operation of a motor vehicle or vessel while the debtor was intoxicated from using alcohol, a drug, or another substance. 11 U.S.C. § 507(a)(10).

*Amounts are subject to adjustment on April 1, 2007, and every three years thereafter with respect to cases commenced on or after the date of adjustment.

_____2_____ continuation sheets attached

Form B6E - Cont.
(10/05)

In re   Carrie Anne Edwards   ,   Case No. _____
                                                     Debtor

SCHEDULE E. CREDITORS HOLDING UNSECURED PRIORITY CLAIMS
(Continuation Sheet)

Domestic Support Obligations

TYPE OF PRIORITY

CREDITOR'S NAME, AND MAILING ADDRESS INCLUDING ZIP CODE, AND ACCOUNT NUMBER (See instructions.)	CODEBTOR	H W J C	DATE CLAIM WAS INCURRED AND CONSIDERATION FOR CLAIM	CONTINGENT	UNLIQUIDATED	DISPUTED	AMOUNT OF CLAIM	AMOUNT ENTITLED TO PRIORITY
			Husband, Wife, Joint, or Community					
Account No.			2005					
Jon Edwards 900 Grand View Jackson, WY 83001		−	Child support				2,500.00	2,500.00
Account No.								
Account No.								
Account No.								
Account No.								

Sheet __1__ of __2__ continuation sheets attached to
Schedule of Creditors Holding Unsecured Priority Claims

Subtotal
(Total of this page)

2,500.00	2,500.00

Form B6E - Cont.
(10/05)

In re   Carrie Anne Edwards   ,   Case No. _____

                               Debtor

SCHEDULE E. CREDITORS HOLDING UNSECURED PRIORITY CLAIMS
(Continuation Sheet)

Taxes and Certain Other Debts
Owed to Governmental Units

TYPE OF PRIORITY

CREDITOR'S NAME, AND MAILING ADDRESS INCLUDING ZIP CODE, AND ACCOUNT NUMBER (See instructions.)	CODEBTOR	Husband, Wife, Joint, or Community			DATE CLAIM WAS INCURRED AND CONSIDERATION FOR CLAIM	CONTINGENT	UNLIQUIDATED	DISPUTED	AMOUNT OF CLAIM	AMOUNT ENTITLED TO PRIORITY
		H W	J	C						
Account No.					April 15, 20XX tax liability and interest					
IRS Columbus, OH 43266		–							3,000.00	3,000.00
Account No.										
Account No.										
Account No.										
Account No.										

Sheet __2__ of __2__ continuation sheets attached to
Schedule of Creditors Holding Unsecured Priority Claims

	Subtotal (Total of this page)	3,000.00	3,000.00
	Total (Report on Summary of Schedules)	5,500.00	5,500.00

Form B6F
(10/05)

In re ____Carrie Anne Edwards_____,   Case No. _____

                                            Debtor

SCHEDULE F. CREDITORS HOLDING UNSECURED NONPRIORITY CLAIMS

State the name, mailing address, including zip code, and last four digits of any account number, of all entities holding unsecured claims without priority against the debtor or the property of the debtor, as of the date of filing of the petition. The complete account number of any account the debtor has with the creditor is useful to the trustee and the creditor and may be provided if the debtor chooses to do so. If a minor child is a creditor, indicate that by stating "a minor child" and do not disclose the child's name. See 11 U.S.C.§112; Fed.R.Bankr.P. 1007(m). Do not include claims listed in Schedules D and E. If all creditors will not fit on this page, use the continuation sheet provided.

If any entity other than a spouse in a joint case may be jointly liable on a claim, place an "X" in the column labeled "Codebtor", include the entity on the appropriate schedule of creditors, and complete Schedule H - Codebtors. If a joint petition is filed, state whether husband, wife, both of them, or the marital community maybe liable on each claim by placing an "H", "W", "J", or "C" in the column labeled "Husband, Wife, Joint, or Community".

If the claim is contingent, place an "X" in the column labeled "Contingent". If the claim is unliquidated, place an "X" in the column labeled "Unliquidated". If the claim is disputed, place an "X" in the column labeled "Disputed". (You may need to place an "X" in more than one of these three columns.)

Report the total of all claims listed on this schedule in the box labeled "Total" on the last sheet of the completed schedule. Report this total also on the Summary of Schedules.

☐   Check this box if debtor has no creditors holding unsecured claims to report on this Schedule F.

CREDITOR'S NAME, AND MAILING ADDRESS INCLUDING ZIP CODE, AND ACCOUNT NUMBER (See instructions above.)	CODEBTOR	Husband, Wife, Joint, or Community			DATE CLAIM WAS INCURRED AND CONSIDERATION FOR CLAIM. IF CLAIM IS SUBJECT TO SETOFF, SO STATE.	CONTINGENT	UNLIQUIDATED	DISPUTED	AMOUNT OF CLAIM
		H	W	J/C					
Account No. Alan Accountant 5 Green St. Cleveland, OH 44118		-			4 /XX Tax preparation				500.00
Account No. 41 89-0000-2613-5556 American Allowance PO Box 1 New York, NY 10001		-			1/xx to 4/xx credit card charges				5,600.00
Account No. Angel of Mercy Hospital 4444 Elevisior St. Belmont, CA 94003		-			12/xx uninsured surgery and medical treatment				34,000.00
Account No. Bob Jones III 4566 Fifth Ave. New York, NY 10020		-			5/xx Auto accident--negligence claim				75,000.00

  __2__ continuation sheets attached

Subtotal (Total of this page)   115,100.00

Form B6F - Cont.
(10/05)

In re   Carrie Anne Edwards   ,   Case No. _____
                                              Debtor

SCHEDULE F. CREDITORS HOLDING UNSECURED NONPRIORITY CLAIMS
(Continuation Sheet)

CREDITOR'S NAME, AND MAILING ADDRESS INCLUDING ZIP CODE, AND ACCOUNT NUMBER (See instructions.)	CODEBTOR	Husband, Wife, Joint, or Community			DATE CLAIM WAS INCURRED AND CONSIDERATION FOR CLAIM. IF CLAIM IS SUBJECT TO SETOFF, SO STATE.	CONTINGENT	UNLIQUIDATED	DISPUTED	AMOUNT OF CLAIM
		H W	J	C					
Account No. Bonnie Johnson 3335 Irving St Clearlake, CA 95422		–			8/xx Personal loan				5,500.00
Account No. 845061-86-3 Citibank 200 East North St Columbus, OH 43266		–			20xx Student loan				10,000.00
Account No. 4401 Dr. Dennis Dentist 45 Superior Way Cleveland, OH 44118		–			12/xx to 6/xx dental work				1,050.00
Account No. 555671 Dr. Helen Jones 443 First St. Soledad, CA 94750		–			4/xx to 8/xx Pediatric Care				5,000.00
Account No. Fannie's Furniture 55544 Grove St. Berkeley, CA 94710	X	–			12/xx used bedroomset				1,300.00

Sheet no. _1_ of _2_ sheets attached to Schedule of
Creditors Holding Unsecured Nonpriority Claims

Subtotal
(Total of this page)   22,850.00

Form B6F - Cont.
(10/05)

In re   Carrie Anne Edwards   ,   Case No. _____
                                    Debtor

SCHEDULE F. CREDITORS HOLDING UNSECURED NONPRIORITY CLAIMS
(Continuation Sheet)

CREDITOR'S NAME, AND MAILING ADDRESS INCLUDING ZIP CODE, AND ACCOUNT NUMBER (See instructions.)	CODEBTOR	Husband, Wife, Joint, or Community			DATE CLAIM WAS INCURRED AND CONSIDERATION FOR CLAIM. IF CLAIM IS SUBJECT TO SETOFF, SO STATE.	CONTINGENT	UNLIQUIDATED	DISPUTED	AMOUNT OF CLAIM
		H	W J	C					
Account No. 222387941 Illuminating Co. 20245 Old Hwy 53 Clearlake, CA 95422	–				3/xx to 7/xx electrical work on house				750.00
Account No. John White Esq. PO Box 401 Finley, CA 95435	–				2/xx to 8/xx Legal representation in lawsuit against neighbor for incursion on property				3,450.00
Account No. 11210550 PG&E 315 North Forbes St. Lakeport, CA 95453	–				12/xx to 6/xx gas and electric service				1,200.00
Account No. 487310097 Sears PO Box 11 Chicago, IL 60619	–				20xx to 200xy Dept store and catalog charges				3,800.00
Account No. 									

Sheet no. _2_ of _2_ sheets attached to Schedule of
Creditors Holding Unsecured Nonpriority Claims

Subtotal (Total of this page)	9,200.00
Total (Report on Summary of Schedules)	147,150.00

Form B6G
(10/05)

In re   Carrie Anne Edwards   ,   Case No. _____

Debtor

SCHEDULE G. EXECUTORY CONTRACTS AND UNEXPIRED LEASES

Describe all executory contracts of any nature and all unexpired leases of real or personal property. Include any timeshare interests. State nature of debtor's interest in contract, i.e., "Purchaser", "Agent", etc. State whether debtor is the lessor or lessee of a lease. Provide the names and complete mailing addresses of all other parties to each lease or contract described. If a minor child is a party to one of the leases or contracts, indicate that by stating "a minor child" and do not disclose the child's name. See 11 U.S.C. § 112; Fed.R. Bankr. P. 1007(m).

☐ Check this box if debtor has no executory contracts or unexpired leases.

Name and Mailing Address, Including Zip Code, of Other Parties to Lease or Contract	Description of Contract or Lease and Nature of Debtor's Interest. State whether lease is for nonresidential real property. State contract number of any government contract.
Beauty Products Leasing Co. 44332 Geismar, LA 70734	Laser skin treatment machine. Lease for 5 year period that expires on 2010
Herman Jones 45543 Woodleigh Court Smith River, CA 95567	Sales contract for debtor's home entered into between debtor and Herman Jones on 2 /1/XX

___0___ continuation sheets attached to Schedule of Executory Contracts and Unexpired Leases

Form B6H
(10/05)

In re ___Carrie Anne Edwards_____,   Case No. _____
                                    Debtor

SCHEDULE H. CODEBTORS

    Provide the information requested concerning any person or entity, other than a spouse in a joint case, that is also liable on any debts listed by debtor in the schedules of creditors. Include all guarantors and co-signers. If the debtor resides or resided in a community property state, commonwealth, or territory (including Alaska, Arizona, California, Idaho, Louisiana, Nevada, New Mexico, Puerto Rico, Texas, Washington, or Wisconsin) within the eight year period immediately preceding the commencement of the case, identify the name of the debtor's spouse and of any former spouse who resides or resided with the debtor in the community property state, commonwealth, or territory. Include all names used by the nondebtor spouse during the eight years immediately preceding the commencement of this case. If a minor child is a codebtor or a creditor, indicate that by stating "a minor child" and do not disclose the child's name. See 11 U.S.C. § 112; Fed. Bankr. P. 1007(m).

☐ Check this box if debtor has no codebtors.

NAME AND ADDRESS OF CODEBTOR	NAME AND ADDRESS OF CREDITOR
Bonnie Johnson 3335 Irving St. Clearlake, CA 95422	Fannie's Furniture 55544 Grove St. Berkeley, CA 94710

___0___ continuation sheets attached to Schedule of Codebtors

Form B6I
(10/05)

In re   Carrie Anne Edwards   Case No. _____
                        Debtor(s)

SCHEDULE I. CURRENT INCOME OF INDIVIDUAL DEBTOR(S)

The column labeled "Spouse" must be completed in all cases filed by joint debtors and by a married debtor in a chapter 7, 11, 12, or 13 case whether or not a joint petition is filed, unless the spouses are separated and a joint petition is not filed. Do not state the name of any minor child.

Debtor's Marital Status:	DEPENDENTS OF DEBTOR AND SPOUSE	
Divorced	RELATIONSHIP: daughter Son	AGE: 12 14

Employment:	DEBTOR	SPOUSE
Occupation	Retail	
Name of Employer	Macy's	
How long employed	2 months	
Address of Employer	2356 Cleveland Ave. Santa Rosa, CA 95402	

INCOME: (Estimate of average monthly income)	DEBTOR	SPOUSE
1. Current monthly gross wages, salary, and commissions (Prorate if not paid monthly.)	$ 3,033.33	$ N/A
2. Estimate monthly overtime	$ 0.00	$ N/A
3. SUBTOTAL	$ 3,033.33	$ N/A
4. LESS PAYROLL DEDUCTIONS		
a. Payroll taxes and social security	$ 541.67	$ N/A
b. Insurance	$ 0.00	$ N/A
c. Union dues	$ 0.00	$ N/A
d. Other (Specify): _____	$ 0.00	$ N/A
	$ 0.00	$ N/A
5. SUBTOTAL OF PAYROLL DEDUCTIONS	$ 541.67	$ N/A
6. TOTAL NET MONTHLY TAKE HOME PAY	$ 2,491.66	$ N/A
7. Regular income from operation of business or profession or farm. (Attach detailed statement)	$ 0.00	$ N/A
8. Income from real property	$ 0.00	$ N/A
9. Interest and dividends	$ 0.00	$ N/A
10. Alimony, maintenance or support payments payable to the debtor for the debtor's use or that of dependents listed above.	$ 500.00	$ N/A
11. Social security or other government assistance (Specify): _____	$ 0.00	$ N/A
	$ 0.00	$ N/A
12. Pension or retirement income	$ 0.00	$ N/A
13. Other monthly income (Specify): royalties from book on bankruptcy _____	$ 1,000.00	$ N/A
	$ 0.00	$ N/A
14. SUBTOTAL OF LINES 7 THROUGH 13	$ 1,500.00	$ N/A
15. TOTAL MONTHLY INCOME (Add amounts shown on lines 6 and 14)	$ 3,991.66	$ N/A

16. TOTAL COMBINED MONTHLY INCOME: $ _____ 3,991.66   (Report also on Summary of Schedules)

17. Describe any increase or decrease in income reasonably anticipated to occur within the year following the filing of this document:

Form B6J
(10/05)

In re   Carrie Anne Edwards _____   Case No. _____
                        Debtor(s)

SCHEDULE J. CURRENT EXPENDITURES OF INDIVIDUAL DEBTOR(S)

Complete this schedule by estimating the average monthly expenses of the debtor and the debtor's family. Pro rate any payments made bi-weekly, quarterly, semi-annually, or annually to show monthly rate.

☐ Check this box if a joint petition is filed and debtor's spouse maintains a separate household. Complete a separate schedule of expenditures labeled "Spouse."

1. Rent or home mortgage payment (include lot rented for mobile home) $	1,500.00
a. Are real estate taxes included? Yes _x_ No ____	
b. Is property insurance included? Yes _x_ No ____	
2. Utilities: a. Electricity and heating fuel $	200.00
b. Water and sewer $	150.00
c. Telephone $	300.00
d. Other See Detailed Expense Attachment $	130.00
3. Home maintenance (repairs and upkeep) $	75.00
4. Food $	500.00
5. Clothing $	125.00
6. Laundry and dry cleaning $	40.00
7. Medical and dental expenses $	175.00
8. Transportation (not including car payments) $	300.00
9. Recreation, clubs and entertainment, newspapers, magazines, etc. $	0.00
10. Charitable contributions $	0.00
11. Insurance (not deducted from wages or included in home mortgage payments)	
a. Homeowner's or renter's $	0.00
b. Life $	0.00
c. Health $	0.00
d. Auto $	100.00
e. Other _____ $	0.00
12. Taxes (not deducted from wages or included in home mortgage payments)	
(Specify) _____ $	0.00
13. Installment payments: (In chapter 11, 12 and 13 cases, do not list payments to be included in the plan.)	
a. Auto $	250.00
b. Other Payment on home equity loan $	100.00
c. Other _____ $	0.00
d. Other _____ $	0.00
14. Alimony, maintenance, and support paid to others $	0.00
15. Payments for support of additional dependents not living at your home $	0.00
16. Regular expenses from operation of business, profession, or farm (attach detailed statement) $	0.00
17. Other _____ $	0.00
Other _____ $	0.00
18. TOTAL MONTHLY EXPENSES (Report also on Summary of Schedules) $	3,945.00

19. Describe any increase or decrease in expenditures anticipated to occur within the year following the filing of this document:

20. STATEMENT OF MONTHLY NET INCOME

a. Total monthly income from Line 16 of Schedule I $	3,991.66
b. Total monthly expenses from Line 18 above $	3,945.00
c. Monthly net income (a. minus b.) $	46.66

Form B6J
(10/05)

In re Carrie Anne Edwards   Case No. _____
                          Debtor(s)

SCHEDULE J. CURRENT EXPENDITURES OF INDIVIDUAL DEBTOR(S)
Detailed Expense Attachment

Other Utility Expenditures:

Satellite TV	$ 90.00
DSL	$ 40.00
Total Other Utility Expenditures	$ 130.00

Official Form 6-Decl.
(10/05)

United States Bankruptcy Court
Northern District of California

In re   Carrie Anne Edwards   Case No. _____

                                    Debtor(s)   Chapter   7   _____

DECLARATION CONCERNING DEBTOR'S SCHEDULES

DECLARATION UNDER PENALTY OF PERJURY BY INDIVIDUAL DEBTOR

        I declare under penalty of perjury that I have read the foregoing summary and schedules, consisting of
___21___ sheets *[total shown on summary page plus 2]*, and that they are true and correct to the best of my knowledge, information, and belief.

Date October 25, 2005 _____   Signature /s/ Carrie Anne Edwards _____
                                           Carrie Anne Edwards
                                           Debtor

Penalty for making a false statement or concealing property: Fine of up to $500,000 or imprisonment for up to 5 years or both.
18 U.S.C. §§ 152 and 3571.

Official Form 7
(10/05)

United States Bankruptcy Court
Northern District of California

In re   Carrie Anne Edwards   Case No. _____

                              Debtor(s)   Chapter   7

STATEMENT OF FINANCIAL AFFAIRS

This statement is to be completed by every debtor. Spouses filing a joint petition may file a single statement on which the information for both spouses is combined. If the case is filed under chapter 12 or chapter 13, a married debtor must furnish information for both spouses whether or not a joint petition is filed, unless the spouses are separated and a joint petition is not filed. An individual debtor engaged in business as a sole proprietor, partner, family farmer, or self-employed professional, should provide the information requested on this statement concerning all such activities as well as the individual's personal affairs. Do not include the name or address of a minor child in this statement. Indicate payments, transfers and the like to minor children by stating "a minor child." See 11 U.S.C. § 112; Fed. R. Bankr. P. 1007(m).

Questions 1 - 18 are to be completed by all debtors. Debtors that are or have been in business, as defined below, also must complete Questions 19 - 25. **If the answer to an applicable question is "None," mark the box labeled "None."** If additional space is needed for the answer to any question, use and attach a separate sheet properly identified with the case name, case number (if known), and the number of the question.

DEFINITIONS

"In business." A debtor is "in business" for the purpose of this form if the debtor is a corporation or partnership. An individual debtor is "in business" for the purpose of this form if the debtor is or has been, within six years immediately preceding the filing of this bankruptcy case, any of the following: an officer, director, managing executive, or owner of 5 percent or more of the voting or equity securities of a corporation; a partner, other than a limited partner, of a partnership; a sole proprietor or self-employed full-time or part-time. An individual debtor also may be "in business" for the purpose of this form if the debtor engages in a trade, business, or other activity, other than as an employee, to supplement income from the debtor's primary employment.

"Insider." The term "insider" includes but is not limited to: relatives of the debtor; general partners of the debtor and their relatives; corporations of which the debtor is an officer, director, or person in control; officers, directors, and any owner of 5 percent or more of the voting or equity securities of a corporate debtor and their relatives; affiliates of the debtor and insiders of such affiliates; any managing agent of the debtor. 11 U.S.C. § 101.

---

1. Income from employment or operation of business

None
☐

State the gross amount of income the debtor has received from employment, trade, or profession, or from operation of the debtor's business, including part-time activities either as an employee or in independent trade or business, from the beginning of this calendar year to the date this case was commenced. State also the gross amounts received during the **two years** immediately preceding this calendar year. (A debtor that maintains, or has maintained, financial records on the basis of a fiscal rather than a calendar year may report fiscal year income. Identify the beginning and ending dates of the debtor's fiscal year.) If a joint petition is filed, state income for each spouse separately. (Married debtors filing under chapter 12 or chapter 13 must state income of both spouses whether or not a joint petition is filed, unless the spouses are separated and a joint petition is not filed.)

AMOUNT   SOURCE
$144,600.00   2003 ($55,100) (employment at Microsoft as software engineer)
                    2004 ($50,100) (employment at Microsoft)

                    Jan-Oct 2005 (39,400) (employment at Microsoft and Macy's)

2

2. Income other than from employment or operation of business

None
☐

State the amount of income received by the debtor other than from employment, trade, profession, or operation of the debtor's business during the **two years** immediately preceding the commencement of this case. Give particulars. If a joint petition is filed, state income for each spouse separately. (Married debtors filing under chapter 12 or chapter 13 must state income for each spouse whether or not a joint petition is filed, unless the spouses are separated and a joint petition is not filed.)

AMOUNT	SOURCE
$32,000.00	Oct 04-Oct 05 (12,000 royalties, 6,000 child support
	October 03-Oct 04 (8,000 royalties, 6,000 child support)

3. Payments to creditors

None
☐

Complete a. or b., as appropriate, and c.

a.   *Individual or joint debtor(s) with primarily consumer debts.* List all payments on loans, installment purchases of goods or services, and other debts to any creditor made within **90 days** immediately preceding the commencement of this case if the aggregate value of all property that constitutes or is affected by such transfer is not less than $600. Indicate with an (*) any payments that were made to a creditor on account of a domestic support obligation or as part of an alternative repayment schedule under a plan by an approved nonprofit budgeting and creditor counseling agency. (Married debtors filing under chapter 12 or chapter 13 must include payments by either or both spouses whether or not a joint petition is filed, unless the spouses are separated and a joint petition is not filed.)

NAME AND ADDRESS OF CREDITOR	DATES OF PAYMENTS	AMOUNT PAID	AMOUNT STILL OWING
Loantree PO Box 305 Lucerne, CA 95458	12/xx	$800.00	$0.00

None
■

b.   *Debtor whose debts are not primarily consumer debts:* List each payment or other transfer to any creditor made within **90 days** immediately preceding the commencement of the case if the aggregate value of all property that constitutes or is affected by such transfer is not less than $5,000. (Married debtors filing under chapter 12 or chapter 13 must include payments by either or both spouses whether or not a joint petition is filed, unless the spouses are separated and a joint petition is not filed.)

NAME AND ADDRESS OF CREDITOR	DATES OF PAYMENTS/ TRANSFERS	AMOUNT PAID OR VALUE OF TRANSFERS	AMOUNT STILL OWING

None
■

c.   *All debtors:* List all payments made within **one year** immediately preceding the commencement of this case to or for the benefit of creditors who are or were insiders. (Married debtors filing under chapter 12 or chapter 13 must include payments by either or both spouses whether or not a joint petition is filed, unless the spouses are separated and a joint petition is not filed.)

NAME AND ADDRESS OF CREDITOR AND RELATIONSHIP TO DEBTOR	DATE OF PAYMENT	AMOUNT PAID	AMOUNT STILL OWING

4. Suits and administrative proceedings, executions, garnishments and attachments

None
☐

a. List all suits and administrative proceedings to which the debtor is or was a party within **one year** immediately preceding the filing of this bankruptcy case. (Married debtors filing under chapter 12 or chapter 13 must include information concerning either or both spouses whether or not a joint petition is filed, unless the spouses are separated and a joint petition is not filed.)

CAPTION OF SUIT AND CASE NUMBER	NATURE OF PROCEEDING	COURT OR AGENCY AND LOCATION	STATUS OR DISPOSITION
Bob Jones III v. Carrie Edwards Case # cv34457	Negligence action for auto accident	Lake County Superior Court 255 N. Forbes St. Lakeport, CA 95453	Trial pending

3

None ☐ b. Describe all property that has been attached, garnished or seized under any legal or equitable process within **one year** immediately preceding the commencement of this case. (Married debtors filing under chapter 12 or chapter 13 must include information concerning property of either or both spouses whether or not a joint petition is filed, unless the spouses are separated and a joint petition is not filed.)

NAME AND ADDRESS OF PERSON FOR WHOSE BENEFIT PROPERTY WAS SEIZED	DATE OF SEIZURE	DESCRIPTION AND VALUE OF PROPERTY
JNR Adjustment Co. PO Box 27070 Minneapolis, MN 55427	4/XX	wage garnishment for two months totaling $510 for judgment on debt owed to DVD club.

5. Repossessions, foreclosures and returns

None ☐ List all property that has been repossessed by a creditor, sold at a foreclosure sale, transferred through a deed in lieu of foreclosure or returned to the seller, within **one year** immediately preceding the commencement of this case. (Married debtors filing under chapter 12 or chapter 13 must include information concerning property of either or both spouses whether or not a joint petition is filed, unless the spouses are separated and a joint petition is not filed.)

NAME AND ADDRESS OF CREDITOR OR SELLER	DATE OF REPOSSESSION, FORECLOSURE SALE, TRANSFER OR RETURN	DESCRIPTION AND VALUE OF PROPERTY
Eskanos & Adler 2325 Clayton Rd. Concord, CA 94520	4/XX	Repossessed furniture worth $800

6. Assignments and receiverships

None ■ a. Describe any assignment of property for the benefit of creditors made within **120 days** immediately preceding the commencement of this case. (Married debtors filing under chapter 12 or chapter 13 must include any assignment by either or both spouses whether or not a joint petition is filed, unless the spouses are separated and a joint petition is not filed.)

NAME AND ADDRESS OF ASSIGNEE	DATE OF ASSIGNMENT	TERMS OF ASSIGNMENT OR SETTLEMENT

None ■ b. List all property which has been in the hands of a custodian, receiver, or court-appointed official within **one year** immediately preceding the commencement of this case. (Married debtors filing under chapter 12 or chapter 13 must include information concerning property of either or both spouses whether or not a joint petition is filed, unless the spouses are separated and a joint petition is not filed.)

NAME AND ADDRESS OF CUSTODIAN	NAME AND LOCATION OF COURT CASE TITLE & NUMBER	DATE OF ORDER	DESCRIPTION AND VALUE OF PROPERTY

7. Gifts

None ■ List all gifts or charitable contributions made within **one year** immediately preceding the commencement of this case except ordinary and usual gifts to family members aggregating less than $200 in value per individual family member and charitable contributions aggregating less than $100 per recipient. (Married debtors filing under chapter 12 or chapter 13 must include gifts or contributions by either or both spouses whether or not a joint petition is filed, unless the spouses are separated and a joint petition is not filed.)

NAME AND ADDRESS OF PERSON OR ORGANIZATION	RELATIONSHIP TO DEBTOR, IF ANY	DATE OF GIFT	DESCRIPTION AND VALUE OF GIFT

8. Losses

None ■ List all losses from fire, theft, other casualty or gambling within **one year** immediately preceding the commencement of this case **or since the commencement of this case.** (Married debtors filing under chapter 12 or chapter 13 must include losses by either or both spouses whether or not a joint petition is filed, unless the spouses are separated and a joint petition is not filed.)

DESCRIPTION AND VALUE OF PROPERTY	DESCRIPTION OF CIRCUMSTANCES AND, IF LOSS WAS COVERED IN WHOLE OR IN PART BY INSURANCE, GIVE PARTICULARS	DATE OF LOSS

4

9. Payments related to debt counseling or bankruptcy

None
☐   List all payments made or property transferred by or on behalf of the debtor to any persons, including attorneys, for consultation concerning debt consolidation, relief under the bankruptcy law or preparation of the petition in bankruptcy within **one year** immediately preceding the commencement of this case.

NAME AND ADDRESS OF PAYEE	DATE OF PAYMENT, NAME OF PAYOR IF OTHER THAN DEBTOR	AMOUNT OF MONEY OR DESCRIPTION AND VALUE OF PROPERTY
Jim McDonald Esq. 444 State St. Ukiah, CA	7/xx	$100 for bankruptcy telephone advice

10. Other transfers

None
■   a. List all other property, other than property transferred in the ordinary course of the business or financial affairs of the debtor, transferred either absolutely or as security within **two years** immediately preceding the commencement of this case. (Married debtors filing under chapter 12 or chapter 13 must include transfers by either or both spouses whether or not a joint petition is filed, unless the spouses are separated and a joint petition is not filed.)

NAME AND ADDRESS OF TRANSFEREE, RELATIONSHIP TO DEBTOR	DATE	DESCRIBE PROPERTY TRANSFERRED AND VALUE RECEIVED

None
■   b. List all property transferred by the debtor within **ten years** immediately preceding the commencement of this case to a self-settled trust or similar device of which the debtor is a beneficiary.

NAME OF TRUST OR OTHER DEVICE	DATE(S) OF TRANSFER(S)	AMOUNT OF MONEY OR DESCRIPTION AND VALUE OF PROPERTY OR DEBTOR'S INTEREST IN PROPERTY

11. Closed financial accounts

None
☐   List all financial accounts and instruments held in the name of the debtor or for the benefit of the debtor which were closed, sold, or otherwise transferred within **one year** immediately preceding the commencement of this case. Include checking, savings, or other financial accounts, certificates of deposit, or other instruments; shares and share accounts held in banks, credit unions, pension funds, cooperatives, associations, brokerage houses and other financial institutions. (Married debtors filing under chapter 12 or chapter 13 must include information concerning accounts or instruments held by or for either or both spouses whether or not a joint petition is filed, unless the spouses are separated and a joint petition is not filed.)

NAME AND ADDRESS OF INSTITUTION	TYPE OF ACCOUNT, LAST FOUR DIGITS OF ACCOUNT NUMBER, AND AMOUNT OF FINAL BALANCE	AMOUNT AND DATE OF SALE OR CLOSING
WestAmerica Bank 444 North Main St. Lakeport, CA 95453	Checking Acct #4444444 Final balance ($50)	

12. Safe deposit boxes

None
■   List each safe deposit or other box or depository in which the debtor has or had securities, cash, or other valuables within **one year** immediately preceding the commencement of this case. (Married debtors filing under chapter 12 or chapter 13 must include boxes or depositories of either or both spouses whether or not a joint petition is filed, unless the spouses are separated and a joint petition is not filed.)

NAME AND ADDRESS OF BANK OR OTHER DEPOSITORY	NAMES AND ADDRESSES OF THOSE WITH ACCESS TO BOX OR DEPOSITORY	DESCRIPTION OF CONTENTS	DATE OF TRANSFER OR SURRENDER, IF ANY

5

13. Setoffs

None
■

List all setoffs made by any creditor, including a bank, against a debt or deposit of the debtor within **90 days** preceding the commencement of this case. (Married debtors filing under chapter 12 or chapter 13 must include information concerning either or both spouses whether or not a joint petition is filed, unless the spouses are separated and a joint petition is not filed.)

NAME AND ADDRESS OF CREDITOR   DATE OF SETOFF   AMOUNT OF SETOFF

14. Property held for another person

None
☐

List all property owned by another person that the debtor holds or controls.

NAME AND ADDRESS OF OWNER	DESCRIPTION AND VALUE OF PROPERTY	LOCATION OF PROPERTY
Bonnie Johnson 3335 Irving St Clearlake, CA 95422	Poodle (Binkie) $300	Edwards residence

15. Prior address of debtor

None
☐

If the debtor has moved within **three years** immediately preceding the commencement of this case, list all premises which the debtor occupied during that period and vacated prior to the commencement of this case. If a joint petition is filed, report also any separate address of either spouse.

ADDRESS	NAME USED	DATES OF OCCUPANCY
21 Scarborough Rd. South Cleveland Heights OH 41118	Carrie Edwards	1/1/XX-- 5/1/XX

16. Spouses and Former Spouses

None
☐

If the debtor resides or resided in a community property state, commonwealth, or territory (including Alaska, Arizona, California, Idaho, Louisiana, Nevada, New Mexico, Puerto Rico, Texas, Washington, or Wisconsin) within **eight years** immediately preceding the commencement of the case, identify the name of the debtor's spouse and of any former spouse who resides or resided with the debtor in the community property state.

NAME
Torrey Edwards

17. Environmental Information.

For the purpose of this question, the following definitions apply:

"Environmental Law" means any federal, state, or local statute or regulation regulating pollution, contamination, releases of hazardous or toxic substances, wastes or material into the air, land, soil, surface water, groundwater, or other medium, including, but not limited to, statutes or regulations regulating the cleanup of these substances, wastes, or material.

"Site" means any location, facility, or property as defined under any Environmental Law, whether or not presently or formerly owned or operated by the debtor, including, but not limited to, disposal sites.

"Hazardous Material" means anything defined as a hazardous waste, hazardous substance, toxic substance, hazardous material, pollutant, or contaminant or similar term under an Environmental Law

None
■

a. List the name and address of every site for which the debtor has received notice in writing by a governmental unit that it may be liable or potentially liable under or in violation of an Environmental Law. Indicate the governmental unit, the date of the notice, and, if known, the Environmental Law:

SITE NAME AND ADDRESS	NAME AND ADDRESS OF GOVERNMENTAL UNIT	DATE OF NOTICE	ENVIRONMENTAL LAW

6

None ■   b. List the name and address of every site for which the debtor provided notice to a governmental unit of a release of Hazardous
Material. Indicate the governmental unit to which the notice was sent and the date of the notice.

SITE NAME AND ADDRESS   NAME AND ADDRESS OF   DATE OF   ENVIRONMENTAL
                               GOVERNMENTAL UNIT   NOTICE   LAW

None ■   c. List all judicial or administrative proceedings, including settlements or orders, under any Environmental Law with respect to which
the debtor is or was a party. Indicate the name and address of the governmental unit that is or was a party to the proceeding, and the
docket number.

NAME AND ADDRESS OF
GOVERNMENTAL UNIT   DOCKET NUMBER   STATUS OR DISPOSITION

18 . Nature, location and name of business

None ■   a. *If the debtor is an individual,* list the names, addresses, taxpayer identification numbers, nature of the businesses, and beginning
and ending dates of all businesses in which the debtor was an officer, director, partner, or managing executive of a corporation,
partner in a partnership, sole proprietor, or was self-employed in a trade, profession, or other activity either full- or part-time within
six years immediately preceding the commencement of this case, or in which the debtor owned 5 percent or more of the voting or
equity securities within **six years** immediately preceding the commencement of this case.

If the debtor is a partnership, list the names, addresses, taxpayer identification numbers, nature of the businesses, and beginning and
ending dates of all businesses in which the debtor was a partner or owned 5 percent or more of the voting or equity securities, within
six years immediately preceding the commencement of this case.

If the debtor is a corporation, list the names, addresses, taxpayer identification numbers, nature of the businesses, and beginning and
ending dates of all businesses in which the debtor was a partner or owned 5 percent or more of the voting or equity securities within
six years immediately preceding the commencement of this case.

NAME	LAST FOUR DIGITS OF SOC. SEC. NO./ COMPLETE EIN OR OTHER TAXPAYER I.D. NO.	ADDRESS	NATURE OF BUSINESS	BEGINNING AND ENDING DATES

None ■   b. Identify any business listed in response to subdivision a., above, that is "single asset real estate" as defined in 11 U.S.C. § 101.

NAME   ADDRESS

The following questions are to be completed by every debtor that is a corporation or partnership and by any individual debtor who is or has
been, within **six years** immediately preceding the commencement of this case, any of the following: an officer, director, managing executive, or
owner of more than 5 percent of the voting or equity securities of a corporation; a partner, other than a limited partner, of a partnership, a sole
proprietor or self-employed in a trade, profession, or other activity, either full- or part-time.

*(An individual or joint debtor should complete this portion of the statement **only** if the debtor is or has been in business, as defined above,
within six years immediately preceding the commencement of this case. A debtor who has not been in business within those six years should go
directly to the signature page.)*

19. Books, records and financial statements

None ■   a. List all bookkeepers and accountants who within **two years** immediately preceding the filing of this bankruptcy case kept or
supervised the keeping of books of account and records of the debtor.

NAME AND ADDRESS   DATES SERVICES RENDERED

None ■   b. List all firms or individuals who within the **two years** immediately preceding the filing of this bankruptcy case have audited the
books of account and records, or prepared a financial statement of the debtor.

NAME   ADDRESS   DATES SERVICES RENDERED

7

None ■ c. List all firms or individuals who at the time of the commencement of this case were in possession of the books of account and records of the debtor. If any of the books of account and records are not available, explain.

NAME   ADDRESS

None ■ d. List all financial institutions, creditors and other parties, including mercantile and trade agencies, to whom a financial statement was issued by the debtor within **two years** immediately preceding the commencement of this case.

NAME AND ADDRESS   DATE ISSUED

20. Inventories

None ■ a. List the dates of the last two inventories taken of your property, the name of the person who supervised the taking of each inventory, and the dollar amount and basis of each inventory.

| DATE OF INVENTORY | INVENTORY SUPERVISOR | DOLLAR AMOUNT OF INVENTORY (Specify cost, market or other basis) |

None ■ b. List the name and address of the person having possession of the records of each of the two inventories reported in a., above.

| DATE OF INVENTORY | NAME AND ADDRESSES OF CUSTODIAN OF INVENTORY RECORDS |

21 . Current Partners, Officers, Directors and Shareholders

None ■ a. If the debtor is a partnership, list the nature and percentage of partnership interest of each member of the partnership.

| NAME AND ADDRESS | NATURE OF INTEREST | PERCENTAGE OF INTEREST |

None ■ b. If the debtor is a corporation, list all officers and directors of the corporation, and each stockholder who directly or indirectly owns, controls, or holds 5 percent or more of the voting or equity securities of the corporation.

| NAME AND ADDRESS | TITLE | NATURE AND PERCENTAGE OF STOCK OWNERSHIP |

22 . Former partners, officers, directors and shareholders

None ■ a. If the debtor is a partnership, list each member who withdrew from the partnership within **one year** immediately preceding the commencement of this case.

| NAME | ADDRESS | DATE OF WITHDRAWAL |

None ■ b. If the debtor is a corporation, list all officers, or directors whose relationship with the corporation terminated within **one year** immediately preceding the commencement of this case.

| NAME AND ADDRESS | TITLE | DATE OF TERMINATION |

23 . Withdrawals from a partnership or distributions by a corporation

None ■ If the debtor is a partnership or corporation, list all withdrawals or distributions credited or given to an insider, including compensation in any form, bonuses, loans, stock redemptions, options exercised and any other perquisite during **one year** immediately preceding the commencement of this case.

| NAME & ADDRESS OF RECIPIENT, RELATIONSHIP TO DEBTOR | DATE AND PURPOSE OF WITHDRAWAL | AMOUNT OF MONEY OR DESCRIPTION AND VALUE OF PROPERTY |

8

24. Tax Consolidation Group.

None

■   If the debtor is a corporation, list the name and federal taxpayer identification number of the parent corporation of any consolidated group for tax purposes of which the debtor has been a member at any time within **six years** immediately preceding the commencement of the case.

NAME OF PARENT CORPORATION   TAXPAYER IDENTIFICATION NUMBER (EIN)

25. Pension Funds.

None

■   If the debtor is not an individual, list the name and federal taxpayer identification number of any pension fund to which the debtor, as an employer, has been responsible for contributing at any time within **six years** immediately preceding the commencement of the case.

NAME OF PENSION FUND   TAXPAYER IDENTIFICATION NUMBER (EIN)

DECLARATION UNDER PENALTY OF PERJURY BY INDIVIDUAL DEBTOR

I declare under penalty of perjury that I have read the answers contained in the foregoing statement of financial affairs and any attachments thereto and that they are true and correct.

Date ___October 25, 2005___   Signature ___/s/ Carrie Anne Edwards___
                                              Carrie Anne Edwards
                                              Debtor

Penalty for making a false statement: Fine of up to $500,000 or imprisonment for up to 5 years, or both. 18 U.S.C. §§ 152 and 3571

B 201 (10/05)

UNITED STATES BANKRUPTCY COURT
NORTHERN DISTRICT OF CALIFORNIA

NOTICE TO INDIVIDUAL CONSUMER DEBTOR UNDER § 342(b)
OF THE BANKRUPTCY CODE

In accordance with § 342(b) of the Bankruptcy Code, this notice: (1) Describes briefly the services available from credit counseling services; (2) Describes briefly the purposes, benefits and costs of the four types of bankruptcy proceedings you may commence; and (3) Informs you about bankruptcy crimes and notifies you that the Attorney General may examine all information you supply in connection with a bankruptcy case. You are cautioned that bankruptcy law is complicated and not easily described. Thus, you may wish to seek the advice of an attorney to learn of your rights and responsibilities should you decide to file a petition. Court employees cannot give you legal advice.

1. Services Available from Credit Counseling Agencies

With limited exceptions, § 109(h) of the Bankruptcy Code requires that all individual debtors who file for bankruptcy relief on or after October 17, 2005, receive a briefing that outlines the available opportunities for credit counseling and provides assistance in performing a budget analysis. The briefing must be given within 180 days **before** the bankruptcy filing. The briefing may be provided individually or in a group (including briefings conducted by telephone or on the Internet) and must be provided by a nonprofit budget and credit counseling agency approved by the United States trustee or bankruptcy administrator. The clerk of the bankruptcy court has a list that you may consult of the approved budget and credit counseling agencies.

In addition, after filing a bankruptcy case, an individual debtor generally must complete a financial management instructional course before he or she can receive a discharge. The clerk also has a list of approved financial management instructional courses.

2. The Four Chapters of the Bankruptcy Code Available to Individual Consumer Debtors

Chapter 7: Liquidation ($220 filing fee, $39 administrative fee, $15 trustee surcharge: Total Fee $274)
1. Chapter 7 is designed for debtors in financial difficulty who do not have the ability to pay their existing debts. Debtors whose debts are primarily consumer debts are subject to a "means test" designed to determine whether the case should be permitted to proceed under chapter 7. If your income is greater than the median income for your state of residence and family size, in some cases, creditors have the right to file a motion requesting that the court dismiss your case under § 707(b) of the Code. It is up to the court to decide whether the case should be dismissed.
2. Under chapter 7, you may claim certain of your property as exempt under governing law. A trustee may have the right to take possession of and sell the remaining property that is not exempt and use the sale proceeds to pay your creditors.
3. The purpose of filing a chapter 7 case is to obtain a discharge of your existing debts. If, however, you are found to have committed certain kinds of improper conduct described in the Bankruptcy Code, the court may deny your discharge and, if it does, the purpose for which you filed the bankruptcy petition will be defeated.
4. Even if you receive a general discharge, some particular debts are not discharged under the law. Therefore, you may still be responsible for most taxes and student loans; debts incurred to pay nondischargeable taxes; domestic support and property settlement obligations; most fines, penalties, forfeitures, and criminal restitution obligations; certain debts which are not properly listed in your bankruptcy papers; and debts for death or personal injury caused by operating a motor vehicle, vessel, or aircraft while intoxicated from alcohol or drugs. Also, if a creditor can prove that a debt arose from fraud, breach of fiduciary duty, or theft, or from a willful and malicious injury, the bankruptcy court may determine that the debt is not discharged.

Chapter 13: Repayment of All or Part of the Debts of an Individual with Regular Income ($150 filing fee, $39 administrative fee: Total fee $189)
1. Chapter 13 is designed for individuals with regular income who would like to pay all or part of their debts in installments over a period of time. You are only eligible for chapter 13 if your debts do not exceed certain dollar amounts set forth in the Bankruptcy Code.
2. Under chapter 13, you must file with the court a plan to repay your creditors all or part of the money that you owe them, using your future earnings. The period allowed by the court to repay your debts may be three years or five years, depending upon your income and other factors. The court must approve your plan before it can take effect.
3. After completing the payments under your plan, your debts are generally discharged except for domestic support obligations; most student loans; certain taxes; most criminal fines and restitution obligations; certain debts which are not properly listed in your bankruptcy papers; certain debts for acts that caused death or personal injury; and certain long term secured

B 201 (10/05)

obligations.

Chapter 11: Reorganization ($1000 filing fee, $39 administrative fee: Total fee $1039)

Chapter 11 is designed for the reorganization of a business but is also available to consumer debtors. Its provisions are quite complicated, and any decision by an individual to file a chapter 11 petition should be reviewed with an attorney.

Chapter 12: Family Farmer or Fisherman ($200 filing fee, $39 administrative fee: Total fee $239)

Chapter 12 is designed to permit family farmers and fishermen to repay their debts over a period of time from future earnings and is similar to chapter 13. The eligibility requirements are restrictive, limiting its use to those whose income arises primarily from a family-owned farm or commercial fishing operation.

3. Bankruptcy Crimes and Availability of Bankruptcy Papers to Law Enforcement Officials

A person who knowingly and fraudulently conceals assets or makes a false oath or statement under penalty of perjury, either orally or in writing, in connection with a bankruptcy case is subject to a fine, imprisonment, or both. All information supplied by a debtor in connection with a bankruptcy case is subject to examination by the Attorney General acting through the Office of the United States Trustee, the Office of the United States Attorney, and other components and employees of the Department of Justice.

WARNING: Section 521(a)(1) of the Bankruptcy Code requires that you promptly file detailed information regarding your creditors, assets, liabilities, income, expenses and general financial condition. Your bankruptcy case may be dismissed if this information is not filed with the court within the time deadlines set by the Bankruptcy Code, the Bankruptcy Rules, and the local rules of the court.

Certificate of Attorney

I hereby certify that I delivered to the debtor this notice required by § 342(b) of the Bankruptcy Code.

X /s/   October 25, 2005

_____   _____
Printed Name of Attorney   Signature of Attorney   Date
Address:

Certificate of Debtor

I (We), the debtor(s), affirm that I (we) have received and read this notice.

Carrie Anne Edwards   X /s/ Carrie Anne Edwards   October 25, 2005

_____   _____
Printed Name(s) of Debtor(s)   Signature of Debtor   Date

Case No. (if known) _____   X _____
                                       Signature of Joint Debtor (if any)   Date

Form B22A (Chapter 7) (10/05)

In re   Carrie Anne Edwards
_____
                    Debtor(s)

Case Number: _____
                    (If known)

According to the calculations required by this statement:

■ The presumption arises.

☐ The presumption does not arise.

(Check the box as directed in Parts I, III, and VI of this statement.)

STATEMENT OF CURRENT MONTHLY INCOME AND MEANS TEST CALCULATION
FOR USE IN CHAPTER 7 ONLY

In addition to Schedules I and J, this statement must be completed by every individual Chapter 7 debtor, whether or not filing jointly, whose debts are primarily consumer debts. Joint debtors may complete one statement only.

	Part I. EXCLUSION FOR DISABLED VETERANS
1	If you are a disabled veteran described in the Veteran's Declaration in this Part I, (1) check that box at the beginning of the Veteran's Declaration, (2) check the box for "The presumption does not arise" at the top of this statement, and (3) complete the verification in Part VIII. Do not complete any of the remaining parts of this statement. ☐ Veteran's Declaration. By checking this box, I declare under penalty of perjury that I am a disabled veteran (as defined in 38 U.S.C. § 3741(1)) whose indebtedness occurred primarily during a period in which I was on active duty (as defined in 10 U.S.C. § 101(d)(1)) or while I was performing a homeland defense activity (as defined in 32 U.S.C. §901(1)).

	Part II. CALCULATION OF MONTHLY INCOME FOR § 707(b)(7) EXCLUSION			
2	Marital/filing status. Check the box that applies and complete the balance of this part of this statement as directed. a. ■ Unmarried. Complete only Column A ("Debtor's Income") for Lines 3-11. b. ☐ Married, not filing jointly, with declaration of separate households. By checking this box, debtor declares under penalty of perjury: "My spouse and I are legally separated under applicable non-bankruptcy law or my spouse and I are living apart other than for the purpose of evading the requirements of § 707(b)(2)(A) of the Bankruptcy Code." Complete only column A ("Debtor's Income") for Lines 3-11. c. ☐ Married, not filing jointly, without the declaration of separate households set out in Line 2.b above. Complete both Column A ("Debtor's Income") and Column B ("Spouse's Income") for Lines 3-11. d. ☐ Married, filing jointly. Complete both Column A ("Debtor's Income") and Column B ("Spouse's Income") for Lines 3-11.			

All figures must reflect average monthly income for the six calendar months prior to filing the bankruptcy case, ending on the last day of the month before the filing. If you received different amounts of income during these six months, you must total the amounts received during the six months, divide this total by six, and enter the result on the appropriate line.

			Column A	Column B
			Debtor's Income	Spouse's Income
3	Gross wages, salary, tips, bonuses, overtime, commissions.		$ 3,800.00	$
4	Income from the operation of a business, profession or farm. Subtract Line b from Line a and enter the difference on Line 4. Do not enter a number less than zero. Do not include any part of the business expenses entered on Line b as a deduction in Part V.			
		Debtor	Spouse	
	a. Gross receipts	$ 0.00	$	
	b. Ordinary and necessary business expenses	$ 0.00	$	
	c. Business income	Subtract Line b from Line a		$ 0.00	$
5	Rents and other real property income. Subtract Line b from Line a and enter the difference on Line 5. Do not enter a number less than zero. Do not include any part of the operating expenses entered on Line b as a deduction in Part V.			
		Debtor	Spouse	
	a. Gross receipts	$ 0.00	$	
	b. Ordinary and necessary operating expenses	$ 0.00	$	
	c. Rental income	Subtract Line b from Line a		$ 0.00	$
6	Interest, dividends, and royalties.			$ 1,000.00	$
7	Pension and retirement income.			$ 0.00	$
8	Regular contributions to the household expenses of the debtor or the debtor's dependents, including child or spousal support. Do not include contributions from the debtor's spouse if Column B is completed.			$ 500.00	$

9	Unemployment compensation. Enter the amount in column A and, if applicable, Column B. However, if you contend that unemployment compensation received by you or your spouse was a benefit under the Social Security Act, do not list the amount of such compensation in Column A or B, but instead state the amount in the space below: Unemployment compensation claimed to be a benefit under the Social Security Act Debtor $ 0.00 Spouse $	$ 0.00	$
10	Income from all other sources. If necessary, list additional sources on a separate page. Do not include any benefits received under the Social Security Act or payments received as a victim of a war crime, crime against humanity, or as a victim of international or domestic terrorism. Specify source and amount. Debtor Spouse a. $ $ b. $ $ Total and enter on Line 10	$ 0.00	$
11	Subtotal of Current Monthly Income for § 707(b)(7). Add Lines 3 thru 10 in Column A, and, if Column B is completed, add Lines 3 through 10 in Column B. Enter the total(s).	$ 5,300.00	$
12	Total Current Monthly Income for § 707(b)(7). If Column B has been completed, add Line 11, Column A to Line 11, Column B, and enter the total. If Column B has not been completed, enter the amount from Line 11, Column A.	$ 5,300.00	

Part III. APPLICATION OF § 707(b)(7) EXCLUSION

13	Annualized Current Monthly Income for § 707(b)(7). Multiply the amount from Line 12 by the number 12 and enter the result.	$ 63,600.00
14	Applicable median family income. Enter the median family income for the applicable state and household size. (This information is available by family size at www.usdoj.gov/ust/ or from the clerk of the bankruptcy court.) a. Enter debtor's state of residence: _____CA_____ b. Enter debtor's household size: ___3___	$ 59,633.00
15	Application of Section 707(b)(7). Check the applicable box and proceed as directed. ☐ The amount on Line 13 is less than or equal to the amount on Line 14. Check the box for "The presumption does not arise" at the top of page 1 of this statement, and complete Part VIII; do not complete Parts IV, V, VI or VII. ■ The amount on Line 13 is more than the amount on Line 14. Complete the remaining parts of this statement.

Complete Parts IV, V, VI, and VII of this statement only if required. (See Line 15).

Part IV. CALCULATION OF CURRENT MONTHLY INCOME FOR § 707(b)(2)

16	Enter the amount from Line 12.	$ 5,300.00
17	Marital adjustment. If you checked the box at Line 2.c, enter the amount of the income listed in Line 11, Column B that was NOT regularly contributed to the household expenses of the debtor or the debtor's dependents. If you did not check box at Line 2.c, enter zero.	$ 0.00
18	Current monthly income for § 707(b)(2). Subtract Line 17 from Line 16 and enter the result.	$ 5,300.00

Part V. CALCULATION OF DEDUCTIONS UNDER § 707(b)(2)

Subpart A: Deductions under Standards of the Internal Revenue Service (IRS)

| 19 | National Standards: food, clothing, household supplies, personal care, and miscellaneous. Enter "Total" amount from IRS National Standards for Allowable Living Expenses for the applicable family size and income level. (This information is available at www.usdoj.gov/ust/ or from the clerk of the bankruptcy court.) | $ 1,156.00 |
| 20A | Local Standards: housing and utilities; non-mortgage expenses. Enter the amount of the IRS Housing and Utilities Standards; non-mortgage expenses for the applicable county and family size. (This information is available at www.usdoj.gov/ust/ or from the clerk of the bankruptcy court). | $ 449.00 |

20B	Local Standards: housing and utilities; mortgage/rent expense. Enter, in Line a below, the amount of the IRS Housing and Utilities Standards; mortgage/rent expense for your county and family size (this information is available at www.usdoj.gov/ust/ or from the clerk of the bankruptcy court); enter on Line b the total of the Average Monthly Payments for any debts secured by your home, as stated in Line 42; subtract Line b from Line a and enter the result in Line 20B. Do not enter an amount less than zero.		
	a.	IRS Housing and Utilities Standards; mortgage/rental expense	$ 749.00
	b.	Average Monthly Payment for any debts secured by your home, if any, as stated in Line 42	$ 0.00
	c.	Net mortgage/rental expense	Subtract Line b from Line a.
			$ 749.00

21	Local Standards: housing and utilities; adjustment. If you contend that the process set out in Lines 20A and 20B does not accurately compute the allowance to which you are entitled under the IRS Housing and Utilities Standards, enter any additional amount to which you contend you are entitled, and state the basis for your contention in the space below:
	$ 0.00

22	Local Standards: transportation; vehicle operation/public transportation expense. You are entitled to an expense allowance in this category regardless of whether you pay the expenses of operating a vehicle and regardless of whether you use public transportation. Check the number of vehicles for which you pay the operating expenses or for which the operating expenses are included as a contribution to your household expenses in Line 8. ☐ 0 ■ 1 ☐ 2 or more. Enter the amount from IRS Transportation Standards, Operating Costs & Public Transportation Costs for the applicable number of vehicles in the applicable Metropolitan Statistical Area or Census Region. (This information is available at www.usdoj.gov/ust/ or from the clerk of the bankruptcy court.)
	$ 305.00

23	Local Standards: transportation ownership/lease expense; Vehicle 1. Check the number of vehicles for which you claim an ownership/lease expense. (You may not claim an ownership/lease expense for more than two vehicles.) ■ 1 ☐ 2 or more. Enter, in Line a below, the amount of the IRS Transportation Standards, Ownership Costs, First Car (available at www.usdoj.gov/ust/ or from the clerk of the bankruptcy court); enter in Line b the total of the Average Monthly Payments for any debts secured by Vehicle 1, as stated in Line 42; subtract Line b from Line a and enter the result in Line 23. Do not enter an amount less than zero.		
	a.	IRS Transportation Standards, Ownership Costs, First Car	$ 475.00
	b.	Average Monthly Payment for any debts secured by Vehicle 1, as stated in Line 42	$ 0.00
	c.	Net ownership/lease expense for Vehicle 1	Subtract Line b from Line a.
			$ 475.00

24	Local Standards: transportation ownership/lease expense; Vehicle 2. Complete this Line only if you checked the "2 or more" Box in Line 23. Enter, in Line a below, the amount of the IRS Transportation Standards, Ownership Costs, Second Car (available at www.usdoj.gov/ust/ or from the clerk of the bankruptcy court); enter in Line b the total of the Average Monthly Payments for any debts secured by Vehicle 2, as stated in Line 42; subtract Line b from Line a and enter the result in Line 24. Do not enter an amount less than zero.		
	a.	IRS Transportation Standards, Ownership Costs, Second Car	$ 0.00
	b.	Average Monthly Payment for any debts secured by Vehicle 2, as stated in Line 42	$ 0.00
	c.	Net ownership/lease expense for Vehicle 2	Subtract Line b from Line a.
			$ 0.00

25	Other Necessary Expenses: taxes. Enter the total average monthly expense that you actually incur for all federal, state and local taxes, other than real estate and sales taxes, such as income taxes, self employment taxes, social security taxes, and Medicare taxes. Do not include real estate or sales taxes.
	$ 500.00

26	Other Necessary Expenses: mandatory payroll deductions. Enter the total average monthly payroll deductions that are required for your employment, such as mandatory retirement contributions, union dues, and uniform costs. Do not include discretionary amounts, such as non-mandatory 401(k) contributions.
	$ 0.00

27	Other Necessary Expenses: life insurance. Enter average monthly premiums that you actually pay for term life insurance for yourself. Do not include premiums for insurance on your dependents, for whole life or for any other form of insurance.
	$ 0.00

28	Other Necessary Expenses: court-ordered payments. Enter the total monthly amount that you are required to pay pursuant to court order, such as spousal or child support payments. Do not include payments on past due support obligations included in Line 44.	$	0.00
29	Other Necessary Expenses: education for employment or for a physically or mentally challenged child. Enter the total monthly amount that you actually expend for education that is a condition of employment and for education that is required for a physically or mentally challenged dependent child for whom no public education providing similar services is available.	$	0.00
30	Other Necessary Expenses: childcare. Enter the average monthly amount that you actually expend on childcare. Do not include payments made for children's education.	$	300.00
31	Other Necessary Expenses: health care. Enter the average monthly amount that you actually expend on health care expenses that are not reimbursed by insurance or paid by a health savings account. Do not include payments for health insurance listed in Line 34.	$	300.00
32	Other Necessary Expenses: telecommunication services. Enter the average monthly expenses that you actually pay for cell phones, pagers, call waiting, caller identification, special long distance or internet services necessary for the health and welfare of you or your dependents. Do not include any amount previously deducted.	$	100.00
33	Total Expenses Allowed under IRS Standards. Enter the total of Lines 19 through 32	$	4,334.00

Subpart B: Additional Expense Deductions under § 707(b)

Note: Do not include any expenses that you have listed in Lines 19-32

34	Health Insurance, Disability Insurance and Health Savings Account Expenses. List the average monthly amounts that you actually expend in each of the following categories and enter the total.		
	a. Health Insurance $ 0.00		
	b. Disability Insurance $ 0.00		
	c. Health Savings Account $ 0.00		
	Total: Add Lines a, b and c	$	0.00
35	Continued contributions to the care of household or family members. Enter the actual monthly expenses that you will continue to pay for the reasonable and necessary care and support of an elderly, chronically ill, or disabled member of your household or member of your immediate family who is unable to pay for such expenses.	$	0.00
36	Protection against family violence. Enter any average monthly expenses that you actually incurred to maintain the safety of your family under the Family Violence Prevention and Services Act or other applicable federal law.	$	0.00
37	Home energy costs in excess of the allowance specified by the IRS Local Standards. Enter the average monthly amount by which your home energy costs exceed the allowance in the IRS Local Standards for Housing and Utilities. You must provide your case trustee with documentation demonstrating that the additional amount claimed is reasonable and necessary.	$	0.00
38	Education expenses for dependent children less than 18. Enter the average monthly expenses that you actually incur, not to exceed $125 per child, in providing elementary and secondary education for your dependent children less than 18 years of age. You must provide your case trustee with documentation demonstrating that the additional amount claimed is reasonable and necessary and not already accounted for in the IRS Standards.	$	0.00
39	Additional food and clothing expense. Enter the average monthly amount by which your food and clothing expenses exceed the combined allowances for food and apparel in the IRS National Standards, not to exceed five percent of those combined allowances. (This information is available at www.usdoj.gov/ust/ or from the clerk of the bankruptcy court.) You must provide your case trustee with documentation demonstrating that the additional amount claimed is reasonable and necessary.	$	41.00
40	Continued charitable contributions. Enter the amount that you will continue to contribute in the form of cash or financial instruments to a charitable organization as defined in 26 U.S.C. § 170(c)(1)-(2).	$	0.00
41	Total Additional Expense Deductions under § 707(b). Enter the total of Lines 34 through 40	$	41.00

	Subpart C: Deductions for Debt Payment				
42	**Future payments on secured claims.** For each of your debts that is secured by an interest in property that you own, list the name of creditor, identify the property securing the debt, and state the Average Monthly Payment. The Average Monthly Payment is the total of all amounts contractually due to each Secured Creditor in the 60 months following the filing of the bankruptcy case, divided by 60. Mortgage debts should include payments of taxes and insurance required by the mortgage. If necessary, list additional entries on a separate page.				

		Name of Creditor	Property Securing the Debt	60-month Average Payment		
	a.	-NONE-		$		
					Total: Add Lines	$	0.00

43	**Past due payments on secured claims.** If any of the debts listed in Line 42 are in default, and the property securing the debt is necessary for your support or the support of your dependents, you may include in your deductions 1/60th of the amount that you must pay the creditor as a result of the default (the "cure amount") in order to maintain possession of the property. List any such amounts in the following chart and enter the total. If necessary, list additional entries on a separate page.

		Name of Creditor	Property Securing the Debt in Default	1/60th of the Cure Amount		
	a.	-NONE-		$		
					Total: Add Lines	$	0.00

44	**Payments on priority claims.** Enter the total amount of all priority claims (including priority child support and alimony claims), divided by 60.		$	0.00

45	**Chapter 13 administrative expenses.** If you are eligible to file a case under Chapter 13, complete the following chart, multiply the amount in line a by the amount in line b, and enter the resulting administrative expense.		
	a.	Projected average monthly Chapter 13 plan payment.	$	0.00
	b.	Current multiplier for your district as determined under schedules issued by the Executive Office for United States Trustees. (This information is available at www.usdoj.gov/ust/ or from the clerk of the bankruptcy court.)	x	9.90
	c.	Average monthly administrative expense of Chapter 13 case	Total: Multiply Lines a and b	$	0.00

46	**Total Deductions for Debt Payment.** Enter the total of Lines 42 through 45.	$	0.00

	Subpart D: Total Deductions Allowed under § 707(b)(2)		
47	**Total of all deductions allowed under § 707(b)(2).** Enter the total of Lines 33, 41, and 46.	$	4,375.00

	Part VI. DETERMINATION OF § 707(b)(2) PRESUMPTION		
48	Enter the amount from Line 18 (Current monthly income for § 707(b)(2))	$	5,300.00
49	Enter the amount from Line 47 (Total of all deductions allowed under § 707(b)(2))	$	4,375.00
50	**Monthly disposable income under § 707(b)(2).** Subtract Line 49 from Line 48 and enter the result.	$	925.00
51	**60-month disposable income under § 707(b)(2).** Multiply the amount in Line 50 by the number 60 and enter the result.	$	55,500.00

52	Initial presumption determination. Check the applicable box and proceed as directed. ☐ The amount on Line 51 is less than $6,000. Check the box for "The presumption does not arise" at the top of page 1 of this statement, and complete the verification in Part VIII. Do not complete the remainder of Part VI. ■ The amount set forth on Line 51 is more than $10,000. Check the box for "The presumption arises" at the top of page 1 of this statement, and complete the verification in Part VIII. You may also complete Part VII. Do not complete the remainder of Part VI. ☐ The amount on Line 51 is at least $6,000, but not more than $10,000. Complete the remainder of Part VI (Lines 53 through 55).	
53	Enter the amount of your total non-priority unsecured debt	$
54	Threshold debt payment amount. Multiply the amount in Line 53 by the number 0.25 and enter the result.	$
55	Secondary presumption determination. Check the applicable box and proceed as directed. ☐ The amount on Line 51 is less than the amount on Line 54. Check the box for "The presumption does not arise" at the top of page 1 of this statement, and complete the verification in Part VIII. ☐ The amount on Line 51 is equal to or greater than the amount on Line 54. Check the box for "The presumption arises" at the top of page 1 of this statement, and complete the verification in Part VIII. You may also complete Part VII.	

Part VII. ADDITIONAL EXPENSE CLAIMS

56 — Other Expenses. List and describe any monthly expenses, not otherwise stated in this form, that are required for the health and welfare of you and your family and that you contend should be an additional deduction from your current monthly income under § 707(b)(2)(A)(ii)(I). If necessary, list additional sources on a separate page. All figures should reflect your average monthly expense for each item. Total the expenses.

Expense Description	Monthly Amount
a.	$
b.	$
c.	$
d.	$
Total: Add Lines a, b, c, and d	$

Part VIII. VERIFICATION

57 — I declare under penalty of perjury that the information provided in this statement is true and correct. (If this is a joint case, both debtors must sign.)

Date: October 25, 2005   Signature: /s/ Carrie Anne Edwards
Carrie Anne Edwards
(Debtor)

Form 8
(10/05)

United States Bankruptcy Court
Northern District of California

In re   Carrie Anne Edwards

Debtor(s)

Case No.

Chapter   7

CHAPTER 7 INDIVIDUAL DEBTOR'S STATEMENT OF INTENTION

■   I have filed a schedule of assets and liabilities which includes debts secured by property of the estate.

■   I have filed a schedule of executory contracts and unexpired leases which includes personal property subject to an unexpired lease.

■   I intend to do the following with respect to property of the estate which secures those debts or is subject to a lease:

Description of Secured Property	Creditor's Name	Property will be Surrendered	Property is claimed as exempt	Property will be redeemed pursuant to 11 U.S.C. § 722	Debt will be reaffirmed pursuant to 11 U.S.C. § 524(c)
2002 Buick LeSabre fully loaded in good condition (replacement value from nada.com)	GMAC				X
Residence Location: 3045 Berwick St, Lakeport CA	Grand Junction Mortgage				X
Residence Location: 3045 Berwick St, Lakeport CA	Lending Tree				X

Description of Leased Property	Lessor's Name	Lease will be assumed pursuant to 11 U.S.C. § 362(h)(1)(A)
Laser skin treatment machine. Lease for 5 year period that expires on 2010	Beauty Products Leasing Co.	X

Date   October 25, 2005

Signature   /s/ Carrie Anne Edwards

Carrie Anne Edwards

Debtor

Form B 21 Official Form 21
(12/03)

FORM 21. STATEMENT OF SOCIAL SECURITY NUMBER

United States Bankruptcy Court
Northern District of California

In re Carrie Anne Edwards
_____
                           Debtor   Case No. _____

         3045 Berwick St
Address Lakeport, CA 95453   Chapter _7_

Employer's Tax Identification (EIN) No(s). [if any]: _____
Last four digits of Social Security No(s).: _xxx-xx-6287_

STATEMENT OF SOCIAL SECURITY NUMBER(S)

1. Name of Debtor (enter Last, First, Middle): Edwards, Carrie, Anne
(Check the appropriate box and, if applicable, provide the required information.)

    / x /Debtor has a Social Security Number and it is: _573-55-6287_
          (If more than one, state all.)

    / /Debtor does not have a Social Security Number.

2. Name of Joint Debtor (enter Last, First, Middle): _____
(Check the appropriate box and, if applicable, provide the required information.)

    / /Joint Debtor has a Social Security Number and it is: __
          (If more than one, state all.)

    / /Joint Debtor does not have a Social Security Number.

I declare under penalty of perjury that the foregoing is true and correct.

    X /s/ Carrie Anne Edwards   October 25, 2005
       Carrie Anne Edwards   Date
       Signature of Debtor

    X _____
       Signature of Joint Debtor   Date

Joint debtors must provide information for both spouses.
Penalty for making a false statement: Fine of up to $250,000 or up to 5 years imprisonment or both. 18 U.S.C. §§ 152 and 3571.

United States Bankruptcy Court
Northern District of California

In re   Carrie Anne Edwards

_____   Case No. _____

Debtor(s)   Chapter   7   _____

STATEMENT PURSUANT TO RULE 2016(B)

The undersigned, pursuant to Rule 2016(b), Bankruptcy Rules, states that:

1. The undersigned is the attorney for the debtor(s) in this case.

2. The compensation paid or agreed to be paid by the debtor(s), to the undersigned is:
    a)   For legal services rendered or to be rendered in contemplation of and in
         connection with this case $ _____ 0.00
    b)   Prior to the filing of this statement, debtor(s) have paid $ _____ 0.00
    c)   The unpaid balance due and payable is $ _____ 0.00

3. $ _____ 0.00 _____ of the filing fee in this case has been paid.

4. The Services rendered or to be rendered include the following:
    a.   Analysis of the financial situation, and rendering advice and assistance to the debtor(s) in determining
         whether to file a petition under title 11 of the United States Code.
    b.   Preparation and filing of the petition, schedules, statement of affairs and other documents required by the
         court.

5. The source of payments made by the debtor(s) to the undersigned was from earnings, wages and compensation for
    services performed, and

6. The source of payments to be made by the debtor(s) to the undersigned for the unpaid balance remaining, if any,
    will be from earnings, wages and compensation for services performed, and

7. The undersigned has received no transfer, assignment or pledge of property from debtor(s) except the following for
    the value stated:

8. The undersigned has not shared or agreed to share with any other entity, other than with members of undersigned's
    law firm, any compensation paid or to be paid except as follows:

Dated: October 25, 2005
_____

                                        Respectfully submitted,

                                        /s/
                                        _____
                                        Attorney for Debtor:

United States Bankruptcy Court
Northern District of California

In re   Carrie Anne Edwards _____   Case No. _____

                            Debtor(s)   Chapter   7 _____

CREDITOR MATRIX COVER SHEET

     I declare that the attached Creditor Mailing Matrix, consisting of ____3____ sheets, contains the correct, complete and current names and addresses of all priority, secured and unsecured creditors listed in debtor's filing and that this matrix conforms with the Clerk's promulgated requirements.

Date: October 25, 2005 _____   /s/ _____
                                                 Signature of Attorney

Alan Accountant
5 Green St.
Cleveland, OH 44118

American Allowance
PO Box 1
New York, NY 10001

Angel of Mercy Hospital
4444 Elevisior St.
Belmont, CA 94003

Bob Jones III
4566 Fifth Ave.
New York, NY 10020

Bonnie Johnson
3335 Irving St
Clearlake, CA 95422

Citibank
200 East North St
Columbus, OH 43266

Dr. Dennis Dentist
45 Superior Way
Cleveland, OH 44118

Dr. Helen Jones
443 First St.
Soledad, CA 94750

```
Fannie's Furniture
55544 Grove St.
Berkeley, CA 94710


GMAC
PO Box 23567
Duchesne, UT 84021


Grand Junction Mortgage
3456 Eight St.
Clearlake, CA 95422


Illuminating Co.
20245 Old Hwy 53
Clearlake, CA 95422


IRS
Columbus, OH 43266


John White Esq.
PO Box 401
Finley, CA 95435


Jon Edwards
900 Grand View
Jackson, WY 83001


Lending Tree
PO Box 3333
Palo Alto, CA 94310
```

```
Loantree
PO Box 305
Lucerne, CA 95458


PG&E
315 North Forbes St.
Lakeport, CA 95453


Sears
PO Box 11
Chicago, IL 60619
```

Worksheets

Worksheet A: Current Monthly Income

Use this worksheet to calculate your current monthly income; use figures for you and your spouse if you plan to file jointly.

Line 1. Calculate your total income over the last six months from wages, salary, tips, bonuses, overtime, and so on.

   A. Month 1 $ _____

   B. Month 2   _____

   C. Month 3   _____

   D. Month 4   _____

   E. Month 5   _____

   F. Month 6   _____

   G. TOTAL WAGES (add Lines A–F) $ _____

Line 2. Add up all other income for the last six months.

   A. Business, profession, or farm income   _____

   B. Interest, dividends, and royalties   _____

   C. Rents and real property income   _____

   D. Pension and retirement income   _____

   E. Alimony or family support   _____

   F. Spousal contributions (if not filing jointly)   _____

   G. Unemployment compensation   _____

   H. Workers' compensation   _____

   I. State disability insurance   _____

   J. Annuity payments   _____

   K. Other   _____

   L. TOTAL OTHER INCOME $ _____

Line 3. Calculate total income over the six months prior to filing.

   A. Enter total wages (Line 1G)   _____

   B. Enter total other income (Line 2L)   _____

   C. TOTAL INCOME OVER THE SIX MONTHS PRIOR TO FILING. Add Lines A and B together. $ _____

Line 4. Average monthly income over the six months prior to filing. This is called your "current monthly income."

   A. Enter total six-month income (Line 3C)   _____

   B. CURRENT MONTHLY INCOME. Divide Line A by six. $ _____

Worksheet B: Allowable Monthly Expenses

Use this worksheet to calculate the monthly expenses allowed by the IRS.

Calculate total allowable monthly expenses.

A. Food, clothing, and so on $ _____

B. Transportation   _____

C. Housing & utilities   _____

D. Domestic violence   _____

E. Dependent care   _____

F. Education   _____

G. Taxes   _____

H. Mandatory payroll deductions   _____

I. Insurance   _____

J. Court-ordered payments   _____

K. Charitable contributions   _____

L. Child care   _____

M. Health care   _____

N. Communications   _____

O. Business expenses   _____

P. Total allowable monthly expenses. Add lines A–N together $ _____

Current Monthly Income (from Worksheet A, Line 4B). $ _____

Total Allowable Monthly Expenses (from Line P above).   _____

Net monthly income. $ _____

● If net monthly income is less than $100, you have passed the means test
  and you do not need to continue.

● If net monthly income is $100 or more, complete Worksheet C.

Worksheet C: Monthly Disposable Income

Use this worksheet to find out how much income you would have left over, after paying the IRS expenses calculated in Worksheet B, your secured and priority debts, any arrearages on your secured debts, and the administrative costs associated with a Chapter 13 bankruptcy, to devote to your unsecured, nonpriority debts.

Line 1. Figure out what you would have to pay each month over the next five years on your secured debts.

    A. Total amount due over the next five years for a mortgage or second deed of trust. $ _____

    B. Total amount due over the next five years on a car note.   _____

    C. Total amount due over the next five years on all other secured debts.   _____

    D. Add Lines A–C together to figure out the total amount you owe on all secured debts for the next five years.   _____

    E. Divide Line D by 60 to determine how much you would have to pay each month on these debts for the next five years.   _____

Line 2. Figure out what you would have to pay each month over the next five years to make up your arrearages (missed payments) on secured debts.

    A. Total arrearage on mortgage or second deed of trust.   _____

    B. Total arrearage on car note.   _____

    C. Total arrearage on all other secured debts.   _____

    D. Add Lines A–C together to figure out your total arrearage on secured debts.   _____

    E. Divide Line D by 60 to determine how much you would have to pay each month to pay off these arrearages over the next five years.

Line 3. Figure out how much you will owe on your priority debts for the next five years.

    A. Back child support and alimony you owe. $ _____

    B. Priority income taxes you owe.   _____

    C. Other priority debts you owe.   _____

    D. Add Lines A–C together to figure out the total priority debt you owe.   _____

    E. Divide Line D by 60 to determine how much you would have to pay each month to pay off these priority debts over the next five years.   _____

Line 4. Calculate the total amount you would have left over each month after paying allowable expenses and the debts you would have to pay in full in a Chapter 13 plan.

   A. Enter your current monthly income (from Line 4B on Worksheet A). _____

   B. Enter your allowable monthly expenses (from Line P on Worksheet B). _____

   C. Subtract Line B from Line A to calculate your net income, after allowable expenses. _____

   D. Enter your total monthly payments for secured debts, arrearages on secured debts, and priority debts (the sum of Lines 1E, 2E, and 3E, above). _____

   E. Subtract Line D from Line C to calculate how much you would have left over each month, after paying your allowable expenses and your monthly payments on the debts you would have to pay in full in a Chapter 13 plan. _____

Line 5. Calculate your monthly disposable income.

   A. Enter your leftover monthly income from Line 4E, above. _____

   B. Multiply Line A by the administrative expense multiplier for your judicial district to calculate how much you would have to pay each month for administrative costs. _____

   C. MONTHLY DISPOSABLE INCOME. Subtract Line B from Line A. $ _____

● If your monthly disposable income (Line 5C) is less than $100, you have passed the means test and you do not need to continue.

● If your monthly disposable income (Line 5C) is $100 or more, complete Worksheet D.

Worksheet D: The Means Test

Use this worksheet to figure out whether you will be allowed to file for Chapter 7 bankruptcy, or whether you will be limited to Chapter 13.

Line 1. Figure out how much disposable income you will have over the next five years.

A. Enter your monthly disposable income (from Line 5C of Worksheet C). $ _____

B. Multiply Line A by 60 to calculate your monthly disposable income for the next five years.   _____

● If Line B is more than $10,000, you have failed the means test. Do not continue.

● If Line B is less than $6,000, you have passed the means test. Do not continue.

● If Line C at least $6,000 but not more than $10,000, continue to Line 2.

Line 2. Add up your unsecured, nonpriority debts.

A. Back rent   _____

B. Medical bills   _____

C. Alimony and child support   _____

D. Student loans   _____

E. Utility bills   _____

F. Loans from friends or relatives   _____

G. Health club dues   _____

H. Lawyer and accountant bills   _____

I. Union dues   _____

J. Church or synagogue dues   _____

K. Money judgments arising out of contract disputes _____

L. Money judgments arising out of negligent behavior _____

M. Deficiency judgments from secured loans   _____

N. Credit and charge card purchases and cash advances   _____

O. Department store credit card purchases   _____

P. Other   _____

Q. TOTAL UNSECURED, NONPRIORITY DEBT.
Add Lines A–P.   _____

R. Divide Line Q by four to calculate 25% of your total
unsecured, nonpriority debt. $ _____

- If Line 2R is larger than Line 1B, you have passed the means test and you do not need to continue.

- If Line 1B is equal or larger than Line 2R, you have failed the means test unless you can prove special circumstances.

Worksheet E: Personal Property Checklist

Cash on hand (include sources)
- ☐ In your home
- ☐ In your wallet
- ☐ Under your mattress

Deposits of money (include sources)
- ☐ Bank account
- ☐ Brokerage account (with stockbroker)
- ☐ Certificates of deposit (CDs)
- ☐ Credit union deposit
- ☐ Escrow account
- ☐ Money market account
- ☐ Money in a safe deposit box
- ☐ Savings and loan deposit

Security deposits
- ☐ Electric
- ☐ Gas
- ☐ Heating oil
- ☐ Security deposit on a rental unit
- ☐ Prepaid rent
- ☐ Rented furniture or equipment
- ☐ Telephone
- ☐ Water

Household goods, supplies, and furnishings
- ☐ Antiques
- ☐ Appliances
- ☐ Carpentry tools
- ☐ China and crystal
- ☐ Clocks
- ☐ Dishes

- ☐ Food (total value)
- ☐ Furniture (list every item; go from room to room so you don't miss anything)
- ☐ Gardening tools
- ☐ Home computer (for personal use)
- ☐ Iron and ironing board
- ☐ Lamps
- ☐ Lawn mower or tractor
- ☐ Microwave oven
- ☐ Patio or outdoor furniture
- ☐ Radios
- ☐ Rugs
- ☐ Sewing machine
- ☐ Silverware and utensils
- ☐ Small appliances
- ☐ Snow blower
- ☐ Stereo system
- ☐ Telephone and answering machines
- ☐ Televisions
- ☐ Vacuum cleaner
- ☐ Video equipment (VCR, camcorder)

Books, pictures, and other art objects; stamp, coin, and other collections
- ☐ Art prints
- ☐ Bibles
- ☐ Books
- ☐ Coins
- ☐ Collectibles (such as political buttons, baseball cards)
- ☐ Family portraits

☐ Figurines

☐ Original artworks

☐ Photographs

☐ Records, CDs, audiotapes

☐ Stamps

☐ Videotapes

Apparel

☐ Clothing

☐ Furs

Jewelry

☐ Engagement and wedding rings

☐ Gems

☐ Precious metals

☐ Watches

Firearms, sports equipment, and other hobby equipment

☐ Board games

☐ Bicycle

☐ Camera equipment

☐ Electronic musical equipment

☐ Exercise machine

☐ Fishing gear

☐ Guns (rifles, pistols, shotguns, muskets)

☐ Model or remote-controlled cars or planes

☐ Musical instruments

☐ Scuba diving equipment

☐ Ski equipment

☐ Other sports equipment

☐ Other weapons (swords and knives)

Interests in insurance policies

☐ Credit insurance

☐ Disability insurance

☐ Health insurance

☐ Homeowners' or renters' insurance

☐ Term life insurance

☐ Whole life insurance

Annuities

Pension or profit sharing plans

☐ IRA

☐ Keogh

☐ Pension or retirement plan

☐ 401(k) plan

Stock and interests in incorporated and unincorporated companies

Interests in partnerships

☐ Limited partnership interest

☐ General partnership interest

Government and corporate bonds and other investment instruments

☐ Corporate bonds

☐ Municipal bonds

☐ Promissory notes

☐ U.S. savings bonds

Accounts receivable

☐ Accounts receivable from business

☐ Commissions already earned

Family support

- [ ] Alimony (spousal support, maintenance) due under court order

- [ ] Child support payments due under court order

- [ ] Payments due under divorce property settlement

Other debts for which the amount owed is known and definite

- [ ] Disability benefits due

- [ ] Disability insurance due

- [ ] Judgments obtained against third parties you haven't yet collected

- [ ] Sick pay earned

- [ ] Social Security benefits due

- [ ] Tax refund due under returns already filed

- [ ] Vacation pay earned

- [ ] Wages due

- [ ] Workers' compensation due

Any special powers that you or another person can exercise for your benefit, other than those listed under "real estate"

- [ ] A right to receive, at some future time, cash, stock, or other personal property placed in an irrevocable trust

- [ ] Current payments of interest or principal from a trust

- [ ] General power of appointment over personal property

An interest in property due to another person's death

- [ ] Any interest as the beneficiary of a living trust, if the trustor has died

- [ ] Expected proceeds from a life insurance policy where the insured has died

- [ ] Inheritance from an existing estate in probate (the owner has died and the court is overseeing the distribution of the property), even if the final amount is not yet known

- [ ] Inheritance under a will that is contingent on one or more events occurring, but only if the owner has died

All other contingent claims and claims where the amount owed you is not known, including tax refunds, counterclaims, and rights to setoff claims (claims you think you have against a person, government, or corporation, but you haven't yet sued on)

- [ ] Claims against a corporation, government entity, or individual

- [ ] Potential tax refund on a return that is not yet filed

Patents, copyrights, and other intellectual property

- [ ] Copyrights

- [ ] Patents

- [ ] Trade secrets

- [ ] Trademarks

- [ ] Trade names

Licenses, franchises, and other general intangibles

- [ ] Building permits

- [ ] Cooperative association holdings

- [ ] Exclusive licenses

- [ ] Liquor licenses

☐ Nonexclusive licenses
☐ Patent licenses
☐ Professional licenses

Automobiles and other vehicles
☐ Car
☐ Minibike or motor scooter
☐ Mobile or motor home if on wheels
☐ Motorcycle
☐ Recreational vehicle (RV)
☐ Trailer
☐ Truck
☐ Van

Boats, motors, and accessories
☐ Boat (canoe, kayak, rowboat, shell, sailboat, pontoon, yacht)
☐ Boat radar, radio, or telephone
☐ Outboard motor

Aircraft and accessories
☐ Aircraft
☐ Aircraft radar, radio, and other accessories

Office equipment, furnishings, and supplies
☐ Artwork in your office
☐ Computers, software, modems, printers
☐ Copier
☐ Fax machine
☐ Furniture

☐ Rugs
☐ Supplies
☐ Telephones
☐ Typewriters

Machinery, fixtures, equipment, and supplies used in business
☐ Military uniforms and accoutrements
☐ Tools of your trade

Business inventory

Livestock, poultry, and other animals
☐ Birds
☐ Cats
☐ Dogs
☐ Fish and aquarium equipment
☐ Horses
☐ Other pets
☐ Livestock and poultry

Crops—growing or harvested

Farming equipment and implements

Farm supplies, chemicals, and feed

Other personal property of any kind not already listed
☐ Church pew
☐ Health aids (such as a wheelchair or crutches)
☐ Hot tub or portable spa
☐ Season tickets

Worksheet F: Property Value Schedule

List the total replacement value of each item in your Personal Property Checklist.

Item	Replacement Value
1. Cash	$ _____
2. Bank accounts	_____
3. Security deposits	_____
4. Household goods & furniture	_____
5. Books, pictures, etc.	_____
6. Clothing	_____
7. Furs & jewelry	_____
8. Sports & hobby equipment	_____
9. Interest in insurance	_____
10. Annuities	_____
11. Pensions & profit sharing plans	_____
12. Stock & interest in business	_____
13. Interest in partnership & ventures	_____
14. Bonds	_____
15. Accounts receivable	_____
16. Alimony & family support	_____
17. Other liquidated debts, tax refund	_____
18. Future interests & life estates	_____
19. Interests due to another's death	_____
20. Other contingent claims	_____
21. Intellectual property rights	_____
22. Licenses & franchises	_____
23. Vehicles	_____
24. Boats, motors, & accessories	_____
25. Aircraft & accessories	_____
26. Office equipment, furniture, & supplies	_____
27. Machinery, fixtures etc.	_____
28. Inventory	_____
29. Animals	_____
30. Crops—growing or harvested	_____
31. Farm equipment	_____
32. Farm supplies, chemicals, & feed	_____
33. Anything not listed above	_____
TOTAL	$ _____

Index

··

A

F

CATALOG

...more from nolo

CONSUMER

	PRICE	CODE
How to Win Your Personal Injury Claim	$29.99	PICL
Nolo's Encyclopedia of Everyday Law	$29.99	EVL
Nolo's Guide to California Law	$24.99	CLAW

ESTATE PLANNING & PROBATE

	PRICE	CODE
8 Ways to Avoid Probate	$19.99	PRAV
Estate Planning Basics	$21.99	ESPN
The Executor's Guide: Settling a Loved One's Estate or Trust	$34.99	EXEC
How to Probate an Estate in California	$49.99	PAE
Make Your Own Living Trust (Book w/CD-ROM)	$39.99	LITR
Nolo's Simple Will Book (Book w/CD-ROM)	$36.99	SWIL
Plan Your Estate	$44.99	NEST
Quick & Legal Will Book	$16.99	QUIC
Quicken Willmaker: Estate Planning Essentials (Book w/ Interactive CD-ROM)	$49.99	QWMB
Special Needs Trust: Protect Your Child's Financial Future	$34.99	SPNT

FAMILY MATTERS

	PRICE	CODE
Building a Parenting Agreement That Works	$24.99	CUST
The Complete IEP Guide	$34.99	IEP
Divorce & Money: How to Make the Best Financial Decisions During Divorce	$34.99	DIMO
Do Your Own California Adoption: Nolo's Guide for Stepparents and Domestic Partners (Book w/CD-ROM)	$34.99	ADOP
Every Dog's Legal Guide: A Must-Have for Your Owner	$19.99	DOG
Get a Life: You Don't Need a Million to Retire Well	$24.99	LIFE
The Guardianship Book for California	$39.99	GB
A Legal Guide for Lesbian and Gay Couples	$34.99	LG
Living Together: A Legal Guide (Book w/CD-ROM)	$34.99	LTK
Living Wills and Powers of Attorney in California (Book w/CD-ROM)	$21.99	CPOA
Nolo's IEP Guide: Learning Disabilities	$29.99	IELD
Prenuptial Agreements: How to Write a Fair & Lasting Contract (Book w/CD-ROM)	$34.99	PNUP
Using Divorce Mediation: Save Your Money & Your Sanity	$29.99	UDMD

GOING TO COURT

	PRICE	CODE
Beat Your Ticket: Go To Court and Win! (National Edition)	$21.99	BEYT
The Criminal Law Handbook: Know Your Rights, Survive the System	$34.99	KYR
Evrybody's Guide to Small Claims Court (National Edition)	$26.99	NSCC
Everybody's Guide to Small Claims Court in California	$29.99	CSCC
Fight Your Ticket and Win in California	$29.99	FYT
How to Change Your Name in California	$34.99	NAME
How to Collect When You Win a Lawsuit (California Edition)	$29.99	JUDG
The Lawsuit Survival Guide	$29.99	UNCL
Nolo's Deposition Handbook	$29.99	DEP
Represent Yourself in Court: How to Prepare & Try a Winning Case	$34.99	RYC
Win Your Lawsuit: A Judge's Guide to Representing Yourself in CA Superior Court	$29.99	SLWY

HOMEOWNERS, LANDLORDS & TENANTS

	PRICE	CODE
California Tenants' Rights	$27.99	CTEN
Deeds for California Real Estate	$24.99	DEED
Every Landlord's Legal Guide (National Edition, Book w/CD-ROM)	$44.99	ELLI
Every Landlord's Tax Deduction Guide	$34.99	DELL
Every Tenant's Legal Guide	$29.99	EVTEN
For Sale by Owner in California	$29.99	FSBO
How to Buy a House in California	$34.99	BHCA
The California Landlord's Law Book: Rights & Responsibilities (Book w/CD-ROM)	$44.99	LBRT
The California Landlord's Law Book: Evictions (Book w/CD-ROM)	$44.99	LBEV
Leases & Rental Agreements	$29.99	LEAR
Neighbor Law: Fences, Trees, Boundaries & Noise	$26.99	NEI
The New York Landlord's Law Book (Book w/CD-ROM)	$39.99	NYLL
New York Tenants' Rights	$29.99	NYTEN
Renters' Rights (National Edition)	$24.99	RENT

IMMIGRATION

	PRICE	CODE
Becoming a U.S. Citizen: A Guide to the Law, Exam and Interview	$24.99	USCIT
Fiancé & Marriage Visas (Book w/ CD-ROM)	$44.99	IMAR
How to Get a Green Card	$29.99	GRN
Student & Tourist Visas	$29.99	ISTU
U.S. Immigration Made Easy	$44.99	IMEZ

MONEY MATTERS

	PRICE	CODE
101 Law Forms for Personal Use (Book w/CD-ROM)	$29.99	SPOT
Bankruptcy: Is It the Right Solution to Your Debt Problems?	$21.99	BRS
Chapter 13 Bankruptcy: Repay Your Debts	$36.99	CHB
Credit Repair (Book w/CD-ROM)	$24.99	CREP
Getting Paid: How to Collect from Bankrupt Debtors	$29.99	CRBNK
How to File for Chapter 7 Bankruptcy	$29.99	HFB
IRAs, 401(k)s & Other Retirement Plans: Taking Your Money Out	$34.99	RET
Solve Your Money Troubles	$29.99	MT
Stand Up to the IRS	$29.99	SIRS
Surviving an IRS Tax Audit	$24.95	SAUD
Take Control of Your Student Loan Debt	$26.95	SLOAN

PATENTS AND COPYRIGHTS

	PRICE	CODE
All I Need is Money: How to Finance Your Invention	$19.99	FINA
The Copyright Handbook: How to Protect and Use Written Works (Book w/CD-ROM)	$39.99	COHA
Copyright Your Software (Book w/CD-ROM)	$34.95	CYS
Getting Permission: How to License and Clear Copyrighted Materials Online and Off (Book w/CD-ROM)	$34.99	RIPER
How to Make Patent Drawings Yourself	$29.99	DRAW
The Inventor's Notebook	$24.99	INOT
License Your Invention (Book w/CD-ROM)	$39.99	LICE
Nolo's Patents for Beginners	$29.99	QPAT
Patent, Copyright & Trademark	$39.99	PCTM
Patent It Yourself	$49.99	PAT
Patent Pending in 24 Hours	$29.99	PEND
The Public Domain	$34.99	PUBL
Trademark: Legal Care for Your Business and Product Name	$39.99	TRD
Web and Software Development: A Legal Guide (Book w/ CD-ROM)	$44.99	SFT
What Every Inventor Needs to Know About Business and Taxes (Book w/ CD-ROM)	$34.99	ILAX

RESEARCH & REFERENCE

	PRICE	CODE
Legal Research: How to Find & Understand the Law	$39.99	LRES

SENIORS

	PRICE	CODE
Long-Term Care: How to Plan & Pay for It	$21.99	ELD
Social Security, Medicare & Goverment Pensions	$29.99	SOA

SOFTWARE

Call or check our website at www.nolo.com for special discounts on Software!

	PRICE	CODE
Incorporator Pro	$89.99	STNC1
LLC Maker—Windows	$89.95	LLP1
Patent Pending Now!	$19.99	PP1
PatentEase—Windows	$349.00	PEAS
Personal RecordKeeper 5.0 CD—Windows	$59.95	RKD5
Quicken Legal Business Pro 2006—Windows	$109.99	SBQB6
Quicken WillMaker Plus 2006—Windows	$79.99	WQP6

SPECIAL UPGRADE OFFER—Get 35% off the latest edition of your Nolo book

It's important to have the most current legal information. Because laws and legal procedures change often, we update our books regularly. To help keep you up-to-date we are extending this special upgrade offer. Cut out and mail the title portion of the cover of your old Nolo book and we'll give you 35% off the retail price of the NEW EDITION of that book when you purchase directly from us. For more information call us at 1-800-728-3555. This offer is to individuals only.

Order Form

Name _____

Address _____

City _____

State, Zip _____

Daytime Phone _____

E-mail _____

Our "No-Hassle" Guarantee

Return anything you buy directly from Nolo for any reason and we'll cheerfully refund your purchase price. No ifs, ands or buts.

☐ Check here if you do not wish to receive mailings from other companies

Item Code	Quantity	Item	Unit Price	Total Price

Method of payment

☐ Check   ☐ VISA   ☐ MasterCard
☐ Discover Card   ☐ American Express

Subtotal	
Add your local sales tax (California only)	
Shipping: RUSH $9, Basic $5 (See below)	
"I bought 3, ship it to me FREE!"(Ground shipping only)	
TOTAL	

Account Number _____

Expiration Date _____

Signature _____

Shipping and Handling

Rush Delivery—Only $9

We'll ship any order to any street address in the U.S. by UPS 2nd Day Air* for only $9!

* Order by noon Pacific Time and get your order in 2 business days. Orders placed after noon Pacific Time will arrive in 3 business days. P.O. boxes and S.F. Bay Area use basic shipping. Alaska and Hawaii use 2nd Day Air or Priority Mail.

Basic Shipping—$5

Use for P.O. Boxes, Northern California and Ground Service.

Allow 1-2 weeks for delivery. U.S. addresses only.

For faster service, use your credit card and our toll-free numbers

**Call our customer service group
Monday thru Friday 7am to 7pm PST**

Phone   1-800-728-3555

Fax   1-800-645-0895

Mail   Nolo
950 Parker St.
Berkeley, CA 94710

Order 24 hours a day @
www.nolo.com

Remember:

Little publishers have big ears.
We really listen to you.

Take 2 Minutes & Give Us Your 2 cents

Your comments make a big difference in the development and revision of Nolo books and software. Please take a few minutes and register your Nolo product—and your comments—with us. Not only will your input make a difference, you'll receive special offers available only to registered owners of Nolo products on our newest books and software. Register now by:

PHONE
1-800-728-3555

FAX
1-800-645-0895

EMAIL
cs@nolo.com

or **MAIL** us
this registration card

fold here

NOLO

Registration Card

NAME _____ DATE _____

ADDRESS _____

CITY _____ STATE _____ ZIP _____

PHONE _____ EMAIL _____

WHERE DID YOU HEAR ABOUT THIS PRODUCT? _____

WHERE DID YOU PURCHASE THIS PRODUCT? _____

DID YOU CONSULT A LAWYER? (PLEASE CIRCLE ONE)   YES   NO   NOT APPLICABLE

DID YOU FIND THIS BOOK HELPFUL?   (VERY)   5   4   3   2   1   (NOT AT ALL)

COMMENTS _____
_____
_____

WAS IT EASY TO USE?   (VERY EASY)   5   4   3   2   1   (VERY DIFFICULT)

We occasionally make our mailing list available to carefully selected companies whose products may be of interest to you.
❑ If you do not wish to receive mailings from these companies, please check this box.
❑ You can quote me in future Nolo promotional materials.
   Daytime phone number _____.

FIBA 1.0

Nolo
in the
NEWS

"Nolo helps lay people perform legal tasks without the aid—or fees—of lawyers."

—USA TODAY

Nolo books are ..."written in plain language, free of legal mumbo jumbo, and spiced with witty personal observations."

—ASSOCIATED PRESS

"...Nolo publications...guide people simply through the how, when, where and why of law."

—WASHINGTON POST

"Increasingly, people who are not lawyers are performing tasks usually regarded as legal work... And consumers, using books like Nolo's, do routine legal work themselves."

—NEW YORK TIMES

"...All of [Nolo's] books are easy-to-understand, are updated regularly, provide pull-out forms...and are often quite moving in their sense of compassion for the struggles of the lay reader."

—SAN FRANCISCO CHRONICLE

fold here

- -

```
┌─────────────────┐
│                 │
│     Place       │
│  stamp here     │
│                 │
└─────────────────┘
```

Nolo
950 Parker Street
Berkeley, CA 94710-9867

Attn: `FIBA 1.0`